~ *A View from the Home Front* ~

Royal Leamington Spa

1939 - 1945

Best wishes

Allan Jennings

SYDNI
BOOKS

First published in 2017 by: -

Sydni Books
9, Amroth Mews
Sydenham
LEAMINGTON SPA
CV31 1NZ

www.sydni.org

ISBN: 978-0-9932980-7-3

Printed in Great Britain by Warwick Printing Company Limited.

Dedication

This book is dedicated to the men, women and children of Royal Leamington Spa - when called upon to do their duty, they did their bit!

At the Thanksgiving Service for Victory in Europe, on Sunday 13th May 1945, the Mayor of Leamington [Alderman C. W. Gardner] said, "I share with you a great feeling of thankfulness to Almighty God that we have been spared to see this day. In many hearts, there will be grief at the loss of dear ones, but to those we hope it will be some comfort to know that their sons and husbands did not die in vain."

"I feel it would be the wish of the Town Council to thank you all for the part you have played during the past six years. We are proud to salute the members of the Armed Forces, men and women, the Home Guard, the Civil Defence in all its branches, the youth organisations and the war workers, both those from factories and those who have worked on the land. To those who have not been in uniform, particularly the womenfolk, I would say you have all played your part splendidly."

This memorial to those who worked on the Home Front during World War Two is one of over 300 memorials at the National Memorial Arboretum at Alrewas Staffordshire. It is well worth a visit, so why not go and give them your support.

Contents

Preface

Many books have been written about the Second World War, but there are two aspects of the war that, as a Leamingtonian and as a local historian, interest me.

The first is the detail of the six main enemy bombing raids on Leamington. No one had explored the subject in detail in 75 years. That has now been put right with the 2015 publication of my book, "The Bombing of Royal Leamington Spa" which details the raids and names the unfortunate people that died.

The second is the quest to discover what happened in Leamington Spa itself and again publish the detail - which is exactly what this book is all about.

Also, it seemed strange to me that in all this time since the Second World War, no specific memorial to the 13 people who died in Leamington Spa had been erected. However, following a fund-raising exercise by Barry Franklin and the Leamington History Group this was put right on 11th October 2017 when Adam Anders and Paul Swinson from Swinson's Masonry installed this memorial close to the main war memorial on the Parade.

I hope that you will find this book interesting and informative. And now, to quote one of the most well-known sayings from that most popular of TV programmes 'Only Fools and Horses': -

During the war.........

Preparations

It is difficult for anyone to be fully prepared for war, but Leamington Spa and Warwickshire did have a number of measures in place. As early as Monday 23rd March 1936, the first meeting took place of the general committee formed in connection with the preparation of a scheme for the protection of the civil population of Warwickshire against air attacks. At that meeting, it was agreed to spend £50 on sending trainees to the civilian anti-gas school. By October 1936 arrangements had been made for every member of the Warwickshire Police Force to undergo a fortnight's training in air raid precautions and anti-gas instruction.

By the beginning of the war, official buildings such as the Town Hall, Police Station, the Post Office, Warneford Hospital and other public buildings had sand-bags piled on the outside of the buildings.

In March 1939, experimental work was being carried out in connection with 'trench revetment' [a retaining wall or facing to protect the sides] at Eagle Recreation Ground.

In this photograph, notice the air-raid siren on top of the Police Station in High Street.

On 24th March 1939, the Borough Engineer was authorised to purchase six sand bag filling machines. Urgent work was continuing in the basement of the Report and Control Centre for the A.R.P. [Air Raid Precautions] which was set up in Hamilton House, at No.4 Hamilton Terrace on the corner of Rosefield Place, which in later years became the site of the police station. Other urgent work continued at the 'temporary centre' at the Town Hall, and at the Decontamination Centre, Central Depot, Lillington Avenue.

The telephone communications systems at the various depots were authorised and then installed in April 1939. A First Aid Post was set up at Warneford Hospital along with a mobile surgical unit. The provision of 12 Wardens Posts was approved and permission obtained for the installation of telephones.

On 12th April 1939, the A.R.P. Committee recommended the appointment of 62 recently selected senior and deputy senior air-raid wardens. Police Inspector Bastock and P.C. 38 Knifton became civilian Anti-Gas School Instructors.

On 21st April 1939, it was reported that the refuge room for staff at the Town Hall was almost complete and that volunteers had been trained on first aid and anti-gas measures.

In April 1939 as war was looking more and more likely, Leslie Hore-Belisha, the Secretary of State for War, persuaded the Government to introduce a limited form of conscription. Single men aged 20 to 22 years old were liable to be called up. The intention was for the first intake to undergo six months of basic training before being discharged into an active reserve. The men could be recalled for ongoing training as well as attending an annual camp.

On 25th May 1939, it was reported that the telephone system in the Report and Control Centre was now complete; concrete lining of the trenches on the Eagle Recreation Ground had commenced; 178 men and women had been enrolled for first aid posts - 56 were now fully trained; 41 people had been enrolled for first aid parties - 12 were now fully trained; and 55 people had been enrolled as ambulance drivers and attendants - 35 were now fully trained.

On 28th July 1939, it was reported that all Wardens would be required to take training on high explosives and incendiary bombs and that a class for instructors was already in progress. Hamilton House Report and Control Centre was now complete. Trenches for people caught in the streets during an air raid were being completed at the Eagle Recreation Ground, Cashmore Avenue Recreation Ground, Victoria Park and Shrubland Recreation Ground - the four sites could accommodate 1,230 people.

On 1st September 1939, it was reported that the staff of the A.R.P. Department of the County Medical Officer of Health had been working until midnight each day during the past fortnight, and a fleet of lorries had been carrying supplies to every town and hamlet in the administrative county. An official stated on Monday 28th August, that 20 tons of cotton wool had so far been sent out. First-aid posts were fully equipped and in most areas personnel were allocated and instructed in their duties. The nine mobile first-aid units had all been fitted up, and were ready for immediate use. They were converted motor buses, the personnel manning them consisting of a doctor, a trained nurse, and 18 auxiliary nurses. They were to be used chiefly in rural areas.

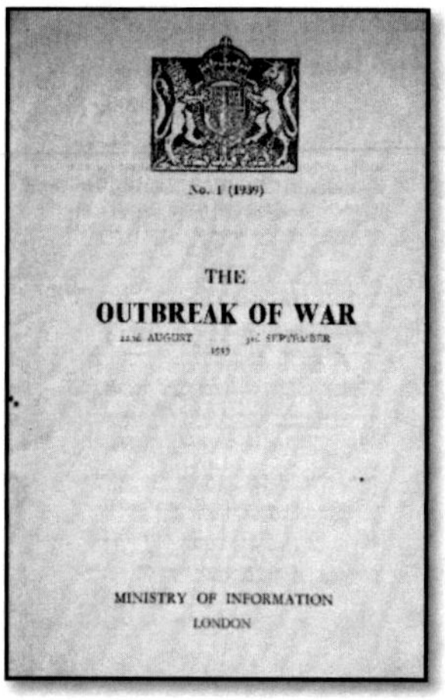

The Leamington Spa Courier dated Friday 8th September 1939 reported: - **Leamington's Conversion To War Time Conditions** – After a week of suspense in the course of which it became more and more clear that hostilities would be unavoidable, Great Britain has declared war against Germany, - as from 11 o'clock on Sunday morning.

A final British note presented to Berlin at 9.00am gave the German Government two hours in which to give an undertaking that they would withdraw their troops from Poland. They had invaded Poland on 1st September 1939.

At 11.15am on 3rd September 1939, the Prime Minister broadcast to the nation the news, "that no such undertaking has been received and that consequently this country is at war with Germany."

On the announcement of war Leamington Town Council set up an Emergency Committee and the Town Clerk, Mr. A. F. Greenwood, became Leamington's War Time Controller. A Food Control Committee was established consisting of 15 members.

Lighting regulations were put in place with advice that "very careful attention should be paid to skylights, for these can be seen from above."

Conscription - The Emergency Powers [Defence Act] of August 1938 empowered the British Government to take certain measures for the defence of the nation. It contained around 100 measures aimed at calling up military reservists and Air Raid Precautions [A.R.P.] volunteers. However, it required more than just volunteers.

The Military Training Act of 27th April 1939 required all British men aged 20 and 21 who were fit and able, to do six months' military training. Even so, at the outbreak of war the British Army only totalled 897,000 men. On 3rd September 1939, the day Britain declared war on Germany, the Act was overtaken by the National Service [Armed Forces] Act which introduced conscription of all able men aged 18 to 41 into the Army, Navy or Air Force. Men could be rejected for medical reasons and those involved in vital industries or occupations classed as "reserved occupations" could be exempt. Single men were called up before married men. By the end of 1939 more than 1.5 million men had been conscripted into the British armed forces. By 1942 all male British subjects between 18 and 51 years of age, as well as all females between 20 and 30 years of age and resident in Britain were liable to be called up, although there were some limited exemptions.

Saturday 21st October 1939 was a registration day for National Service when 'local youths' visited the local Employment 'Labour' Exchange to make their applications. In the Coventry area, which included Leamington, Rugby, Nuneaton and the surrounding villages, the number dealt with was 2,945. Of these, 441 expressed a preference for the Royal Navy and 1,061 for the Air Force. Presumably the other 1,443 preferred the Army.

On Saturday 9th December 1939, it was time for the age 22 group to register for military service. 292 men from Leamington, Warwick and the surrounding area presented themselves at the local Labour Exchange. Only three of them claimed exemption as conscientious objectors.

The first 'war wedding' of a Leamington man took place on Monday 4th September 1939 at Warwick Register Office. It had been brought forward in view of the fact that bridegroom, Sergeant Pilot Terence Frank Kennan, a reservist, had been ordered to re-join the Royal Air Force. He married Miss Thelma Barford Ward.

The Morning News dated Monday 11th September 1939 gave the following housekeeping advice to its readers: -

Housekeeping in War Time – The order restricting the use of electricity and gas to 75 per cent of the usual consumption is now in force. Housewives should find it quite easy to adapt their households to the new requirements without hardship.

How to Save Electricity

1. Look around the house and see where the use of equipment can be limited.
2. Lower the wattage of lamps where possible.
3. Plan meals so that several dishes are prepared together. The Electrical Association for Women, 20, Regent Street, S.W.1, will supply menus that reduce consumption.
4. In order to avoid the use of many fires, get the persons in the house to use only one sitting room. This will make it possible for one wireless set only to be run.
5. Limit the number of baths as much as possible.

How to Save Gas

The Gas Light and Coke Co. suggest the following ways of reducing gas consumption simply and satisfactorily: -

Cooking

1. Never leave a burner alight when not in use, never allow flames to show outside the sides of the pan.
2. Use a small burner instead of a large one unless speed is necessary.
3. When using a griller, put something on top at the same time.
4. Have a steamer with two or more compartments; you can then cook several dishes, possibly a whole meal, on one gas ring.
5. Keep the lid on your pans; the contents will cook more quickly. When the pan comes to the boil, turn the burner down.
6. Never heat more liquid than you need. Remember this when you fill the kettle, as you use gas unnecessarily. Do not keep the kettle on the boil.
7. When you use the oven try to put a complete meal into it at once. Turn the flame out as soon as the dinner is cooked, the food will keep hot for some time. Casserole dishes are economical.

Water Heating

1. When cooking put a bowl of water in the oven at the same time. This will give you hot water for washing up.
2. Never wash up, or your hands, under a running tap.
3. The less crockery you use, the less water you will need for washing up.
4. Be careful when you take your bath to keep it shallow.

Room Warming

1. When you have turned the fire on keep the door closed.
2. Turn the fire down when the room is warmed. If in sections, some can be turned off.
3. If you have more than one sitting room, try to get everyone to use the same one.
4. Never leave a gas fire on when a room is not in use.

On 24th Oct 1939, the Town Clerk, Mr. A. F. Greenwood updated members of the Leamington and Warwick Rotary Club on the war emergency arrangements. "Following months of preparation, and immediately after the outbreak of hostilities, civil defence schemes had to be brought into operation very speedily, with somewhat disturbing results. Faced with the necessity of speedy decisions, many local authorities delegated full powers to Emergency Committees for the duration of the war. In many places, ordinary committees were now in abeyance, power having been given to chairmen of committees and the officials. This tendency towards bureaucracy was undesirable, and had certain disadvantages. For instance, it deprived the Council of the services of men of experience, cast an unfair burden on the few, and invited extensive criticism. Such criticism was mostly unjustified in that if the elected representatives on the Council knew the full facts they would undoubtedly have come to decisions similar to those taken by the few."

Mr. Greenwood was happy to say that in Leamington, after having an Emergency Committee for the first four weeks of the war, they had reverted to the routine committees, with adequate safeguards for action in an emergency. He hoped this would continue.

"The Council has been faced with the difficulty of discharging efficiently peacetime functions, and duties imposed by war conditions. Regarding A.R.P., the Government, in 1935, urged local authorities to consider this question, and to those who were brought in contact with emissaries from London a vague impression grew up that it had to do with a number of wardens about the street. It was not until 1937 that A.R.P. was placed on a proper basis after the passing of the Act, which made counties and county boroughs responsible for schemes. In Leamington, the Town Council acted as the agent of Warwickshire County Council."

"The construction of trenches for the protection of the public during an air raid was proceeding in Leamington, and we hope to have shelters available in the course of a week or two. There is a very efficient wardens' service under the control of Rotarian Mr. E. Sidwell, and at the 'Old Brewery' there are decontamination squads, ambulance parties, rescue and demolition parties, etc. Anyone paying a visit to that centre and seeing how the squads are organised would agree that the arrangements were a model of efficiency. If the state of preparedness in Leamington had not reached that peak of perfection which the man in the street considered desirable, it was not the fault of the Council or the County Authority. It was due to the Government's decision, on a basis known to themselves, as to what constituted vulnerable areas. Supplies of materials and equipment have first been issued to those places which are regarded as especially vulnerable. We have to be thankful that Leamington is a 'reception area'."

"It was difficult to describe the extent of A.R.P. The task of wrestling with official circulars and documents was almost Herculean. Since the outbreak of war, I have received on A.R.P. alone over 100 circulars from the Home Office, apart from correspondence with and instructions from the County Council. These are in addition to the instructions relating to the Auxiliary Fire Service and the Police."

"On the question of evacuation, the reception arrangements have been organised and carried out admirably under very difficult circumstances. There have been a devoted band of helpers from the W.V.S. [Woman's Voluntary Service], and residents of all classes. The children have, on the whole, been well behaved and the foster-parents have been splendid. The tolerance and adaptability of both foster-parents and children have been such that it is not necessary to invoke compulsory billeting in Leamington, and no case has been brought before the Billeting Tribunal set up to deal with complaints."

This photo of 'an ambulance group' taken with an ambulance in the background was taken at the Central Depot on 29th May 1945.

Mr. Greenwood paid tribute to the billeting officer, who with the aid of the head teachers, had carried out the work. "It is due mainly to their great efforts that the difficulties had been amicably settled, and where necessary re-arrangements and interchange of billets have been effected. The reception of evacuees however, was only the fringe of the general question." They now had to consider welfare and after care, in which connection Mr. Greenwood referred to the establishment of the centre at No.25 Warwick Place, and the setting up of a panel system under which the medical practitioners looked after the health of the children.

"The Police and Fire Services are conducted in a manner characteristic of the efficiency of this department. As to Food Control, I fear that shortly members of the public will become familiar with their ration cards. Leamington has the advantage of having a thoroughly representative and enthusiastic Food Control Committee. The writing up of the ration cards has almost been completed, and will be in advance of the scheduled time. There will be no difficulty in residents receiving their rations when it becomes necessary."

One common feature to all these services was the voluntary aspect of the work continued Mr. Greenwood, "Sometime we hear criticisms of paid personnel for war-time services, but it should not be forgotten that the vast majority are volunteers of whose efforts and enthusiasm one could not speak too highly. Last week the Town Hall was humming with activity, and there were no fewer than 40 voluntary workers fully employed in the various sections of the services. War had necessitated the intensification of the Town Council's peace-time activities. Evacuation, for instance, had meant more work for the Health Committee, the Education Committee, and the Water Committee, whilst the black-out was responsible for increased demands on the Public Library, and also greater activity on the part of the C.I.D."

Turning to the Rotary Clubs part in the national effort, Mr. Greenwood spoke appreciatively of the Club's offer to assist the Council in the formation of a Citizen's Advice Bureau. He had been authorised to accept this offer with sincere appreciation. The purpose of such a bureau would be the setting-up of a clearing house for personal problems. There were many peace-time problems which assumed an added importance in war-time, such as National Health Insurance, Old Age Pensions, housing difficulties etc., which gave great anxiety to the average person. The existence of such a bureau would be of the greatest advantage. He assured the Club that if members were prepared to conduct the bureau they would have every assistance from the Borough officials. He made suggestions for the staffing of the bureau and its office equipment, and observed that in a town the size of Leamington it might be sufficient for it to open on two afternoons and one evening each week.

The Leamington Spa Courier dated 15th December 1939 gave advice to its readers under the heading: - **Salvage of Waste Materials** - In view of the urgent need to avoid unnecessary imports, it has become important that further use should be made of many materials which are now wasted. The Council are therefore organising a salvage scheme, and all residents and shop keepers are asked to assist by keeping separate from their ordinary refuse NOW, all CLEAN WASTE PAPER. TINS and other SCRAP METAL. BOTTLES and GLASS. These items will be collected separately at the same time as the house refuse and returned to industry. The Council's arrangements are intended to supplement and not to replace those already in existence.

The same Leamington Spa Courier also gave **Advice to Water Consumers**: - In the event of an air raid, enemy action may cause damage to the water distribution system. The water authority would take prompt action to deal with damaged mains, but consumers are reminded that the maintenance of all pipes, tanks and fittings in private premises is the responsibility of the owner or occupier. In order to avoid waste of water and damage to property, consumers are advised to make themselves familiar with their own installations; it is especially important that they should know the position of the stop-cock and make sure that it can be closed quickly in case of need. If no stop-cock exists, one should be fixed as soon as possible in order that the supply can be shut off to prevent flooding should the internal pipes be damaged. It is important that the consumption of water should be kept as low as possible, as large quantities would probably be required in the event of an air raid for firefighting, decontamination and other essential services.

In May 1940, an Air Raid Information Bureau was set up at the Public Health Office under Mr. G. H. Hammond the Casualty Information Officer. Any lists of casualties would be published at the Bureau, Warneford Hospital, the Police Station and the Town Hall.

In 1940, Lord Beaverbrook, then Minister of Aircraft Production, made a desperate appeal for aluminium pans. The idea was to turn the aluminium into duralumin, a metal used to build the lightweight Spitfire frame. In Leamington, there was an amazing response to the appeal, as can be seen from this July 1940 Leamington Spa Courier photograph that was taken at Oakfield, Binswood Avenue. Miss Milne and Mrs. Kerr Chalmers are seen helping to pile up the pots and pans. Somewhere in the heap is a piece of the first Zeppelin brought down in England during the First World War.

On 25th November 1940 Borough Engineer Mr. J. Sutcliffe issued the following notice about an acute water shortage: - **Acute Water Shortage** - It is imperative that the consumption of the town's water be reduced immediately by at least one-third to prevent failure of supply. Town water must not be used for washing vehicles or yards. Water for baths must be drastically reduced. Use alternative sources of supply wherever available, and as far as possible use all water more than once. Domestic water softeners must be discontinued wherever possible, in order to avoid waste of water in regeneration. **AVOID ALL WASTE.**

Information Posters and Leaflets – Various posters and leaflets were issued to tell people what to do and what not to do. One of these was an instruction poster giving information about invasion. Posters carried various messages such as, "Careless talk costs lives"; "Be like dad, keep mum"; "Hitler will send no warning, so always carry your gas mask".

This leaflet issued by the Ministry of Information is entitled, "**If the INVADER comes - What To Do - And How To Do It.**"

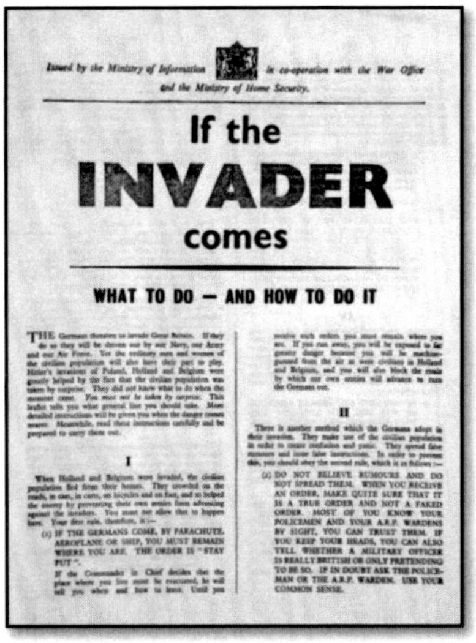

Issued by the Ministry of Information in co-operation with the War Office and the Ministry of Home Security.

If the INVADER comes

WHAT TO DO – AND HOW TO DO IT

The Germans threaten to invade Great Britain. If they do they will be driven out by our Navy, our Army and our Air Force. Yet the ordinary men and women of the civilian population will also have their part to play. Hitler's invasion of Poland, Holland and Belgium were greatly helped by the fact that the civilian population was taken by surprise. They did not know what to do when the moment came. *You must not be taken by surprise.* This leaflet tells you what general line you should take. More detailed instructions will be given you when the danger comes nearer. Meanwhile, read these instructions carefully and be prepared to carry them out.

I. When Holland and Belgium were invaded, the civilian population fled from their homes. They crowded on the roads, in cars, in carts, on bicycles and on foot, and so helped the enemy by preventing their own armies from advancing against the invaders. You must not allow that to happen here. Your first rule, therefore is: -

(1) If the Germans come, by parachute, aeroplane or ship, you must remain where you are. The order is "Stay Put". If the Commander in Chief decides that the place where you live must be evacuated, he will tell you when and how to leave. Until you receive such orders you must remain where you are. If you run away, you will be exposed to far greater danger because you will be machine-gunned from the air as were civilians in Holland and Belgium, and you will also block the roads by which our own armies will advance to turn the Germans out.

II. There is another method which the Germans adopt in their invasion. They make use of the civilian population in order to create confusion and panic. They spread false rumours and issue false instructions. In order to prevent this, you should obey the second rule, which is as follows: -

(2) Do not believe rumours and do not spread them. When you receive an order, make quite sure that it is a true order and not a faked order. Most of you know your policemen and your A.R.P. Wardens by sight, you can trust them. If you keep your heads, you can also tell whether a military officer is really British or only pretending to be so. If in doubt, ask the policeman or the A.R.P. Warden. Use your common sense.

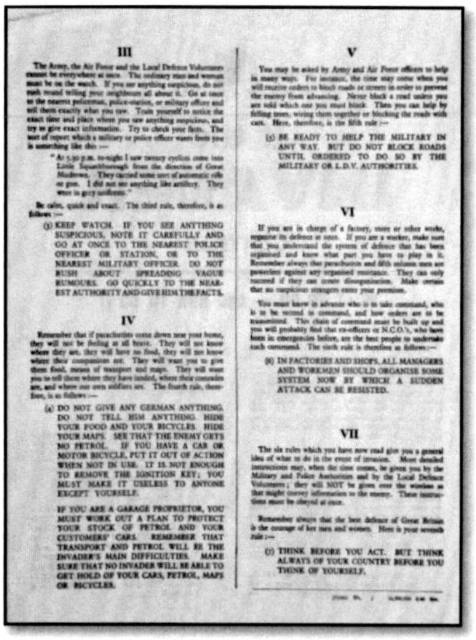

III

(3) KEEP WATCH. IF YOU SEE ANYTHING SUSPICIOUS, NOTE IT CAREFULLY AND GO AT ONCE TO THE NEAREST POLICE OFFICER OR STATION, OR TO THE NEAREST MILITARY OFFICER. DO NOT RUSH ABOUT SPREADING VAGUE RUMOURS. GO QUICKLY TO THE NEAREST AUTHORITY AND GIVE HIM THE FACTS.

IV

(4) DO NOT GIVE ANY GERMAN ANYTHING. DO NOT TELL HIM ANYTHING. HIDE YOUR FOOD AND YOUR BICYCLES. HIDE YOUR MAPS. SEE THAT THE ENEMY GETS NO PETROL. IF YOU HAVE A CAR OR MOTOR BICYCLE, PUT IT OUT OF ACTION WHEN NOT IN USE. IT IS NOT ENOUGH TO REMOVE THE IGNITION KEY; YOU MUST MAKE IT USELESS TO ANYONE EXCEPT YOURSELF.

IF YOU ARE A GARAGE PROPRIETOR, YOU MUST WORK OUT A PLAN TO PROTECT YOUR STOCK OF PETROL AND YOUR CUSTOMERS' CARS. REMEMBER THAT TRANSPORT AND PETROL WILL BE THE INVADER'S MAIN DIFFICULTIES. MAKE SURE THAT NO INVADER WILL BE ABLE TO GET HOLD OF YOUR CARS, PETROL, MAPS OR BICYCLES.

V

(5) BE READY TO HELP THE MILITARY IN ANY WAY. BUT DO NOT BLOCK ROADS UNTIL ORDERED TO DO SO BY THE MILITARY OR L.D.V. AUTHORITIES.

VI

(6) IN FACTORIES AND SHOPS, ALL MANAGERS AND WORKMEN SHOULD ORGANISE SOME SYSTEM NOW BY WHICH A SUDDEN ATTACK CAN BE RESISTED.

VII

(7) THINK BEFORE YOU ACT. BUT THINK ALWAYS OF YOUR COUNTRY BEFORE YOU THINK OF YOURSELF.

III. The Army, Air Force and the Local Defence Volunteers cannot be everywhere at once. The ordinary man and women must be on the watch. If you see anything suspicious, do not rush around telling your neighbours all about it. Go at once to the nearest policemen, police-station, or military officer and tell them exactly what you saw. Train yourself to notice the exact time and place where you saw anything suspicious, and try to give exact information. Try to check your facts. The sort of report which a military or police officer wants from you is something like this: - "At 5.30pm tonight I saw twenty cyclists come into Little Squashborough from the direction of Great Mudtown. They carried some sort of automatic rifle or gun. I did not see anything like artillery. They were in grey uniforms."

Be calm, quick and exact. The third rule, therefore, is as follows: -

(3) Keep watch. If you see anything suspicious, note it carefully and go at once to the nearest police officer or station, or to the nearest military officer. Do not rush about spreading vague rumours, go quickly to the nearest authority and give him the facts.

IV. Remember that if parachutists come down near your home, they will not be feeling at all brave. They will not know where they are, and will have no food, they will not know where their companions are. They will want you to give them food, means of transport and maps. They will want you to tell them where they have landed, where their comrades are, and where our own soldiers are. The fourth rule, therefore, is as follows: -

(4) Do not give any German anything. Do not tell him anything. Hide your food and your bicycles. Hide your maps. See that the enemy gets no petrol. If you have a car or motor bicycle, put it out of action when not in use. It is not enough to remove the ignition key; you must make it useless to anyone except yourself.

If you are a garage proprietor, you must work out a plan to protect your stock of petrol and your customers' cars. Remember that transport and petrol will be the invader's main difficulties. Make sure that no invader will be able to get hold of your cars, petrol, maps or bicycles.

V. You may be asked by Army and Air Force officers to help in many ways. For instance, the time may come when you will receive orders to block roads or streets in order to prevent the enemy from advancing. Never block a road unless you are told which one you must block. Then you can help by felling trees, wiring them together or blocking the roads with cars. Here, therefore, is the fifth rule: -

(5) Be ready to help the military in any way. But do not block roads until ordered to do so by the military or L.D.V. authorities.

VI. If you are in charge of a factory, store or other works, organize its defence at once. If you are a worker, make sure that you understand the system of defence that has been organized and know what part you have to play in it. Remember always that parachutists and fifth column men are powerless against any organized resistance. They can only succeed if they can create disorganization. Make certain that no suspicious strangers enter your premises.

You must know in advance who is to take command, who is to be second in command, and how orders are to be transmitted. This chain of command must be built up and you will probably find that ex-officers or N.C.O.'s who have been in emergencies before, are the best people to undertake such command. The sixth rule is therefore as follows: -

(6) In factories and shops, all managers and workmen should organize some system now by which a sudden attack can be resisted.

VII. The six rules which you have now read give you a general idea of what to do in the event of an invasion. More detailed instructions may, when the time comes, be given you by the Military and Police Authorities and by the Local Defence Volunteers; they will **NOT** be given over the wireless as that might convey information to the enemy. These instructions must be obeyed at once.

Remember always that the best defence of Great Britain is the courage of the men and women. Here is your seventh rule: -

(7) Think before you act. But think always of your Country before you think of yourself.

Sir Robert Anthony Eden

Robert Anthony Eden was born on 12th June 1897 at Rushyford County Durham. He was educated at Eton and Christ Church College Oxford. At the age of 57 he became Prime Minister for a short period from April 1955 until 9th January 1957. He became the Earl of Avon in 1961 and died on 14th January 1977.

As Member of Parliament for Warwick and Leamington, Anthony Eden stood for peace, but he was resolutely opposed to appeasement and resigned as Foreign Secretary in Neville Chamberlain's 1938 government disagreeing with his policy towards Hitler and Mussolini. In his resignation speech, Eden said, "I do not feel we can make progress in European Appeasement."

That struck a chord with Winston Churchill who was soon to assume the mantle of power. Churchill wrote, "There seemed one strong young figure standing up against long, dismal, drawling tides of drift and surrender." The Churchill - Eden partnership grew out of that moment. When war was declared 19 months later, Eden was back in the Government, first as Secretary of State for Dominion Affairs, then Secretary of State for War and, in 1940, Foreign Secretary.

On 15th May 1940 Leamington Town Council resolved that the Town Clerk would convey to Mr. Eden the Council's congratulations on his new appointment as Secretary of State for War in Mr. Winston Churchill's new administration.

As Churchill's right-hand man, and heir apparent, he played a decisive role in the conduct of the war, whilst remaining in close touch with his Warwick and Leamington constituency - which he represented for 34 years - being first elected in 1923.

Anthony Eden was predicting early in 1939 the "universal disaster" to which Europe was hurtling. After Hitler's subjugation of Czechoslovakia in March of that year he said, "We can hug no more comfortable illusions. The truth is - and must be bluntly stated - that if the present methods are allowed to continue unchecked we are heading straight for anarchy, for a universal tragedy which will involve us all. This is neither the time for recriminations, nor for self-justification. It is essentially a time for action."

"It may be that the struggle upon which we are engaged must prove both long and harsh, but whatever the duration, or its intensity, there can be no doubt of the determination of the people of the British Commonwealth, side by side with our French and Polish allies to see it through to the end."

Eden said the world could not continue to live indefinitely under the threat or the fact of constantly recurring aggression. "There have been too many victims of Nazi Germany already. At this hour, foreign peoples, whose only crime is that they are not Germans, are being brutally ill-treated in Bohemia, in Poland, and elsewhere. Each in turn the neighbours of Nazi Germany have been cajoled, menaced and overrun."

"The Nazi system knows no rule but force and the advance to power has been marked by ruthless disregard of every engagement entered into. Each concession made has only been used as a pretext for some fresh act of arms against some weaker neighbour. Twenty years ago, we thought to have made an end of Prussian militarism and its plans for world hegemony."

"The British people are now united in their determination to make a supreme effort to ensure for the nations of Europe, whether small or great, freedom to live their own lives in a world at peace."

Gas Masks and Identity Cards

Gas Masks [Respirators] - The Leamington authorities moved quickly, even before war broke out, to distribute 35,000 civilian respirators. On 28th July 1939, it was reported that, "very few people are now without respirators".

Thirty-eight million standard civilian gas masks were issued across Britain.

Members of the civilian services were issued with a different type of gas mask that had a separate larger filter.

The gas masks which were issued to every man, woman and child in the country soon came to be regarded as a nuisance rather than a necessary precaution. Thankfully, they were never needed on the Home Front. It is thought by some people that Adolf Hitler had decided that it was pointless to gas a population when the people were so well prepared.

The size of the normal civilian respirator would, in general, fit children down to 4-5 years of age. Below that age a special design of respirator, known as a 'Small Child's Respirator', was provided for young children from that age down to at least two years of age. For babies whose faces were too small for the Small Child's Respirator, a Protective Helmet was provided. Its use necessitated the attention of an older person to provide air by means of a pump. The helmet consisted of a hood, fitted with a large window, which enclosed the head, shoulders and arms, and was tied around the waist by means of a draw tape. The baby was able to get its hand to its mouth.

Public Information Leaflet No.1 dated July 1939 stated: - 'If you have already got your gas mask, make sure that you are keeping it safely and in good condition for immediate use. If you are moving permanently, or going away for any length of time, remember to take your gas mask with you. The special anti-gas mask for babies and the respirator for small children will not be distributed in any district before an emergency arises.'

I am grateful to Derek Billings of Whitnash for this photo of people queuing for their gas masks.

Derek says, "This is 28th September 1938 at Bath Place Church of England School in Bath Place, and is the queue for gas masks as war loomed over us. The children were issued with Mickey Mouse masks; I saw one recently in a museum. I was too young to remember this day as I was only two and in my mother's arms, directly behind the dog. Peter and Mrs Fleming are also in the photo; he is the lad wearing a beret to the left of the man in the bowler hat [centre]. I believe that the lady fifth from the right in the long coat is Mary Churchill, her husband worked for Burgis and Colbourne. Myself, Peter Fleming and the Churchill's lived in Victoria Street. The last I heard of Peter, he was living in Canada. I wonder how many more of the young people are still around Leamington today?"

As the school was in use for the issue of gas masks, Mr. Stokes the teacher took the school children for a walk to Campion Hills.

Your Gas Mask - Civil Defence Public Information Leaflet No.2 - July 1939

'Take care of your gas mask and your gas mask will look after you. It is possible that in war your life might depend on your gas mask and the condition in which it had been kept. The official gas mask, or respirator, consists of a metal container filled with a material which absorbs the gas, and a rubber face piece with a non-inflammable transparent window. Some people seem to think that this mask does not look as if it would offer very good protection. Actually, it has been most carefully designed and fully tested, and will give you adequate protection against breathing any of the known war gases. But remember it will not protect you from the ordinary gas that you burn in a gas cooker or gas fire.

How to Store it - Your mask should be kept carefully. Never hang it up by the straps which fasten it over the head. This will pull the rubber face piece out of shape so that it no longer fits you properly. It should be kept in the special box provided, where this has been issued, but any box which is air tight, or nearly so, will do. When placed in the box the metal container should lie flat with the rubber face piece uppermost, the transparent window lying evenly on top at full length. Great care should be taken not to bend or fold the window, or to let it get scratched, cracked or dented.

Keep the box in a cool place away from strong light. Exposure to heat or prolonged exposure to strong light will spoil the material of the mask and it may cease to give complete protection. It should never be held close to a fire or hot water pipes, or left lying out in the sun.

How to put it on and take it off - It is important to know how to put on your mask quickly and properly. You might need to do this in a hurry. To put it on, hold the mask by each of the side straps with the thumbs underneath and the inside of the window facing you. Then lift the mask to your face, push your chin forwards into it and draw the straps over the top of your head as far as they will go. See that the straps are properly adjusted and leave them so.

To remove the mask, insert the thumb under the buckle at the back of your head and then pull it forward over the top of your head so that the mask is lowered downwards from the face. Never try to lift the mask off upwards or by pulling the container or the edge of the rubber at the chin. To prevent the window from misting over when the mask is worn, wet the end of a finger and rub it on a piece of toilet soap. Then rub the finger all over the inside of the window so as to leave a thin film of soap.

Putting your mask away - After the mask has been used you will find that it is wet on the inside with moisture from the breath. This should be wiped off with a soft dry cloth and the mask allowed to dry before it is put away in its box. Do not try to dry it by applying heat.

The contents of the container do not deteriorate either with age or with wearing the mask when gas is not present. But if you suspect any flaw in your gas mask you should inform your local air raid warden. It is a good thing to get out your gas mask occasionally and put it on, so as to get used to wearing it, and if you take the simple precautions set out above you will ensure that it is always ready for your protection.'

The Morning News dated Wednesday 11th October 1939 reported that 5000 gas-mask satchels were being provided for school children by the Leamington Education Committee. The cost to the committee was 1s. 0½d. per satchel.

The Morning News dated Friday 5th January 1940 reported that, a supply of Anti-Gas Helmets for children up to the age of two years, has now been received for distribution. Parents should apply at once at the Air Raid Wardens' Headquarters, Jephson Villa, 6 Hamilton Terrace, or at any of the under-mentioned Air Raid Wardens' Posts, to register their children who are now under two years of age and make application for the issue of Anti-Gas Helmets.

After registration has been effected, Anti-Gas Helmets will be delivered at the parents' house, and the use of the Helmet will be demonstrated by an Air Raid Warden. The Air Raid Wardens Posts to which application may be made are as follows: -

Central Hotel Post, Euston Place; Leicester Street Schools Post, Leicester Street; Union Road Post, Sub-Police Station, Union Road; Lillington Library, Lillington; Weights and Measures Post, Police Station, High Street; R.M.C. Post, Home for Incurables, Tachbrook Street entrance; Avenue Road Post, Garage at rear of 26, Avenue Road; Shrubland Street Schools Post, Shrubland Street. - E. Sidwell Divisional Air Raid Warden January 2, 1940.

On 27th January 1940, it was reported that 760 babies' helmets and 390 babies' respirators had been received.

On 26th July 1940, the Divisional Warden reported that up to 34,000 'Contex' filters had been fitted in a week.

The Morning News dated 19th March 1941 reported that a respirator had caused a soldier's death – 'A soldier's respirator, provided to save his life, caused his death. This was revealed at the Leamington inquest on Gunner Frank Abbott, of an A.A. battery, who was killed in a singular accident in Leicester Lane on Friday morning. Evidence was given that as an Army lorry carrying soldiers passed another lorry, driven by a Rugby man, the reflecting mirror or some projecting part tore the canvas covering off the Army lorry, caught Abbott's respirator strap, and pulled him into the road. He sustained a fractured skull. A verdict of "Accidental Death" was recorded.'

Identity Cards

The 1939 Register, similar to a census, was taken on Friday 29th September 1939 having been introduced by Parliament as an emergency measure at the start of the war.

The information giving details of name, address, date of birth, gender, marital status and occupation, was used to provide a snapshot of the 40 million population of England and Wales just as the war started.

It provided current population statistics and was used for the issuing of National Registration Identity Cards, and later to facilitate the issuing of ration books.

Everyone, including children had to carry their ID cards.

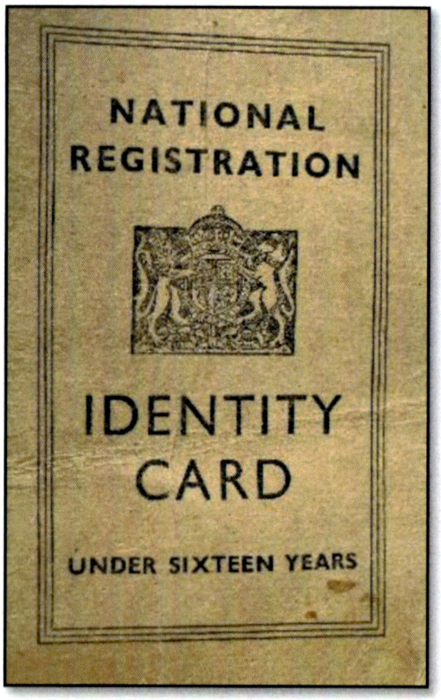

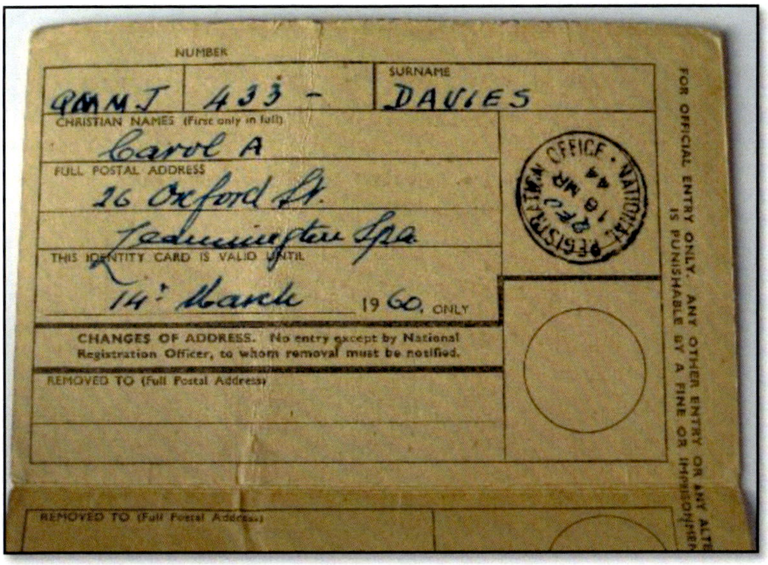

Initially they were brown for both adults and children under 16 years of age, but in 1943 a blue version was issued to adults.

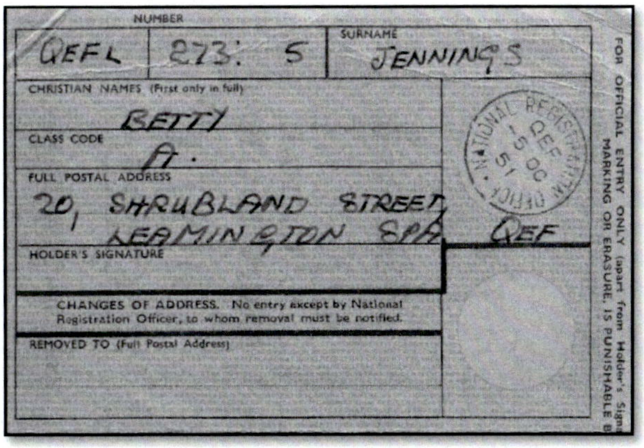

You may be forgiven for thinking that the scheme would have ended in 1945; however, it was 7 years later on 21st February 1952 before this happened when it was no longer necessary to carry an identity card.

Identity Labels - Public Information Leaflet No.1 stated: - In war you should carry about with you your name and address clearly written. This should be on an envelope, card or luggage label, not on some odd piece of paper easily lost. In the case of children, a label should be fastened, e.g. sewn, on to their clothes, in such a way that it will not readily become detached.

Black-outs and Lighting Restrictions

Prior to the war starting, warnings were already being issued about lighting restrictions: - 'If war should come all windows, sky-lights, glazed doors, or other openings which would show a light, will have to be screened in war time with dark blinds or blankets, or brown paper pasted on the glass, so that no light is visible from outside. You should obtain now any materials you may need for this purpose. No outside lights will be allowed, and all street lighting will be put out. Instructions will be issued about the dimming of lights on vehicles.'

On the 1st September 1939, two days before the outbreak of war, the black-out restrictions started as the Government attempted to make the enemy bombers job more difficult. No chinks of light, no see-through curtains, no car headlights. Even the red glow of a cigarette was banned. In the event of an air raid at night, people were warned to be extremely careful not to switch on the lights in their bedroom. Britain was plunged into complete darkness.

In order to assist car drivers and pedestrians a little, some trees and bridges had white stripes painted on them as this photo taken in Avenue Road shows.

It was reported on 8th September 1939 that Messrs. E. Francis & Sons 34-40 Bath Street had been paid £33. 11s. 9d. for blacking out the windows at Hamilton House Report and Control Centre.

At the very beginning of the war, Leamington appealed to its citizens to take part in a black-out, but it wasn't very successful. A Leamington Spa Courier correspondent was quoted as saying, "A lot has been done to secure a real and honest black-out in Leamington, but the Upper Parade is really pathetic. On the other hand, the efforts of people in King Street, Queen Street and gallant Windmill Road have been wholehearted and immensely successful."

As far as children were concerned, one of the biggest problems caused by the black-out, was that Guy Fawkes night was cancelled for the duration of the war halting a tradition that dates back to 1605. The sight of bonfires and fireworks by the likes of Brocks and Standard would have to wait until the war ended.

A safety-first poster was issued to cyclists giving advice/instructions about their cycles. **Look Out in the Black-out** – 'There should be a regulation white patch on the rear mudguard - Good tyres and brakes - The rear lamp must have only one aperture, no bigger than a one inch circle, the light from which must be clearly visible from 30 yards but not visible at 300 yards - the upper half of the front lamp glass and whole of the side or rear panels must be completely obscured; the lower half of the reflector must be painted with black matt paint or otherwise rendered ineffective.'

Masking your windows - Public information leaflet No.2 - July 1939

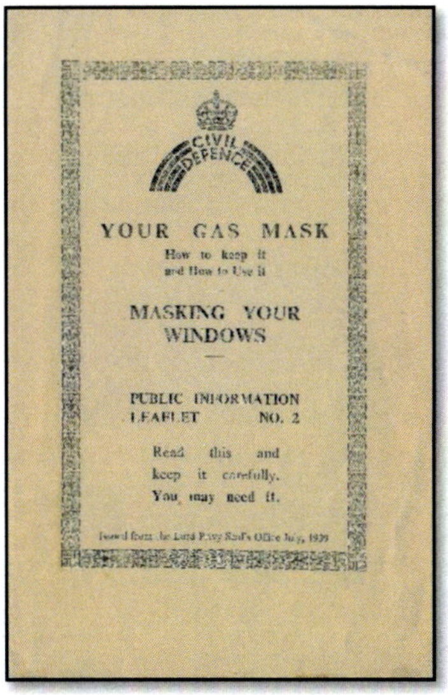

'In war, one of our great protections against the dangers of air attack after nightfall is the "black-out". On the outbreak of hostilities all external lights and street lighting will be totally extinguished so as to give hostile aircraft no indication as to their whereabouts. But this will not be fully effective unless ***you*** do your part, and see to it that no lighting in the house where you live is visible from the outside. The motto for safety will be "Keep it dark!"

Every occupier of rooms, house or flat will be responsible for darkening his own lights. Lights in the halls or on the staircases of blocks of flats or dwellings will be the responsibility of the landlord or owner.

The most convenient way of shutting in the light is to use close fitting blinds. These can be of any thick, dark coloured material such as dark blue or black or dark green glazed Holland, Lancaster or Italian cloth. If you cannot manage this, you could obscure your windows by fixing up sheets of black paper or thick dark brown paper mounted on battens.

Possibly you have blinds already fitted to your windows. If the material is not sufficiently opaque, you can treat it with Oil Bound Water Paint or Distemper of some dark colour. The following mixture can be applied with a brush: 1lb of concentrated size, 3lb lamp black in powder form, 1.2 gill of gold size. The size and lamp black should be thoroughly mixed and 2½ gallons of boiling water added. This quantity will cover about 80 square yards of material.

If your blinds do not fit very closely, you could paint the edges of the window panes all round with dark paint. It will, of course, help you if you also shade your lights so as to prevent any light falling directly on the window.

Most important - do not forget your skylight if you have one, or glazed doors or even fanlights. You may find it simplest to make these permanently obscure by applying sufficient coats of some dark distemper or paint, or pasting them over with thick brown paper.

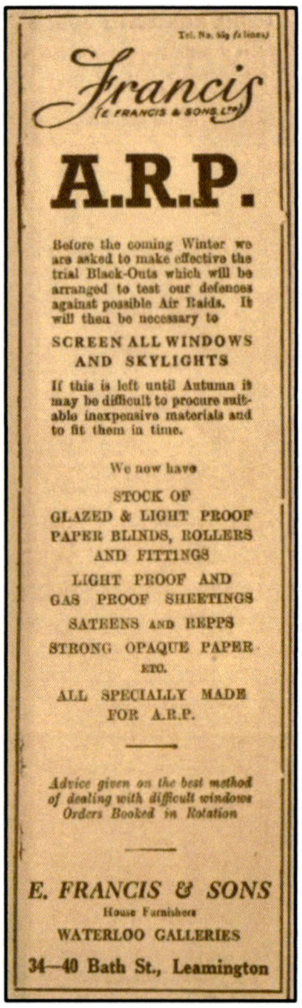

Advert: Leamington Spa Courier dated 1st July 1939.

There is another thing to remember - make sure that no light shows when your front door or back door is open. In some cases, it may be possible to fix a curtain in the hall or passage to form a "light lock", but if this cannot be done, the light must be turned off before the door is opened.

Some people perhaps will only use one or two rooms at night in war time. This, of course, would simplify matters considerably, as the precautions indicated would only have to be taken for those particular rooms. But you would have to take care not to show by mistake any light in a room where the windows were not screened, and also to see that the light did not reach the window of an unoccupied room through some open door.

Do not leave things until the last, but get together the materials which you think you would need. If you wait, you might find that you had difficulty in getting what you wanted. Besides, your help is wanted in making effective the "black-outs" for the A.R.P. exercises which are being arranged to try out our defences from time to time. After all, it is only common sense to make our preparations in advance to meet a possible emergency.'

Interviewed on Wednesday 6th September 1939, the Acting Chief Constable, Mr. A. E. Young said that generally speaking, Leamington people had complied very well with the lighting regulations.

"Very careful attention should be made to skylights, however," said Mr. Young. "For these can only be seen from above. Shops should conform a little better than at present, especially at the doors. The regulations suggest the use of a light trap, but only a few have been erected and the result is that the public using the shops allow a rather dangerous light to appear."

Speaking of vehicles, the Acting Chief Constable said, "I should like to remind the public that slits in headlamp screens do not comply with the lighting regulations unless they are also provided with a hood. In many cases, lights have been slotted but no hood is provided. Generally speaking, people should be discouraged from using even these head-lights. Good advice is to keep off the roads altogether at night."

Advert: Leamington Spa Courier dated 8th December 1939.

"This last injunction could also apply to pedestrians. Roads are not as safe now as they usually are, and unless people are forced to go out, they should stay at home. I should be glad if they would comply with the Chamber of Trade's appeal to 'shop early'. Very few cyclists are exhibiting the red rear-light which is now compulsory, but I understand that this may partly be due to the fact that such rear-lights are practically unobtainable."

"All lighting regulations will now be rigidly enforced by the police, who are being assisted by the Air-Raid Wardens. If anyone has any doubt about anything, he or she should enquire from any member of the Force, who will be glad to help. One final word. Pedestrians should remember that they should be careful about the use of torches and the striking of matches during the black-out. Torches are subject to the same restrictions as car lights, and are forbidden unless covered by a hood."

At first owners of motor vehicles had to severely dim their car headlights, but a proper hood became compulsory on 22nd January 1940. The hood or mask was fitted to either the nearside or offside; the bulb from the one not being used had to be removed. Reflectors had to be painted black or rendered non-reflective. In order to identify emergency vehicles during the blackout, the blanked off headlamp could have on it the service it belonged to e.g. W [Warden], FAP [First Aid Party], VCP [Volunteer Car Pool] etc. By 1942, some restrictions were lifted and the full aperture of rear lamps could be used.

Despite the warnings, a number of people were prosecuted in the local Magistrates Court for a variety of offences that wouldn't necessarily have been brought in peace time.

Although I don't want to give particular details of individuals, this is a summary of one day in Leamington Spa Police Court: - For black-out offences two people were fined £1 with 2s. 6d. costs and one person in Greatheed Road was fined £2 with 2s. 6d. costs. For a chimney fire in the blackout, one person was fined 15s. and for a similar offence in daylight a person in Brunswick Street was fined 5s. For failing to immobilise her car which had been left on the Parade, a lady from Holly Walk was fined 10s. For riding a 'lightless' bicycle in Lower Avenue, a man from Pound Lane was fined £1 and for displaying unauthorised lights on a motor car, a man from Clemens Street was fined 5s. and 2s. 6d. costs.

In November 1940, a pensioner who had lost an eye in the First World War, was fined five shillings at Leamington Police Court for using an unscreened hand torch in the black-out while passing through Church Walk. He said that the light was necessary for him to get along. Thirteen other people were also fined on the same day for black-out offences.

On 21st November 1941, the Leamington Spa Courier reported a man being fined £1 for failing to immobilise a car in Kenilworth Street. Another was fined £2 for driving a car at a speed exceeding 20 miles per hour in Rugby Road and four people who were on the 'Black Out List' were fined for breaches of the Lighting Restrictions Order. In mitigation one person stated that "a dog had opened the door of a room from which the offending light was showing".

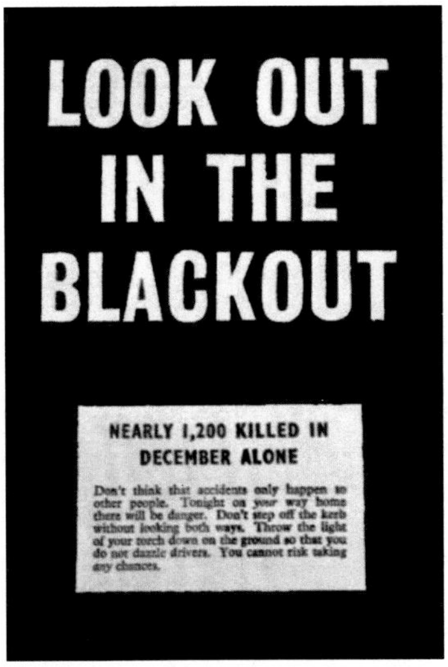
LOOK OUT IN THE BLACKOUT

NEARLY 1,200 KILLED IN DECEMBER ALONE

Don't think that accidents only happen to other people. Tonight on your way home there will be danger. Don't step off the kerb without looking both ways. Throw the light of your torch down on the ground so that you do not dazzle drivers. You cannot risk taking any chances.

Image: Leamington Spa Courier dated 9th February 1940.

Although there was a good reason for blackouts, being that light helped German bomber pilots, they did cause some serious problems as the Morning News dated Friday 15th September 1939 shows: - **Leamington's First Black-Out Victim – Inquest on Cyclist Knocked Down at Cubbington – Witness Says "Car Lights Were Insufficient to Pick up Object"** – The first Leamingtonian to be killed in the black-out was Valentine Dighton [52], a single man, of 14, Vincent Street, who was employed as a storekeeper at a Coventry factory. On Monday night, while pushing his pedal-cycle near to the Rugby Tavern at New Cubbington, he was struck by a motor-car, sustaining serious injuries from which he died in the Warneford Hospital the following day. The Coroner, Mr. E. F. Hadow, said he expected more such occurrences. Sympathising with the driver of the car involved, he said, "He is not to blame, but the lighting restrictions are."

The Morning News dated Wednesday 8th July 1942 reported: - **Leamington Club Tragedy – Steward Mistook Stairs in Dark** – It was surmised at an inquest at the Warneford Hospital, on Monday, that Harry Weston, 69-year-old steward of the Trades Hall, High Street, met his death when, while using the stairs at the club in the dark, he stepped on to a flight he thought ascended when in reality they were a flight descending. He fell to the bottom of the stairs, striking his head on the rails and sustaining a fractured spine. The mishap occurred on Thursday last, and Mr. Weston died the following day. He had been at the Trades Hall since August, 1940. Recording a verdict of "Accidental Death," the Coroner, Mr. E. F. Hadow, expressed sympathy with Mrs. Weston.

Throughout the war people were reminded about the blackout as this article from the Morning News dated Thursday 13th August 1942 shows: - '**Please to Remember** – "Put that light out!" This is a saying most people will have heard and will associate with past winter months when the black-out has been one of the most noticeable features of our daily lives and has caused us to look for chinks of light in our windows and grope about in pitch dark streets with the aid of torches. Now that the hour has been taken off double Summer Time, winter months lie ahead and nights begin to lengthen; we must once more look to those curtains and see that the wardens and firewatchers do not catch us napping. In view of recent events no stress need be laid on the fact that we must not relax in this matter. It is to be noticed that in a large number of lighting cases brought before the magistrates it is revealed that the offending light was switched on during the daytime and forgotten until the person responsible was roused from sleep to put it out. In some homes "hubby's" last duty at night is to make a round of the house to see that all lights are switched off – a five minutes job that may save no end of trouble. This, too, should be the practise of every Fire Guard and persons in charge of business premises.'

'**Forgotten Fires** – A similar thing happens with fires – during daylight they are frequently forgotten by those away from home until a late hour and are left burning in unscreened rooms. Get those black-out curtains or boards fixed up to your windows again and [another job for "hubby"] see that no ray of light is visible from outside. Keep your outer doors closed. A curtain fixed a short space inside the door is essential in some public establishments where people are continually coming and going. If you use a torch when walking in the street during the black-out, see that it is properly screened. Do not flash it about. Keep to the left and if possible wear something white. Be careful where you walk. Make sure after a spell of work on the allotment that the refuse heap is not still smouldering.'

'**Road Users** – Travel carefully, see that your lights and masks are in working order. A common offender last winter was the cyclist without a rear light, a danger not only to himself but to other people on the road. A rather more unusual point is the land mark afforded by washing hanging on a line in the backyard after dark. So mother – when you put up the black-out take down the washing. Black-out times appear daily in the press. **Remember** Those who commit these breaches of the regulations may not only be endangering their own lives, but the lives of others, too.'

The Morning News dated Saturday 8th January 1944 reported a further death as a result of the blackout: - **Death of Leamington Licensees' Manager – Victim of Black-Out Accident** – Mr. Thomas David Dickinson, who died in the Warneford Hospital, on Thursday, was manager of Messrs. Brett's Wine Vaults, 27, Bedford Street, Leamington. Mr. Dickinson, who was 60 and married, had been in the hospital since December 8, when he sustained injuries on being knocked down by a motor vehicle in the black-out.

On 29th December 1944, the Watch Committee decided on the possible relaxation of street lighting restrictions and the experimental repainting of twenty-seven lamp posts in the Borough by Messrs. Lewis & Watters at a cost of £32.

Lighting restrictions were lifted on 30th April 1945, five years and 123 days since the blackout started. Big Ben was lit up for the first time. This was the same day that Adolf Hitler committed suicide. However, the Ministry of Fuel & Power asked local authorities, in the interest of fuel economy, to extinguish all street lights from 1st May until 15th June 1945 when full street lighting, up to pre-war standards, could be resumed.

Civil Defence

The Ministry of Home Security was established by the Government in 1939. Its function was to direct the civil defence work of government departments and local authorities. Their responsibilities for civil defence covered many aspects, from the emergency services to A.R.P. Wardens, and included the provision of air raid shelters, ambulances and casualty services, a gas identification service, decontamination, report centres, messenger service, rescue operations and mortuary service. The Ministry also had the task of making preparations for the possibility of an invasion.

In 1980 Nora Henn and Norah Prosser recalled: - "During World War Two Harrington House was requisitioned and it became the Headquarters of Civil Defence. We did our W.V.S. training there. It was a huge house with huge rooms and a beautiful staircase with a stained-glass window at the top of the stairs. There were glass-houses and conservatories all-round the house with palms and peaches etc., and there were beautiful trees in the garden. We had lectures there and training. We had to read maps and do stirrup pump practice and build fires and cook outside etc. There was also a Civil Defence Club there with a canteen and a bar, and there were social evenings. Brigadier J.G.S. Ross, who lived in Newbold Terrace was in charge."

Harrington House was designed by Edward Pugin in 1869 and built by William Gascoyne. It was the largest Victorian Gothic Villa in the town. It was demolished in 1967 and the Royal Spa Centre, which was opened on 15th June 1972 by the Earl of Avon, now occupies the site.

The top floor of Radford Brewery at Radford Semele was used to produce blueprints for the war effort. Wrens [Women's Royal Naval Service] were involved in decoding work at the brewery. The Wrens lived in Leamington.

Freda Watson recalled in 1977, "The Wrens were here too, billeted at Harrington House and working on the top floor of Thornley's Brewery at Radford. They were doing decoding and were afraid people would try and find out about this, but the public firmly believed they were bottling beer for the navy and never questioned them. Mrs. Watson's cousin was in the Wrens with me. There were 30 to 40 of us. At first I lived at home, but later we had quarters, at 10 and 12 Newbold Terrace, where the Spa Centre is now. We biked to Thornley's Brewery at first, but later had a minibus. It went from High Street Post Office to Radford. We had to march from the quarters to High Street to get it. We had a very strict C.O., Captain Sutton. He was well liked and respected but had a strict routine. There was no talking in the office. We had to concentrate for we were doing important confidential work. We had a Royal Marine guard, and the Marines got out the books for us and put them away safely when work was over. Later on, I went to Poole. I loved it there. At Leamington, the Wrens had parties at the quarters and dancing in the Parthenon. We had the Marines band. Captain Vivian Dunn was bandmaster."

Leamington's Civil Defence officials on 25th September 1939 on the balcony of the Town Hall.

Seated L-R: Dr. E. R. Gilmore [First Aid Commandant]; Mr. A. E. Young, Acting Chief Constable of the Police and Fire Brigades, Head of the Special Constables, Police War Reserve and Auxiliary Fire Service; Mr. Alan F. Greenwood [Town Clerk], Sub-Controller of A.R.P. Services, National Registration Officer, Food Executive Officer and Chief Billeting Officer; and Mr. J. Sutcliffe, Head of Engineering Services.

Standing L-R: Mr. Arthur J. Smith, Decontamination Officer, Mr. Ernest Sidwell, Chief Air Raid Warden; Mr. Peter Clarke, Deputy Sub-Controller of A.R.P. Services; Mr. C. O. Innes-Jones [Chief Engineering Assistant], Deputy Head of Engineering Services; Mr. G. J. W. Hellon, District A.R.P. Officer; and Mr. L. Mallinson, Evacuation and Chief Reception Officer.

MIDLAND (No. 9) REGION

CIVIL DEFENCE

WOMEN'S ORGANISATION

ADMIT ONE

To CALTHORPE PARK, BIRMINGHAM,
REGIONAL EXERCISE,

THURSDAY, 18th APRIL, 1940.

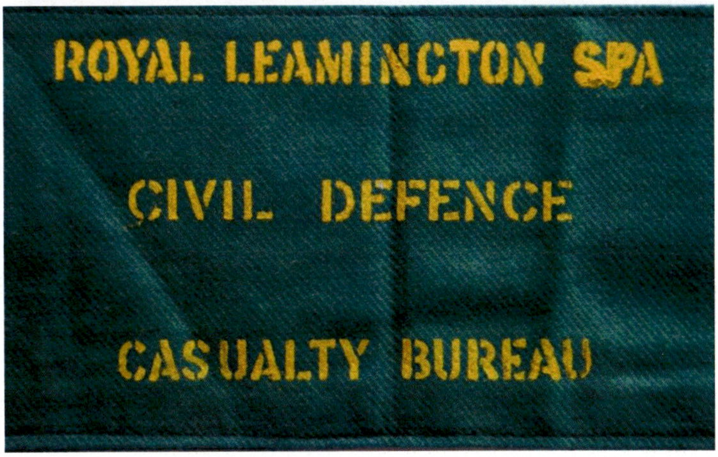

Photographs of a Civil Defence tunic button, an admittance ticket to a Civil Defence women's organisation exercise in Birmingham, and two Civil Defence arm bands.

Report and Control Centre

The Report and Control Centre was at Jephson Villa 4 Hamilton Terrace at the corner of Rosefield Place, the site of the old Police Station. It was on the ground floor, heavily reinforced and had cellars beneath. On 25th May 1939, it was reported that the telephone system had been installed in the Centre. On 28th July 1939, it was reported that the Report and Control Centre was now complete.

The function of the Report Centre was to receive messages concerning air raid damage and other reports covering secret and confidential information, and also reports of damage caused by enemy action. Upon receiving such reports action had to be taken immediately to see that services were sent to the incidents. The police and National Fire Service [N.F.S.] were notified so that they could immediately take action if their services were required. Further arrangements were made at all times to see that adequate reinforcements were in place, and that the feeding of Civil Defence personnel was maintained under prolonged raid conditions. Rest Centres were opened if required for homeless persons or persons whose homes may have been threatened owing to the presence of unexploded bombs. Information concerning casualties was received and passed on to the relevant people.

The following were some of the members of the team: - Divisional Controller Mr. A. F. Greenwood; Clerk to the Divisional Controller, Mrs. D. Griffiths; Divisional A.R.P. and Liaison Officer, Mr. D. L. Ryrie Butler; Officer-in-Charge, Mr. W. Egerton; Assistant to the Officer-in-Charge, Mr. A. H. Wilson; Operations Officer and Deputy Borough Engineer, Mr. C. O. Innes Jones; Clerk to the Operations Officer, Mrs. I. R. Rolfe; Plotting Clerk, Mr. F. E. Johnson; Incident Board Officer, Mr. H. F. Rolfe; Doctor in Charge of Casualty Services, Dr. E. R. Gilmore; Senior Telephonist, Miss V. R. Hughes; Assistant Telephonists, Miss B. E. Sargent, Miss M. Pain, Miss D. M. Toull, Mrs. E. Hill, Mrs. P. H. Yates and Miss E. R. Chamberlain. Head Messenger [Outside Duty] Mr. E. A. Bloxham; Assistant Messengers, Mr. M. D. Gardner, Mr. D. N. O'Dell and Mr. N. S. Lawson. Head Messenger [Inside Duty] Mrs. D. M. Baskott, Miss J. Healey, Miss M. Worledge and Miss D. M. Batkin. Rendevous Messengers, Mr. G. W. J. Franklin, Mr. J. H. F. Randell and Miss P. B. U. Wilson.

On 23rd February 1940, it was stated at the A.R.P. committee meeting that the previous staffing establishment was nine men and 21 women. At the time of the meeting five men and six women were employed and it was proposed that the new establishment should be two men and three women. However, it was resolved that four men would be employed full time and that the present female staff would be discharged. It was said that, "After consideration we are of the opinion that the dramatic reduction in paid personnel must inevitably have a detrimental effect on the efficiency of the whole organisation." A resolution was then passed, "It is the earnest hope of this committee that additional volunteers will enrol so as to maintain the services." It was reported at the A.R.P. committee meeting on 21st June 1940 that the Report Centre was manned each night by six volunteers, all of whom were Town Hall staff.

In June 1943, Leamington Report Centre won the cup presented by the County War Emergency Committee in a competition to test the efficiency of the Civil Defence nerve centres. For the purpose of the competition, the County was split into three sections depending on the size of the Report Centre. The first section consisted of four towns with large Report Centres. The second section, of which Leamington was the winner, consisted of eight towns and the third section comprised three rural districts. Three neutral umpires were appointed from Staffordshire.

A.R.P. Control Centre on 22nd June 1945. Photo courtesy of Warwickshire County Record Office. Ref: PH(N)600/720/25.

A.R.P. Control Centre on 22nd June 1945. Photos courtesy of Warwickshire County Record Office. Refs: PH(N)600/720/26 & 27.

A.R.P. Control Centre on 22nd June 1945. Photo courtesy of Warwickshire County Record Office. Ref: PH(N)600/720/29.

On 26th July 1945, it was decided that once Jephson Villa was no longer needed by the Report & Control Centre, the rooms on the 1st floor would be offered to the National Fire Service and the Warwickshire County Probation Office as office accommodation.

Messenger Service

There were 40 men and eight women in the Civil Defence Messenger Service, although these numbers did fluctuate slightly. In early 1941 appeals were made for more volunteers for the Messenger Service. On 2nd January 1942, approval was given for four messengers to be allocated to the rest and information centres.

Pauline Zwicker, a second cousin of mine, lived at 25 Chandos Street during the war. In 1964, she sailed to Canada and eventually settled in Lunenburg, Nova Scotia, Canada. In 1980, she recalled some of her war time memories: - "Having left Milverton Senior School I started work in the Filing Office at Lockheed Hydraulic Brake Company for the princely sum of ten shillings a week. I still have the diaries I kept, with the exception of 1944. On 3rd September 1939, I wrote simply **WAR**. I was still working at Lockheed's and sometimes we had to go to the air-raid shelters. On one occasion, I returned to the office to find that the steel grating from high up in the wall above my place had been loosened by the bomb blast and had landed on my chair, better that than on my head."

"During the war, we had a Civil Defence Messengers Service. Our Report Centre was at Jephson Villa, a house on the corner of the street behind Euston Place, at the Holly Walk end. Our job was to deliver civil defence messages via bicycle to fire-watchers at the depots and to collect report sheets from them. Mostly, it was great fun."

"We were a young crowd and had our own recreation room somewhere along Holly Walk near the British Restaurant. There we used to dance, play cards and rehearse our play, which never did come off. The recreation room was officially opened on 11th September 1941."

"We were required to attend evening rota duty and all-night duty at the Report Centre, and also to turn out during the night if there was an air-raid. It seemed a bit of a lark in those far-off days to jump out of bed, in uniform and tin hat as quickly as possible, hop on a bike and tazz down Holly Walk, perhaps see a little red light in front and call out, "Is that you Jean [Wills]?" "Yes, is that you Paul?"

"After we had reached the Report Centre and signed on, I think the first thing that we all did was to make tea. Every so often we would have squad-drill and be put through our paces by Captain D. L. Ryrie-Butler who was the A.R.P. officer and training officer. We each had a number, mine was 66, and I was always slightly embarrassed when I had to call out my number and Captain Ryrie-Butler responded with 'clickety-click'."

"Our chief messenger was Edgar Palmer who lived at 23 Highland Road, Lillington. Sometimes he would organise long cycle rides for us. We swam a lot together too. It was all rather fun and like belonging to a youth social club. I suppose in a way it was a bitter-sweet night for us all when on 28th May 1945 we had our Messengers' farewell dinner at Bobby's. On 30th May 1945, the Report Centre was opened to the public for inspection."

Top: Control Centre messengers, telephonists and other staff. Bottom: Civil Defence Messengers at the Report Centre. Seated left is Pauline Zwicker née Wilson, seated centre is Mary Jackson and standing on the right is Mrs. D. Baskott. It is not known who the three men are.

Civil Defence Messengers.

Air Raid Precautions

The biggest perceived threat to our country was from the air, and so the Air Raid Precautions organisation was formed as early as March 1935 to supervise civil defence measures throughout the UK in order to minimise the dangers. In July 1936, the Air Raid Precautions [A.R.P.] Department became the central civil defence authority. By 1938, Leamington A.R.P Centre had been set up and instructor Mr. A. J. Smith was talking at public meetings where hundreds turned out. Housewives, in particular, seemed anxious to hear what they could do in their homes to be safe. Demonstrations were promised on types of gas bombs and incendiary devices likely to be used. Knowledge was vital, said Mr. Smith.

Arthur Smith's A.R.P. instructor badge.

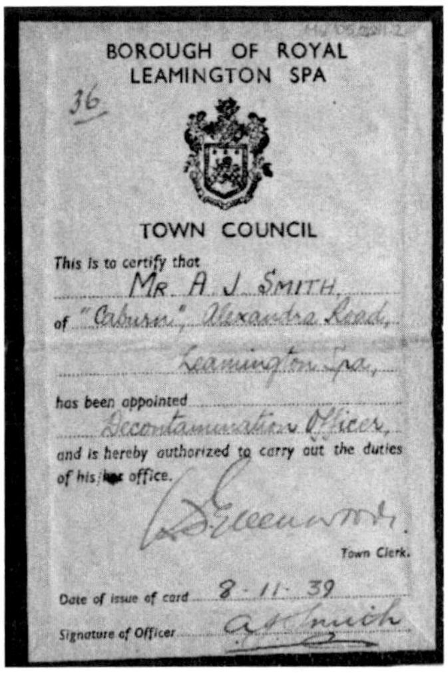
BOROUGH OF ROYAL LEAMINGTON SPA

36

TOWN COUNCIL

This is to certify that Mr. A. J. Smith,

of "Coburn" Alexandra Road,

Leamington Spa,

has been appointed Decontamination Officer,

and is hereby authorized to carry out the duties of his/her office.

Town Clerk.

Date of issue of card 8-11-39

Signature of Officer A J Smith

This is Arthur Smith's authorisation pass which was issued to him on 8th November 1939. He qualified as an A.R.P. instructor in 1938. Throughout the war, he was the Deputy Training Officer and Decontamination Officer for Leamington Spa and Officer in Charge of the South Warwickshire Civil Defence Equipment Repair Depot. He also undertook a range of other civil defence duties and was later awarded the defence medal.

The Air Raid Precautions Committee consisted of: - The Mayor and representatives of the following committees: - Education, Finance, Health, Highways and Town Planning, Pump Room, Watch, and Water and Sewage; as well as Alderman Davis and Gardner; Councillors Mrs. Bragg, Pain and Wallsgrove. Co-opted members were Messrs. I. A. A. Macdonald, deputy manager of the Midland Electric Light and Power Company, R. J. Pressney, R. S. Ramsden, Director, Engineer and Manager of Leamington Priors Gas Company, E. Sidwell, Chief Air Raid Warden and Stanley Wood, Manager of the Regent Garage. The first meeting of the Leamington A.R.P. Committee took place in December 1938 and the last one was on 22nd June 1945.

In September 1938, the Leamington Spa Courier carried an advertisement from the local Officer of Health, under the heading "Air Raid Precautions", appealing for supplies of blankets and clothes to stock the First Aid posts in readiness for the coming crisis.

In January 1939, Parliament brought in the A.R.P. [Air Raid Precautions] Act, making councils responsible for setting up an organisation to deal with such things as blackouts, air raid warnings and air raid shelters to protect civilians, emergency casualty services, air raid wardens and rescue squads. In March, the Home Secretary made an appeal on radio for one million A.R.P. volunteers.

The Morning News dated Wednesday 7th June 1939 reported: - '**A.R.P. in the Schools – Leamington Plans for the Protection of Scholars – Teachers Asked to Undergo Training** – In the event of an air raid occurring while schools are in session, it is recommended at Leamington that children who could get home within seven minutes should be sent home, and that protection should be provided for the remainder. Plans have been prepared of the proposed lay-out of trenches adjacent to all the elementary schools with the exception of Leicester Street School, where the basement could be adapted. These would afford protection to all children unable to reach their homes within five minutes. The total cost would be approximately £7,500, of which the Board of Education would pay 50 per cent, if the proposals were approved on their behalf.

Appeal to Teachers - Following the receipt of a Board of Education circular, teachers in all elementary schools are being asked to undergo training in air raid precautions, and respirator drills and air raid drills are to be organised in the schools.' [Ed's note: Approval for the scheme was given on Monday 12th June 1939. 900 children could get home in five minutes, 2,572 children plus the staff had to be provided for at a cost of just under £3 per head].

The Morning News dated Thursday 27th July 1939 reported: - **Warwickshire to Spend £75,000 on Air Raid Trenches – One Hundred Wardens' Posts to be Provided – Good Recruiting at Leamington** – It has been decided by the Home Office that air raid wardens' posts shall be provided in peace time instead of the period between "diplomatic relations becoming strained and the falling of the first bomb," and authority has been given for 100 posts to be equipped in Warwickshire at a cost not exceeding £4,500. Leamington is marked for 12 posts and Warwick 6. This was announced at the quarterly meeting of Warwickshire County Council, yesterday, when the Air Raid Precautions Committee expressed the view that every effort should be made to utilise existing buildings by rendering them blast and splinter proof. It was reported that Leamington had 505 wardens recruited, this number being 117 in excess of requirements. The Committee's report stated the provision of A.R.P. shelters by means of trenches was preferable, where possible, to the means of basement strengthening. The committee made a total of £75,000 available for public shelters.

The Leamington Spa Courier dated Friday 8th September 1939 reported that extra duties occasioned by the A.R.P. and additional fire brigade responsibilities necessitated the strength of the Leamington Borough Police Force being increased to 55. At the Borough Petty Sessions on Monday 5th some 34 special constables were sworn in. At a special meeting of the Watch Committee on Tuesday 6th several promotions were also approved. Inspector R. W. Bastock became Chief Inspector, a rank held only once previously in the Borough Force - by Inspector William Edwards in 1908. Mr. Bastock who was 41 years of age had been a member of the Force since 1920, having previously served in the war.

Sergeant John Edgington was promoted to Inspector having been commended by the Watch Committee for his work with the Fire Brigade. He saw service in the Great War, during which he was severely wounded. Detective E. T. Woodward became a Detective Sergeant in charge of the Criminal Investigation Department.

P.C. Thomas Knifton, who had been lecturing on A.R.P. Duties, was appointed A.R.P. Sergeant. He had been a member of the Force for 10 years, having previously served with the Coldstream Guards. P.C. H. French, who had served since 1920 was promoted to Sergeant, and P.C.'s Manley and Cuttriss were appointed Detective Constables.

In December 1939, the Borough Engineer reported to the A.R.P. Committee that the work on the construction of trenches was proceeding satisfactorily and that, as soon as the equipment had been delivered, all trenches commenced upon could be completed. The Committee then resolved that the County should be asked to acquire a derelict piece of land in Satchwell Street [behind the Baptist Church] for the construction of a trench.

Leamington held its first large-scale A.R.P. test on Sunday 14th January 1940. The tests took place in the vicinity of the Town Hall, and were witnessed by a good-sized crowd, which was kept informed of the progress of events by loud speakers. Wardens, Ambulances, First Aid Parties, Rescue and Demolition Squads, Road Repair Gangs, Auxiliary Fire Brigade, Gas Company's Repair Squad, Decontamination Squad, Report Centre Staff, cars for 'sitting cases' and Mobile Units were all involved. First-Aid units from Warwick, Stratford and Kenilworth were also present.

Three main incidents were dealt with. The first related to gas bombs. Wardens proceeded to the area of contamination, put on respirators, and tested for the kind of gas employed. On finding it to be mustard gas, one warden reported it to Euston Place Post, and called out two wardens in anti-gas clothing, who plotted out the contaminated area. In the meantime, the Wardens' Post had communicated with the Report Centre requesting the despatch of the decontamination squad. The Report Centre instructed the squad to proceed from the Depot. Gas casualties having been discovered, another report was transmitted to the Report Centre, which sent for a first-aid party. Clad in anti-gas clothing, the decontamination squad and first-aid party arrived in eight minutes after the report of the incident. The decontamination squad cleansed the road surface affected by the mustard gas, and the first-aid party conveyed the casualties to Warneford Hospital, and then returned to the Depot for cleansing.

The second incident concerning a high explosive bomb took place outside Jephson Villa, the walls of which were noticed by wardens to be 'shaking badly' and liable to fall at any moment. There were also many casualties, represented by 26 Boy Scouts, each of whom was labelled with the description of a particular injury. It was assumed that communication by telephone was not possible, and so the wardens informed the Report Centre personally. The Report Centre then sent messengers by bicycle to summon further first-aid services, ambulances, first-aid parties, mobile ambulance unit, 'sitting case' cars, rescue and demolition squads, road repair gangs, a Water Department party, and Gas and Electricity Companies' gangs, all of which were on the scene in about ten minutes.

Fire was the predominant feature of the third incident, an incendiary bomb and smoke-bombs being set off by the Town Hall. Wardens reported the incident to the Post, and three wardens proceeded to extinguish the incendiary bomb by means of a stirrup-pump. The fire was assumed to be getting out of control, and the Auxiliary Fire brigade was summoned.

The Morning News dated Saturday 7th February 1940 reported: - **Leamington to be "Bombed" on Sunday – Another A.R.P. Exercise – Where to see Milverton and Lillington Incidents** – Extensive areas of Milverton and Lillington will be the scene of A.R.P. exercises to be held tomorrow [Sunday] between the hours of 10.00am. and 11.30a.m. At a number of points the public will be able to see the progress of the trial. The first incident will be in Gaveston Road, where a "mustard gas" bomb will explode. This will be discovered by a warden, whose message to the report centre will set the whole machinery of Leamington's A.R.P. organisation into motion. Personnel of every section will be in operation. Other incidents will be staged in the following order: - Beech Lawn, high explosive bomb. Woodcote Road, high explosive bomb. Lillington sandpits, fire. Kinross Road [West End], mustard gas bomb. Corner of Telford Avenue, Kinross Road, high explosive bomb.

Following an order from Government, church bells across the country were to remain silent as from 13th June 1940, and only be rung in the event of an invasion. The ringing of the bells would enable people in the locality to know immediately what was happening and respond accordingly. As the German invasion failed to materialise, the Government decided that the ringing of church bells could be recommenced on Easter Sunday 25th April 1943. However, due to the lack of bell ringers, as many were on active service, not all bells could be rung.

On 29th November 1940, the A.R.P. Officer who was based at Jephson Villa, Hamilton Terrace again advertised for men aged between 32 and 50 for full time First Aid Parties. He preferred that they were experienced in first aid and they would be paid £3. 5s. per week from their commencement of appointment which included the training period. He also required a few Rescue Workers. In May 1941 battle dress clothing was received for the First Aid Parties.

On 16th December 1941, the Emergency Committee approved extra responsibilities for a number of people: - Sanitory Inspector Mr. G. Hammond took control of the Casualty Information Bureau, Mr. J. W. McNab, the Municipal Restaurant Manager, took responsibility for emergency feeding schemes, Mr. L. Mallinson, Director of Education, took responsibility for evacuation, Mr. W. May, Borough Treasurer, took responsibility for mortuary and funeral arrangements and Mr. C. Clarke, Deputy Town Clerk took responsibility for the Blitz Intelligence Centre.

The A.R.P. Committee continued to meet, discuss and take action throughout the war. In September 1942, they discussed Fire Watching at business premises during the hours of daylight, particularly on Saturdays, Sundays and Thursday afternoons [half-day closing], when business premises were normally unoccupied. They concluded that to require parties to stand by on the premises during these periods would be tedious and demoralising to the personnel, and an unnecessary waste of manpower. Nevertheless, it was felt essential that some precautions should be taken and so Alan Greenwood, the Town Clerk and Sub Controller was instructed to ask businesses to arrange for at least one Stirrup Pump Party to immediately report for duty on the sounding of an 'alert' or obvious enemy activity. The plans were required to be notified to the Fire Guard Office at Regent Grove.

The Leamington and District Branch of the Midland Regional Association of A.R.P. Instructors held its annual meeting in November 1942 when they elected Mr. A. J. Smith, Deputy Training Officer Leamington, as Branch chairman; Major F. W. K. Blackwell, A.R.P. Officer Southam, as vice-chairman; and Mr. Jenner Stratton, A.R.P. Officer Leamington, as hon secretary and treasurer.

Arthur Smith's Civil Defence Corps badge.

The Leamington Branch was a development of the original Instructors Discussion Group formed by Mr. A. J. Smith in 1939 with the object of passing on to local instructor's up-to-date information on Civil Defence matters, and the provision of a means of discussing problems identified in carrying out duties as instructors.

The membership in 1942 was 35 and was open to all instructors holding one or other of the official qualifications - A.R.P.S; C.A.G.S; A.A.R.P; or L.A.G.C. The object of the Association was three-fold - a. The holding of meetings for mutual discussion of problems arising out of their duties - b. The delivery of lectures and addresses on subjects relating to Civil Defence - c. The dissemination among members of all available information regarding the latest developments and other matters concerning Civil Defence.

Arthur Smith's 'decontamination' shoulder patch.

In 1942 alone, lectures were given on bomb disposal, a new technique for dealing with incendiary bombs, rescue of crews from crashed aircraft, revised technique for decontaminating roads, the work of the roof-spotter, industrial camouflage and recent developments in the gas identification service.

The Morning News dated Wednesday 28th October 1942 reported: - **Civil Defence Duties – 8,000 Leamington Women Registered This Month** – A rough summary of the numbers of women who have registered during the month for civil defence duties shows that 8,000 enrolled and 5,500 claimed exemption of which 3,000 were women with children under 14. 500 women claimed hardship or medical unfitness; 750 were already performing fire-watching duties; 550 were members of the Civil Defence, Nursing Reserve, N.F.S., etc., and 700 were working long hours or were night shift workers.

Air Raid Wardens

The Air Raid Wardens Service was established in 1937 as the Government prepared for war. Altogether there were around 1,400,000 wardens in the country during the war, almost all of them were unpaid volunteers who also held day-time jobs. Air Raid Wardens were part of the A.R.P. organisation. Initially, wardens were expected to be on duty 3 nights a week, but as bombing intensified across the country this was increased.

The Chief Air Raid Warden for Leamington Spa was Ernest Sidwell. On 24th March 1939 arrangements were made for the use of Oxford House, 35 Oxford Street to be used as the Wardens Headquarters. A telephone line was to be installed between the headquarters and the police station. On 6th September 1939, it was reported that 35 Oxford Street was now empty.

On 6th September 1939, the Town Clerk reported that Ansell's Brewery had offered the use of their basement, in Lillington Avenue, free of charge, to be used as a dormitory for the Rescue and Demolition Services. It was resolved that armlets would be provided for Wardens and ID cards would be provided for A.R.P. officials.

At the end of August 1939, Ernest Sidwell said, "We have been working on Wardens' posts, of which Leamington's full war-time strength is 25. Of this number, eight have got to be built, and the County authorities officially sanctioned their construction on Saturday. Work had commenced on Monday 28th August."

He continued, "The town has been divided into four sections by drawing imaginary lines down the Kenilworth Road, Parade and Clemens Street, and along the course of the river."

"The position of the Wardens' posts will be: - Section 'A' – Union Road Police Station; the basement of No.1 Northumberland Road; the Adelaide Road Depot; and the basement of the R.D.C. Offices in Waterloo Place. These are all ready for occupation, and one new post is to be built in Woodcote Road. Section 'B' – The Board Room of the Lillington Library; Chandos Street Sub-Police Station; Basement of the Central Hotel, Euston Place, and a room in Leicester Street Schools. The following are to be built: - A protected post at the sand-pits, Cubbington Road; one in Campion Terrace, and one in Regent Grove."

"Section 'C' – Basement of St. John's Lodge, Charlotte Street; a room at the Home for Incurables; the Bath Street Schools, and the garage at 'Cranbrook', Adelaide Road. Another protected post is to be built on the site of the Booster Station by the Canal bridge. Section 'D' – Room at the Police Station, High Street; the Parochial Hall, New Street, and Shrubland Street School. Three protected posts are to be built – one on the Eagle Recreation Ground, one in Mill Road, and one at the Oak Inn. With the exception of those being built, the posts will be ready for Wardens to occupy as soon as instructions for us to continue on a war-time basis are received. They will not be occupied until war starts; but in every district, when an emergency arises, two or three will be occupied to form a nucleus for the service. They will be manned the whole time, so that someone will always be on duty."

Prior to the introduction and issue of uniforms, wardens were issued with a black steel helmet with a white 'W' on it. The only exception was Chief Wardens who wore a white helmet with black lettering, an armlet, and a silver badge, worn with their civilian clothes. The wardens were issued with a uniform of heavy cotton dark blue overalls and wellington boots, and later a dark blue battledress.

Whistles were issued to warn people to take cover, or just to get them to notice and listen before being told to do something. Other equipment available included a ceiling pike which could be used to explore bomb damaged buildings whilst ladders were strategically placed in an area. The ladder in the photograph was in Neilston Street on the Althorpe Street Estate.

The Warden is Doris 'Doss' Underhill, one of three wardens in the area. The A.R.P. wardens were almost always local as it was essential that they knew their sector and the people living there. Doris lived at 2 Neilston Street with her husband Jack.

Photo: Doris Underhill's uniform was on display at the Leamington Spa Art Gallery and Museum from 22nd July – 16th October 2016.

A gas rattle gave a warning of a gas attack whilst the all clear was given by the ringing of a hand bell. The Wardens were responsible for notifying the fire brigade of any fires and would use report forms to notify the report centre of bomb damage, where they were dropped, types of bombs dropped, any damage to mains water, gas, electricity as well as sewers. Wardens were trained in first aid and a first aid kit was issued to them for treating the injured. They had access to stirrup pumps for putting out incendiaries and small fires. Mainly it was a two-man operation, one working the pump in a bucket of water and the other pointing the jet at the fire, although it could be done by one person.

Helmets for other services had other letters on them. Rescue services had an 'R' on them which was later changed to 'HR' and 'LR' for heavy and light rescue parties. First Aid Parties had 'FAP', Messengers had 'M', Ambulance drivers had 'A' and Stretcher Parties had 'SP'.

To start with wardens were paid, but that didn't last for long, and it soon became a voluntary service as the A.R.P. Committee minutes dated 23rd February 1940 show. Prior to February 1940 the warden's authorised staffing establishment was 50 men and 12 women. At the time of the meeting there were 22 men and 4 women in post. The Town Clerk stated at the meeting that all paid Wardens would be discharged on 24th February 1940 and that the new establishment would be nil! After that it was all down to volunteers!

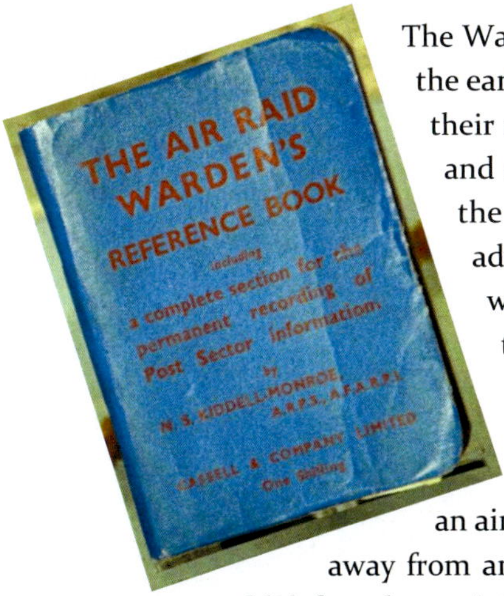

The Warden's job included a number of responsibilities. In the early stages of the war, before any bombing had started, their main duties were to register everyone in their sector and enforce the black-out. They needed to know where the shelters were located in their sector so they could advise people during an air raid warning as to the whereabouts of their nearest shelter. They patrolled the streets of their area ensuring that everyone obeyed the 'black-out' regulations. Often a shout of, **"Put that light out"** was heard with persistent offenders being reported to the police. If there was an air raid they needed to make sure that the public stayed away from any unexploded bombs until the bomb disposal unit could defuse them. A 600-yard radius had to be enforced around the bomb. They encouraged people to carry their gas masks with them at all times. A.R.P. Wardens had to carry out monthly gas mask checks in their area. First aid skills were important, quite often they could be first on the scene after a bomb had been dropped and so their ability to cope in an emergency and act quickly and correctly was important.

Wardens reported fires to the fire brigade. Although they were not expected to put themselves in dangerous situations, as it was more important for them to remain able to send in their reports, they helped householders to fight fires before the arrival of the fire brigade. They guided the police, fire brigade, first aid parties, rescue parties etc. to the scene of damage and assisted occupants of buildings which had been damaged to find new shelter.

They liaised with the police force, fire service and bomb disposal teams and informed them as soon as they could about emergency situations. If the presence of gas was suspected they would report it and would sound the alarm.

Leamingtonian Ernest Sidwell, the Divisional Air Raid Warden attended a course on gas attacks. He said, "It was held at the old police station in High Street, and about 100 people joined. Inspector Bastock took it. He was a marvellous lecturer and very thorough. One night Inspector Bastock called me into his office and said the outfit needed a Chief Warden and I'd been chosen. I'd never done anything like that before. I was head boy at school and I'd been a Scout master but other than that I'd just controlled my own business and minded my own business. So, I said I'd think about it and let him know. 'There's no thinking', he said. 'You've been appointed and 50,000 gas masks are coming to Leamington and they've all got to be assembled. There's the door. You go in, stand on a chair, and tell them you're their boss'. 'I can't do that', I said. 'You've got to'... When he opened the door, and put a chair for me the people pretty well fell out, the crush was so great. He shouted, 'Silence, here's the Chief Warden', so I got on the chair and told them I'd done the course thoroughly and so on."

"Our first job was to get these gas masks assembled. We approached Gulliman's the photographic film makers and developers in Warwick Place, and all their girls agreed to work all night and they never took a penny. They assembled the face pieces. George Wright came forward and he set up a huge assembly depot where we fixed the face pieces to the respirator part. We all worked all night. I was down at the Police Station. It was the moment when we thought it was going to start."

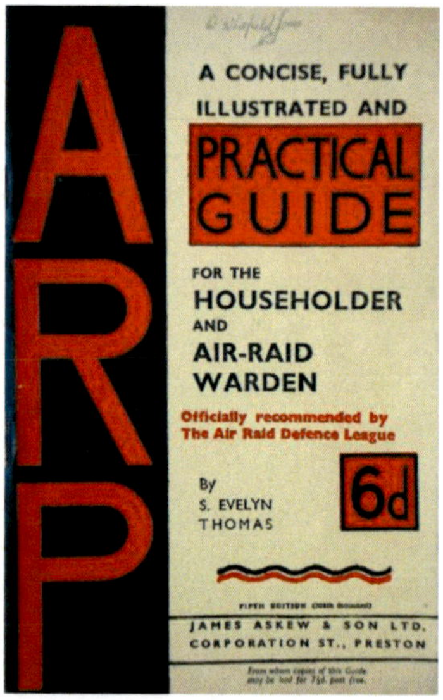

"The next problem was how to register the whole population. You couldn't just hand a gas mask over to anybody. I think the press helped. We had hundreds of volunteers. We took the Urquhart Hall

and turned the large room into an office, and had benches and tables and Kelly's directory and wrote down the name and address of every house in Leamington, and each had to have its required number of gas masks. Then there was the fitting. The Wardens did that. It was a marvellous effort really."

"Next we had to divide up the town for the purpose of organising the Wardens. We divided it into four divisions by a line running down the Parade, Bath Street and Brunswick Street, and the river. This left Lillington. It was nothing like the size it is now but is was very important from a population point of view as it had women and children... So we had five divisions in Leamington in all."

"Each division had a number of Wardens' Sectors, and each Sector had its Wardens' posts. Each division had a Head Warden and an H.Q. The H.Q. for Lillington was the old Lillington Library in Pound Lane, and a very good H.Q. it was too. The H.Q. for North West Leamington was the library in Union Road."

"The Wardens came from all walks of life. I can't remember if there were women at the beginning; there certainly were later. But the pride of those fellows was marvellous. Many were old soldiers and they did drill on Sunday mornings at the Eagle Recreation Ground behind Brunswick Street and had marching and parades. We had no uniform at the beginning. Then we got A.R.P. armbands; that took a bit of getting! When we got great-coats we thought the end of the world had come! Eventually we got uniforms - navy."

"All the Wardens had to do the Wardens' Course. We trained about 1500 but my quota for Leamington was 550. Later we were asked to take on some full-time Wardens. When war started, there was some unemployment, for many trades closed down."

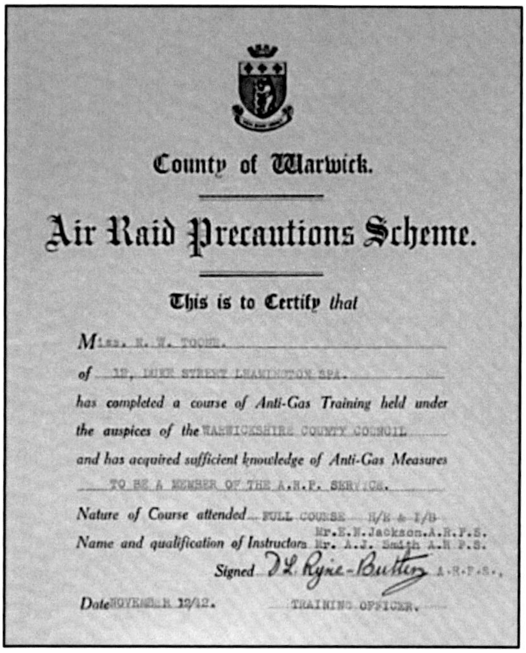

County of Warwick.

Air Raid Precautions Scheme.

This is to Certify *that*

M [illegible]

of 12, DUKE STREET LEAMINGTON SPA.

has completed a course of Anti-Gas Training held under the auspices of the WARWICKSHIRE COUNTY COUNCIL

and has acquired sufficient knowledge of Anti-Gas Measures

TO BE A MEMBER OF THE A.R.P. SERVICE.

Nature of Course attended FULL COURSE [illegible]

Name and qualification of Instructors Mr.E.N.Jackson.A.R.P.S. Mr. A.J. Smith A.R.P.S.

Signed J.L. Ryrie-Butler A.R.P.S.,

Date NOVEMBER 12/42. TRAINING OFFICER.

"I took a further course at a naval establishment near Bristol so that I was entitled to lecture. I didn't do as much of it as many did, but I took the course so that I would be their equal in knowledge."

"Soon after the war started we realised that we had to deal with incendiaries rather than gas. The Wardens' posts needed stirrup pumps for firefighting. At first, we raised money by calling on people to give 6d. or 1s. or more if they wished, and bought them ourselves, but official stirrup pumps were issued later. Wardens instructed people in their use. The Wardens' posts were also supplied with bunks. They were a Government Issue."

"We started by manning quite a number of posts, and soon realised this was an absolute waste of effort. People were losing sleep unnecessarily. So, we manned the H.Q. for the purpose of the telephone, and if a 'warning yellow' was received at the Report Centre, each H.Q. was asked to open up another post, as required."

"We were on the ground floor which was heavily reinforced and had cellars beneath. It was only a short walk from the Town Hall to the Report Centre so that the Town Clerk could get across if a warning came through. He was the chief man in the area."

"The Police had a separate H.Q. at the old Drill Hall in Adelaide Road. At first Leamington's Wardens were under the control of the Police. I had Inspector Bastock's office at the Police Station in High Street, but it was put to me that I was under the wrong authority and that it would be better if Leamington's Wardens went with the County; we would have a bigger voice in the Ministry of Defence, so we transferred and it turned out to be the right decision. I then had as assistant Captain Scott, an ex-military man."

By 8th September, 1939, A.R.P. men, reserves and special constables, all wearing their special helmets were a familiar site in the streets. One of the posts was in Charlotte Street and was known as 113c; they used the basement of a private house. This 1939 photo of the voluntary Wardens was sent in to the Leamington Spa Courier in 1987 by Mrs. Betty Hull née Wrighton, who is front row second right. In the front row from left to right are Helen Green, Marjorie Wrighton, unknown, Phillip Labrum, Mr. Quail, Betty Wrighton [now Hull] and Winifred Badger. In the back row, the first two are unknown, then it's Arthur Dawkes, Charlie Parkin, Mr. Davis, Mr. Franklin, Charlie Rowley, Frank Cattell, Mr. Harris and Charlie Jeffrey.

The Morning News dated Monday 30th October 1939 reported: - **Civil Defence Services – Things the Leamington Public Should Know** – The following statement, which gives the location of Leamington's civil defence services, may prove of interest and value to the public: -

Wardens' Posts – Union Road Wardens' Post, Sub. Police Station, Union Road [tel. 2103]; Lillington Wardens' Post, Boardroom, Lillington Library [tel. 2106]; Leicester Street Wardens' Post, Leicester Street Schools [tel. 2098]; Euston Place Wardens' Post, Central Hotel Basement, Euston Place [tel. 2101]; Charlotte Street Wardens' Post, St.

John's Lodge, Charlotte Street [tel. 2099]; R.M.C. Wardens' Post, Home for Incurables' Basement, Tachbrook Street, [tel. 2105]; Avenue Road Wardens' Post, Garage, 26, Avenue Road [tel. 2154]; Police Station Wardens' Post, Central Police Station, High Street [tel. 2097]; Shrubland Street Wardens' Post, Shrubland Street Schools [tel. 2107].

Auxiliary Fire Service Action Stations – Central Fire Station, Adelaide Road Depot, Bowell's Garage [Clarendon Avenue], Jewel Factory [Tachbrook Road], Central Depot [Lillington Avenue], Campion Terrace Waterworks, Crown Hotel Yard, Chandos Street Sub. Police Station, Midland Autocar [Russell Street], Milverton Garage [Rugby Road], Lillington Garage.

Central Police Station – High Street [tel. 2222].

First Aid Post – Warneford Hospital, Radford Road [tel. 1420].

Public Shelters, for those caught in the streets and who cannot get home in seven minutes. A number of public shelters are almost complete, and their situations and capacity will be published in the papers as soon as they are ready. Find out from your nearest Wardens' Post who is the Warden for your road. If there is no Warden in your road, why not find a suitable man and get him to enrol for training.

Cut This Out For Reference.

On 24th May 1940, it was decided to produce cards containing information on Wardens Posts etc. and supply them to householders - the cost of producing the cards was estimated at the time to be approximately £15.

On 13th August 1940, it was recommended at the A.R.P. committee meeting, that if an adequate rota can be provided, then permission should be given to use the Town Hall tower as a Warden's observation post. In September 1940, the County Architect was asked to install heating and lighting in the Warden's post at the Oak Inn, Radford Road.

This December 1940 photo is of members of the A.R.P. first-aid party and rescue party enjoying their Christmas dinner in what had been the grain store at Leamington Brewery in Lillington Avenue. Numbering about 30, they sat down to dinner provided by Mr. Eden, members of the A.R.P. committee, and others.

On 2nd September 1941, the fire party organiser reported the current position on recruitment and training to the A.R.P. Emergency Sub-Committee meeting. It was recommended that he be authorised to purchase 400 practise incendiary bombs at a cost of £35, as well as 300 whistles at approximately £16 for use by fire party leaders, and that demonstration huts for training fire parties be erected in each of the five Warden's Districts at a cost of approximately £35 each.

On 12th June 1942 readers of the Leamington Spa Courier were reminded that there were now 20 Wardens' Posts and they were situated at: -

Milverton Station	Euston Place	Lillington Library	Eagle Recreation Ground
Union Road	Church Walk	Sand Pits	Home for Incurables
Waterloo Place	Mill Gardens	Binswood Avenue	Charlotte Street
Boys' College	Farley Street	Campion Terrace	Booster Station
Woodcote Road	Oak Inn	Regent Grove	Technical College

The Home for Incurables post was set up in a gardener's tool shed. It was "equipped into a highly efficient unit of the A.R.P. service with every necessary comfort for the personnel in attendance." A report at the time said, "A number of female wardens are attached to the post and their influence has been felt."

JOLLITY IN AN AIR RAID WARDENS' POST

The Leamington Spa Courier dated 10th March 1941 reported: - 'An air-raid wardens' post is not normally a pleasant resort – certainly not at 2 o'clock in the morning with a telephone ringing! But there are occasions, as seen in our picture [above], when the relief comes from sterner duties, and members of this branch of the A.R.P. Service give themselves over to merry-making. Tuesday night's party at the Home for Incurables Post was a great success, thanks to the vigour of a few bright spirits. Mr. G. M. Webber added to his duties as chairman the role of conjurer. The excellence of his performance, and the range of other talent revealed, led the Matron of the Home [who was the guest of honour] to invite members of the Post to provide an entertainment for the Home. This they have undertaken to do.'

Mrs. Margaret Francis nee Hollingsworth – Air Raid Warden

Margaret Hollingsworth was born on 16th January 1920 at Lansdowne Crescent where her mother was in service, and is the eldest of five children.

Prior to the Second World War, the family had moved to 11, Althorpe Street. Margaret said, "I was 19 when the war started and was working at Hitchman Road laundry. I was told to take the job as I would be well paid at 28s. a week – a working man with a family only got 32s. a week. My mother worked as a cleaner at the White Lion pub in Althorpe Street."

Althorpe Street in 1957.

"The Second World War started and Police Sergeant Knifton came to our house and said he was looking for someone to do A.R.P. work [Air Raid Precautions], and it was decided that I would do it. The volunteers had to go to the Boy's Mission in George Street where we had our training. Sergeant Knifton was the training officer and taught us the job including such things as how to use a stirrup pump for fighting fires. I don't know how useful that would have been, it took ages for the water to come through and there wasn't much water in the bucket anyway."

"Around 1941, the Government decided that we had to register for conscription; we were being called up and had to decide whether to work in the factories, the Women's Land Army or go into the forces. I decided to work in the factory and started at Lockheed as a capstan operator. We worked two weeks of days and two weeks of nights. When you did nights, it was so difficult to sleep with the noise going on and the kids running around. We worked a 12-hour shift from 7.30am-7.30pm and then had to fit in our air raid warden duties around work. I seemed to go through the war in a trance because I was so tired; I was either working at Lockheed, doing A.R.P. work, sometimes right through the night or trying to catch up on a little sleep."

Arthur Reading taken around 1958 in the Althorpe Arms.

"There were three air raid wardens to cover the Althorpe Street estate up to the canal; Doris [Doss] Underhill, Arthur Reading and myself. Arthur's parents ran the Althorpe Arms in Althorpe Street. Our A.R.P. shelter and offices were at the old Town Hall in High Street; in fact, the office was where the lads who had done something wrong used to get birched."

"As soon as we had reported in to the A.R.P. office, our first job was to check every street to make sure that the black-outs were in place and that no light could be seen, not even a candle. This was our top priority before we started checking if people were alright. We had a lot of old people around the Althorpe Street area and they were grateful to see us, it seemed to boost their morale and give them confidence – sometime we would stop for a cup of tea, but every two hours we had to report in. We didn't have a uniform to start with but as time went by we were issued with a uniform and a tin hat."

"The air raid shelters at Lockheed were all outside to start with – it took a long time to get there and we could be in there for a couple of hours, which wasn't any good as we weren't getting paid because we weren't working. Sometime later they moved some shelters inside. They couldn't understand why people were almost falling asleep in the workshops and were always tired until they realised that working for that long in an enclosed space without any fresh air was causing it. And so, an hour before we finished our shift they would open a huge door to let in the fresh air and that seemed to do the trick and made things better."

"I was working during one of the air raids on Lockheed on 16th July 1942. It was about twenty past six in the morning, just before knocking off time at the end of our shift. The workshops were damaged and they had to put tarpaulin over – four men were killed."

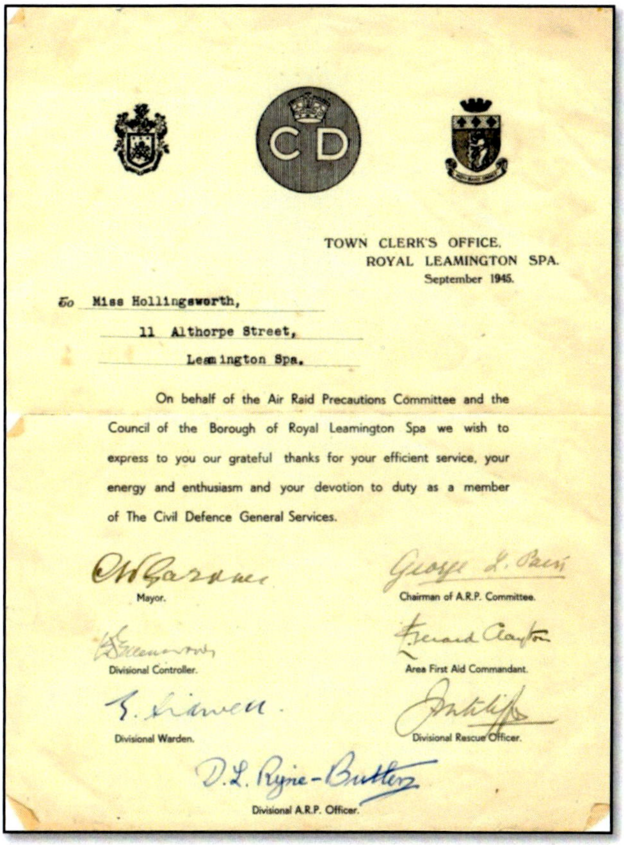

CD

TOWN CLERK'S OFFICE,
ROYAL LEAMINGTON SPA.
September 1945.

To Miss Hollingsworth,
11 Althorpe Street,
Leamington Spa.

On behalf of the Air Raid Precautions Committee and the Council of the Borough of Royal Leamington Spa we wish to express to you our grateful thanks for your efficient service, your energy and enthusiasm and your devotion to duty as a member of The Civil Defence General Services.

Mayor.
Chairman of A.R.P. Committee.
Divisional Controller.
Area First Aid Commandant.
Divisional Warden.
Divisional Rescue Officer.
Divisional A.R.P. Officer.

"Some of the men didn't turn up for the next shift, but all of the women went in. There were crowds of people hanging around on the main road."

"Win Underhill lived by me. When she got married she became Mrs. Herbert and they moved to 119 Kinross Road. One of the two landmines that dropped on Lillington on 14th November 1940 fell in her back garden and she was seriously injured. Her face was badly disfigured and glass was still coming to the surface of her face years later. She came back to live by me with the family and they had to take down all of the mirrors in the house so she couldn't see her face."

"I worked at Lockheed for five years and became the first female union shop steward. I still remember the end of the war; the Parade was packed and everyone was dancing. How we ever survived all that time I don't know, food was so scarce, we were always hungry, there was just enough to keep us going. In September 1945, I was sent a letter to thank me for the work I did as an air raid warden, and I still have the letter. No one mentions the A.R.P. people much, but they did a good job across the country – they certainly did their bit. After the war, I got a job at Flavel's."

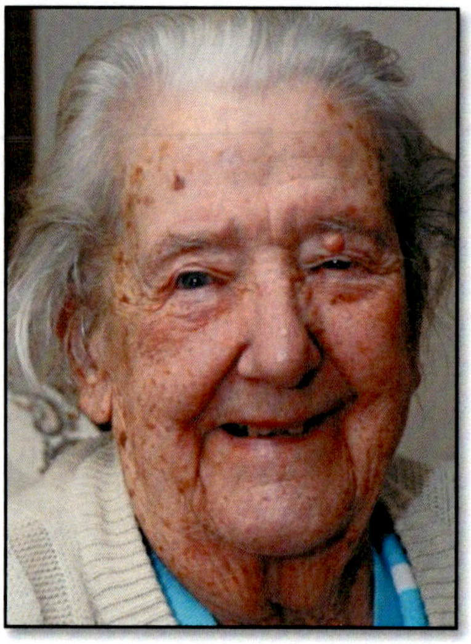

When interviewed in 2013 Margaret was living independently in Leamington and was very much looking forward to her 94th birthday in the New Year.

Local historian Terry Gardner tells me that this water pumping station [below], which is situated on the south side of the canal bridge at Tachbrook Road, was used as an A.R.P. post during the war, and later as a pumping station. It was used to pump water to the Lockheed factory further along the Tachbrook Road. The Grand Union Canal Co. had an air raid shelter at Tachbrook Road bridge and it is likely that it is the same building.

Rescue Parties / Decontamination Parties

Rescue Parties were required to assess and then try to gain access to bombed-out buildings in order to retrieve injured or dead people. They would turn off gas, electricity and water supplies, and repair or pull down unsteady buildings. Leamington had three light duty Rescue Parties and one heavy duty Rescue Party. Mr. J. Eaton was the Superintendent in charge of the Rescue Parties.

Decontamination parties were provided with protective clothing and were responsible for dealing with gas attacks. As stated previously, Arthur Smith was the Deputy Training Officer and Decontamination Officer for Leamington.

On 13th March 1939, the Clerk of Works was nominated as one of the Instructors - particularly for the practical drilling of the Rescue and Demolition Parties. It was intended that he should attend the Civilian Air Raid Precautions School at Falfield.

On 27th December 1939, there was a 'strong recommendation' from the A.R.P. Committee that a first aid post, as part of the decontamination arrangements, should be provided at Warneford Hospital.

On 23rd February 1940, it was decided by the A.R.P. Committee to no longer have paid rescue parties. Previously the authorised establishment for rescue and decontamination parties was 15 persons. At the time of the A.R.P. meeting there were no full-time posts and it was decided that in future the authorised establishment would be nil. The Borough Engineer would try to arrange for two men [volunteers] to be on stand-by and also look into the possibility of obtaining assistance from builders and contractors.

Cyril Carter said in June 1990, "I was leader of Rescue Squad No.1. Soon after 10.15pm on 14th November 1940, a stick of bombs fell on Leamington and we made our way to Dormer Place, where we rescued both the dead and the living, then we went to number 15 York Road where the house was destroyed, with only one wall and the staircase left standing. Czech soldiers had surrounded the house and guarded the site. I believe I am the last living survivor of the rescue squads, although there may be one other, Bill Blower, who on several occasions was in action with our squad when Birmingham was bombed."

Following the destruction and damage to two houses in Dormer Place, the wrecked buildings were later used for training purposes.

On 23rd May 1941, the A.R.P. Committee resolved to purchase 20 sets of overalls for the decontamination squads at a cost of approximately £18.

As from 14th June 1943, the Rescue Services and First-Aid Services were amalgamated.

Mortuary Services

In December 1939, the Borough Engineer reported on enquiries he had made on behalf of the A.R.P. Committee for premises for the purpose of mortuary accommodation in the event of air raids. He submitted plans for suggested alterations to the Nonconformist Chapel in Leamington Cemetery providing the necessary facilities.

On 28th May 1941, the Borough Engineer said that in the event of a heavy air raid, the Revd. G. Rolfe had agreed to permit the use of the All Saints Church chapel to be used for all burial services. Revd. Rolfe also agreed that the chapel at Brunswick Street cemetery could be used as a temporary mortuary.

Following a letter from the Ministry of Supply, the A.R.P. Emergency Committee recommended on 2nd September 1941 that 50 shrouds [emergency supply of coffins] be purchased at a cost of approximately £25. An application was sent to the Ministry of Health asking for permission to purchase timber for the 50 shrouds which would be stored ready for assembly when necessary.

On 16th December 1941, Mr. W. May, the Borough Treasurer, was given the added responsibility of Mortuary and Funeral arrangements.

On 12th January 1942, the Chief Constable was authorised to purchase equipment for the mortuary at the Adelaide Road sub-station.

On 23rd January 1942, Mr. A. L. Stapleton, Borough Treasurer in the Rates department was formerly appointed as A.R.P. Mortuary Superintendent.

Parades

Throughout the war there were various parades down the Parade, many as a way of raising money for the war effort. They included War Weapons Week parades, Salute the Soldier parades, Warship parades, Women's Land Army parades, Battle of Britain Sunday and Wings for Victory parades to name but a few. Civil defence detachments, military detachments, mechanised units and civilian mechanised units also formed part of the parades.

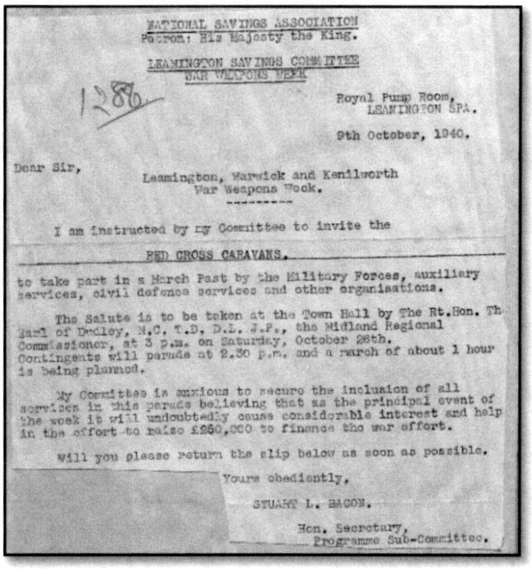

NATIONAL SAVINGS ASSOCIATION
Patron: His Majesty the King.

LEAMINGTON SAVINGS COMMITTEE
WAR WEAPONS WEEK

1286

Royal Pump Room,
LEAMINGTON SPA.

9th October, 1940.

Dear Sir,

Leamington, Warwick and Kenilworth
War Weapons Week.

I am instructed by my Committee to invite the

RED CROSS CARAVANS.

to take part in a March Past by the Military Forces, auxiliary services, civil defence services and other organisations.

The Salute is to be taken at the Town Hall by The Rt.Hon. The Earl of Dudley, M.C, T.D, D.L. J.P., the Midland Regional Commissioner, at 3 p.m. on Saturday, October 26th. Contingents will parade at 2.30 p.m. and a march of about 1 hour is being planned.

My Committee is anxious to secure the inclusion of all services in this parade believing that as the principal event of the week it will undoubtedly cause considerable interest and help in the effort to raise £250,000 to finance the war effort.

Will you please return the slip below as soon as possible.

Yours obediently,

STUART L. BACON.

Hon. Secretary,
Programme Sub-Committee.

Invitations were send out early in October for the War Weapons Week parade. This is the invite for the Red Cross caravans.

Members of the Women's Land Army took part in a parade at Leamington on Saturday, and the wide range of mechanical implements now used in agriculture were demonstrated. During the afternoon the Mayor of Leamington, Alderman A. Ashton, inspected a guard of honour at the Town Hall.

Members of the Women's Land Army.

One of these was the War Weapons Week parade on Saturday 26th October 1940 which was organised by the National Savings Association and the Leamington Savings Committee.

At the parade, the Earl of Dudley, Commissioner for the West Midlands, announced that £110,000 had been subscribed towards the £250,000 which the organisers had set as their objective. He said, "This is a fight not for England or Great Britain, but for the free peoples of the world. We must give everything we have got to the national cause. The enemy was realising that he is not fighting an army but a whole nation. Women, men and children would sooner die than lose their freedom, their religion, their history and their tradition. The enemy could turn houses into dust and rubble. He could not make dust and rubble out of the spirit of the British Empire." Afterwards, Lord Dudley, accompanied by the Mayors of Leamington and Warwick, the chairman of Kenilworth U.D.C. and military officers, took the salute at the Town Hall.

LEAMINGTON, WARWICK and KENILWORTH
WAR WEAPONS WEEK PARADE
Saturday, Oct. 26th, 1940

PARADE INSTRUCTIONS

Parade to be carried through wet or fine weather.

ASSEMBLE. Beauchamp Avenue - Dismounted detachments.
Binswood Avenue - Mechanised detachments
(West of Kenilworth Road)

TIME. 2.30 p.m.

ROUTE. Parade will move off at 2.50 via Kenilworth Road and the Parade and turn into Newbold Terrace for dismissal.

SALUTING BASE The Rt. Hon. the Earl of Dudley, M.C., T.D. D.L. J.P. will take the Salute at the Town Hall at 3 p.m. General Blakiston Houston, Commander Central Midland Area, the Mayors of Leamington and Warwick and Chairman of the Kenilworth U.D.C. will also be present.

TRAFFIC AND MARSHALLING ARRANGEMENTS. Will be carried out by Leamington Police and Military Traffic Control Group.

ORDER OF PARADE

MILITARY DETACHMENTS
Police.
Band - Royal Warwickshire Regt.
Royal Tank Regt. Detachment.
Royal Warwickshire Regt. Detachment.
Company of Czechs.
Home Guards - Leamington.
Lockheed.
Warwick.
Kenilworth.

CIVIL DEFENCE DETACHMENTS (Leamington and Warwick)
1. Special Constabulary.
2. St. John Ambulance Brigade.
3. British Legion.
4. Auxiliary Firemen.
5. Air Raid Wardens (5 detachments)
6. Women's Voluntary Service.
7. Church Lad's Brigade and Band.
8. Boy Scouts.
9. Girl Guides.

Mechanised Units
Military - Royal Tank Regt.
2 Light Tanks.
2 Carriers.
1 Motor Cycle Combination.
2 Motor Cycles.
1 Mobile Office.
1 Staff Car.
3 Bren Gun Carriers
(Royal Warwickshire Regt)
Bomb Disposal Squad.
2 Armoured Cars
(Lockheed)

2 Anti-Tank Guns.
2 75 Guns
Machine Gun Co.
(Czechs)
Daimler & Standard Co
Vehicles.

Mechanised Civilian Units.
1. Special Constabulary Cars.
2. 4 A.R.P.First Aid Units.
3. 2 Red Cross Caravans.
4. Fire Brigade Pumps.
5. 3 Rescue Lorries
6. 1 Decontamination Lorry.
7. Marshal's Car.

The various units of the Civil Defence Services will parade in the order of procession indicated above and will assemble at points at which their number will be displayed.

Hon.Secretary's Office.
Pump Room, Leamington Spa.

A.E.Young,
Parade Marshal, Chief Constable.

On Wednesday afternoon 15th April 1942, the Duke of Kent inspected contingents from Leamington's Civil Defence units at Victoria Park. He wore the uniform of a flying officer in the Royal Air Force. On arrival at Leamington, the Duke was received by the Mayor [Alderman M. S. Moore], the Town Clerk and Sub-Controller of the Borough [Mr. A. F. Greenwood], and the Chief Constable [Mr. C. Carnegie Martin]. The Duke was accompanied by the Regional Commissioner [Lord Dudley], Group Captain Bone, and the principal Regional Officers, Sir William Dugdale [Chairman of the County Council], and Mr. L. Edgar Stephens [County Controller].

The Duke inspected the units, chatting to both the leaders and other ranks, for just over half-an-hour. Leaders of the units presented were: - Chief Inspector R. W. Bastock [police], Divisional Officer Tanner [N.F.S.], Matrons E. J. Harrison and Holl-Edwards [nurses from Warneford Hospital and the Midland Counties Home], Divisional Warden Sidwell [Air Raid Wardens and Fire Guards], Dr. Cheyne [nurses attached to first-aid post], Deputy Sub-Controller C. Peter Clarke [Report Centre staff], Mrs. Kerr Chalmers [Women's Voluntary Services], Mr. W. A. James [Hospital Stretcher-bearers], and Senior Messenger Palmer [messengers].

The Duke then passed to the mobile units: - Casualty Services [under Dr. E. R. Gilmore, the First-Aid Commandant], ambulances [Mrs. Smallwood], first-aid parties [Mr. Walton Cliffe], mobile unit [Dr. Edmondson], and Gas Cleansing unit [Dr. Clayton]; Engineering Services [Mr. J. Sutcliffe, Borough Engineer, and his deputy Mr. C. O. Innes Jones], rescue parties [Mr. J. Eaton], and Decontamination Squad [Mr. A. J. Smith]. Emergency food vans [Mr. J. W. McNab], mobile canteens [Mrs. Kerr Chalmers], first-aid caravan [Mrs. M. M. Maitland Fowler O.B.E.], and the mobile special constabulary [Chief Inspector Bastock].

H.R.H. the Duke of Kent being introduced to Mrs. M. M. Maitland Fowler O.B.E. following the Civil Defence parade.

Following the parade on 15th April, the Town Clerk was congratulated by the Duke of Kent on the excellent turn-out.

He later received a letter of thanks from the Regional Commissioner and the County Controller and passed on the details to those concerned.

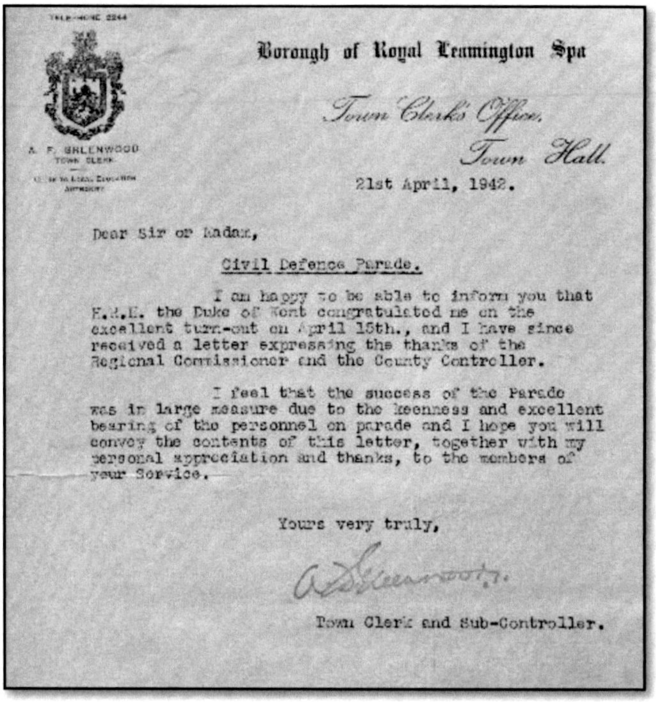

TELEPHONE 2244

Borough of Royal Leamington Spa

A. F. GREENWOOD
TOWN CLERK

Town Clerk's Office,
Town Hall.

21st April, 1942.

Dear Sir or Madam,

Civil Defence Parade.

I am happy to be able to inform you that H.R.H. the Duke of Kent congratulated me on the excellent turn-out on April 15th., and I have since received a letter expressing the thanks of the Regional Commissioner and the County Controller.

I feel that the success of the Parade was in large measure due to the keenness and excellent bearing of the personnel on parade and I hope you will convey the contents of this letter, together with my personal appreciation and thanks, to the members of your Service.

Yours very truly,

Town Clerk and Sub-Controller.

Winding up the Civil Defence

On 22nd September 1944, the Town Clerk reported to the A.R.P. Committee on Home Office circulars [115 and 116/1944] relating to the reduction in hours of the Civil Defence and Fire Guard organisations.

He also mentioned Home Security circular 111/44 which included the preliminary instructions for the collection and disposal of civil defence equipment.

By the end of 1944, a number of post-war development [council] committees had been introduced and were meeting.

On 6th November 1944, A. J. Smith submitted proposals for a local Association of Civil Defence services – it would be open to all members of the Civil Defence services within the purview of the A.R.P. Committee.

On 1st June 1945, the A.R.P. Committee discussed a number of circulars dealing with the winding up of the Civil Defence services, including the collection of equipment, release of office staff, removal of air-raid shelters and sundry other matters.

The Morning News dated Tuesday 12th June 1945 reported that the Leamington A.R.P. Committee would not meet again after 22nd June 1945.

On Wednesday 2nd May 1945 the Civil Defence Service was officially disbanded. The final parade of the Civil Defence services took place on the evening of 12th July 1945. The salute was taken by Capt. C. S. Kitchen, the Deputy Inspector General of Civil Defences. Photos courtesy of Warwickshire County Record Office Ref: PH(N)600/720/30 & 31.

The parade assembled in Regent Street and headed by the Civil Defence Band, marched down the Parade to the Pump Room Gardens. The procession consisted of wardens, messengers, report centre personnel, regional Reserve Column personnel, Women's Voluntary Service, Fire Guards, nurses from Warneford Hospital and Midland Counties Home, the Special Constabulary and National Fire Service.

The Civil Defence Colours took up position, the Colour Party being Mr. J. T. Creelman [officer-in-charge], Mr. W. T. Payne [Rescue Service] and Mr. W. A. Haynes [Messenger Service]. The inspection followed the playing of the National Anthem.

Mr. A. F. Greenwood [Divisional Controller] said that it was the last time he would have the privilege of addressing them in that position. He expressed his very sincere appreciation of their very valuable services for the town rendered for more than six years by every branch of the Services. He paid tribute to the many helpers including the Police Force and those in their ranks who rendered valuable assistance in Coventry and Birmingham. Mr. Greenwood said he was very grateful to everyone and in saying farewell he wished them peace and prosperity in the future.

The ceremony of handing over the Civil Defence Colours for safe keeping to the Mayor then took place. Alderman Gardner expressed his appreciation of the magnificent response which had been made by the members in turning up in such numbers for the final parade. Then came the final march past at which Capt. Kitchen took the salute. The parade was followed at 8.30pm with a reception and dance in the Town Hall.

By the end of the war, 1,900,000 men and women had served in various parts of the Civil Defence organisation across the country – 6,200 of them had died. One of those was 47-year-old William Alfred Cooper, a fire warden and fire watcher from Coventry.

He was injured on 8th April 1941, at the St. John's Ambulance Hall in Coventry during an air raid, and died in an ambulance on 9th April on his way to Warneford Hospital in Leamington Spa.

This memorial to the men and women of the Civil Defence is situated at the National Memorial Arboretum at Alrewas in Staffordshire.

Air Raids

Full details of the six main bombing raids on Leamington Spa can be found in my 2015 book, "The Bombing of Royal Leamington Spa", ISBN: 978-0-9932980-4-2. However, the following is some extra information: -

Before Hitler could contemplate invading England, he knew that he had to destroy the Royal Air Force. From 10th July 1940, the German Air Force *[Luftwaffe]* attacked airfields and aircraft factories - this became known as the 'Battle of Britain'. Despite huge losses, the RAF still managed to defend the country and maintain control of the skies. If these attacks had carried on a little longer it is likely that there would have been a different outcome. Hitler suddenly switched to the large-scale bombing of London and other major cities and towns *[The Blitz or Blitzkreig - lightning war]*. Despite around 42,000 deaths and the destruction of many thousands of homes, he did not succeed in his objective and the invasion was postponed indefinitely and eventually cancelled.

The first air raid warning was put out in Leamington Spa on Wednesday, 6th September 1939, just before 8 o'clock in the morning. Although no enemy planes appeared over Leamington, and the siren was never sounded, there was a good response from the emergency services, all 20 of the full-time wardens who had been employed at the time turned out for duty. On the same day, the Acting Chief Constable reported that the new air raid warning sirens were installed and satisfactory.

The public were told of the warnings that would be given in the event of enemy planes approaching the Midlands via Public Information Leaflet No.1 dated July 1939 and the Leamington Spa Courier dated 8th September 1939: - "In the event of enemy planes approaching the Midlands the public will receive these warnings: - A fluctuating or warbling signal of varying pitch, or a succession of intermittent blasts sounded by hooters and sirens. The warning may also be given by the Police or Air Raid Wardens blowing short sharp blasts on whistles."

Air Raid Warden's wood and metal hand rattle.

"When you hear the warning, take cover at once. Remember that most of the injuries in an air raid are caused not by direct hits by bombs, but by flying fragments of debris or bits of shells. Stay under cover until you hear the hooters sounding continuously for two minutes on the same note, which is the signal for "Raiders Past"."

Air Raid Warden's wooden hand rattle.

"If poison gas has been used, you will be warned by means of hand rattles. Keep off the streets until the poison gas has been cleared away. Hand bells will be rung when there is no longer any danger. If you hear the rattle when you are out, put on your gas mask at once and get indoors as soon as you can. Make sure that all members of your household understand the meanings of these signals. In the event of an air-raid warning sounding at night, people should be extremely careful not to switch on lights in their bedrooms."

In September 1939 Head Postmaster, Major Lockerbie informed the Leamington Spa Courier that all members of staff, including the female telephone operators had expressed readiness to remain at their posts in the event of an air raid. "Not a single member hesitated to come forward," he declared. "The response to my appeal was wonderful." Major Lockerbie added that they will do all in their power to maintain essential services.

The General Post Office in 1940 courtesy of Warwickshire County Record Office Ref:PH(N)600/334/2.

The first few months of the war were eerily quiet and the authorities were accused of over-reacting. Five people were injured in black-out accidents, three of them fatally, prompting Warneford Hospital coroner, Mr E. F. Hadow, to say that the lighting restrictions were making a better "bag" than the Germans.

A.R.P. message - Incident 26th August 1940 01.05 - 5/ISEFG
Incendiary bomb dropped at Blackdown Mill two miles north of Leamington STOP.
Leamington fire brigade report having received a call for assistance. End of Message.

A.R.P. message - 26th August 1940 01.42 – 11/ISEFG
Reference my 01.05/63012 fire at Blackdown Mill now extinguished STOP. No casualties.

A.R.P. message - 26th August 1940 03.06
Police report no fires burning. Number of incendiary bombs in field at Bericote Wood all burnt out. Blackdown Mills several small incendiary bombs in open field all burnt out. A large incendiary bomb at Hill Wootton in open field now burning out. No trace of H.E. [high explosive] bomb.

A.R.P. Message - Incident - 8th October 1940 – 10.20
I have received information from outside source that an aeroplane landed at Whitnash about 18.45 yesterday the 7th October. Will you please let me know if this is so and full details available? – Group Controller Warwick.

A.R.P. message - 8th October 1940 – 11.12
A guard was placed on the plane throughout the night and R.A.F experts picked up the machine and pilot at 08.30 hours today.

A.R.P. message - 8th October 1940 – With reference your message 10.20 hours of today 8/10/40 Warwick County Police inform us that the plane which landed at Whitnash last night 7th October at 18.50 hours was a De Haviland training plane from Chipping Norton R.A.F Training School. The pilot had lost his bearings.

A.R.P. message - 30th October 1940 - 00.10am An unexploded incendiary bomb has been found in Lillington Road Leamington and has been removed by the Auxiliary Fire Service at 22.38 on 29th October.

This photo of an unexploded incendiary bomb is not the actual bomb found in Lillington Road.

Following the Blitz on Coventry on 14th November 1940, many 'bombed out' Coventrian's walked to friends and relatives at Leamington. They were 'put up' wherever there was space, even if that meant sleeping on a floor in a room or in the hallway. The Leamington Spa Courier dated 22nd November 1940 reported: - **Valuable Humanitarian Work** – Mr. Eden has sent the following telegram to the Mayor of Leamington: - "I have been greatly interested to learn of the wonderful work done by Leamington for the victims of the bombardment of Coventry. I congratulate everyone, and have no doubt that you will continue this most valuable humanitarian work."

Pauline Zwicker said, "From my diary I find that on 15th October 1940, a night before a full moon, my Coventry cousins suddenly arrived and stayed with us for two nights. My younger cousin, June, stayed with us for several months and went to school at the Central. My diary for 14th November 1940, again a night before a full moon, states, "We had an awful air-raid. Coventry 1,000 killed."

Freda Watson said, "In the Coventry Blitz, Trinity Church and Dale Street were opened to take people whose homes had been bombed. There were straw palliasses for them to sleep on. They didn't look very comfortable, but one woman told me it was wonderful to be able to lie down flat to sleep. She and others had been sitting up in air-raid shelters and slept with their heads on their knees. The Leamington buses were organised to take the men at 6.00am into Coventry for work, before starting their normal bus service at 7.30am, but they had a job to get the men off so early as their work didn't start till 8.00am."

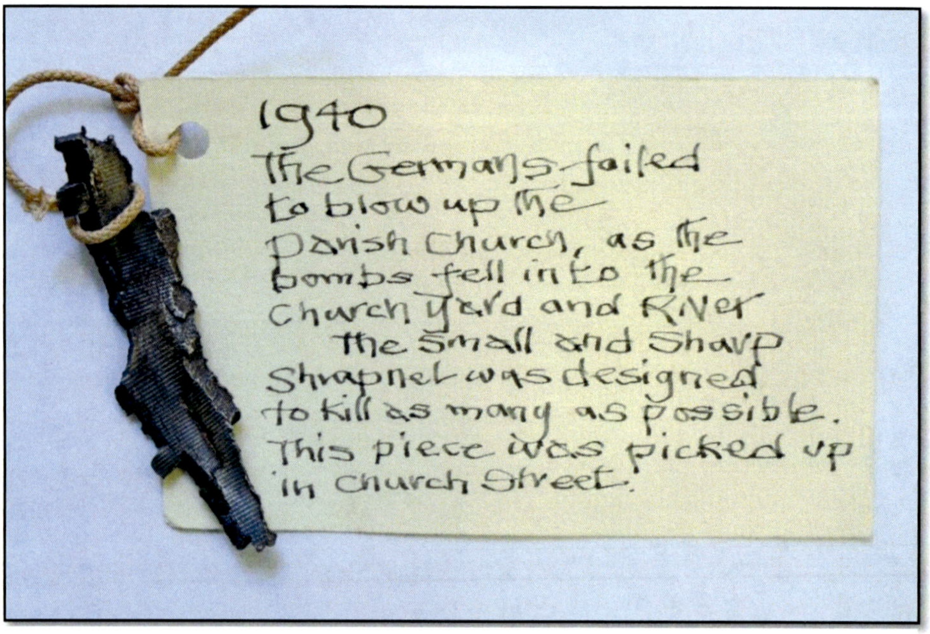

This piece of sharp jagged edged shrapnel was picked up by Kit Smith, then a child, in Church Street on 19th October 1940; He has kept it for the last 77 years.

The war wasn't all bad news for children and Kit wasn't the only child to look for shrapnel. Many youngsters were excited about finding such things as well as seeing German aeroplanes flying across the skies of Leamington - no doubt they were unaware of the dangers. Some developed a life time interest in aviation and aeroplanes as a result - David Brown was one of these children and he is certainly someone to go to now for information about aeroplanes. On 13th June 1942 at the age of 13 he was at his home at Maple Road when a German aeroplane flew over his house prior to bombing the Lockheed factory and on his second run he machine gunned the office block. In places such as London and Coventry the children had many bombed-out houses that they would use as playgrounds, Leamington didn't have anywhere near as many but there were still some around and local children thought it good fun to explore with their friends.

A.R.P. message - Incident 13th January 1941 at 11.45 - Leamington Sub Control report that a balloon has been found at rear of Heathcote Hospital, Heathcote, Warwick. Police state that it is a meteorological balloon bearing a cable directing it to be returned to The Supt, Radio dept., Teddington, Middlesex and that they are attending to its despatch.

A.R.P. message - 14th March 1941 – 23.38/21386
Leamington Sub Control state that a report has been received from Milverton L.M.S. Railway Station, that a green rocket was seen descending in direction of south end of Leamington at 23.15 hours. Rocket broke into 3 sections, giving three vertical queer lights, coming down together in a string.

Tony Tricker said, "I remember being in the Anderson air-raid shelter at the bottom of our garden, slightly frightened but mostly excited. We could hear the German planes going over, and the sounds of the bombs and the anti-aircraft fire. We had gone down to the shelter during a lull in the firing – the biggest risk was being hit by a piece of falling shrapnel from our anti-aircraft shells. Afterwards, when we were able to get back to the house, we found the back door had been blown open by the blast of what turned out to be a land-mine dropped a hundred yards or so away. That was the only damage we sustained. Farther away from the bomb, two houses across the end of our street fared much worse than us. The roofs were blown in by the blast, which must have travelled straight down the street."

Rose McKie formerly McGlasson said, "I was six years old when we were bombed out of our home in Kinross Road, Lillington. We had two cousins staying with us and my father and their father were away on business. When the air-raid siren went off, we children were excited – it was lovely to watch the big silver barrage balloons and the searchlights raking across the sky, even if it was very noisy, with all the A.R.P. men shouting in the road about keeping the lights covered."

"All our windows were covered with criss-crossed strips of sticky brown paper, to lessen the damage caused by flying glass if a bomb was to go off and shatter the windows. We also had blackout curtains, like everyone else. After a while it wasn't quite so exciting because my mother and auntie were getting very frightened and would scream when another bang went off, which made the children start to get very edgy."

"We learned afterwards that two landmines had exploded in the road, killing some people and badly injuring others. Eventually, it got so bad that we heard a loud banging at the door, the A.R.P. men had come to take us out of the road and we were all passed high up from hand to hand into a waiting lorry, you couldn't walk as the ground was covered in broken glass. From there we were taken to a very large and crowded house where there seemed to be hundreds of people, just like us in their night clothes – the house was called The Grange, but that's all I know about it. The next thing I remember was going back with my mother and sister the next day to our house to see if mum could find a change of clothing for us, but the house was in too bad a condition to allow us in. The front door was open and there was a big gaping hole in the wall which adjoined the garage and my uncle's car was in there sitting under a huge heap of rubble."

"We had to move to Cumberland, as it was called then, as our house was declared to be uninhabitable and so my granny up north found us a house where we lived for a few months all together until we moved back down south."

The Morning News dated 12th June 1942 reported: - **It Might Happen To You Tonight** – If you are injured in an air raid we will help you, if you are buried in the debris of your house we will dig you out – but if you are homeless and uninjured you **MUST** be able to help yourself and maybe help us to help others. Have you fixed up your good neighbour? Do you inform your Warden when the number of persons residing in your house increases or decreases? Many valuable hours after heavy raiding are wasted digging for people who have taken shelter elsewhere – if you help your Warden it will help him in his job if your house is hit.

Incident Reports: - 19th October 1940 – 20.15. Reports so far received indicate H.E. Bombs dropped at 2 or 3 separate incidents in Borough and one at Whitnash. No fires reported. No information received as to casualties etc. Mutual aid is requested for rescue parties 3 parties possible. Suggested R.P Central depot Lillington Avenue Leamington Spa.

29th October 1940 – 21.40. Preliminary report – Message received from Leamington. Unexploded bomb reported dropped at Golf Lane, Whitnash about ¼ to ½ mile from house occupied by Dr. Howell Jones – Briar Hill, Golf Lane in direction of Banbury. Time of occurrence 20.30 hours.

30th October 1940 – 22.00. Reports have been received from Wardens that a heavy detonation was heard at 21.15 hours which on investigation appears to have been a delayed action H.E. bomb exploding in the Heathcote – Tachbrook district. It would appear that this may be the delayed action bomb mentioned in the report to the County

Control timed 20.46 hours yesterday and referred to as No.1 in the situation report of 05.55 hours.

31st October 1940 – 17.00. Leamington Sub Control report that the British Barrage Balloon on show for War Weapons Week broke away at 15.15 hours today from moorings at Leamington. Proceeding N.E. with S.W. wind.

20th November 1940 – 14.45. Police report – In rear garden of Hall's Close, Whitnash at 20.20 hrs on 19/11/40. Unexploded shell fell in open ground. Diameter of hole 6″ estimated depth of shell 5ft. No part of shell exposed. No crater formed, no windows broken, and no splinter marks to be found. No signs of blackening. Remarks: side of hole smooth and not curved in.

20th November 1940 – 09.53. Wardens report 1/9B 23.30 Tuesday [19th]. A.A. shell burst in Lillington Avenue opposite No.7 doing damage to windows and fence wall of No.10a. People at No.10a did not report occurrence last night and have taken steps over damage.

5th December 1940 – 05.55. Situation Report – Some damage to windows in Willes Road and Lansdowne Street caused by A.A. shell fragments during last night's alert period.

9th April 1941 – 22.57. Three incendiary bombs fell upon Hawkes Farm, Heathcote and have been put out. They fell at 22.40.

In September 1986 crane driver Robert Hildred showed off an old air raid siren that he discovered during demolition work at the district council's former depot at Lillington Avenue. The site was the former Leamington Brewery and was used by the Air Raid Wardens.

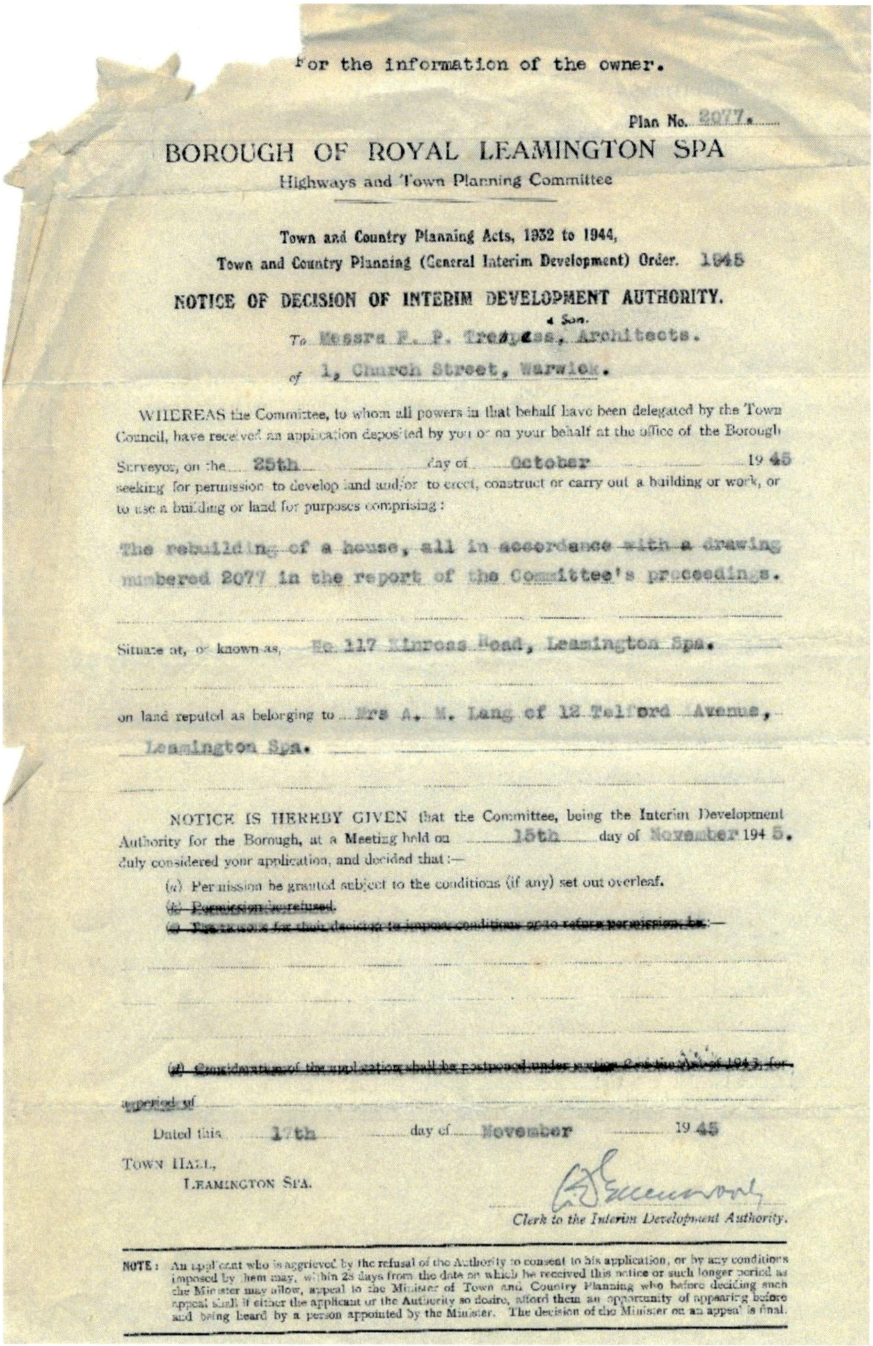

For the information of the owner.

Plan No. 2077.

BOROUGH OF ROYAL LEAMINGTON SPA

Highways and Town Planning Committee

Town and Country Planning Acts, 1932 to 1944,

Town and Country Planning (General Interim Development) Order. 1945

NOTICE OF DECISION OF INTERIM DEVELOPMENT AUTHORITY.

To Messrs F. P. Trepass & Son, Architects.

of 1, Church Street, Warwick.

WHEREAS the Committee, to whom all powers in that behalf have been delegated by the Town Council, have received an application deposited by you or on your behalf at the office of the Borough Surveyor, on the 25th day of October 1945 seeking for permission to develop land and/or to erect, construct or carry out a building or work, or to use a building or land for purposes comprising:

The rebuilding of a house, all in accordance with a drawing numbered 2077 in the report of the Committee's proceedings.

Situate at, or known as, No. 117 Kinross Road, Leamington Spa.

on land reputed as belonging to Mrs A. M. Lang of 12 Telford Avenue, Leamington Spa.

NOTICE IS HEREBY GIVEN that the Committee, being the Interim Development Authority for the Borough, at a Meeting held on 15th day of November 1945. duly considered your application, and decided that:—

(a) Permission be granted subject to the conditions (if any) set out overleaf.

~~(b) Permission be refused.~~

~~(c) The reasons for their decision to impose conditions or to refuse permission be:—~~

~~(d) Consideration of the application shall be postponed under section ... of the Act of 1943, for a period of~~

Dated this 17th day of November 1945

TOWN HALL,
LEAMINGTON SPA.

Clerk to the Interim Development Authority.

NOTE: An applicant who is aggrieved by the refusal of the Authority to consent to his application, or by any conditions imposed by them may, within 28 days from the date on which he received this notice or such longer period as the Minister may allow, appeal to the Minister of Town and Country Planning who before deciding such appeal shall if either the applicant or the Authority so desire, afford them an opportunity of appearing before and being heard by a person appointed by the Minister. The decision of the Minister on an appeal is final.

117 Kinross Road Lillington was the home of Annie Louise Freeman, the only woman to die [on 14th November 1940] in Lillington as a result of enemy bombing. Authority to rebuild the house was obtained in 1945.

Evacuation and Billeting

Evacuation

It wasn't only adults that were affected by the war, children were also affected. In certain parts of the country many were separated from their parents and evacuated to 'safer' areas - and Leamington did its fair share when it came to helping out some of these children.

On 3rd February 1939 the Deputy Town Clerk reported that the Women's Voluntary Service for Civilian Defence [W.V.S.] had already visited two thirds of the houses in the Borough in connection with the proposed evacuation scheme.

It was agreed on 24th March 1939 that a subcommittee of the A.R.P. Committee would be appointed to set up the necessary organisation in connection with the arrival of evacuees in time of an emergency. Mr. Jenner Stratton was temporarily engaged in the Town Clerk's office to work on the preparation of the Evacuation Register. The Ministry of Health produced a window card for circulation to householders who undertook to accommodate unaccompanied schoolchildren.

It was reported on 19th June 1939 that the survey for evacuees had been completed and that the total number that could be accommodated was 12,128. However, some accommodation was unsuitable and so the area could only accommodate 4,539 unaccompanied children, 573 teachers and helpers and 1,513 others. Leamington itself was allocated 5,000 of which 1,670 were expected to arrive during the first two days of the operation.

The Borough was split into seven districts with reception centres for evacuees at the following schools: - Lillington Church of England, Rugby Road, Augusta Place Roman Catholic, Leicester Street, Shrubland Street, New Street R.C. and Clapham Terrace.

Organisation for the reception of evacuees at the railway station, provision of a first aid party, transport to the centres, refreshment at the centres and for guiding evacuees to billets was undertaken by teachers. The W.V.S. were responsible for the recruitment of reception personnel.

Evacuation - Civil Defence Public Information Leaflet No.3 - **Evacuation Why and How?** was issued to the public in July 1939.

Why Evacuation?

There are still a number of people who ask, "What is the need for all this business about evacuation? Surely if war comes it would be better for families to stick together and not go breaking up their homes?"

It is quite easy to understand this feeling, because it is difficult for us in this country to realise what war in these days might mean. If we were involved in war, our big cities might be subjected to determined attacks from the air - at any rate in the early stages - and although our defences are strong and are rapidly growing stronger, some bombers would undoubtedly get through.

We must see to it then that the enemy does not secure his chief objects - the creation of anything like panic, or the crippling dislocation of our civil life.

One of the first measures we can take to prevent this is the removal of the children from the more dangerous areas.

The Government Evacuation Scheme
The Government have accordingly made plans for the removal from what are called "evacuable" areas to safer places called "reception" areas, of school children, children below school age if accompanied by their mothers or other responsible persons, and expectant mothers and blind persons.

The scheme is entirely a voluntary one, but clearly the children will be much safer and happier away from the big cities where the dangers will be the greatest.

There is room in the safer areas for these children, householders have volunteered to provide it. They have offered homes where the children will be made welcome. The children will have their schoolteachers and other helpers with them and their schooling will be continued.

What You Have To Do
Schoolchildren would assemble at their schools when told to do so and would travel together with their teachers by train. The transport of some 3,000,000 in all is an enormous undertaking. It would not be possible to let all parents know in advance the place to which each child is to be sent but they would be notified as soon as the movement is over.

If you have children of school age, you have probably already heard from the school or the local education authority the necessary details of what you would have to do to get your child or children taken away. Do not hesitate to register your children under this scheme, particularly if you are living in a crowded area. Of course it means heartache to be separated from your children, but you can be quite sure that they will be well looked after. That will relieve you of one anxiety at any rate. You cannot wish, if it is possible to evacuate them, to let your children experience the dangers and fears of air attack in crowded cities.

Children Under Five - Children below school age must be accompanied by their mothers or some other responsible person. Mothers who wish to go away with such children should register with the local authority. Do not delay in making enquiries about this. A number of mothers in certain areas have shown reluctance to register.

Naturally, they are anxious to stay by their menfolk. Possibly they are thinking that they might wait and see, that it may not be so bad after all. Think this over carefully and think of your child or children in good time. Once air attacks have begun it might be very difficult to arrange to get away.

Expectant Mothers can register at any maternity or child welfare centre. For further information inquire at your Town Hall.

The Blind - In the case of the blind, registration to come under the scheme can be secured through the home visitors or enquiry may be made at the Town Hall.

Private Arrangements - If you have made private arrangements for getting your children away to relatives or friends in the country, or intend to make them, you should remember that while the Government evacuation scheme is in progress ordinary railway and road services will necessarily be drastically reduced and subject to alteration at short notice. Do not, therefore, in an emergency leave your private plans to be carried out at the last moment. It may then be too late. If you happen to be away on holiday in the country or at the seaside and an emergency arises, do not attempt to take your children back home if you live in an "evacuable" area.

Work Must Go On - The Purpose of evacuation is to remove from the crowded and vulnerable centres, if an emergency should arise, those, more particularly the children, whose presence cannot be of any assistance. Everyone will realise that there can be no question of wholesale clearance. We are not going to win a war by running away.

Most of us will have work to do, and work that matters, because we must maintain the nation's life and the production of munitions and other material essential to the war effort. For most of us therefore, who do not go off into the Fighting Forces our duty will be to stand by our jobs or those new jobs which we may undertake in war.

Some people have asked what they ought to do if they have no such definite work or duty. You should be very sure before deciding that there is really nothing you can do. There is opportunity for a vast variety of services in civil defence. YOU must judge whether in fact you can or cannot help by remaining. If you are sure you cannot, then there is every reason why you should go away if you can arrange to do so, but you should take care to avoid interfering with the official evacuation plans. If you are proposing to use the public transport services, make your move either BEFORE the evacuation of the children begins or AFTER it has been completed. You will not be allowed to use transport required for the official evacuation scheme and other essential purposes, and you must not try to take accommodation which is required for the children and mothers under the Government Scheme.

For the rest, we must remember that it would be essential that the work of the country should go on. Men and women alike will have to stand firm, to maintain our effort for victory. Such measures of protection as are possible are being pushed forward for the large numbers who have to remain at their posts. That they will be ready to do so, no one doubts.

On the morning of 31st August 1939, three days before war broke out, the order was given by the Ministry of Health for the national evacuation plans to be put into operation. During the next four days, nearly 1.9 million people were evacuated, including nearly 1.5 million children, as well as their teachers and other priority people.

The evacuee children were allowed to take with them their gas mask, a change of underclothes, night clothes, house shoes or plimsolls, spare stockings or socks, a toothbrush and comb, a knife, fork and spoon, a mug and plate, a towel and handkerchiefs and a warm coat or mackintosh if possible. Any suitcases or bags that the child carried needed to be labelled with his or her name, their home address and name of school. They also needed sufficient food for one day.

Sandwiches were made by parents, gas masks were carried around the children's necks, name badges or labels were attached to say who the children were, and bags and suitcases were carried by the children. It was now down to luck whether or not they would end up with a good caring family or not.

On the same day, 31st August 1939, Miss Loveday, H.M. Inspector of Schools, called at Bath Street School and informed them that the school would be closed at 4.15pm owing to the arrival of evacuated children the next day from Coventry and Birmingham. The handicraft form was used as a reception centre. The school reopened on Monday 25th September. On re-opening, all local schools, with the exception of the Boys' Central School, which was attached to John Gulson's Senior Boys School Coventry, worked 'double shift'. Where 'double shift' was worked the Leamington school occupied the school in the morning and the evacuated schools in the afternoon. The morning session was from 8.15am to 12.15pm and the afternoon session was from 1.15pm to 4.45pm. On 16th October, some of the children from Bath Street School started using Urquhart Hall in Leam Terrace.

Kit Smith, a member of Leamington History Group is now a sprightly 91-year-old [2017]. His family owned a boot and shoe makers in Bath St, close to the Parthenon. Kit was a pupil at Warwick School when war broke out and he remembers half-time schooling and sharing time with evacuees - some of them he says were billeted at Warwick Castle!

The arrival of Leamington's first batch of "refugee children from Birmingham" at the L.M.S. railway station was reported in the Leamington Spa Courier dated 1st September 1939, two days before Mr. Chamberlain was forced to abandon his dreams of "peace in our time" and declared war on Germany. Those first evacuees were 298 children from five Birmingham schools, accompanied by 57 head-teachers, staff and helpers. The children came from Aston Hill Road senior, junior and infants, and the Aston Brook senior, mixed and infant schools. Each child carried a parcel, some a suitcase and others a kit-bag or brown paper bag. From the L.M.S. station, the first children called out were taken to Clapham Terrace, the Aston Brook senior children went to Shrubland Street, and the infants to St. Peter's. At the schools, teachers were waiting to distribute the day's food supplies, after which they escorted the evacuees to their new 'homes'. The following week, another 915 children arrived from Coventry with 121 staff.

Joan Holmes lived in Coventry – "There were tears as we boarded the bus for Leamington Spa, and then later as we filed around the streets to be taken in. I was lucky enough to stay with my sister Doris. Owing to the influx of children part-time school became the norm." After a while her dad decided that nothing was happening so it was back to Coventry.

Although 14-year-old May Slater wasn't evacuated to Leamington, she was evacuated in the summer of 1940 to a Warwickshire village. She said, "We were herded into one end of the village hall. At the other end stood a group of adults. One by one, the women came over and picked the children they wanted. It was like a cattle market." She was put in a separate billet to her brothers Edward, 12, and Norman, 8. May was one of the older children in the group of 72 Dagenham children, many of whom were being evacuated for a second time, having first been sent to Suffolk.

Lillington Church of England School - It was not the case that children came to Leamington at the start of war and went home at the end. At Lillington Church of England School, the first group of eight children arrived on 25th September 1939. The first evacuee to be registered at the school was Margaret Jarnett from Walthamstow who was sent to live with Mrs. Warr at 9 Highland Road. On 28th June 1940, she was sent with other Walthamstow children to Wellingborough in Northamptonshire.

Maureen Keen and Vivien Benbow, both from Coventry, went to live with Mrs. Keen at 102 Kinross Road, but they only stayed until 13th October 1939 when they both returned to Coventry. This begs the question why they went back? In some instances, children became very home-sick, in others parents quite naturally missed their children and decided they couldn't bear to be parted from them. In many cases parents decided that the 'hype' regarding bombing raids by the Germans had been overplayed; war had started and throughout the winter of 1939/1940 very little happened - and it wasn't going to until the second half of 1940 - but they didn't know that! [The first bombing raid on Leamington wasn't until Friday 23rd August 1940. The first night of the blitz on London was Saturday 7th September 1940.] Parents and people started to think that evacuation was a little unnecessary - and so more and more evacuees went home.

Donald and Adele Holman had lived in London - they went to live with Mrs. Gregory at the 'old' Rugby Tavern in Lillington. On 30th August 1940, Donald went on to the Boys College and on 20th December 1940, Adele left the district, presumably to go home.

Marjorie Hunt and Sylvia Rea moved from the Lozells area of Birmingham on 25th September 1939 to live with Mrs. Cotton at 232 Cubbington Road. They returned to Birmingham on 16th February 1940. James Lewis came from Sparkhill Birmingham on the same day to live with Mrs. Palmer at 23 Highland Road. He only stayed until 29th September when he returned to Birmingham.

Between September 1939 and 3rd April 1940, it was mainly children from the local area joining the school, although there were children from West Drayton, Yeovil, Banbury, Bristol, Oxford, Birmingham, Leicester, Coventry and Ashford.

On 3rd April 1940, 24 children joined the school, but only six of them were local. June Tew originally came from Oxford on 9th January 1940, but left temporarily on 9th February. On 3rd April, she came back again having been to Ashford in Kent, but then left again for Oxford on 3rd September 1940. On 17th February 1941, she is back from Adderbury School and living once again at 16 Avondale Road until 1st August 1944 when she went to Warwick High School. I can only think that this was to do with her parent's work. The other 17 children all came from Coventry. Pamela Ward stayed at 4 Farm Road, Sheila Stanley at 125 Kinross Road, Iris Hughes at 2 Pound Lane, Betty Hughes at 62 Braemar Road, June Dixon at 16 Lime Avenue, Sylvia Villiers at 104 Cubbington Road, Derek Sanders at 109 Kinross Road, James Moore at 5 Farm Road, Robert Piller at 2 Burns Road, Edward Young at 30 Manor Road, Ernest Hughes at 2 Pound Lane, Maurice Sanders at 60 Braemar Road, Arthur Brown at 64 Braemar Road, Sylvia Price at 4 Manor Road, Lilian Dixon at 16 Lime Avenue, Jean Pratley at 17 Manor Road, Brenda Villiers at 104 Cubbington Road and Stanley Lodge at 19 Lime Avenue.

From 9th April until 9th September 1940 it was relatively quiet. Some 34 children started at various times, some of them local and others coming from Feltham, Birmingham, Guernsey, Bradford, London, Monmouthshire, Coventry and Brighton.

From 9th September until 12th December 1940, 71 children started at Lillington, many of them from Coventry including five-year-old Margaret Cobley whose home address is given as Coventry [demolished]. Others came from Devon, Sunderland, London and Durham.

On 27th December 1940, the Chief Billeting Officer reported that the current position as of 20th December, was that 707 persons, including 100 children, were officially billeted in the Borough under the Government Evacuation Scheme. By 24th January

1941 the numbers had increased to 954 persons, including 196 children - 83 of them being between 2-5 years of age.

Surprisingly, even in 1944 and 1945, and for a time after the end of war, children were still coming to Lillington from places such as Barnsley, London, Devon, Scotland, Birkenhead, Sheffield and Middlesborough. All in all, over 400 children started at Lillington School between the start and end of the war. Many were local children, 63 came from Coventry and the rest from a variety of other towns and cities.

Shrubland Street School

Tom Williams recalled in 1980:

"The broadcast by the Prime Minister, Neville Chamberlain, that we were at war was heard in a crowded Shrubland Street school hall on, I think, a Sunday morning. Other teaching colleagues and I had gathered to receive coachloads of children who were being evacuated from Coventry. The outbreak of war had been anticipated and children were being removed from large cities to escape from the dangers of the expected bombing; an action which subsequent events proved to be a wise one. Having registered each child, we took groups of the somewhat bewildered youngsters along the neighbouring streets, knocking on doors and eventually finding "homes" where they could stay. The innate kindness of the good folk of Leamington was demonstrated by the finding of a place of refuge for all."

Shrubland Street School accepted 125 evacuee children during the conflict and the vast majority of the children came from different areas of Great Britain. They didn't all come together, they could arrive on their own or they could come as part of a group. The first child, a nine-year-old girl, came from Berlin in Germany to stay at Heathcote Road and started at school on 29th August 1939. The second child arrived from Sydenham in London on 25th September 1939 and stayed in Hitchman Road.

Children were accepted from London, Birmingham, Coventry, Norwich, Wolverhampton, Essex, Surrey, Glamorgan, Glasgow, Clydebank, Isle of Wight, Acton Wells, Thornton Heath, Croydon, Portsmouth, Worthing, Great Yarmouth, Leigh on Sea, Bristol, Plymouth, Hull and Burton on Trent – as well as Berlin, Belgium and Prague, the capital of Czechoslovakia – now the capital of the Czech Republic.

The children stayed with families at Alexander Road, Althorpe Street, Baker Avenue, Brunswick Street, Charlotte Street, Claremont Road, Clemens Street, Eagle Street, East Grove, Grove Place, Heathcote Road, Hitchman Road, Kennan Avenue, Landor Road, Lillington Avenue, Llewellyn Road, Maple Road, Northway, Offa Road, Prospect Road, Ranelagh Terrace, Scotland Place, Scott Road, Shrubland Street, Southlea Close, St. Georges Road, St. Helen's Road, St. John's Road, Swadling Street, Tachbrook Road, Tachbrook Street, The Close, Waverley Road, West Street, and Windmill Road.

The Leamington Spa Courier dated Friday 8th September 1939 reported: - "As indicated in our last issue, the reception of evacuated children from Coventry was bringing a sharp reminder of the precautionary measures necessary in case of air raids. During the weekend the process was continued - another 915 Coventry children arrived accompanied by 121 staff."

"Splendid work was done by a large body of voluntary workers, including many school teachers, whose assistance was invaluable. All the children scheduled for transference to Leamington have not yet arrived, it being understood that in some cases parents in Coventry have not at the moment taken advantage of the facilities provided."

"Nevertheless, large numbers are already adjusting themselves to their new surroundings, and ways and means are being explored by voluntary organisations to render their absence from home as tolerable as possible. Until the settling down process has had a chance to operate it will not be possible to decide what can best be done; but we can state that the question is receiving every consideration by various religious and social bodies."

"Mr. A. F. Greenwood, the Chief Billeting Officer, has expressed his great appreciation of all the voluntary workers who took part in the arrangements, and particularly pays tribute to the organising ability displayed by Mr. L. Mallinson [Director of Education] in his capacity of Chief Reception Officer."

On 7th November 1940, the Chief Billeting Officer stated that the Dale Street and Lillington feeding centres had been utilised in recent weeks and that all evacuees had been satisfactorily billeted.

In December 1939, the Town Clerk reported to the A.R.P. Committee that the proposals relating to the Children's Welfare Centre and Sick Bay at 25 Warwick Place

Young evacuee painters helping to get the Milverton Children's Centre for Evacuees at 25, Warwick Place ready for use.

had been approved by the Minister of Health, but the Minister had requested the reconsideration of the proposal for a house in the southern district of the borough to be used as a day nursery and for sewing parties. It was recommended that in view of the small number of evacuated children under school age remaining in the borough the proposal for a day nursery not be pursued but that the Town Clerk and the Director of Education endeavour to arrange for the use of suitable premises for the sewing parties, without charge. The Director of Education reported the establishment of a play centre for certain Coventry evacuees in the Lillington area.

The Town Clerk went on to report the receipt of a circular relating to Christmas festivities for evacuated children. It was recommended that the Chairman of the A.R.P. Committee, together with councillors Mrs. Brinton and Mrs. Bragg, be requested to meet the evacuated Head Teachers with a view to organising recreational activities and pastimes for the evacuated children during the Christmas holidays.

Evacuation ended officially on 2nd May 1945. In all, 1,334,358 children parents and teachers were evacuated across the country by trains, to areas considered to be safe from the bombing - but around 38,000 children across the country were not reunited with their families. Some had no homes to return to as they had been destroyed by the bombing, some parents had died, and tragically some parents had moved having chosen to abandon their children.

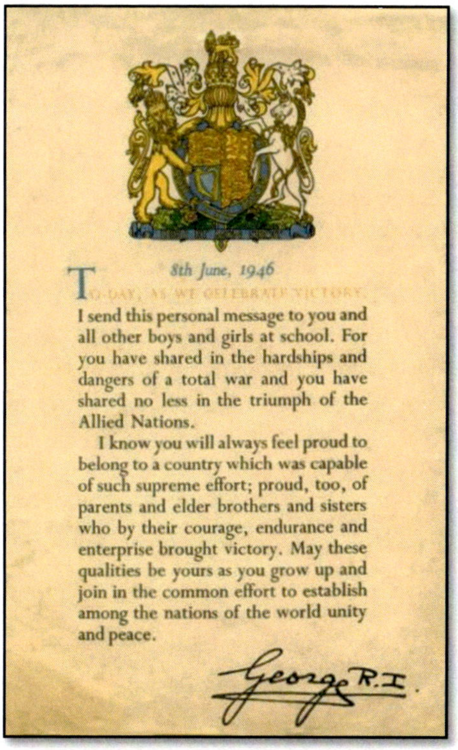

8th June, 1946

TO-DAY, AS WE CELEBRATE VICTORY, I send this personal message to you and all other boys and girls at school. For you have shared in the hardships and dangers of a total war and you have shared no less in the triumph of the Allied Nations.

I know you will always feel proud to belong to a country which was capable of such supreme effort; proud, too, of parents and elder brothers and sisters who by their courage, endurance and enterprise brought victory. May these qualities be yours as you grow up and join in the common effort to establish among the nations of the world unity and peace.

George R.I.

A Royal certificate of thanks for school children.

At the end of the war, many people, including children then at school, received a certificate of thanks signed by Royalty for their fortitude and help in winning the war. The certificate for school children was signed by King George VI.

Certificates were also sent a little earlier by Queen Elizabeth [mother of Queen Elizabeth II] to the people who took evacuees into their homes in the reception areas. It read: - 'I wish to mark, by this personal message, my appreciation of the service you have rendered to your Country in 1939 - In the early days of the War you opened your door to strangers who were in need of shelter, and offered to share your home with them. I know that to this unselfish task you have sacrificed much of your own comfort and that it could not have been achieved without the loyal co-operation of all in your household. By your sympathy, you have earned the gratitude of those to whom you have shown hospitality and by your readiness to serve you have helped the State in a work of great value. Elizabeth R.'

Billeting

The setting up of a billeting office in the Town Hall was approved on 25th October 1940. In December 1940, the Ministry of Health approved a £25 per annum car allowance for the Chief Billeting Officer. In January 1941, there was a request from the Ministry of Health to the Council to set up an organisation for securing lodgings in the town for transferred war workers on a voluntary basis. The Highways Committee were asked to allow the use of a room in the Town Hall annexe.

Margaret Tinsley said, "My office was next to the BBC in London, and one night in 1940 it took a direct hit. I was 17 and working in the office of a munitions factory. When we arrived for work next morning, we were told to go home and wait for a letter. Eventually, my parents received a letter from the management to say that all factory employees were being relocated to Leamington Spa."

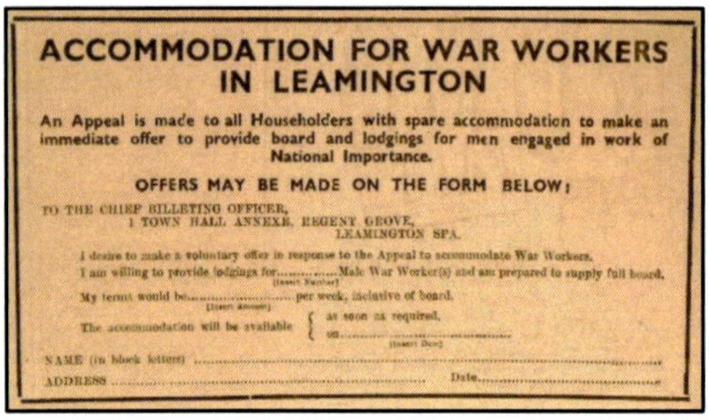

ACCOMMODATION FOR WAR WORKERS IN LEAMINGTON

An Appeal is made to all Householders with spare accommodation to make an immediate offer to provide board and lodgings for men engaged in work of National Importance.

OFFERS MAY BE MADE ON THE FORM BELOW:

TO THE CHIEF BILLETING OFFICER,
1 TOWN HALL ANNEXE, REGENT GROVE,
LEAMINGTON SPA.

I desire to make a voluntary offer in response to the Appeal to accommodate War Workers.
I am willing to provide lodgings for .... Male War Worker(s) and am prepared to supply full board.
My terms would be .... per week, inclusive of board.
The accommodation will be available { as soon as required. / on ....
NAME (in block letters) ....
ADDRESS .... Date ....

The Morning News dated 6th March 1941 carried this advertisement: - **Lodgings for War Workers** – Full board and lodgings are urgently required this week for 100 war workers [men] engaged on work of vital national importance. Offers of accommodation with terms should be sent immediately to: - The Chief Billeting Officer, No.1 Annexe, Town Hall, Regent Grove.

The Morning News dated 13th May 1941 reported: - '**Accommodation for War Workers** – Compulsory billeting at Leamington was foreshadowed in a report of the Evacuation sub-committee at yesterday's meeting of the Town Council. The Billeting Officer [Mr. L. Mallinson] stated that although at the present time he has a reserve of voluntary lodgings available, compulsory billeting would almost certainly be necessary in the near future. It was recommended that the Officer be authorised to exercise, as and when necessary, the billeting powers conferred on the local authority by the Ministry of Health for their compulsory billeting of war workers and their wives and families. The Town Clerk reported on unoccupied premises in the Borough, and it was recommended, that subject to them being satisfactory, the houses now specified be requisitioned for use by families whose homes have been damaged by enemy action.'

On 23rd May 1941, the Billeting Officer reported that 400 transferred industrial workers had now been placed by the Lodgings Bureau in voluntary lodgings in the Borough. In July 1941, he reported that it was now 658 persons and that accommodation had been found for 780 workers. Only 11 persons had been compulsorily billeted. Workers from nine companies were being lodged by the Bureau.

On 1st August 1941, Mr. Mallinson informed the Evacuation Sub-Committee of his difficulties in coping with the work in view of his other duties. It was recommended that the Mayor be requested to appoint Councillor Fetherston-Dilke as Chief Billeting Officer in place of Mr. Mallinson.

In October 1941, James Thorburn of 1, Euston Place was appointed Lodgings Bureau Supervisor and Billeting Officer.

On 20th February 1942, the Lodgings Bureau Supervisor reported that 34 firms had received help in finding accommodation for their workers. There were 2,043 persons billeted and lodged, as well as 36 families.

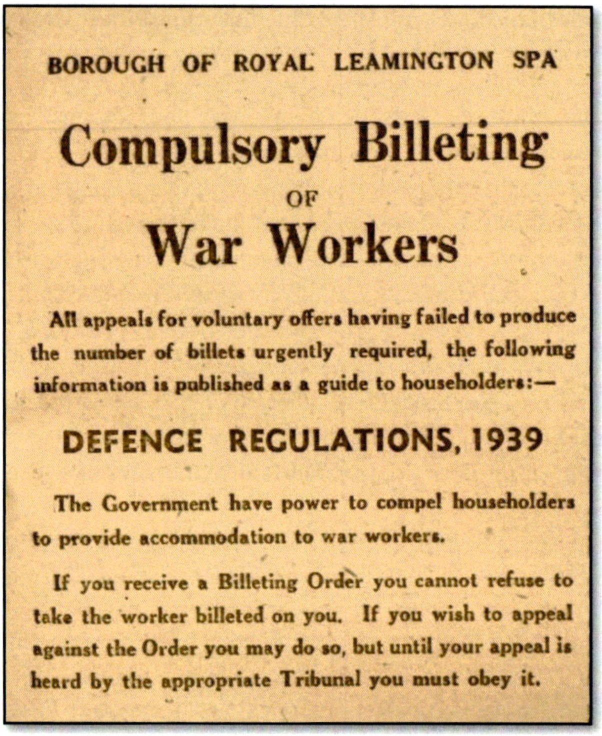

BOROUGH OF ROYAL LEAMINGTON SPA

Compulsory Billeting

OF

War Workers

All appeals for voluntary offers having failed to produce the number of billets urgently required, the following information is published as a guide to householders:—

DEFENCE REGULATIONS, 1939

The Government have power to compel householders to provide accommodation to war workers.

If you receive a Billeting Order you cannot refuse to take the worker billeted on you. If you wish to appeal against the Order you may do so, but until your appeal is heard by the appropriate Tribunal you must obey it.

Compulsory Billeting of War Workers appeal.

The Leamington Spa Courier dated 4th June 1943 carried the following appeal: -

'Compulsory Billeting of War Workers –

All appeals for voluntary offers having failed to produce the number of billets urgently required, the following information is published as a guide to householders: -

DEFENCE REGULATIONS, 1939
The Government have powers to compel householders to provide accommodation to war workers. If you receive a Billeting Order you cannot refuse to take the worker billeted on you. If you wish to appeal against the Order you may do so, but until your appeal is heard by the appropriate tribunal you must obey it.'

On 24th November 1944, the Town Clerk recommended to the Billeting Committee, that due to the reduced amount of business now being conducted, the committee only be called as and when necessary.

On 22nd June 1945, the office used by the Billeting Officer was earmarked for use by Mr. R. Hewitt, the Town Hall porter as living accommodation, once he returns from service in H. M. Forces.

Fire Service / Fire Guard Service

By 1937 the Home Office had set up a separate Fire Brigades Division and in February of that year, a memorandum on an Emergency Fire Brigade Organisation was issued to local fire authorities. This required local authorities to prepare and submit schemes for air raid precautions and for fire protection in the event of war.

With the international situation deteriorating still further, two separate Acts of Parliament were presented to the House of Commons which further prepared the nation's fire services for the threat of aerial warfare.

The Air Raid precautions Act of 1937 came into force on 1st January 1938 and provided for a grant from central government of up to 75% of the cost of A.R.P and of the funding of a volunteer force to be called the Auxiliary Fire Service [A.F.S.] which would work alongside the existing brigades.

The Fire Brigade Act 1938, which received Royal Assent on 28th July 1938, constituted all local authorities above parish level [county boroughs and county districts] as fire authorities with an obligation to provide a fire brigade for the protection of their own area. Towns were required to make sufficient firefighting arrangements for a war situation. At the same time, the service was put under the control of the Home Secretary with assistance from a Fire Service Commission and a Central Advisory Council.

The A.F.S. was mobilised on 1st September 1939. The strength of the Leamington A.F.S. at the time was 130; some 70 more than required as it was thought that a number of the personnel would be called up. On 22nd May 1941 the Fire Services [Emergency Provisions] Bill became law, and then on 18th August 1941, the A.F.S. became the National Fire Service [N.F.S.] and was merged with the existing local fire brigades.

The volunteers were required to undergo weekly training totalling 60 hours, at the end of which was a passing-out examination. Only at the completion of the training was a full issue of uniform made along with a small A.F.S. buttonhole badge. There were two categories of auxiliary; those who in the event of war would give up their normal occupation and would become full-time firemen and the others who would serve as part-timers devoting what time they could to fire services duties when required.

The rate of pay for a full-time auxiliary was fixed at £3 for men and £2 for women. The part-timers were unpaid but might be lucky enough to get a free breakfast following a night's stand-by duty at the fire station.

Public Information Leaflet No.1 dated July 1939 stated: - 'An air attack may bring large numbers of small incendiary bombs, which might start so many fires that the Fire Brigades could not be expected to deal with them all. Everyone should be prepared to do all he can to tackle a fire started in his own house. Most large fires start as small ones.

Clearing the top floor of all inflammable materials, lumber, etc., will lessen the danger of fire and prevent a fire from spreading. See that you can reach your attic or roof space readily. Water is the best means of putting out a fire started by an incendiary bomb. Have some buckets handy. But water can only be applied to the bomb itself in the form of a fine spray, for which a hand pump with a length of hose and special nozzle are needed. **If you throw a bucket of water on a burning incendiary bomb it will explode and throw burning fragments in all directions.** You may be able to smother it with sand or dry earth.'

The nation listened with some trepidation when at 11.15am on Sunday 3rd September 1939, Prime Minister Neville Chamberlain announced on the wireless that a state of war existed between Britain and Germany. There was a general feeling of expectation, not least among the members of the fire service who waited day by day for the wailing of the air raid siren and the anticipated aerial bombardment. Surprisingly, nothing at all happened and as the days ran into weeks and the year drew to a close the winter of 1939/1940 ushered in a period which came to be known as the 'phoney war'. In the absence of any activity on the home front, many men drifted away from the service or volunteered for the armed forces.

The public esteem in which the A.F.S. was held reached an all-time low. The winter was bitterly cold and it seemed that the months of inactivity might last for the duration of the war. There was a feeling that the A.F.S. was an unnecessary drain on national resources and that those who served in it were enjoying a 'cushy number'. Firemen were insulted and referred to as 'Idlers', 'Parasites' and 'the Darts Brigade'. This public antipathy was reflected in a continuous exodus from the A.F.S. ranks, a situation that became so serious that in June 1940 the Government made an order which forbade full-time members of the service from resigning and effectively 'froze' them in post.

In May 1940, a payment of £6. 6s. was paid to Police Surgeon Dr. Lisle Croft in respect of instruction in first aid given to 42 auxiliary firemen.

The fire service of 1940 was much different to that of a few years earlier. Brigades in the larger towns had set up sub-stations in convenient buildings where basic sleeping accommodation and messing facilities were provided. The red appliances of the regular brigades were often divided among the sub-stations and were supplemented by the grey-liveried equipment provided by the Home Office. The principal item of apparatus in most stations was the trailer pump designed for towing behind a suitable vehicle. One of the principal manufacturers of these trailer pumps was a local company, Coventry Climax. The engines developed for the Climax range of pumps were superbly efficient and were later adapted with great success to provide the power units for racing cars. Towing vehicles for the trailer pumps were however not provided and the brigades and A.F.S. were expected to make their own arrangements to secure towing vehicles. A wide variety of requisitioned cars, vans and trucks were pressed into service during the early months of the war.

In many respects the long period of inactivity proved to be invaluable for the Nation's fire services. It enabled the A.F.S. crews to be worked up to a much greater level of efficiency and provided a breathing space in which many of the early teething problems were ironed out. By mid-August 1940 the war had entered a decidedly more serious phase and the first high explosive bombs fell in Warwickshire. The first high explosive bombs to fall on Leamington was on 19th October 1940. The months of waiting were over and from then on the chilling sound of the air-raid siren would be heard with increasing frequency.

On Saturday 29th September 1940, the Leamington Auxiliary Firemen held their first competitions and display in Victoria Park. The Challenge Cup, presented by Alderman K. R. England [Chairman of the Watch Committee] for the best action station went to Adelaide Road [Zone 1]. The crew, under Leading Fireman L. F. Martin, consisted of Firemen Rogers, Davies, Gallagher, Edwards and Lane. Chandos Street [Campion Terrace] crew were awarded the shield for the runners-up, the team being Leading Fireman Barnacle and Firemen Ives, Badger, Groom, Kimble and Wickes. The Crown Hotel action station, under Leading Fireman Faulkner took third place. The competition for the England Cup was judged on two events – a dry drill of four men running out 10 lengths of hose, and a wet drill – which began with the crews dressing, getting a light trailer pump to work from a dam of water with a line of hose and knocking down the target.

The placings in the tug of war contest were as follows: [1] Leamington; [2] Stratford; [3] Warwick. The obstacle race, which included the risk of a fall by competitors and plunging into a portable dam of water, was won by Fireman Davies, with Firemen Postlethwaite and Kellas second and third respectively. Leamington Fire Brigade gave a display with their new machine and demonstrated their rescue and life-saving apparatus. A humorous interlude was provided by Leading Fireman Fred Carno and his crew, who, by a happy combination of entertainment and instruction, showed the spectators how **not** to deal with an incendiary bomb. The finale included a parade of firemen and a cascade of jets.

The heavy raids of 1940 had shown up serious deficiencies in the fire services nationally. There had been major difficulties in co-ordinating the many separate fire authorities of which there were over a thousand in number at the commencement of war. There was little or no standardisation of equipment and each brigade had a rank structure of its own, which caused much friction. Following a conference in London in April 1941, the Home Secretary, Mr. Herbert Morrison, announced his intention of nationalising the service. On 18th August, all the old independent brigades were disbanded and the National Fire Service came into existence. The Auxiliary Fire Service was incorporated into the N.F.S. which had a national establishment figure of 102,000 men and women.

For the very first time, ranks, equipment, and training were standardised and a nationwide system of communications was established. The rate of pay for a fireman was fixed at £3. 10s. a week. Many of the men who entered the service as members of the A.F.S. in 1938 now found themselves with substantive rank for the first time. Much of the southern half of Warwickshire became part of a Division within No.23 Fire Force commanded by Commander Kerr and centred on Worcester.

On 28th October 1941, the Highways and Planning Committee reported the necessity of erecting an air-raid shelter in the yard of the Chandos Street Depot. However, on 21st November 1941 it was reported to the A.R.P. Committee that the Chandos Street Depot was now required by the National Fire Service.

On the communications front, all mobilising was controlled from the brigade's Operational Control Room situated at Leamington fire station.

Apart from the fire cover provided by the local authority brigade, there were also in the county a number of Industrial Fire Brigades providing protection for particular industrial premises and funded by the premises concerned. In Leamington, the Lockheed Hydraulic Brake Co. at Tachbrook Road was one of these. The large Army Ammunition Depot at Kineton was protected by a unit of the Army Fire Service.

A new training school for firewomen opened on Wednesday 18th March 1942, it was the first in the Midland Region. These trainee A.F.S. women, outside the headquarters in Holly Walk, include a former milliner, hairdresser, domestic servant and a cashier. The instructress is on the right. [Photo courtesy of Alan Griffin].

A.F.S. Adelaide Road. [Photos courtesy of Warwickshire County Record Office Ref: PH852/4-5].

Leamington Fire Brigade taken in 1941 at Riverside Buildings, Adelaide Road. Walter Owen is top row on the right. [Photo courtesy of Kenneth Owen].

Women members of the National Fire Service learn how to operate a large Coventry Climax trailer pump in the yard at the Adelaide Road fire station, Leamington, in 1942. The instructor is Company Officer Joe Fessey. [Photo courtesy of Alan Griffin].

Chandos Street Fire Brigade circa 1941. [Photo courtesy of Alan Griffin].

Adelaide Road Fire Station circa 1944. [Photo courtesy of Alan Griffin].

On Monday 14th September 1942, Mr. Herbert Morrison, the Home Secretary and Minister of Home Security, inspected personnel of the N.F.S. at Adelaide Road station. He was accompanied by Lord Dudley, the Deputy Regional Commissioner [Major G. Dennison], the Chief Regional Fire officer [Mr. B. A. Westbrook], and the Senior Regional Woman Officer [Mrs. R. M. Marshall]. He was appreciative of the many improvements carried out by the men in their spare time. These included sleeping quarters, a canteen and social club, which included a bar, which was opened on Saturday 19th September. He was also interested in a mobile workshop, a large lorry fitted out with all the necessary lathes, tools and other appliances for carrying out speedy repairs on the fire-ground and elsewhere. He chatted to the repair team, including firewomen, who had undergone special training in mechanics.

N.F.S. Presentation to the Adelaide Road Messengers in 1944. [Photo courtesy of Warwickshire County Record Office Ref: PH(N)600/720/22].

Members of the A.F.S. based at Adelaide Road. [Photo courtesy of Warwickshire County Record Office Ref: PH852/3].

Column Officer Calypso Clarence Gammon [George Medal], who was known as 'Clip', had been District Officer in the Birmingham Fire Brigade until his subsequent promotion to Column Officer in the National Fire Service. He was awarded his George Medal in 1941, for bravery during the 1940 blitz on Birmingham, when he put his own safety at risk in order to save another fireman from death. He was posted to Leamington to take command of all firefighting arrangements in central Warwickshire. In 1943, he went on to be the Chief of Fire and Security for Lockheed Hydraulic Brake Company at Tachbrook Road where he stayed until his retirement in 1957.

This photo is of a portrait of 'Clip' Gammon painted by the noted war artist Bernard Hailstone who was commissioned to portray a typical British wartime fireman. Courtesy of Leamington Spa Art Gallery & Museum [Warwick District Council].

Holy Trinity Church was better prepared for the worst than most as they trained themselves a voluntary squad of firemen. The committee that decided this was led by Dr. W. Edmund Jones and as well as starting their own service they took other precautions including the supply of a hydrant, the laying of new water pipes and the provision of hosepipes and buckets.

The Whitnash National Fire Service unit operated during the Second World War from a yard near to 21 Heathcote Road. Back row: L-R: Mr. Underhill [snr], Mr. Hill, Mr. Underhill [jnr], F. Roberts, W. Roberts, J. Dolden, G. Marlow, D. Jacobs and A. Martin. Front row: L-R: S. Thornton, A. Batchelor, R. Hall, J. Bullock, P. Smith and S. Addicott.

Lola Dorothy Hall lived at 102, Plymouth Place and worked at Adelaide Road fire station as a telephonist on the switchboard. She was very proud to wear her National Fire Service uniform as this 1943 photo shows.

Effie Small said, "I worked in the Leamington Spa control room for the National Fire Service. We worked 48 hours on duty and 24 hours off, but we were always on call. One night when we were on duty on the switchboard, the overhead light seemed too bright to allow my friend and I to go to sleep on the collapsible beds by the switchboard, so we decided to cover the light. We used a cloth that we also used to dust the place – and eventually dozed off. We woke up to the smell of burning to find the control on fire!! Of course, there was lots of paper around and we panicked. We phoned the officer's dormitory which was next door and they came and put the fire out with stirrup pumps. We weren't put on a charge but we certainly didn't do it again."

Leamington 'Wings for Victory Week' opened on Saturday 8th May 1943 when Mr. Anthony Eden, Foreign Secretary, took the salute at an impressive march-past of fighting and civil defence units on a miserable rainy day outside the Town Hall. Despite the weather a large crowd witnessed the parade. Alongside Mr. Eden were the Town Clerk [Mr. A. F. Greenwood], the Mayor [Councillor R. S. Salt], Colonel N. Blacker [Deputy Commander for the Central Midland District] who paid tribute to the Home Guards and Group Captain R. B. Jordan [R.A.F Station Commander]. The Mayor said, "Leamington and district with an estimated population of considerably less than 40,000 has already subscribed £3½ million to the various Government loans since the outbreak of war; and by raising, as we intend to do this week, a further £500,000, we shall reach the magnificent total of £4 million, or well over £100 per head of population."

Mr. Eden said that the parade was to celebrate particularly the achievements of Bomber Command. The man in the photograph leading the contingent is Column Officer Calypso 'Clip' Gammon of the National Fire Service with 'Sunny' Ayres on the right and Joe Fessey on the left.

The parade, which included an aeroplane fly-past took 25 minutes to pass. Motor cyclists of the Military Police headed the procession followed by the band of the Life Guards which halted and remained opposite the Town Hall. Then came the Royal Navy followed by the Wrens, a military section, members of the Pioneer Corps, a company from 1st Battalion Warwickshire Home Guard, a company of the A.T.S., and a contingent from the R.A.F headed by their band and accompanied by women of the Air Force.

Then came the R.A.F Medical Services, followed by Cadets and Girls Training Corps, a company of Belgian troops, members of the National Fire Service and the St. John Ambulance Brigade. Leamington's Civil Services were headed by their band, followed by Wardens, Fire Guards and First Aid Post representatives. The Women's Land Army made an impressive sight with two of the girls driving Fordson tractors. The W.V.S were followed by the Boy Scouts, Church Lads Brigade and the Girl Guides. Mr. Eden called it a "very remarkable sight" and said that "it was fitting that the parade should have taken place in the vicinity of a spot which still bears the scars of enemy action".

The Leamington Spa Courier dated 2nd June 1944 reported that firewoman Betty Heath, of 113 Shrubland Street, a former diamond setter of engagement rings, now worked at the Rugby N.F.S coachworks shop. She was the only firewoman to be directly concerned in the building of vehicles for the Volunteer Overseas Contingent.

On Saturday 3rd March 1945, some 60 firemen, wives and friends assembled in the function room at Adelaide Road station to mark the 'standing down' of many of the part-time personnel of Chandos Street station. Section Leader Barnacle [Station Officer at Chandos Street] presided.

Following the introduction of the Fire Services Act 1947, the N.F.S. was disbanded in 1948. Control of fire brigades then came under the control of county council and county boroughs under the general guidance of the Home Secretary.

Fire Guard Service

Britain's Fire Guard Service was formed as an essential factor in the defence of this country against the attempts of the enemy to destroy its homes and industries. The Fire Guard organisation was constituted as part of the Wardens' Service. The smallest unit in the Wardens' organisation covered a sector containing an average of 500 people, the smallest operational unit in the Fire Guard Service was the stirrup pump team, of which there was, in a built-up area, at least one for approximately every 150 yards of street or for every 30 houses if there were more than that number of houses in 150 yards of street. A stirrup pump team usually consisted of three people. All large factories and business premises were required to maintain their own Fire Guard organisation.

On 2nd October 1940, the Borough Engineer reported to the Watch Committee the necessity to provide a hut for the fire watcher on the Parish Church tower. The committee recommended that one be provided at an approximate cost of £15.

The Morning News dated 8th January 1941 reported: - **Fire Watching in Leamington** – Vigorous action is to be taken by the authorities at Leamington to protect the town against fire raids. Fire-watchers are required for any building, the whole or any part of which is used as a warehouse of more than 50,000 cubic feet capacity, or any sawmill or timber yard containing more than 50,000 cubic feet of timber, and the borough is to be combed for premises which come within these requirements. Prosecutions will be made if necessary, but it is realised that fire protection is a matter for co-operation. Occupiers of large premises who are doubtful as to their responsibility are invited to seek advice at the Police Station, and the police appeal to those with fire watching schemes already in operation to notify them. Arrangements will be made to give instructions in fire protection and as a new order is expected extending the scope of fire-watching the public in general should take advantage of this opportunity.

The Morning News dated 3rd February 1941 reported: - **Fire Watchers Order, A.R.P. Section 63** – Will every householder please arrange to attend a meeting, or send a representative, to be held at the Bedford Stores Café on Wednesday next, the 5th February, at 6.30pm., for the purpose of arranging voluntary fire parties under the above scheme. Section 63 comprises: - Rugby Road [South side] from Binswood corner to Union Road, Union Road, Warwick Place [North side] from Union Road to Upper Grove Street, Upper Grove Street, Warwick Terrace, Albany Terrace, Beauchamp Hill, Beauchamp Street, Clarendon Crescent, Strathearn Road, Milverton Crescent, Milverton Crescent West, Garden Place, Stamford Place, Barrett Place and Gulistan Road. Signed: H.C. Burgis, Senior Warden, Section 63.

On 21st February 1941, it was reported that 500 persons had attended the fire protection demonstrations and that more had been arranged.

The Fire Guard Headquarters was at Jephson Villa in Hamilton Terrace. The Chief Fire Guard was E. Sidwell, he was already the Divisional Air-raid Warden; the Deputy Fire Guard was P.G. Baddeley; the Fire Guard Assistant Staff Officer was P.C. Glyn Evans who was formerly appointed on 18th December 1941 and C. G. Ackers was appointed Fire Guard Depot Superintendent on 23rd January 1942. It was their responsibility to ensure that sound fire prevention arrangements were in place.

On 30th September 1941, the Highways and Planning Committee approved the installation of a Fire-Guard training hut in the grounds of Jephson Villa, they agreed the necessity for a telephone to be installed at the top of the Town Hall clock tower and approved plans for a fire-watchers hut to be installed at 14 Kinross Road for a Mr. M. C. Mould.

Fire Guard training commenced at the beginning of autumn 1941. By December 1941, in spite of some serious handicaps caused by a shortage of staff and the difficulty of appointing officers with the necessary qualifications, Leamington had made good progress with its arrangements for guarding the town against incendiary bomb attacks.

Of the 7,250 men registered under the Compulsory Enrolment Order, only 473 were immediately available for Fire Guard duty, 416 had attended the lectures and 237 had attended the 'fire hut' training. However, alongside this, volunteer members of the Street Fire Parties had been undergoing the same training and of the 3,500 members more than 2,000 had already had elementary instruction. In addition, many businesses had sought the council's help in training members of their staff who were engaged in fire-watching duties.

The training which a Fire Guard received fell roughly into three stages. The first stage consisted of lectures on incendiary bombs and fire precautions, followed by a practical drill in the use of a stirrup pump, how a team of three persons should attack a fire, what to do if only two persons were available and how an incendiary bomb had to be tackled single handed. The second stage included demonstrations with practice incendiary bombs and practical training, including a team drill in 'smoke', in one of the 'fire huts' erected in the town. The third [advanced] stage was tactical training, including collective exercises with neighbouring Fire Guard parties and also with Wardens in the area covered by the team concerned.

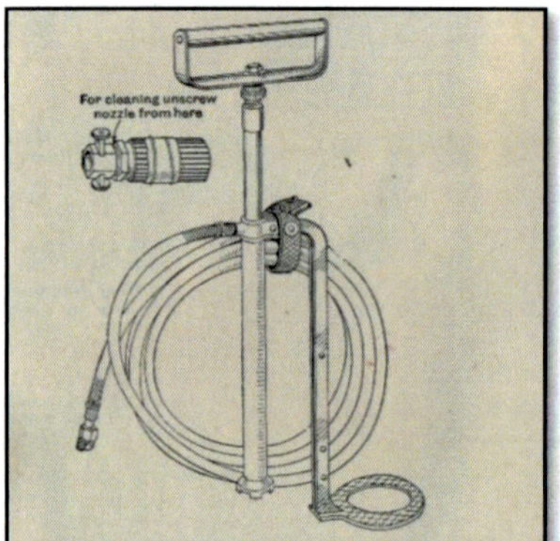

Fig. 8.—The Stirrup Pump with Dual Jet and Spray Nozzle.

A stirrup pump was one of the first lines of defence for Fire Guard parties against incendiary attacks. In addition, each individual Fire Guard was entitled to be supplied with a protective steel helmet and an armlet. Water applied as a jet from the stirrup pump to a magnesium fire bomb had the effect of scattering the burning magnesium whereas a fine jet limited this scattering effect. Therefore, the pumps were fitted with a dual-purpose nozzle. The pump was capable of delivering about 1½ gallons of water per minute in the form of a jet to a distance of 30 feet, or about ¾ gallon of water per minute in the form of a spray to a distance of 15 feet.

The local Fire Guards Handbook stated, "Fire bomb raids are a threat to the very life of the nation. As is well known a very small number of bomber aeroplanes can shower many thousands of small incendiary bombs over a town in the space of a few minutes. And these, if left alone, will start more fires than could possibly be put out either by the National Fire Service or by the efforts of unorganised and untrained individuals, however well-meaning they may be. This is why it becomes the duty of all able-bodied men and women to give whatever service they can in the part-time army of millions of citizens trained to deal with fire bombs promptly whenever and wherever they fall."

"The duty of a Fire Guard is to take turns in watching for the fall of fire bombs; to warn the neighbourhood when they fall in the area for which he is responsible; to help promptly to control them and thus to prevent small fires from becoming big fires; and to fit himself by training to perform this work efficiently."

"It involves the sacrifice of time that can sometimes ill be spared, and often entails a great deal of tedious waiting and watching but it is work which must be done if the homes and industries of the nation are to be saved."

On 24th October 1941, the A.R.P. Officer reported the necessity of an assistant training officer to help him train the Fire Guards. It was resolved that application would be made to the County Council for their approval to appoint A. J. Smith [Decontamination Officer] as Assistant Training Officer.

On 18th November 1941, an application from the A.R.P. officer was made to the Educational Sub-committee requesting use of Shrubland Street School hall on six evenings for lectures to members of the Fire Guard service. The request was agreed subject to a payment of 2s. 6d. to the caretaker and 1s. to the local education authority for each evening.

On 18th December 1941, the A.R.P. Committee authorised one depot superintendent, two male senior fire guards and one female senior fire guard, together with one shorthand typist for the Fire Guards.

On 2nd January 1942, the A.R.P. Officer reported that the first batch of compulsory enrolled Fire Guards would commence duties on 12th January 1942.

On 12th January 1942, the Watch Committee authorised the use of three A.R.P. Committee rooms in the Town Hall annexe for use by the Fire Guard HQ.

On 24th April 1942, the Divisional Warden and Chief Fire Guard reported the appointment of 37 senior fire guards.

The Morning News dated Friday 7th August 1942 reported: - **Women Must Fire-Watch** – Proposals for making fire-watching compulsory for women are to be announced by the Ministry of Home Security today.

On Tuesday 11th August 1942, the Morning News reported: - '**Training of Fire Guards – Leamington Personnel Will be Told About New Incendiaries** – Fire Guards at present undergoing instruction in Leamington, in connection with the Regional Commissioner's training drive, will be told how to combat the three new types of incendiary bomb, which, it was announced recently, enemy aircraft have used in attacks on this country. Women between the ages of 20 and 45, who will be required shortly to register for Fire Guard service, will also receive full training before they perform duties.'

At 3.30pm on 6th October 1942, a meeting was held with representatives of Messrs. Soans, Messrs. Rotherham's, the Regal Cinema and the Employment Exchange in order to discuss and update a joint fire prevention scheme in the Dormer Place area.

Memories of Fire Watching by Betty Thompson [née Kemp] - "Fire watching at Bobby's department store was carried out by all available staff on a rota system. I remember it came round pretty often, once a week and more often if someone was obliged to cancel. We came off duty at 7.00am and returned to work at 10.00am. It was routine to go up to the flat roof which we rather enjoyed! The copper spire of St. Alban's Church [now demolished] showed up strikingly through the darkness when caught in the searchlight beam or in brilliant moonlight."

On 17th October 1943, the local authority introduced a Fire Guard Plan - part of the plan was to issue instructions by poster about fire calls. One poster for the Shrubland Street area instructed: - 'During an alert in the fire guard plan period – get a message to a fire guard or the fire guard assembly point or block point at 39 Alexandra Road. Do not telephone or use a fire alarm system. During other alerts get a message to a warden or policemen or the nearest warden's post at Eagle Recreation Ground. Do not telephone or use a fire alarm system unless you cannot get your message through otherwise.'

Following a request from the Regional Authorities, an exercise was held in Leamington on the evening of Thursday 30th March 1944. The objective was to test the working of the Fire Guard plan in the business premises sector. It was intended to bring out the lessons which would normally be taught in a heavy bombing raid in the shopping centre and tested the general efficiency of the area captains, sector captains, party leaders and fire guards. 26 umpires, all certificated L.F.G.I. instructors [Local Fire Guard Instructors] or sector captains, officiated at the various incidents. The exercise was a complete success and the Borough was congratulated by the Regional Officers upon the efficiency of its Fire Guard Service. The 130 'fires' staged involved 14 calls for the N.F.S.

On 22nd September 1944, the Town Clerk reported to the A.R.P. Committee on Home Office circulars 115 & 116/1944 relating to the reduction in hours of the Civil Defence and Fire Guard organisations.

The uniformed personnel of the Fire Guard Service taken in November 1944. [Photo courtesy of Warwickshire County Record Office Ref: PH(N)600/720/15].

Most of the people in the group are Fire Guard Sector Captains and members of the administrative staff. Those seated are the higher officers of the organisation. L-R: Mr. F. Walker [Deputy Area Captain], Mr. H. W. Crosthwaite [Area Captain], Mr. F. W. Moore [Area Captain], Mr. W. Wilson [Area Captain], Mr. A. S. Dolton [Area Captain], Mr. J. R. Sinclair [Training Officer], Mr. C. G. Ackers [Deputy Fire Guard Officer], Mrs. F. Scott [Assistant Fire Guard Officer], Mr. L. O. Butler [Area Captain], Mr. A. F. Wesley [Area Captain], Mr. G. M. Easterby [Area Captain] and Mr. E. D. Keen [Area Captain].

Mr. C. G. Akers and women members of the Fireguard Service in November 1944. [Photo courtesy of Warwickshire County Record Office Ref: PH(N)600,720-17].

Leamington's Fire Guard service ceased functioning on 7th December 1944. All Fire Guard equipment and signs, which were issued free on loan to street and party areas and business premises occupiers had to be returned to the local authority.

The Morning News dated Thursday 14th December 1944 reported: - '**Leamington's 12,000 Fire Guards** – On December 7 Leamington became a de-prescribed borough under the Fire Prevention Orders, but the present staff in the Fire Guard Department are to be retained for the time being. The position is to be reviewed in two months time. At the meeting of the Town Council this week a resolution was carried expressing appreciation of the services performed by the Fire Guards of whom 12,000 were enrolled in the Borough.'

This was followed up by the Morning News dated Tuesday 13th March 1945: - 'Leamington's Fire Guard Organisation is to be finally wound up on Saturday next, March 17, and the A.R.P. Committee have decided that the remaining members of the office staff shall be given notice terminating their services one month from that date. Similar notice is to be given to all the Fire Guard sector captains, deputy sector captains, and party leaders. The committee have placed on record their appreciation of the valuable services rendered by Mr. C. G. Ackers and his staff, and have extended to them best wishes on the termination of their contracts.'

Camouflage Directorate

Camouflage was a very important and particularly secret aspect of the Second World War. Royal Leamington Spa and the surrounding area played a vital role in this area of work with a number of local establishments being requisitioned for use. It was felt that camouflage could be used to help protect both key civilian sites as well as military sites. As time went on it was decided that concealment and deception could also be useful in protecting naval and merchant shipping.

Before the war, camouflage policy for the military was the responsibility of the various Services. In the civilian area, the Ministry of Home Security, the Ministry of Supply, the Ministry of Aircraft Production and other departments were responsible for buildings or industrial activities.

In 1938 the Air Ministry set up a section in the R.A.F headquarters at Adastral House, London to design camouflage for key civil sites. The Chief Camouflage Officer was Captain Lancelot Glasson. In 1939 Colonel John Turner's department in the Air Ministry, based at Aerial House in London, managed decoy and deception schemes and generally undertook design and construction. The department was initially based at the Strand in London but during 1940 it moved to Sound City at Shepperton.

With war imminent, the Civil Defence Act, which was passed in July 1939, allowed the Camouflage Sub-Committee to insist on essential camouflage work. A Camouflage Advisory Panel was appointed on 2nd August. On 28th August, an emergency instruction for camouflage was issued and on 2nd September 1939 as war was about to be officially declared urgent telegrams were sent out requiring compulsory action on these instructions.

At this crucial moment, the Ministry of Home Security with responsibility for all areas of civil defence, was formed. The Camouflage Section was taken over by the Home Office, and in March 1940 a Camouflage Policy and Organisation Committee was established with senior staff and representatives from each of the Services.

Shortly after this they were evacuated to Leamington Spa under their new name 'The Civil Defence Camouflage Establishment' [CDCE]. Captain Glasson transferred as the head of the CDCE. The headquarters was located at the impressive Regent Hotel on the Parade which was the largest hotel in the town. The hotel was requisitioned in September 1939 under the Emergency Powers [Defence] Act 1939 and de-requisitioned on 25th October 1947. *[It re-opened as a hotel on Saturday 1st May 1948].* The creative [photographic] department for land based camouflage used the disused roller skating rink at Victoria Colonnade on the south bank of the River Leam. *[In 1945 the roller skating rink was sold to the Leamington and Warwick Dramatic Study Group and it opened as the Loft Theatre in 1948].*

It is worth mentioning that there are some reports indicating that the unit was based at the former ice-skating rink in Dormer Place. However, this is incorrect. There was a roller skating rink operated by Leamington and Warwick Skating Rink Ltd at Dormer Place, but much earlier than the Second World War. The Ford car dealership C. H. Soans moved to the Dormer Place site in 1933. At the outbreak of war, the business concentrated on the reconditioning of military vehicles for the Ministry of Defence. I interviewed Barbara Buckley [née Gee], in January 2016, and she told me that she worked for the Camouflage Directorate at the former Colonnade roller skating rink.

The choice of Leamington Spa was due to its central location and the town's proximity to armaments factories in Coventry and Birmingham - and of course Leamington had the Lockheed [Automotive Products] factory along with other factories that were involved in 'war work'. There were also good road and rail links to London, Birmingham and Coventry.

The secret job of the CDCE was to disguise key bombing targets, to undertake experiments in decoy design and to coordinate the use of decoys nationally. It developed an array of camouflage techniques to confuse enemy aircraft. Bombing decoy sites were constructed to deceive and divert enemy bombers from attacking the intended targets. Most of the work was done in the early years of the war when Britain faced the greatest aerial threat.

In 1936 the City of Coventry developed Baginton Coventry as a civil airfield. In May 1939 part of the airfield was granted to the Air Ministry for training of the R.A.F Volunteer Reserve. From October 1939 aircraft based at R.A.F Baginton [Camouflage Flight] were used by the CDCE to assess the effectiveness of camouflage schemes on industrial buildings and airfields using aerial surveys, photographing UK factories, other vital buildings and the decoys. Camouflage Flight became part of No.1 Camouflage Unit on 3rd November 1939.

Compton Verney House, located 11 miles south of Leamington Spa, was requisitioned and used as a Smoke School where soldiers were trained in the production of smoke for use as camouflage. This photo shows a Haslar oil smoke generator. On the top floor of the Regent Hotel, staff in the smoke sub-section worked on camouflage techniques using smoke.

The National Collection of Aerial Photography records that over 650 photographs of locations in Scotland were taken between 1940 and 1943 for No.1 Camouflage Unit. The aircrews of No.1 Camouflage Unit were drawn from the survey arm of the Aircraft Operating Company and reported directly to the CDCE at the Regent Hotel. The back of the photographs were stamped 'Top Secret' and also bore the stamp of the R.A.F Photographic Section, Regent Hotel.

By December 1940 Captain Glasson had recruited 84 technical officers, a subordinate staff of 20 and a clerical staff of 23.

Captain Glasson is in the middle of the second row on this photo of 'Camoufleurs'.

By 6th April 1941 the staffing had increased again - there was now a director, a technical staff consisting of a chief camouflage officer, a senior design officer, a deputy senior design officer, a senior constructional officer, a deputy constructional officer, 30 camouflage officers, a principal technical assistant, 15 senior technical assistants, 20 junior technical assistants, 10 technical officers, 12 assistant technical officers, three in smoke sub-section, five in the horticultural sub-section, two in the map section, four in the photographic section, a storekeeper, a packer and four labourers. The administration and finance department was transferred from London and consisted of a principal, a senior staff officer, four staff officers, 10 executive and higher clerical officers and temporary assistants, 16 clerical officers and clerical assistants, 48 temporary clerical officers, 11 shorthand typists and typists, two telephonists, seven messengers, five night watchmen and 15 cleaners. This totalled 234 people. There were also seven people that remained in London. It was at this time that the name was changed to the Camouflage Directorate and was then headed by Wing Commander T. R. Cave-Brown-Cave.

The responsibilities of the Directorate were later expanded to include work on naval camouflage and included the Admiralty's Naval Camouflage Research Section. The Officer in Charge [Director of Naval Camouflage] was Lt. Commander James Yunge-Bateman and his deputy was Gerald Trice-Martin M.C. Initially there were three camouflage officers, five senior and three junior technical assistants, as well as a model maker. Work on naval camouflage was undertaken at the former Art Gallery and Museum, and the Technical School and Art School, in Avenue Road using two viewing tanks to view the completed camouflage schemes. One viewing tank was inside the building and one outside. The east wing of the Art Gallery and Museum, a single storey building, lighted from the roof and without windows, was used for design and the housing of an experimental tank. Construction of the models was carried out in a sectioned off single room in the basement of the main gallery. The outdoor experimental tank at the rear of the main building was used for daylight work. It was overlooked by windows in the Art Gallery and Technical School.

The Art School, which had been over the Girls' College next to the Library, had to move to Beauchamp Hill. They also changed their evening classes to daytime because of the black-out. Other buildings in Leamington Spa were used or requisitioned during the time the camouflage people were at Leamington. One in particular was The Gables, a large Victorian house in Kenilworth Road. As well as being used for some aspects of camouflage work, it was also the control centre for anti-aircraft gun installations. The Art Gallery was de-requisitioned and handed back to the council on 13th August 1946, but did not reopen as the municipal Art Gallery until 28th July 1947.

Eva Lawrence née Shakespeare who worked at the library as a senior assistant librarian recalled in 1980, "The Art Gallery was joined to the library and the librarians had much to do with it. I remember soon after the war started we had an exhibition in the Art Gallery containing pictures from Manchester, Liverpool, Glasgow etc. and from Dame Laura Knight. The Art Gallery was suddenly taken over by the Camouflage Directorate, and we were asked to get the exhibition down and get out in 48 hours. Of course, we couldn't do it in that short time, but we did it as quickly as we could. All the pictures in the Art Gallery had to be packed up and stored. The magazine room was closed for the duration, and the pictures stored there. A bomb hit the house opposite the library, but the pictures were unharmed. We used the strongroom, behind the reference room as an air raid shelter, and a bolt hole was made in the wall to the outside, in case doors got trapped. The dome in the Art Gallery couldn't be blacked out, and while I was in charge, I was fetched out many times by Air Raid Wardens because the Camouflage people had gone off duty and left the light on in the Art Gallery."

Among the directorate were some of the biggest names in the field of art and movie design. Based at the Regent Hotel, the directorate's artists, designers and technicians worked on various aspects of military and civilian camouflage. More used to living the London high-life, these were the people now called upon to help protect factories, ships, docks and air bases.

Led by Captain Glasson and Christopher Ironside, an opera set designer, the team's sole aim was to disguise key bombing targets. They surveyed and photographed factories and installations from the ground and the air and then used the giant turntable at the Colonnade to create models in a variety of light and weather conditions which would show what the targets looked like from the air.

From this work came a huge array of camouflage schemes and ideas to confuse German pilots. The work involved using techniques to 'break up' the outline of buildings as seen from the air. It is said that some of the techniques employed included draping giant nets over buildings, painting fake road markings onto rooftops and quite bizarrely, even putting concrete cows on the roofs of key buildings so that they might appear as fields from the air. They covered huge areas with lights and steam rising into the air in the hope of diverting the enemy bombers onto open fields.

Another camouflage ploy was to use a modified slurry-spreading machine to spray sump oil across airfields. In Leamington's old Art Gallery and Museum in Avenue Road, the directorate set up two huge water tanks designed to float model boats. The team experimented with different paints to help disguise ships from enemy submarines.

Having designed the effect they would go to the various sites and oversee the painting and camouflage work. However, despite the group's best efforts in using a range of techniques, bombers often hit their targets. The Germans were well aware of what the site looked like prior to the war starting, as in many cases they had maps and photographs. After the war ended it was discovered that in preparation for war, the Germans had set up a unit near Berlin responsible for photographing "everywhere from Hull to the south coast".

One of the factories that had nets draped over parts of it was Lockheed [Automotive Products] on Tachbrook Road, but that didn't stop it being hit twice, once on Saturday 13th June 1942 and again on Thursday 16th July 1942. The factory employed 10,000 people, many of them women, working continuous shifts in the manufacture of undercarriages and aircraft hydraulic equipment for a number of British aircraft including the Armstrong Whitworth Whitley.

Some of the artists, or Camoufleurs as they were known, employed on this important war work included Christopher Ironside, the Deputy Senior Design Officer, who later designed the reverse of our first decimal coinage in 1971, Richard Fairbairn who was also Personal Assistant to Captain Glasson, Tom Rathmell, Guy Roddon and Robin Darwin, the great-grandson of the naturalist Charles Darwin. Robin later became principal of the Royal College of Art and was knighted becoming Sir Robert 'Robin' Vere Darwin. There was also Stephen Bone, a member of the New English Art Club, Adrian Daintrey, Leon Underwood and Hugh Casson. Wilfred Shingleton was brought in to work on naval camouflage. He went on to win an Oscar for the 1946 film Great Expectations. Richard Guyatt, Regional Camouflage Officer for Scotland, went on to be Rector of the Royal College of Art, visiting Professor at Yale University and Governor of the Imperial Society of Science and Technology. He was very much involved with the Festival of Britain in 1951 and designed the mugs for the Coronation in 1953.

Another of these artists was Victorine Anne Foot who worked in oils, watercolours and pastels and is best known for her work during World War II on military camouflage. In 1941 she took a job as a Junior Technical Assistant in the Naval Section of the Directorate of Camouflage based in Leamington Spa. Her duties included painting camouflage designs onto models of ships. The models were all based on real ships. If the actual ship was sunk or lost the model was retired from further use. Whilst at the

Camouflage Directorate, Victorine drew and painted her colleagues at work, both at Leamington Spa and at the docks where they painted their camouflage schemes onto ships. She submitted some of this work to the War Artists' Advisory Committee and had one painting, camouflaging a cruiser in dock, purchased by the committee in June 1943. In 1994 Victorine donated her sketches from Leamington Spa to the Imperial War Museum.

Victorine said, "I joined the Naval Section of the Directorate of Camouflage in the summer of 1941. It was in the Art Gallery of Leamington Spa right in the centre of England. The camouflaging of factories took place in The Rink. The headquarters was in the Regent Hotel in The Parade. The camouflage officers were all artists, while we junior Technical Assistants were still students."

"There was an experimental tank at one end of the Art Gallery - Commander Yunge Bateman was in charge of the naval section. Varying weather conditions were simulated with the use of fans and lighting from sunny, cloudy to moonlight. The model to be camouflaged would be painted and tried out on the tank - the officers sitting at the other end of the gallery with binoculars, their heads covered and in the dark, like an erstwhile photographer, they would then decide whether their design worked in these various conditions. If so the wet model would be placed on one's table and it would be my job to paint the design onto the appropriate plans. Each colour was numbered."

"One job was to cycle with these plans to a brewery *[Thornley Kelsey at Radford Semele]* a few miles outside the town and they would be despatched from there to the Admiralty and then to the ships. I can remember passing German prisoners working in the fields and thinking, "What if they knew what I was carrying?" Sometimes 'the men from the Admiralty' would visit us: Robert Goodden, David Pye, Robin Russell and Oliver Hall. David Pye was in charge of the drawings of the invasion fleet and various tank assault vessels. A blue and white simple design was used for these - I was put in charge of these drawings when he brought them which was very exciting as they were new strange shaped vessels. Models of all the ships were made by a team, I remember the names of Wilcox, Spence and Frank Mason."

"The officers were: Gerald Trice-Martin, Fred Taylor, W. O. Spike, Stanley, and Wilfred Shingleton whose experience in films helped with the lighting of the tank. Stuart Matthew was our draughtsman, Dr. Skoil was a scientific advisor who went to sea in submarines to view ships but was lost in action. Many reconnaissance flights went to Scapa Flow, Rosyth and Belfast."

"There were times when we were very busy and then there would be great gaps in the work. During one of these I was allowed to go to paint something of interest about the war effort. I decided to go to Plymouth where I heard that H.M.S Newcastle was being camouflaged. So, I set out with the necessary permits. I can remember the moment when I had to sit down on the dock and get out my paints. It wasn't long before the officer of the watch flanked by two sailors came down the gangway presented arms and asked for my pass. I handed it up to him and went on squeezing out my paint. This ceremony happened whenever they changed the watch. I was given countless mugs of tea by the sailors who crowded round watching every brush-stroke. I was sketching a man who was way up high painting a sort of yard-arm. He waved at me and I waved back. Sometime later he came running up and wanted to see what I had done and when I showed him, he was so disappointed for he said, "I thought it would be a portrait."

"I was invited on board for tea with the Commander and there in his cabin was the design which we had sent off from Leamington. It was exciting to see and paint the design being applied to a massive great cruiser. Of course, I was overjoyed when the War Artist's Advisory Committee bought my painting for 12 guineas - and delighted for it to be in the Imperial War Museum."

"There were sad days in the Naval Section. The one that I remember specially was when we heard that several ships had been sunk in the Indian Ocean - one I know was H.M.S Prince of Wales - and the models were put up on a special shelf."

"Peter Scott sent us suggestions for pastel coloured designs for the Arctic - which were used. Of course, because of the wake it was impossible to make the ship invisible but it could be made less of a target and disguised so that the enemy would not be able to identify the class of ship and what its armament would be."

Virginia Ironside, daughter of Christopher Ironside, tells of some of her father's work and her own memories - "A couple of weeks after my birth, escaping the nursing home and the bombs, I was taken back by my mother in a basket to our house in Leamington Spa. Much to everyone's relief, both my father and his brother had been spared from actually fighting in the war. While my uncle was safely employed at the Tate Gallery in charge of evacuating hundreds of old masters from London to Upton in Gloucestershire, my father had applied to the Ministry of Home Security Camouflage Unit, and was posted to Leamington Spa as a Camouflage Officer."

"For the inhabitants of the sedate spa town, the invasion of a bunch of artists in their midst must have been a complete shock. My father said that the camouflage people were generally regarded as 'a group of maniacs'. But the task of these maniacs was crucial, to disguise Britain from the enemy. Every so often my father would go up in a plane to take aerial photographs of sensitive targets that the Germans might have their eye on, like factories, and aerodromes, and then, with the aid of paint, netting, seaweed and sludge – the residue of oil from ships' tanks, which was used to darken all kinds of surfaces from roofs to runways – the camouflagers were commissioned with the task of transforming them, using their knowledge about colour, shadows, angles and dimensions, so that from the air they would look like innocent fields of sheep, residential housing estates, or pieces of forest or scrubland."

"Every day my father turned up at the Leamington Skating Rink, which had been converted into a giant studio, and joined the other artists slaving away over enormous turntables on which they had constructed models of factories and aerodromes, lit by ever-moving moons and suns attached to wires, trying out different ways of painting them to make them invisible to enemy aircraft. The models were made to look as if they were being seen from four miles away and lamps were provided with colour filters to simulate different weather conditions."

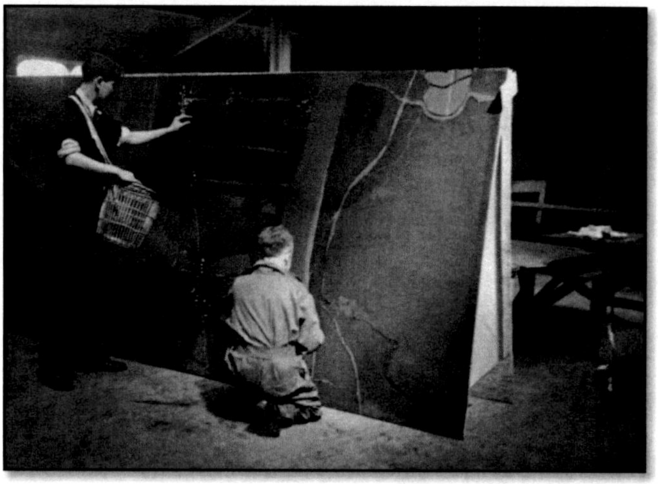

Christopher Ironside and a camoufleur colleague working on a model at the former skating rink.

"The Camouflage Unit teemed with men who would become huge artistic cheeses in the years after the war. There were the painter Tom Monnington and the architect Hugh Casson [both future Presidents of the Royal Academy]; Richard Guyatt, the graphic designer [future Rector of the Royal College of Art]; Eric Schilsky, the sculptor, and Edward Wadsworth, whose later semi-abstract woodcuts were made on the black and white 'dazzle' theme that arose from his experience as a camouflage designer. The painter and lithographer, Julian Trevelyan, and the artist Edward Bawden worked in camouflage units nearby. But the key figure was Robin Darwin. He was secretary of the Camouflage Committee and a man who consistently would play a powerful role in both my parents' lives."

"Robin de Vere Darwin was born in 1910, the great-grandson of Charles Darwin. He had been educated at Eton and Cambridge, and studied at the Slade School of Art. At Eton he not only acquired an excellent education, but further developed what was already a hugely grand and charming manner which made it easy for him not just to hob-nob with but sometimes even to patronise the great and the good. His illustrious family had imbued him with a confidence and certainty that fuelled a driving ambition. Added to this he was a big man, both in height and in breadth. He cut a preposterous figure in Leamington, and caused great amusement when, off-duty, he would set out in an open Rolls Royce, wearing a wide-brimmed hat, to sketch the countryside. On one occasion, when he was out with the sculptor, Leon Underwood, this mildly bohemian behaviour caused him to be arrested as a spy."

Captain Glasson is in the middle of the second row on this photo of 'Camoufleurs'. Christopher Ironside is 2nd from the right on the same row.

"My mother and father had begun their married life in a house in Lansdowne Crescent, where they lived with their tortoiseshell cat and two lodgers, also camouflage artists, who had been foisted upon them by the authorities. Janey bought food for them, cooked for them, made their beds and washed up after them – everything that was still expected of a woman in those early years of the war. One of the lodgers demanded that he be given his egg ration individually so that he could use the yolk for painting in tempera but my mother, desperate for different ingredients to add variety to wartime meals, rightly refused."

"After a spell of 'war work' at Lockheed's Hydraulic Brakes and a brief period in the Records Section of the Camouflage Office, she took on voluntary work at a home for evacuees whose billetters couldn't cope with the nits, scabies, impetigo and bedwetting of unhappy East End children who she entertained by getting them to pose for portraits."

"'Do me now, Mrs. Iminside,' they would beg, as my mother sat, stifling in the antiseptic air of the children's home, with a sketch-pad consisting of thin sheets of paper, drawing these sad children, many of them with their heads shaved to prevent nits, and all dressed in the most unsuitable cast-offs. Tiny boys wore huge grey shorts held up by string, adolescent girls with bosoms burst out of floral dresses suitable for nine-year-olds. My mother always emphasised the clothes in her drawings, she actually drew one poor evacuee from the back, fascinated by the line of her oddly tailored coat."

Christopher Ironside, 3-week-old Virginia and Nurse Horton at 79 Holly Walk in February 1944.

"During her pregnancy, and relieved of war work, my mother made clothes – first, dolls' outfits for Harrods' toy department and then dresses for herself, flowing garments in earth colours *à la* Augustus John's Dorelia, which suited my father because when he came back from work he painted and drew her endlessly."

"Tiny scrap as I was at the time, I still remember Leamington with affection. It's something about the smell. When I returned, at fourteen, for a visit with my father, I breathed in the dank, fetid air of the canals as if I were a Bisto kid because it reminded me of dark, rank waterway paths that I was wheeled along as a baby. And yet these watery memories are inextricably linked with a feeling of melancholy. I had been born between two deaths. Four years before my birth, in the autumn of 1940, my mother had received a telegram informing her that her pilot brother, Jimmy, who had been posted to Norfolk in Coastal Command, was, at only twenty years old, 'Missing, believed killed.'"

Christopher & Janey Ironside with 3-week-old Virginia at 79 Holly Walk in February 1944.

"My mother had been half in love with her dashing, left-wing brother – he'd caused terrible anxiety in the family when, as a boy at Wellington, he'd announced that he was a Communist. He used to motor over from his posting to spend weekends with her, driving her about in an open-topped sports car and taking her from pub to pub. After she died, I found a large suitcase stuffed with his letters. And a year after I was born my mother received another blow. Her sister, Kitty died, also at twenty years old, of a brain tumour at the Military Hospital at Secunderabad in South India where she was serving in the Women's Auxiliary Corps."

"My mother must have felt desperately alone and unhappy. Since I experienced severe post-natal depression when I had my own child, I wouldn't be surprised if my mother hadn't suffered in a similar way. Certainly, I was rather shocked when she told me, years later, that she used simply to dump me in my pram at the bottom of the garden for hours on end 'so I couldn't hear you screaming' - not the action of someone basking in the glow of maternal contentment."

"Life as a housewife and mother in war-time, blacked-out Leamington Spa seemed dreadfully bleak to a beautiful, bereaved and talented young woman. One colleague wrote: 'Her creativity even shone in the unutterable boredom of the Camouflage Records Section.' Although she was indefatigable when it came to cooking and looking after the house, she absolutely loathed housekeeping. When I later asked her what she thought might happen to us when we died, she replied, "Well I suppose if we don't go to heaven, we go to hell. That probably means we have to spend all day and every day washing up.""

"She became completely fed up with queuing, scrimping and saving, mothering, caring for lodgers and provincial artistic life in general. Three years in Leamington Spa was enough. She longed for the bright lights of London, café society, Quaglino's, the Café Royal, the Gargoyle Club in Fitzrovia, black-market booze, famous people, a life that my father used to describe, in a rather jaded, weary voice, as: 'Faster! Faster!'"

In 1940, part of the Royal Pump Room building was taken over by the Ministry of Home Security Camouflage Department. Patients continued to be treated, the annexe being available for those needing to take the waters internally as well as those recuperating after receiving treatment prescribed to them by their medical advisors.

On 23rd February 1945, the Town Clerk reported to the Air Raid Precautions Committee on the closing down, in the near future, of the camouflage establishment. Director Wing Commander T. R. Cave-Brown-Cave was to give a lecture to members of the Council and members of the A.R.P. Committee.

From 1905 until 1939 the resident manager of the Regent Hotel was Herbert Wingfield Sherry. The hotel was requisitioned on 7th September 1939. The 'camouflage' team experimented with mixing different paints in an attempt to help disguise our ships from becoming the targets of enemy submarines. Herbert died just five years later in 1944, aged 69. It is said that he "died broken-hearted because his hotel had been requisitioned by the Ministry of Transport at the outbreak of the war, and was occupied by camouflage experts who reputedly mixed paint in the baths". The hotel was de-requisitioned on 25th October 1947.

The Bath Hotel in Bath Street was another of the town's hotels that was requisitioned, and closed to the public at the beginning of the war. It was handed back at the beginning of August 1946.

The Manor House Hotel was another that was requisitioned by the Ministry of Transport. Messrs. Flowers and Sons. Ltd. of Stratford Upon Avon purchased the hotel at the end of the war, the contract being signed on Tuesday 20th November 1945. A new licence was granted on Monday 21st October 1946 and the hotel reopened to the public on Tuesday 29th October 1946.

Although the Clarendon Hotel at the top of the Parade was requisitioned and closed, its bar remained open with a full publican's licence. During this period, the hotel was occupied by the Ministry of Works. On Monday 16th June 1947, there was a civic dinner party to celebrate the re-opening of the hotel.

The Pioneer Corps day-book tells us that [SO/C8112/F.A.M.P.C.] Smoke Company was formed at Leamington Spa [Regent Hotel] on 11th November 1940 under Major S. Lansley, Officer Commanding. You would have thought that Leamington would be a comparatively safe place for soldiers to be based - after all it was hardly the front line. However, this was not to be so for Serjeant Charles William Welch [3239934] and his colleague Serjeant Thomas Cummings Landles [2745846]. Both had been transferred to the Pioneer Corps [Smoke Company] on 12th November 1940. Two days after arriving in Leamington they sheltered in the doorway of Lipton's grocery shop on the Parade as a German aircraft dropped a stick of bombs across the town. Lipton's suffered a direct hit with the fourth bomb reducing the building to a pile of rubble killing both men. Charles is buried at Brunswick Street Cemetery and Thomas was returned to his home city of Edinburgh where he was cremated.

The Artists International Association [AIA] was formed in 1933 and as early as 1938 attempts had been made to reduce the domination of the art world in London and form regional sub groups. It took the war to firmly establish these groups, partly due to the dispersal of members across the country on various war activities. One of the most interesting groups in terms of scale and activities was the group at Leamington. Many of the artists working for the Camouflage Directorate became affiliated to the AIA. A proposal to provide activities for artists in their spare time was seen as a way of maintaining their psychological well-being, it being well received by the artists. One of the largest schemes was for the British Restaurant at Regent Grove Leamington which was furnished with six panels, ranging from 8 feet x 10 feet to 10 feet x 20 feet. They were the work of separate artists, although in some cases several artists collaborated on individual panels. *[See the British Restaurant section in the Rationing and Food chapter for further details and photographs of the panels].*

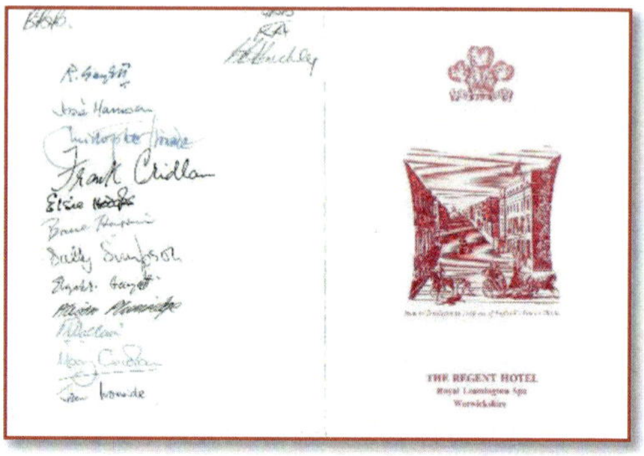

On Saturday 1st February 1992, a Camouflage Directorate reunion was held at the Regent Hotel. The hosts were the hotel's owners Frank and Mary Cridlan. Frank had been a barrister before the war, and served as an intelligence officer in the R.A.F during it. Local artist and cartoonist Ken Aitken also attended and sketched the following cartoons. As a teenager, he 'spied' on the artists at work in Leamington and even got himself a job before joining the R.A.F. For many years his paintings of aircraft made him the pre-eminent artist in that field. A number of celebrated artists attended the reunion including Christopher Ironside, Richard Fairbairn and Richard 'Dick' Guyatt. Welfare Officer Elsie Hodges [née Hicks] was also there. She described her job as visiting "the sick, lame and lazy." Barbara Buckley [née Gee] said in a very understated way, "I worked in the photographic section and was kept busy."

CAPTION:- "OLD FANSHAWE WAS ALWAYS SHORTSIGHTED – HE'S CHATTING UP THE NOTICE BOARD"

The reunion dinner menu comprised cream of tomato and basil soup, fillet of plaice Veronique, entrecote steak Bordelaise, almondene and new potatoes, mange tout, baby carrots, soufflé Grand Marnier and coffee and mints. Drinks included Champagne or Bucks Fizz Rene Tellier, Tokay d'Alsace 1989, Chateau Regent St Emilion 1989 as well as Port, Brandy or Liqueurs.

Barbara Buckley [née Gee]

Barbara Gee was born in 1923. As a 17-year-old teenager Barbara moved with her family at the start of the Second World War from Cromer in Norfolk to No.1 Milverton Terrace in Leamington Spa. The reason for this move was that her engineer father had received a call from Rolls Royce in Coventry to join in the war effort in the aircraft industry working on engines.

Barbara at 18 years of age.

Barbara in 2016.

In 1941 Barbara passed the Civil Service exam, and following an arduous interview at the Labour Exchange, she was sent to work as a technical assistant, which she tells me was basically a photographic assistant, in the photographic section of the Camouflage Unit at the Colonnade. Barbara said, "The photographic section was based in a wooden building that had been a roller skating rink and the staff working in the unit there referred to it as just 'The Rink'."

"The old roller skating rink area was used for the layout of various camouflage schemes. Carpenters and artists would make three-dimensional mock ups on a turntable and then the photographic team would take a number of photos of it using different angles and different lighting. The carpenters were excellent, they worked on schemes for hiding factories, rivers, streams, water towers and the like. They would experiment on disguising water and by floating what looked like mats of grass on rivers. They even covered a whole factory in Wales, disguising it as a village."

"Cyril Jenkins was the head of the photographic department and was therefore my boss. He produced photographic stills and films and I would assist him. We had a Leica and two or three Exacta cameras which were very good cameras at the time. The setting up, developing and production of the images used to take ages. Often we would have very important people from London coming to see one of our various film shows, but we never saw Winston Churchill. On the odd occasion that work was a little slow, we would perhaps make up a montage like this one and photograph it."

A Typical Montage.

"The Rink had two large offices at one end for our various bits of camera equipment. We had a canteen on the premises and the carpenters had their room. We had a number of filing cabinets full of photos and slides and often the artists would come and ask for some to look at."

"I lived at home but many others working for the Camouflage Unit used to rent flats in the town. The arty types working for the unit had mainly come from London and were a novelty to some of the genteel folk of Leamington and they had never seen anything like it. They would walk around town in sandals and no socks, something that was never done. Some people found that type of thing quite shocking."

"Cyril Jenkins often had to fly to various places, including Scotland, to take photos of different camouflage schemes once they were in place. The two planes that were used, a Fairy Battle and a Tiger Moth, were very old and not reliable. Sometimes he would come back looking a little green. There was talk of me going with him on some of the flights but he had one experience when the engine dropped out of his Tiger Moth just outside Manchester and so my husband and I decided that it was not such a good idea."

On 5th July 1941 at the age of 18 Barbara married Peter Buckley, a Major in the Royal Army Service Corps [R.A.S.C] at St. Mark's Church, Rugby Road, Leamington.

On the left of the next photo is Robert 'Bobby' Collingridge who also worked at 'The Rink' in the Colonnade. Then Deborah Gee [Barbara's mother], Patricia Buckley [Peter's sister], Peter, Barbara, Teresa Gee [Barbara's sister], Elvin Gee, [Barbara's father], and Elsie Buckley, [Peter's mother].

"Both Eileen Rhodes and Joan Hollick worked at 'the Rink' mainly doing filing work. They were what you could call Leamington Society girls. One of them had her photo in Picture Post magazine."

Bobby Collingridge was just a junior in the unit at the time but he was a good friend and because my husband was away in the war, Bobby would escort me to parties and the like. Later on he had an art shop in Harbury and also managed the Loft Theatre. He was Chairman of the Loft Theatre on the same site where he worked as a junior."

"A Dr. Sayce also had his offices at 'The Rink'. He did research into pilot's eye sight and night time flying."

"The headquarters of the Camouflage Directorate was based at the Regent Hotel. I didn't have any reason to go there officially although we did go to use the club bar and for social events and I would go to play table tennis. They used other buildings in the town but again I didn't have any reason to go to any of them. Spencer Yard which was very close to us was used but I don't know what they did there."

"It was a good time to be a teenager, everyone seemed to socialise together, but often parties would be in people's own flats. The big thing was ballroom dancing. We used to go three times a week, Friday and Saturday at the Town Hall and Tuesdays at the Palais de Dance in Spencer Street. Many a girl met someone there who would later become their husband. The dances would end around 11.00pm-midnight and afterwards we would go to the Polka Dot café down a small passage off Warwick Street. It was very popular, always packed and there was always a queue. Because of rationing we could only order beans on toast or cheese on toast. As well as the parties and the dancing we would have tickets booked for every Sunday at the Regal cinema."

"On one occasion I went for a dinner at the prisoner of war camp with Marjorie, a friend of mine and an army officer friend of hers. The POWs cooked and served the food, which was all very nice."

"Unfortunately, in 1943 due to a family crisis I had to resign from my job in order to look after my father, sister and brother. It's what girls in a family had to do sometimes."

"As we went through the war, there were many troops from other countries in town. The Czechs came first and then later the Polish and the Americans. I even saw a New Zealand Maori officer in the Haunch of Venison pub. A number of girls married Americans and went off to the States."

"Sad to say but some years later, in 1964, the Loft Theatre, the building where we used to work, was destroyed by fire."

Pauline Ward née Hopkins

Pauline Hopkins was born in 1926 and worked for the Camouflage Directorate at the Regent Hotel in 1943 and 1944. The family lived at 46 Charlotte Street which was very close to Rusina Nursery, the area that was bombed at 11.40am on Friday 23rd August 1940.

Pauline said, "At the age of 15 I went to work at the top of Guys Cliffe Avenue. It was mainly fields in those days although Gulliman's Tennis and Golf Club was there. The drawing office for Armstrong Whitworth was relocated from Coventry and I went to work there as a tracer. I stayed there for two years."

"In 1943 I started work for the Camouflage Directorate at the Regent Hotel. I worked on the top floor doing clerical work. The social side was very good. Often a group of us would go across the road to the Haunch of Venison for a drink either at lunch time or after work. We had a canteen at the hotel as well as the hotel bar. There was a games room on the ground floor and the ballroom, which was also on the ground floor was used for entertaining troops. Often we would go to the Palais de Dance or to the Blue Café that was run by Mrs. Devis. The cinemas were good. We tended to use the Regent, the Regal or the Scala which was always called 'The Flea Pit'. There were plenty of troops in town especially when the Americans entered the war. The Bath Hotel was a popular place for everyone. What I remember most is that everywhere we went it was always very smoky. Nearly everyone smoked in those days."

In 2008 the Sez-U Community Theatre and the Leamington Studio Artists spent a Heritage Lottery grant of £49,900 on celebrating the work of the Civilian Camouflage Directorate. Sez-U project leader Fergus Durrant said, "Surveying factories and installations from the ground and air, the unit created models and designs that could be viewed in all weather and light conditions. The men and women used a large turntable with viewing platforms and giant water tanks constructed in the building that is now the old Art Gallery and Museum in York Road. Can you imagine trying to camouflage a building on the scale of the Ford factory now? That was the enormity of their task. On top of that, resources were so tight. They just did not have the materials to spread the camouflage."

Sez-U and Leamington Studio Artists staged a series of performances, exhibitions, workshops and displays based around the unit's history. Mr. Durrant said at the time, "We have found the blueprints for the original design of the turntable so we're going to reconstruct it as a theatre set and perform a production based around the work of the camouflage unit and the people involved. A range of other activities are also in the pipeline, including a workshop programme during which visual artists will visit more than 70 schools and community venues."

Fast forward to 2016 and this subject is still of interest to people. The Leamington Spa Art Gallery and Museum launched an exhibition called "The Art of Deception" in July 2016 which continued until October 2016. Local curator Alice Swatton said, "A section of the Civil Defence Camouflage Establishment was based in Leamington from 1939 to 1944, where it employed a large number of distinguished artists and designers of the mid-20th century. The exhibition provides an account of the complex tasks of aerial surveillance, design, testing and production of camouflage that was carried out by the Establishment and the smaller naval camouflage unit that was also based in the town."

A book entitled 'Concealment & Deception - The Art of the Camoufleurs of Leamington Spa 1939-45' was also produced to support the exhibition. Other events organised included a camouflage 'Art in the Park', a camouflage quarter in the Jephson Gardens, yarn bombing at the Royal Pump Room and in the Jephson Gardens, camouflaging the Czech memorial fountain, war and camouflage walks by Barry Franklin, secret 'camo' film screening at Foundry Wood, a book of poems 'Party Town' by Matt Black and a display at the Leamington History Day in All Saints' Church.

Local Defence Volunteers / Home Guard

At 9.00pm on the evening of Tuesday 14th May, 1940, Anthony Eden, our Member of Parliament for Warwick and Leamington and Minister of War, made his historic, sombre, wireless broadcast into the homes of millions, bringing into being as if by magic, the most fantastic civilian force ever raised in modern times.

"I want to speak to you to-night about the form of warfare which the Germans have been employing so extensively against Holland and Belgium - namely, the dropping of troops by parachute behind the main defensive lines. Let me say at once that the danger to us from this particular menace, although it undoubtedly exists, should not be exaggerated. We have made preparations to meet it already."

"Let me describe to you the system under which these parachute raids are carried out. The troops arrive by aeroplane - but let it be remembered that any such aeroplane seeking to penetrate here would have to do so in the teeth of the Anti-Aircraft defences of this country. If such penetration is effected, the parachutists are then dropped, it may be by day, it may be by night. These troops are specially armed, equipped, and some of them have undergone specialised training. Their function is to seize important points, such as aerodromes, power stations, villages, railway junctions and telephone exchanges, either for the purpose of destroying them at once, or of holding them until the arrival of reinforcements. The purpose of the parachute attack is to disorganise and confuse, as a preparation for the landing of troops by aircraft."

"The success of such an attack depends on speed. Consequently, the measures to defeat such an attack must be prompt and rapid. It is upon this basis that our plans have been laid. You will not expect me to tell you, or the enemy, what our plans are, but we are confident that they will be effective. However, in order to leave nothing to chance and to supplement, from sources as yet untapped, the means of defence already arranged, we are going to ask you to help us, in a manner which I know will be welcome to thousands of you. Since the war began the Government have received countless enquiries from all over the Kingdom from men of all ages who are for one reason or another not at present engaged in military service, and who wish to do something for the defence of the country."

After spelling out the impending dangers, he went on, "Now is your opportunity. We want large numbers of such men in Great Britain who are British subjects, between the ages of 17 and 65, to come forward now and offer their service in order to make assurance doubly sure. The name of the new force which is now to be raised will be the "Local Defence Volunteers". This name, Local Defence Volunteers, describes its duties in three words. It must be understood that this is, so to speak, a spare-time job, so there will be no need for any volunteer to abandon his present occupation."

"Part-time members of existing civil defence organisations should ask their officers' advice before registering under the scheme. Men who will ultimately become due for calling up under the National Service [Armed Forces] Act may join temporarily, and will be released to join the Army when they are required to serve. Now a word to those who propose to volunteer. When on duty you will form part of the Armed Forces, and your period of service will be for the duration of the war. You will not be paid, but you will receive uniform and will be armed. You will be entrusted with certain vital duties, for which reasonable fitness and a knowledge of firearms are necessary. These duties will not require you to live away from your homes. In order to volunteer, what you have to do is to give in your name at your local police station; and then, as and when we want you, we will let you know."

"This appeal is directed chiefly to those who live in small towns, villages and less densely inhabited suburban areas. I must warn you that, for certain military reasons, there will be some localities where the numbers required will be small, and others where your services will not be required at all. Here then is the opportunity for which so many of you have been waiting. Your loyal help, added to the arrangements which already exist, will make and keep our country safe."

Mr. Eden's plea for men between 17 and 65 years of age to register at their local police stations brought an instant response but in some areas, it brought chaos. The police suddenly realised that they were the ones who were going to be organising the enlistment. In some locations they were swamped with volunteers.

Nationally a million men were enrolled into the Local Defence Volunteers [LDV] almost overnight. Nearly the whole of the local area covered by the 1st Warwickshire [Warwick] Battalion lay within Mr. Eden's constituency. The 1st Warwickshire [Warwick] Battalion was commanded by Lieutenant Colonel J. H. Alexander, D.S.O., M.C. Originally four companies were formed: - "A" Company covered Warwick and its immediate surroundings, under the command of Major H. W. Standring, "B" Company covered Leamington, under the command of Major George Glover, "C" Company covered Kenilworth and the surrounding area, under the command of Major Forwood, O.B.E, D.C.M., and "D" Company, drawn from the employees of Messrs. Lockheed & Co., under the command of Major J. N. Pressney. Colonel R. J. Cash was appointed as the Area Commanding Officer for Warwickshire on 19th June 1940.

LDV's were soon organised into a number of units which continued until March 1941 when the Home Guard Factories Unit was created to group together volunteers from the many industrial concerns. Platoons 1-10 covered particular geographical areas. Platoon No.11 was the Midland Electric & Power Company, platoon No.12 was the Leamington Priors Gas Company, No.13 was the Great Western Railway [GWR], No.14 was the London Midland & Scottish Railway [LMS] Leamington, No.15 was the London

Midland & Scottish Railway [LMS] Milverton, No.16 was Sidney Flavel & Co, and No.17 Ford's Imperial Foundry, A. S. Lines [Timber Merchants], the Post Office and Brico.

Initially ill-equipped and ill-trained, the LDV soon got themselves together and enthusiastically prepared for the task of confronting the enemy, even if it meant training with broom handles. These enthusiastic men soon started making wooden rifles until the real ones arrived, as a wooden rifle looked better than training with a broom handle - and received fewer disparaging comments from onlookers. Starting with a basic design, many started adding embellishments, such as bolts, nails, leather straps and the like until they looked remarkably like the real thing. However, the public still decided that LDV stood for 'Look, Duck & Vanish!'

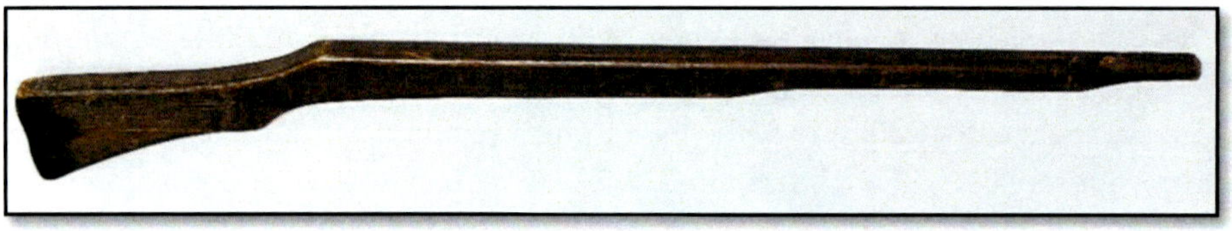

The task of the LDV's was seen early on as purely a nightly guard against possible landings by German parachute troops in this country. For some months, their only uniform was an armband and a few weapons - an assortment of shotguns, revolvers and home-made bombs to guard their own locality. This photo of the volunteers having some rifle 'aiming' practise was taken in Victoria Park.

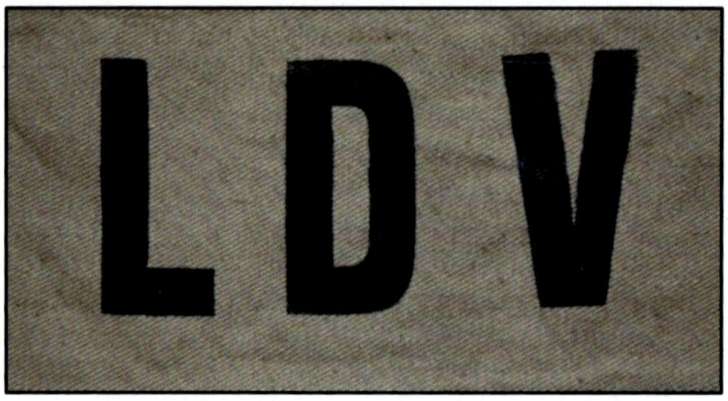

This early photo of the LDV was taken on the banks of the River Leam near Adelaide Road Bridge. It shows a serious looking No.4 platoon, before even the issue of armbands, receiving instruction from a regular Sergeant. The group includes A. J. Brown, Bob Monk, and Herbert [Podge] Robinson.

After three months, it was reported that, "Meeting its increased duties in the defence of our country, the Home Guard is rapidly becoming a highly-trained and efficient organisation. The saying that "Old Soldiers never die" is amply proved by a glance along the lines of this fine body of men [*photo on next page*]. The "Old Soldiers" are easily picked out both by their bearing and by their ribbons. Although many of them went through the Great War, they have to start from scratch in most of the movements of this new Army. They are not used to marching in threes, to the new field drill and to the new method of fixing bayonets, all of which have been introduced in recent years. They are not slow in picking these up though, and the L.D.V.s, or the Home Guard [as they are now called] are a very great force that any German invader will have to reckon with."

"Each night, all over the country, many defence posts are manned and thousands of buildings guarded by this force. They do not grumble at spending a night on guard duty after a long working day in factory or field neither do they mind being drilled for three or four evenings each week in order to make themselves acquainted with the new arts of war."

"The detachment at Leamington under the command of Major G. Glover has been very successful, and the training is proceeding in a very satisfactory way. Use is made of the Pump Room Gardens and Victoria Park for training purposes and the Campion Hills have also been used for field exercises. One platoon requires more men to bring it up to strength. Volunteers for this platoon are requested to report to the Drill Hall at 7.00pm on either Monday, Wednesday or Friday, and to ask for No.6 Platoon. The cheery atmosphere which prevails in the Company was shown at the Smoking Concert held on Wednesday night."

"Second-in-command of the Company is Major A. Giles, while the other officers are Mr. W. Chalmers, Mr. G. R. Gates, Mr. R. B. Rednall, Mr. F. Fennier, Mr. A. E. Malin, Mr. R. B. Lloyd, Mr. J. Sturgess and Mr. F. Wallsgrove. The Company Sergeant-Major is Mr. A. J. Ball and the Quartermaster-Sergeant, Sgt. A. J. Ward, the Army Recruiting Officer."

A Leamington Platoon on the March.

The Local Defence Volunteers, as recalled in March 1979, by Albert Handy who lived at 3, St. Georges Road - "It is 40 years ago, and memories do get a bit dim, but some things can never be forgotten. I sometimes ask myself, "Was I the first volunteer to be promoted to Corporal in the Local Defence Volunteers?"

"In the early days of the war I was working for the Leamington Priors Gas Company, and following the radio speech by Mr. Anthony Eden in which he called upon anyone who could walk, to join the LDV, the manager of the Gasworks, Mr. Dick Ramsden expressed a wish to form a Platoon to guard the works."

"A notice to that effect was put upon the notice board and a couple of nights later about a dozen brave fellows paraded outside the Company office under the command of foreman Bill Rose, a veteran of the First World War and a former Sergeant in the Royal Horse Artillery. Sergeant Rose thought that it would be a good idea for us to learn some arms drill."

"Having no rifles to practise with, some new pickaxe handles were obtained from the stores and these were issued out as a substitute until proper equipment could be obtained. The first attempts at 'slope arms' and 'order arms' were a shambles. Most of the lads hadn't got a clue and that included Sergeant Rose. However, salvation was at hand."

"Among those stout-hearted lads was me, ex-Sergeant Albert Handy, late of the Warwickshire Cadet Battery, Royal Artillery. The Cadet Battery had always been red-hot at arms drill and all the ceremonial carry-on, so presenting arms with a pickaxe handle was no problem."

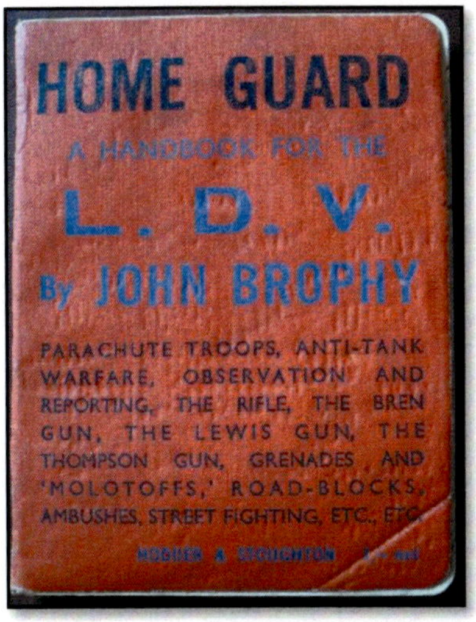

"Observing me going through the motions like a Guardsman, Sergeant Rose called a halt and said, "Albert, you know more about this bloody lark than I do, come out and show us how it's done." After the parade, he promoted me to Corporal."

"Later, equipped with a couple of old shotguns and armbands printed with the letters L.D.V., we mounted guard at the Gasworks and put the wind up old Adolf."

"I enlisted in the Army soon afterwards so I did not experience the change from L.D.V. to Home Guard. A couple of years later I was home on leave and saw the wonderful parade of Home Guard - was it Wings for Victory?" Company after Company of fine lads, armed to the teeth with modern weapons and ready for action. How different to the Local Defence Volunteers."

Memories of Roy Rowberry as recalled in 1980

Sgt. Major A. J. Ball

"I was about 18 years old and well remember those early days at the Drill Hall in Adelaide Road and the 'glint' in the eyes of the older fellows who'd been in the last lot of 1914-18. They relived old battles and prepared the likes of me for battles to come. Sgt. Major Ball was a Boer War veteran, a warrior of 1914-18 who had kept his hand in as an instructor of Drill and Swagger Stick to the local Church Lads' Brigade and came back to do his bit. In the early day's instructors were not easy to come by and anyone with knowledge was used. Things became organised, platoons were formed, and I joined No.8 Platoon, led by Lt. Frank Wallsgrove, who left the army in 1918 as a Captain with the M.C. Frank was as keen as mustard and helped by 2nd in Command, Lt. Harry Clark, built up an enterprising platoon mostly of local fellows but with several whom the war had brought to Leamington from other parts."

"We younger ones sometimes took a dip in the river alongside the Drill Hall after a night on guard. This was one way of getting rid of stale tobacco smoke. I also remember guards at Leamington Parish Church bell tower. The faithful verger, Willie Walton, let us sleep in the bell chamber and to climb out on the 'leads'. I loved the Dawn Watch when with binoculars, I'd scan, half hopeful, half fearful of spotting Nazi paratroopers, jackboots dangling beneath nun's habits, a disguise that popular wartime legend decreed they would wear. Church bells could then be legally rung, giving warning of invasion."

"I was a call out boy and armed with a list of my 'clients' I had to cycle to their homes and "order" them to report. Major Glover of Thornbank [now Mid-Warwickshire College of Further Education] was on my list, but since he was the C.O. at the Drill Hall and on the telephone, I used to think, cycling down his drive, if he didn't know by now, who did? However, I'd have been for the high jump if I'd taken a chance and not called him out. Usually at my ring the door would be opened by a white-frilled maid servant, who would sweetly assure me that Major Glover would be informed."

"I remember, too, digging trenches on Gulliman's Golf Course on the Tachbrook Road, where the Sun-in-Splendour is now. When on the march, we were three abreast [not four as in 1914-18] so that the men on the outside could drop into the ditch and the column present the least possible target for enemy aircraft. In May 1942, I joined the R.A.F taking my issue Home Guard boots with me and found the initial drill was no great hardship."

On 23rd July 1940, at Churchill's insistence, the LDV was renamed the Home Guard, reflecting the fact that they would be the nation's first line of defence if there were to be an invasion. They were supplied with an army type denim uniform and better class weapons – rifles, bayonets, mortars and bombs. From 1941 officers received the King's Commission. The volunteers were all men who had civilian occupations during the day and devoted their evenings and weekends to unpaid military training. Many were veterans of the First World War.

The Home Guard performed an important role in supporting the regular army. They carried out observation duties, occupied defensive positions such as road blocks, defended localities and provided defence against potential airborne landings, as well as assisting the Civil Defence Services before, during, and after air raids where a shortage of Civil Defence necessitated their use. These tasks included dealing with incendiary bombs, rescue work, ambulance work, fire watching, message duties, warden's duties, clearing blocked streets, evacuation of bombed areas and traffic control.

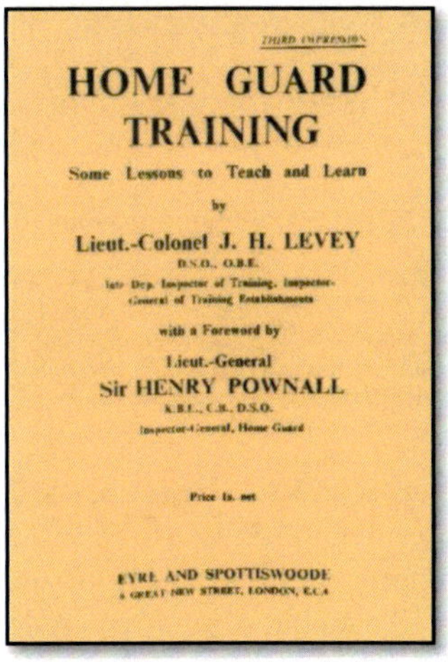

In January 1942 because of a shortage of men caused by the call-up a measure of compulsion was introduced for all men aged 18 to 51 not carrying out work of national importance. On 27th September 1942 the minimum age for joining was reduced from 17 to 16 but the youngsters did require parental consent. From 1943 women 'auxiliaries' aged 18 to 65 were enrolled on a voluntary basis but were only allowed to do work such as cooking, clerical work or driving.

The second anniversary of the formation of the Home Guard was celebrated throughout the country on Sunday 17th May 1942. In Leamington, there was a parade service in Victoria Park where members of the local Company were addressed by the Vicar and Rural Dean [Canon G. C. Rolfe], Colonel Alexander, the Battalion Commander, Major Masters, Major G. Glover [Leamington Company Commander] and the Mayor [Alderman M. S. Moore]. Included in the next photograph are L.Cpl. Bob Atkins, Ron Churches, Frank Bartlett, Capt. Gates, Major Glover, Danny Morgan, Bill Harris and Eric Hancock.

Canon Rolfe's parting message was, "If you would like a text this morning, here it is. Ye shall be my witnesses. Here you have it. Your daily work has never been more important than it is today; your military service has never been so important as it is in these times. But over and above them both there is that higher work and service to which every man is called – to be a witness for Christ. Are you members of the Home Guard giving that with the same readiness and enthusiasm as you are giving service to your King and country? That is a question we must answer. It may be that God is waiting to give us victory and peace until we give witness to His Son, our Saviour Jesus Christ." Following the service a large number of the general public witnessed the various platoons give drill demonstrations, including anti-gas exercises, field-craft, machine gunnery, and bayonet fighting.

On Saturday 15th May 1943, the Morning News advised their readers: - **Home Guard Anniversary – Leamington Parade Tomorrow** – The Home Guard was three years old yesterday, and the anniversary will be celebrated throughout the country tomorrow with parades and demonstrations. At Leamington, there will be a big company parade at which the Salute will be taken by a representative of the Central Midland District outside the Town Hall, at 3pm. The various units will proceed to the Victoria Park, where the platoons will give a display demonstrating the various aspects of Home Guard training, including battle drill and attacks on armoured fighting vehicles.

For over four years the Home Guard was never called upon to resist invasion but many were involved in action against the enemy by manning anti-aircraft batteries. The Home Guard was officially 'stood down' on 3rd December 1944 when it had a strength of 1,794,000 officers and men.

Fred Rogers was in charge of the Flavel's Platoon. He worked as a sales representative for Flavel's but was also in charge of the reconditioned ammunition boxes that the company were producing. In January 1942 Fred, in his role as Defence Officer, started duplicating weekly leaflets, 'The Eagle News', an A.R.P. and Defence Bulletin, giving details of the Home Guard and Fire Guard activities, plus other items designed to keep up morale. In 1950 Fred became the company's Sales Director and was elected to the Board.

Flavel's - No.16 Platoon - one of eight factory units in the area. Fred Rogers is in the middle of the front row. To the right are Sergeants Alf Reading and Jack Redgrave. On the middle row [4th left] is his brother Bill Redgrave, 3rd left is Frank Bushell, extreme left is Corporal Duncan Wright and Bill Brookes is 5th left. Also present are Ernie Bissell, Cpl. Bill Pheasey, Cpl. George Stickley and Bill Payton.

Sidney Drabble, A. John, George Reading, F. Reading, W. Jones, Sgt. W. Parkes, W. Beeby, W. Evans, J. Ashfield, L. Carling, J. Brady, B. Smith, K. Baker, A. Boraston, D. Griffiths, R. Cane, D. Chamberlain, L. Holloway, C. Smith, Cpl. J. Bullimore, C. Mills, E. Davies, W. Bull, H. Caswell, Mr. Robertson, F. Bushell, C. George, A. Pratt, R. Parsons, J. Watkins, A. Hodges, F. Houghton, H. Spittles, J. Elliott, J. Rouse, I. Barton, W. Wells, G. Barrett, S. Bullimore, R. Talbot, F. Caswell and P. Norman were also in the Flavel's platoon but it is not known if any of them are in the photo. Although Bill Pheasey is listed above, both W. Pheasey jnr and snr were in the platoon.

In April 1944, Fred Rogers announced in 'The Eagle News' that "the two pounder anti-tank guns have now been allocated to the platoon. Lieut. Hutchins is in charge and he will commence a hard training programme at once. We are also preparing for some extensive drills on the Smith and Spiget guns, and as the better weather comes along we will practise this mobile warfare as regularly as possible."

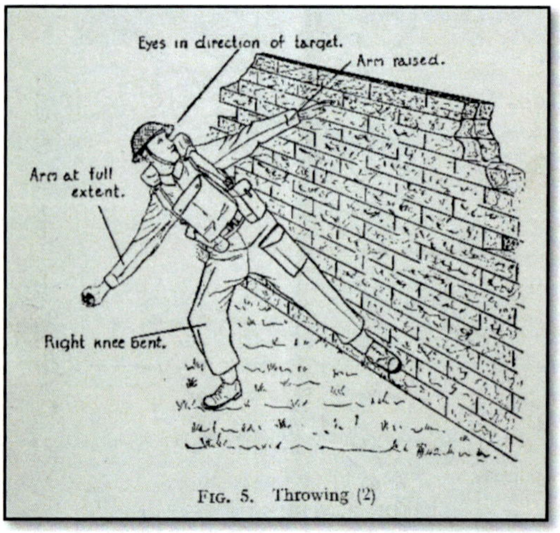

This illustration is from the 48-page Home Guard small arms training booklet, volume 1, grenade. It included instructions for using various types of grenades.

This arm band is self-explanatory - it was used by the Post Office Local Defence Volunteers prior to the name being changed to the Home Guard and prior to having uniforms.

The Post Office Home Guard on 15th October 1944 taken at the rear of the Post Office [The Dock] in Priory Terrace. The back row includes: - A. Johnson, C. Wilson, R. Law, P. Millin, F. Alsop, W. Bennett and Mr. Adams. The middle row includes: - J. Grimster, C. Hesk, M. Smith, J. Grimster, F. Rowlatt, R. Taylor, A. Neale, W. Ayris, R. Lee and F. Bonner. The front row includes: - Mr. McDonagh, H. Boswell, G. Goode, C. Hawkins, H. Keen and C. Dale. I understand that Stan Woods and P. Taylor are also in the photo.

No.1 Platoon and machine gun section 'B' Company, 1st Battalion Royal Warwickshire Regiment of the Home Guard in 1944. Back row far right is Joe Parsons, to the left of Joe is M. G. Robertson. 2nd left on the back row is Albert Batchelor. 3rd right on the front row is Sgt. Eystone. Also on the photo are 'Darkie' Farran, Tommie Clinch, Fred Smith, Harry Walker, Fred Hughes, Reuben Horsley and Messrs. Scott, Lawson and Merrick.

This illustration [right] is from a 20-page Home Guard Drill instruction booklet. It includes instructions for drilling, squad drill, platoon drill and rifle exercises.

'**Falling in with rifles at the order** – The recruit will fall in with rifle held perpendicular at his right side, the butt on the ground, its toe in line with the toe of his right boot. The right arm to be slightly bent, the hand to hold the rifle at or near the band, back of the hand to the right, thumb against the thigh, fingers together and slanting towards the ground, elbow to the rear. [Fig. 3].'

1st Battalion Warwickshire Home Guard - 'B' [Leamington Spa] Company. Officers and NCOs of No.17 [Ford's] Platoon Group in 1944. Back row L-R: Cpl. A. Moss, Sgt. D. Picken, Sgt. N. Turner, Sgt. R. Laming, Cpl. A. Rayment, L/Cpl. G. Cleaver and Cpl. W. Cook. Front row: Sgt. A. Hoffman, Col Sgt. E. Damp, Lt. P. Vass, Lt. W. Wommersley, Lt. G. Laming, Sgt. V. Lillie and armourer Sgt. A. Hibbert.

This photograph of the officers of 'B' Company includes Majors Giles and Glover, Norman Cambray, Fred Rogers [Flavel's], Wilf Wommersley [Ford's], Joe Bodfish and Lt. Malin.

The Home Guard as recalled by Sergeant Robert [Bob] E. Atkins – "During the war I lived in Leamington Spa and was employed at the Lockheed Company in Tachbrook Road. My job was a Jig & Tool Draughtsman designing the jigs and tools to be used for the manufacture of aircraft undercarriages. This was a reserved occupation, i.e. important to the war effort, so I was not called up to serve in the armed forces."

"At the beginning of June 1940, when the Germans were expected to follow up their successes in France by invading Britain, the government appealed to all males aged 18 to 60, not already in full time war service such as Civil Defence, National Fire Service, etc. to join a new force to be called the Local Defence Volunteers [LDV]."

"The LDV would carry on with their normal work during the day and train during the evenings and Sundays as well as mount night guard on important installations, e.g. railway bridges, reservoirs, etc. to prevent sabotage by the placing of explosives or poison in reservoirs."

Local Defence Volunteers in 1940. Uniforms have now been issued but boots are yet to arrive so the men are still wearing their own comfortable shoes. Bob Atkins is 8th left. Also in the line-up are Sgt. Major Corp, W. Harris and Reg Gill.

"As I was then 18 years old, I joined the LDV on 12th June 1940 and was a member of No.2 Platoon 'B' Company, 1st Warwickshire Battalion. The Headquarters of 'B' Company was beside the River Leam adjacent to the bridge over the river at Adelaide Road, Leamington in what was then the Drill Hall." Another to serve there as part of the machine gun platoon was Eric Scrivens.

"Each Company was responsible for the defence of a certain area of the County and 'B' Company was responsible for the defence of Leamington. No.2 Platoon was responsible for the area around Offchurch where we built sandbag emplacements near road junctions and other strategic places. Large metal oil drums filled with highly combustible materials were buried in banks beside roads so that when ignited by an explosive charge at the back would send out great jets of flame and burning oil across the road." These were called 'Flaming Fougasses' [Ed].

"Our Companies responsibility for night guard was the underground reservoir in the Campion Hills on the outskirts of Leamington and the roster was arranged so that each person stood night guard about once every 3 weeks. After all night guard, there was just time to get home, wash and have breakfast before going off to work."

"The ringing of church bells was banned throughout the land; they were only to be rung as a signal the German troops had landed by sea or from the air. They did not ring again until the day the war ended." [*Ed's note: On 13th June 1940, the Order was given out on the wireless that church and chapel bells must not be rung except for air raids. The Government later decided that the ringing of church bells could be recommenced on Easter Sunday 25th April 1943*].

"As our army had lost most of its arms at Dunkirk, the factories were working continuously day and night to replace them and the workforce was working 12 hours a day, 6 days a week. All new arms and equipment went first to the new armies being formed, so the LDV had to train with dummy equipment such as broom sticks."

"As we were untrained and had no arms, equipment or uniforms other than an armband with LDV on it, we were immediately nicknamed the "Looney Dotty Villains" and it was said that our motto was "Look, Duck and Vanish"."

"We were eventually issued with a cheap twill uniform which did not fit very well, but it saved wear and tear on our normal clothing which was rationed and were issued with American First World War rifles still packed in the grease in which they had been stored."

"As more equipment became available we wore the same army battle dress that was worn by the regular army and new weapons were received, such as sten guns, machine guns, anti-tank guns and hand grenades. Winston Churchill, the Prime Minister, ordered that we should now be called The Home Guard."

"I was promoted to Lance Corporal, then full Corporal and finally Sergeant which meant I was in command of a Section of about 12 men and when on night guard I would be the Guard Commander. I went on several weapons courses under regular army instructors and would then instruct our own platoon on the use of these weapons. To practise firing our weapons we would go to the Wedgnock Firing Range at the back of what is now the Woodloes Estate in Warwick which was not built until after the war."

"After 'D' Day when the allied forces landed in France, the Home Guard was trained to operate anti-aircraft guns to release the regular gunners for service in France. We trained on the guns protecting Coventry but as Coventry was not bombed after 'D' Day, we did not go into action."

"The Home Guard was stood down on the 3rd December 1944 as the allied forces were now fighting in Germany itself and the German armies were near defeat so there was no longer a threat to this country. After the war ended all members of the Home Guard were presented with the Defence Medal in recognition of their war time service."

Lockheed Home Guard

"D" [Lockheed] Company, 1st Warwick Battalion Home Guard in November 1941. Sergeant Charles Derek Brown, known as Derek, is third from the right on the front row. Others on the front row from left to right are: Mr. Jakeman, Jack Fahey, H. Clift, Capt. Payne, Major Pressney, M. Smallwood, R. Jewell and Robert 'Bob' Jelfs. Included on the middle row are Mr. Baggott, Mr. Pryne, Reg Aston, S. Emmott, N. Davies and E. Williams. Included on the back row are: E. Myres, S. Grimwood, D. Davies, Jack Calcutt, Mr. Forest, F. Emberton and Norman Cambray. In November 1941 Derek Brown signed up for the R.A.F Volunteer Reserve; on 3rd November 1943, he joined an R.A.F Lancaster crew, but died on the night of 2nd/3rd January 1944 when the plane was shot down over Berlin.

Home Guard snippit No.1

Les Keegan was taking part in a river crossing exercise with No.8 platoon and did not get low enough in his dash across the bridge. Up popped an umpire to say that he had been picked off by a sniper and was therefore adjudged dead.

Les said he was sorry and would try to get down lower next time.

"There is no next time", declared the umpire. "You are dead! Dead! Understand? You will take no further part in this exercise."

Les hung around for ages until a lady came up to him as he leant on the parapet. "Am I going in the right direction for Leamington Spa?" she asked.

"No good asking me, lady" said the bold Les. "I've been dead for nearly an hour."

Lockheed Home Guard's four-gun Lewis mounting - All four guns fired in pairs using a motorcycle clutch Bowden cable. This is Bob Jelfs, who designed and built the four-gun Lewis mounting, and synchronised firing mechanism, at Lockheed's Remote Control Experimental Department. He is showing his work to an Army Major and Captain in 1941. In June 1941, it was fitted to the roof of the Lockheed Works.

Reg Aston remembers his time in the Lockheed Home Guard: -

"The early days of Lockheed Home Guard were more or less treated as an exploration into the unknown, and mainly consisted of drilling with pieces of wood shaped liked rifles, guard duties around the factory and gleaning information on the operation of weapons which might possibly come our way. In those days, I might add, we as the LDV tended to hide from people, since we felt a right bunch of "Charlies" guarding a factory in civvies with pieces of wood. This, mind you, could have been for the best, since no one knew where we were going to pop up."

"As the months passed by, we became more confident in our duties. We grew in strength, denim uniforms arrived and even rifles. By this time there was no holding us, the duties of the Home Guard had taken on a more serious note and when Captain

Payne took over - who, incidentally, was an ex-Sgt. Major of the Coldstream Guards - he soon licked us into shape for things to come."

"We had the odd occasion of heroics, but in those days, they were few and far between. I think the first one came when our rifles were locked and chained in racks in each of the factories and we had a "red alert" come through [enemy aircraft in vicinity]. Chains were unlocked and we lined the boulevards awaiting movement, when suddenly out of the clouds over the factory came a plane in a power dive. Everyone thought "Jerry". Up went the rifles to the volley position. Bang! Bang! We all let go. Unfortunately, it was no Jerry, but a test pilot from Armstrong Whitworth testing a Whitley plane and he had not received the "red alert" and was unaware of enemy aircraft in the vicinity. We shall never know to this day if enemy aircraft was in the vicinity."

"We do, however, know that enemy aircraft was in the vicinity when we were bombed for the second time. Jack Griffin was on the 4-gun Lewis post with Dick Bloxham at the time when Jerry came over, circled the factory, flew off north towards Coventry, turned, opened up his bomb doors and did a run in over the factory. Our instructions were concise: "Never open fire unless he attacks." The stick of bombs was released and straddled the factory. Jack Griffin opened up, and nothing was going to move him from the 4-gun. Fortunately, no one was injured, the 4-gun Lewis post was showered with debris from the factory. I shall always remember Jack's first words, when I took a fresh can of coffee to the post, "The rotten swine, look what he's done to my coffee."

THIRD SUPPLEMENT TO The London Gazette

Published by Authority

The London Gazette dated Friday 18th February 1944 announced a number of awards. One of them reads: - "The King has been graciously pleased to approve of the publication of the names of the under mentioned as having been commended for brave conduct." One of those named was Serjeant Jack Griffin of the Home Guard.

Reg continues, “Life carried on much the same. Field exercises with the Czechoslovakian Army, exercises with the Artillery who were manning the Bofors guns around the factory, more instruction, parades, guards, etc., and then it happened.”

“We were told that it was suspected that German Paratroops, [how many was not known], had been dropped in the Coventry area and we had to send a Platoon out to check on two or three areas. We left Lockheed at about 7.30pm in a hurry and split into sections and were posted to various areas. My section was in some remote spot outside Coventry and we were instructed to stop and challenge everything that breathed. Ten o’clock came, midnight came and, apart from the odd rat, we hadn’t seen a thing and we didn’t know where we were. Two o’clock in the morning, still no sign of life. We were there until 7.30am when, after a roll call, it was realised that we had been forgotten. The search party came for us to tell us that at 10.00pm the previous night the exercise had been called off because it was a false alarm. Everyone else had been called off and recalled to the Gate House at Stoneleigh for hot soup, biscuits, cigarettes and a night’s sleep. We had been forgotten - there were some very red faces after that incident.” *Poster courtesy of Leamington Art Gallery and Museum [Warwick District Council] M.4736.2012.7.*

The following is one day’s aircraft observer’s reports from the Lockheed factory. The date is significant as an early morning air raid on this day resulted in the death of four people: -

AIRCRAFT OBSERVER’S REPORT *Courtesy of Leamington Spa Art Gallery and Museum LeamG:M4736.2012.10*	
0500 Hours to 2300 Hours	Thursday July 16th 1942

0500	Nothing to report
0600	Nothing to report
0613	Stand to from R.O.C.
0614	Message from R.O.C "Plane identified". [But no details as to what]
0616	Message from R.O.C "P98. S.W"

0617 Alert sounded

0619 One aircraft, varying course, 250 feet, direction spotted - north-east, identification - Dornier "217 EJ", function - Long Range Bomber. Remarks: Take cover sounded 06.19 hrs. Aircraft approached from E.N.E. When north of factory banked steeply towards factory. Engaged by spotters with Quad Lewis 218 rounds fired. This fire observed entering aircraft. Enemy ran over factory from north to south dropping 4 H.E. [high explosive] bombs across shops.

0637 All clear sounded

0700 Nothing to report

0800 Nothing to report

0857 Activity commenced by De Havilland "Tiger" Moths

0900 Activity commenced by Airspeed "Oxfords"

1036 One aircraft, course north, height 1200 feet, direction spotted east, identification - Lockheed "Hudson", function - Coastal Command.

1047 One aircraft, course east north-east, height 1000 feet, direction spotted south west, identification - Miles "Master" 1, function - Trainer Command.

1050 One aircraft - Activity commenced by Vickers Armstrong Wellingtons.

1051 One aircraft, course south, height 1200 feet, direction spotted north-east, identification - Lockheed "Hudson", function - Coastal Command.

1058 One aircraft, course north-west, height 200 feet, direction spotted south-east, identification - North American "Mustang", function - Fighter Trainee.

1141 Activity commenced by Avro "Ansons".

1145 One aircraft, course south-west, height 2000 feet, direction spotted north, identification - Aircraft "x", function - Secret List.

1150 One aircraft, course varying, height 1500 feet, direction spotted north-west, identification - Bristol "Beaufighter", function - Fighter Command.

1150 One aircraft, course varying, height 1500 feet, direction spotted north-west, identification - Vickers Supermarine "Spitfire", function - Fighter Command.

1151 Three aircraft, course south, height 2000 feet, course spotted north-east, identification - Bristol "Blenheim", function - Fighter Command.

1210 Two aircraft, course varying, height varying, direction spotted north-west, identification - Bristol "Beaufighter", function - Fighter Command.

1230 One aircraft, course varying, height varying, direction spotted north, identification - Armstrong Whitworth "Whitley", function - Coastal Command.

1314 One aircraft, course south-west, height 1000 feet, direction spotted north, identification - Armstrong Whitworth "Whitley", function - Coastal Command.

1325 One aircraft, course south, height 1000 feet, direction spotted north-west, identification - Vickers Supermarine "Spitfire", function - Coastal Command.

1335 One aircraft, course south, height 1000 feet, direction spotted north-west, identification - Vickers Supermarine "Spitfire", function - fighter command.

1431 One aircraft, course south, height 2000 feet, direction spotted north, identification - Armstrong Whitworth "Whitley" Mark V, function - Bomber Command.

1450 One aircraft, course south, height 1500 feet, direction spotted north-east, identification - Armstrong Whitworth "Whitley" Mark V, function - Bomber Command.

1503 One aircraft, course varying, height 3500 feet, direction spotted north-west, identification - Bristol "Beaufighter" Mark 1, function - Fighter Command.

1506 One aircraft, course north-east, height 1200 feet, direction spotted south-west, identification - Armstrong Whitworth "Whitley" Mark V, function - Bomber Command, returned 1610 hours.

1520 One aircraft, course north-east, height 2000 feet, direction spotted south, identification - North American "Mitchell" III, function - Bomber Command.

1520 Training activity commenced by Avro tutors, function - Training Command.

1529 One aircraft, course north-west, height 1800 feet, direction spotted south, identification - Westland "Lysander", function - Army Co-operation Command.

1530 One aircraft, course south-south-east, height 2000 feet, direction spotted north-west, identification - Phillips & Powis "Miles Master" Mark I, function - Trainer Command.

1530 One aircraft, course varying, height varying, direction spotted, north-east, identification - Bristol "Beaufighter" Mark I, function - Fighter Command.

1534 One aircraft, direction south-west height 1600 feet, direction spotted east, identification - North American "Mustang", function - Fighter Command.

1546 One aircraft, direction west, height 2000 feet, direction spotted south, identification - Phillips & Powis "Miles Master" Mark III, function - Training Command.

1549 One aircraft, direction east, height 30 feet, [as stated], direction spotted south, identification - Douglas "Boston" Mark III, function - Bomber Command.

1550 One aircraft, direction north-east, height 50 feet, [as stated], direction spotted south-west, identification - Douglas "Boston" Mark I, function - Bomber Command.

1550 One aircraft, direction north-east, height 100 feet, [as stated], direction spotted south-west, identification - Douglas "Boston" Mark III, function - Bomber Command.

1551 One aircraft, direction east, height 50 feet, [as stated], direction spotted south-west, identification - Douglas "Boston" Mark III, function - Bomber Command.

1610 One aircraft, course varying, height 2000 feet, direction spotted north-west, identification - Bristol "Beaufighter" II, function - Fighter Command.

1616 One aircraft, course varying, height 2500 feet, course spotted south west, identification - Armstrong Whitworth "Whitley" V, function - Bomber Command.

1702 One aircraft, course north, height 1400 feet, course spotted east-south-east, identification - Westland "Lysander" II, function - Army Co-operation.

1754 One aircraft, course north-west, height 1200 feet, direction spotted south-west, identification - Vickers Supermarine "Spitfire" V, function - Fighter Command.

No.2 Platoon 'B' Company. On the front row, L-R is: L. Harrison, J. Harrison, Sergeant Bob Atkins, Colour Sgt. Collier, Commanding Officer Lt. Gates, Sgt. Fratton, Cpl. Edwards and B. Grane. Note, there is one name missing. On the middle row is: Messrs. Hayes, Buckley, 'Charlie' Cranston, Cpl. Ron Churches [Morning News], Sgt. Randle, Hedley, Sgt. Miles, Jones, Bill Harris, [Councillor], Bromley, Blackwell and Buxton. On the back row is: Messrs. Robinson, Ken Blasdale, Payne, Smith, Oldfield, Petitt, Danny Morgan and Charles Worth.

On Saturday 30th November 1941, the Lockheed Home Guard Company had the honour of competing in a drill demonstration and shooting competition against 'one of best known London Defence Companies' at Buckingham Palace Mews in London. The Leamington men were under the command of Major J. R. Pressney.

The Commanding Officer of the London Company congratulated the Warwickshire boys, saying he had never seen a better drilled squad. He considered that it reflected great credit on the 1st Warwickshire Battalion.

Following the drill parade, a rifle contest took place, resulting in a very comfortable win for the Leamington contingent, the result being as follows: -

London contingent – First team: Lt. Fielding 23, C.S.M. Wyld 22, Cpl. Loper 24, L/Cpl Serjent 24, Cpl. Bannochie 25, Volunteer Holgate 22, Major Williams 24, Vol. Burgess 21, Sgt. Moss 24, Sgt. Jackson 20; **total 229 out of a possible 250.** Second team: Sgt. Seymour 25, Sgt. McIlveen 25, Sgt. Jenkins 22, Vol. Williams 25, C.Q.M.S. Jackson 20, Vol. A. Cole 24, Vol. G. Cole 25, Vol. Garrett 23; **total 189 out of a possible 200.**

Warwickshire contingent – First team: Vol. Cayzer 25, Vol. Walters 25, Vol. Jack Calcutt 25, Vol. Yates 25, Sgt. Hall 24, Capt. Payne 25, Major Pressney 25, Vol. Norman Cambray 24, Vol. Wheeler 25, L/Cpl. Baggott 24; **total 247 out of a possible 250.** Second team: L/Cpl. Payne 25, Sgt. Jewell 24, Sgt. Clift 25, Sgt. Fahey 23, Vol. Greenwood 23, Sgt. Bob Jelfs 24, Cpl. Lawrence 24, L/Cpl. Reg Aston 22; **total 190 out of a possible 200.**

After the contest the detachment marched to the West End, where, after placing their arms and equipment in safe keeping, the men visited a theatre before returning to the Midlands.

D Company 1st Warwickshire Home Guard in 1942.

Members of Home Guard No.6 Platoon circa 1943 courtesy of Warwickshire County Record Office Ref: CR2134/6.

No.3 Platoon outside the Town Hall in 1945 - courtesy of Warwickshire County Record Office Ref: PH(N)600-720-12. Front row L-R: Sgt. Allibon, Sgt. Savage, Lt. Bodfish, 2nd Lt. Parsons, Sgt. Thorner and Sgt. Lawrence. Also included are: - Sgt. Vere, Pte. Atkins, Pte. Appleton, Pte. Bench, Cpl. Astell, Pte. Ward, Cpl. Cashing, Pte. F. Bench, Pte. George Rogers of Queen Street, [Second from the right on the second row from the back], Cpl. Wild, Pte. Owen, Pte. Pitt, Pte. Balesbarrow and Pte. Chandler.

This photo of the Great Western Railway Platoon includes Commanding Officer Lt. Cowley, Company Sgt. Major Williams, Sgt. Phil Young, Bill Hawkins, A. H. James, B. Adams, A. Gibbons, Frank Cale, Sid Squires, Sid Smith, Mark Daniels, Jack Lock, Tommy Devanny, J. Bishop, W. Maynard, E. Jeffries, A. E. Smith, F. Shillito and Albert Springthorpe who is 5th left on the front row.

Home Guard snippit No.2

Volunteers were placed at strategic points with labels attached to say what their injuries were, e.g. broken arm, leg, etc.

The idea was for the first aid people to find them on a map reference and to treat their 'injuries'.

Later, back at headquarters it was found that one of the volunteer injured was missing.

A car rushed to the spot where he was supposed to be and was confronted by a large notice which read, "Bled to death. Gone home."

The Lillington Home Guard. No information is available on the names.

This is thought to be No.4 Platoon Home Guard celebrating at the White Lion pub at Radford Semele. It is said that 'Auntie' the charming hostess of the 'Lion' could always be relied upon to look after the Home Guard.

No.8 Platoon celebrated victory at Milverton School, by kind permission of Sergeant Tom Harrison, the Headmaster.

Home Guard snippit No.3
We belonged to the firm's Home Guard Unit and were involved in a heavy street fighting exercise.

The local pub was the established prisoner-of war camp.

The licensee was our commander.

As opening time drew near, the prisoners began voluntarily surrendering, and the numbers increased so much that I was given a communique to take to the front line: - "Shoot to kill. Take no more prisoners. We've run out of beer."

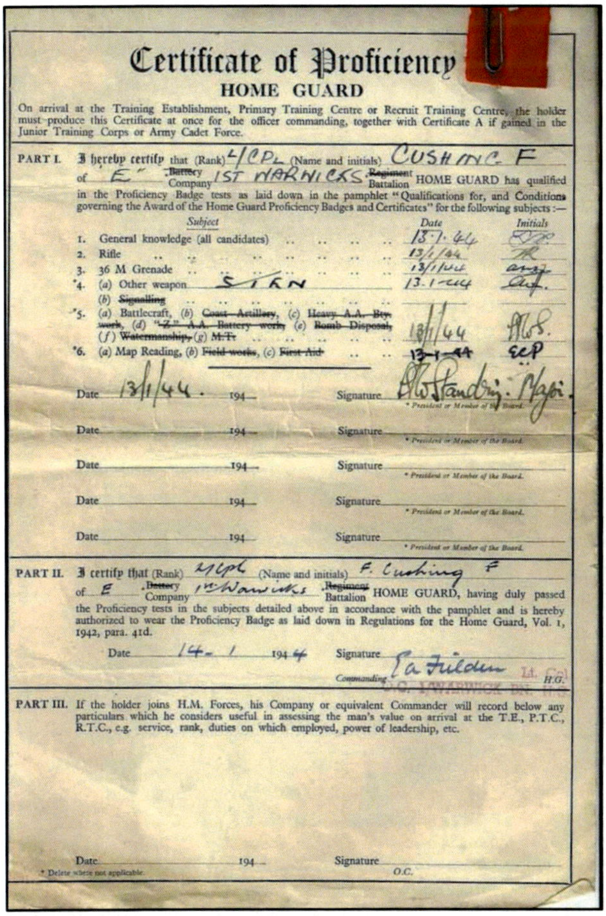

Certificate of Proficiency

HOME GUARD

On arrival at the Training Establishment, Primary Training Centre or Recruit Training Centre, the holder must produce this Certificate at once for the officer commanding, together with Certificate A if gained in the Junior Training Corps or Army Cadet Force.

PART I. I hereby certify that (Rank) L/CPL (Name and initials) CUSHING F of "E" ~~Battery~~ Company 1ST WARWICKS ~~Regiment~~ Battalion HOME GUARD has qualified in the Proficiency Badge tests as laid down in the pamphlet "Qualifications for, and Conditions governing the Award of the Home Guard Proficiency Badges and Certificates" for the following subjects :—

Subject	Date	Initials
1. General knowledge (all candidates)	13.1.44	
2. Rifle	13/1/44	
3. 36 M Grenade	13/1/44	
*4. (a) Other weapon STEN	13.1.44	
(b) ~~Signalling~~		
*5. (a) Battlecraft, (b) ~~Coast Artillery~~, (c) ~~Heavy A.A. Bty. work~~, (d) ~~"Z" A.A. Battery work~~, (e) ~~Bomb Disposal~~, (f) ~~Watermanship~~, (g) ~~M.T.~~	13/1/44	
*6. (a) Map Reading, (b) ~~Field works~~, (c) ~~First Aid~~	13-1-44	ECP

Date 13/1/44. 194— Signature [signature] Major. *President or Member of the Board.

Date 194— Signature *President or Member of the Board.

Date 194— Signature *President or Member of the Board.

Date 194— Signature *President or Member of the Board.

Date 194— Signature *President or Member of the Board.

PART II. I certify that (Rank) L/Cpl (Name and initials) F. Cushing F of E ~~Battery~~ Company 1st Warwicks ~~Regiment~~ Battalion HOME GUARD, having duly passed the Proficiency tests in the subjects detailed above in accordance with the pamphlet and is hereby authorized to wear the Proficiency Badge as laid down in Regulations for the Home Guard, Vol. I, 1942, para. 41d.

Date 14-1 1944 Signature [signature] Lt. Col. Commanding H.G.

PART III. If the holder joins H.M. Forces, his Company or equivalent Commander will record below any particulars which he considers useful in assessing the man's value on arrival at the T.E., P.T.C., R.T.C., e.g. service, rank, duties on which employed, power of leadership, etc.

Date 194— Signature O.C.

* Delete where not applicable.

This certificate of proficiency was awarded to Lance Corporal F. Cushing of 'E' Company 1st Warwickshire Home Guard.

Anthony Eden Tells Home Guards "Your Spirit Needed to Help Win the Peace – Sunday 3rd December 1944 was a memorable day for members of the Home Guard, for it marked the official stand down of the Force. Farewell parades were held in all parts of the country and at Leamington the ceremony was for the 1st Warwickshire Battalion. Large numbers of men who saw service with the Home Guard went into the Regular Army or became members of the other services. Many of those who took part in the parade were originally volunteers thus having completed more than 4½ years with the Force.

The Leamington parade was lent additional significance by the presence of Mr. Eden, the Foreign Secretary, whose broadcast to the nation in May, 1940, led to the creation of the LDV. He was present to watch the march-past of the various units comprising the Battalion, and afterwards at Victoria Park, he witnessed the dismissal of some 3,000 personnel which his original appeal had brought into being.

The Battalion, commanded by Lt. Colonel E. A. Fielden, paraded at Beauchamp Avenue West at 10.30am. Headed by the Band of the Royal Warwickshire Regiment, the parade, which consisted of general service companies, anti-aircraft detachments and mobile units – made its way from Beauchamp Avenue via the Parade, Victoria Terrace, Spencer Street and Avenue Road to Victoria Park. At the Town Hall, the salute was taken by Colonel R. J. Cash, C.B.E., M.C., T.D., the Zone Commander, who, in addition to Mr. Eden, was accompanied by the Mayor [Alderman C. W. Gardner] and deputy Mayor of Leamington, the Mayor of Warwick, [councillor W. V. Collier], the chairman of Kenilworth Urban District Council [Frank Weetman], and Mr. Hamilton Armstrong [assistant to Mr. J. Winant, U.S. Ambassador]. Despite the inclement weather large crowds assembled in the vicinity of the Town Hall. Other parts of the route were well lined with spectators.

To the left of Colonel Cash on this photograph is Minister of War and local M.P. Mr. Anthony Eden, to the left of the dais is Leamington Mayor Alderman Charles Gardner, to the right of the dais is the Mayor of Warwick with Warwick officials. Colonel Alexander of the Home Guard stands centre right of the dais. Photo courtesy of Warwickshire County Record Office Ref: PH(N)600/720/46.

The Leamington Priors Gas Company, Midland Electric and Great Western Railway Platoon.

Photo of the Home Guard Stand Down parade - courtesy of Warwickshire County Record Office Ref: PH(N)600/720/33.

Home Guard Stand Down parade courtesy of Warwickshire County Record Office. Ref: PH(N)600/720/34 & 35.

Home Guard Stand Down parade courtesy of Warwickshire County Record Office. Ref: PH(N)600/720/36 & 37. It is interesting to see shops such as Boots, Stead & Simpson, Bobby & Co, Maypole, Agers and Burton's, as well as the Gaiety Restaurant [in between Maypole grocers and Agers]. The space to the left of Stead & Simpson is the site of the Lipton's grocery store that was destroyed by enemy action on 14th November 1940.

Home Guard Stand Down parade courtesy of Warwickshire County Record Office. Ref: PH(N)600/720/38 & 39. Bottom photo: Flavel's No.16 Platoon, led by Fred Rogers.

At Victoria Park, a low flying R.A.F. aeroplane passed over the assembly. Following the hymn 'Now thank we all our God', there was a short drumhead service, conducted by the Vicar of Leamington [Rev. R. C. Streatfeild], following which Mr. Eden gave an address. In this he said he was glad the Battalion had invited him to attend their stand down parade, so that he could thank them for the services they had rendered in the last four and a half years, during which time they had been members of our splendid army. He thought that the 'Stand Down' ceremony would be remembered all their days.

Mr. Anthony Eden addressing the Home Guard Stand Down parade. Ref: PH(N) 600/720/42 img:4889 (3/4462). Photo courtesy of Warwickshire County Record Office.

He continued, "It fell to my lot to issue the first appeal for Local Defence Volunteers, and I looked up the message I sent. "May I quote one sentence – 'Your loyal help will make and keep our country safe'. Well, that is what you and the other battalions have done. You have made and kept our country safe and as you leave this parade you can take back with you into your homes a feeling of pride and thankfulness that our country has been spared the horrors of the foreign invader."

Alluding to the presence of Mr. Hamilton Armstrong [the U.S. Ambassador's assistant], he said he was sure we in this country would never forget that in those dark days, when the Home Guard rallied so splendidly in numbers far greater than had been thought or prepared for, there were no weapons to put into their hands. It was the action of the United States alone which in those days gave us the weapons. We should never forget that. [Applause].

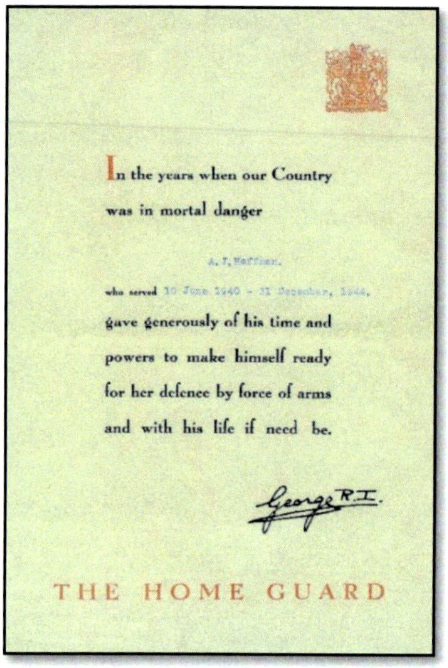
In the years when our Country
was in mortal danger

who served

gave generously of his time and
powers to make himself ready
for her defence by force of arms
and with his life if need be.

George R.I.

THE HOME GUARD

"We look back with thankfulness, and I say to you, on behalf of my colleagues in the Government, thank you for what you have done. Good luck, and be proud of your service now and always."

The parade was dismissed by the Commanding Officer [Lt. Colonel E. A. Fielden], who added his thanks to all ranks, and this signified the standing down of the Battalion.

At the end of the war, by the command of King George VI, every member of the Home Guard was issued with a certificate and some like Sergeant Ralph Rowberry from No.8 Platoon were also awarded a defence medal.

Fast forward to 2017 and there are still signs of past Home Guard activity in the town. This rusted and worn Home Guard muster point metal plate is attached to the wall at the right side of the door at 21 Church Street.

Milkman Vernon [happy] Willis stands in front of a 'pre-metal' Home Guard sign – in the doorway of his shop at Russell Street. The signs were used for emergency call-outs. The paper sign on the right of Vernon informs customers – "Regret no cigarettes, No soap, No chocolate – There's a war on!"

The Home Guard Social Club

The Home Guard Social Club was registered on 26th March 1943. It was originally located at 6, Gloucester Street before moving to its current address [2017] at [Portland Villa] 4, Portland Street on 8th December 1945.

On Monday 10th May 1943, the Home Guard Social Club Committee were supported by Colonel Erskine-Murray, Major Chubberley, Captain G. R. S. Williams, Captain Davies, Captain Lloyd and others, for the opening of Leamington's Home Guard Club at 6, Gloucester Street. The premises were formerly the Boys Club. Major Giles [president] declared the club open. The chairman was Lieutenant D. H. N. Ashdown. The Committee was formed in June 1941 and had held a number of fund raising functions. Initially membership was open to all Home Guards with the annual subscription being 1s [one shilling - 5p], but in February 1945 the Committee let it be known that membership of the club was now open to all former members of the 1st Warwickshire Home Guard; the annual subscription cost 5s.

In May 1945, an Old Comrades Association was formed for the 2,000 or so members of the Home Guard's Leamington companies. Mr. T. Harrison, the secretary of the Home Guard Club said, "It is recognised that all Home Guards are not in a position to enjoy the amenities of the club at Gloucester Street owing to their work or in some cases to their having removed from the district but the committees feel that these Home Guards would enjoy renewing their old comradeship". For that reason, they could be members of both the club and/or the Old Comrades Association. Membership of the Home Guard Rifle Club was automatic and free. With the end of the war, in October 1945 conditions governing the occupation of 6, Gloucester Street had changed and a new home had to be obtained.

Roy Rowberry and Norrys Harrison recalled in 1995, that they had their own songs, traditions and even their own beer which was how the social club came to be formed. They rented an attic room for 1/- [5p] a week, the beer being supplied by members who were in the brewing trade. They fitted it up with a bar and other essentials such as a darts board and by the end of the war, they had surplus funds of £600 which paid for a round of farewell parties. Roy recalled, "The final one was in the Town Hall. After the janitor had thrown everyone out we decided on the steps of the Town Hall to start the club up again." A building was soon acquired at 4 Portland Street, which had previously been used by the Friendly Societies Medical Association.

In December 1945, 'Tommy' wrote to the Courier: - "Twas back in 1940, the merry month of May, when our own Mr. Eden on the wireless did say, men of 17 to 60 hark to me, this country's free 'twill always be, if you all come forward and form the L.D.V. [Local Defence Volunteers]."

So goes the first verse of 'The Song of the Home Guard' written by T. C. Harrison [club Secretary] and L. M. Keegan. "Many will remember Mr. Eden's broadcast after the 9 o'clock news on that evening of May 14th, 1940. To us here in Leamington, it came almost as a personal appeal which few veterans of the 1914-18 war failed to answer. In addition, hundreds of younger men came forward prepared to learn the mysteries of musketry and fit themselves to fight any airborne troops or saboteurs who might be landed in this country."

"The Drill Hall in Adelaide Road became the scene of great activity. Men in caps, trilbies and bowlers, wearing their L.D.V. armlets, 'fell-in' in threes in their newly formed platoons and marched off with arms swinging and shoulders erect to Victoria Park, New River Walk or York Walk, to learn or re-learn how to slope, order, and trail arms, to take a correct aim and not forget the first and second pressures. Proud indeed were those favoured few who carried the precious weapons."

Then [the next verses]: - "They issued us with denims, blimey what a fit, you could get inside 'em, with all your blinking kit" and: - "Then good old Winston Churchill thought he'd change our name, so we lost the L.D.V. and Home Guard we became" and finally: - "Soon we were 'pukka' infantry, in uniform and armed were we, prepared to fight for England, to keep old England free".

"At the drill hall each evening might be seen groups gathered around our old friends the P.S.I.'s, [Permanent Staff Instructors], who explained the workings of the Browning automatic rifle, machine gun or a grenade. Four years rolled by while this enthusiastic band of spare time soldiers, "Britain's cheapest army" became more and more proficient in the arts of war. We grumbled, all soldiers grumble, but we were happy and above all a grand spirit of comradeship grew up amongst us."

"Thanks to the hard work and enthusiasm of a small committee, club premises were acquired in Gloucester Street where thirsts might be quenched after a Sunday morning's exercise or an evening's battle drill. The war is over, the Home Guard stood down but the Leamington Home Guard Club moves on. We feel that the good fellowship formed during the years of war is too valuable a thing to be allowed to die in the days of peace."

"New premises have been bought at Portland Villa, Portland Street, and the Rt. Hon. Anthony Eden, M.C; P.C; M.P. has consented to become our president. We in Leamington are proud indeed that the man, who as War Minister, sent out the appeal for volunteers in the grim days of 1940, is now our peace-time president."

The Leamington Spa Courier dated 7th September 1973 reported: - "Ex-soldiers paid tribute on Friday night to the man who fathered the Leamington Home Guard Club. The club donated £250 to the Parish Church Restoration Fund as a memorial to

Mr. Ralph Rowberry who died on 19th April this year. Mr. Rowberry, who was 77, bought the Portland Street premises in 1945, two years after the club had been formed in a Gloucester Street flat. "He managed to get this place at more than a reasonable price," said vice-chairman of the club, Mr. Norrys Harrison. "I came back from the war and found that all things from the flat had moved up there," he said. An old Leamingtonian, Mr. Rowberry had a great ability to get on with people. He had a close association with St. Alban's Church in Leamington. "He was a master craftsman and spent all his life repairing or renovating valuable furniture. He had a little workshop in Windsor Street," said Mr. Harrison. Mr. Rowberry, who was a sergeant in the war, was living near Edge Hill when he died. In presenting the cheque to Canon Idwal Jones, Mr. Harrison said, "He was wonderful to lads growing up in the area. He was a community minded man and a strong man. There are so many stories one can tell about him." Canon Idwal Jones said, "I must express my very warm thanks for this cheque. I do remember Ralph Rowberry as a very cheerful man and a craftsman. He had a love of Christian faith and made no bones about it. This donation is a tribute to a great man," he said.

On Wednesday 9th October 1990 Princess Alice, Duchess of Gloucester visited the Leamington Home Guard Club where she was greeted by club president Roy Rowberry [behind the Princess] and Betty Stellard. She toured an exhibition of club photographs marking the 50th anniversary of the Home Guard.

50th Anniversary celebrations of the Home Guard on Thursday 10th October 1990. President Roy Rowberry is in all three photos. In the bottom left photo, he is wearing the armband. Councillor Peter Byrd is centre of the top photo. The man on the left and right of the bottom photos is Viscount Daventry, Lord Lieutenant of Warwickshire.

Anthony Eden - later the First Earl of Avon, [He received his Earldom in 1961], chatting in the Home Guard Club. Fred Rogers is in the middle.

In May 1995 veterans of Leamington Home Guard appeared on BBC television amidst national celebrations to mark VE Day. The programme went out to 50 nations during the Veterans' march on Saturday 6th May. Filming took place in the Home Guard Club at 4 Portland Street, which at the time was one of only half a dozen still in existence. The film showed the third club president, Roy Rowberry, dressed up as Corporal Jones from the BBC's Dad's Army programme. Actor Bill Pertwee, [on the right of the photo] joined the veterans in his role as Warden Hodges. Alan Stellard is at the back in the blue shirt.

V E Day celebrations in May 1995. Kate Middleton is on the left.

Former Leamington Boys' College schoolboy Norrys Herbert Charlton Harrison, a founder member of the Home Guard Club died aged 73 on 2nd September 1996. He was blown up in France on his 21st birthday, seven days after D-Day. He had volunteered for special services in 1941 and became a commando. He was invalided home, recovered and returned to serve with an airborne division.

However, before enlisting he was a member of the LDV / Home Guard. On hearing the famous call to arms on the radio in May 1940, Norrys along with his life-long friend, Roy Rowberry immediately joined the LDV. They were 17 and 18 respectively. After the war he joined the Triumph Motor Cycle Company. When the firm closed Norrys proved a popular superintendent of the three swimming baths at Leamington, Kenilworth and Warwick. He retired when the baths closed.

He served as Chairman of the Home Guard Club from 1963 to 1970, was also a vice-president and trustee and for a long period took on the duties of Welfare Officer. Norrys won the club snooker championship three times. His final achievement, the day before he died, was to 'pull' the heaviest single fish [11lb] in a club fishing contest.

He lived at Radcliffe Gardens with his wife Phil until she died in November 1995. He suffered a heart attack and died while he was visiting his wife's grave.

Women in the War

The Second World War brought about significant changes in the role and position of women in society. Men soon became short on the home front and women were at first encouraged and later compelled to fill the gap. From the outset of war, a propaganda campaign called on women without family ties to volunteer for a variety of civilian and military jobs.

The Leamington Spa Courier [Warwickshire at War] dated 1st September 1989 reported: 'With so many men going away to war, women were left to fight the battle on the home front. Some women enlisted in the forces some went into factories or joined the Land Army but for many the battle was fought over the sink, the stove and the sewing machine. A constant stream of government information poured out to remind the nation's house-wives that theirs was a war against waste. Rationing and short supply were only part of the story. Stretching what you were able to get as far as possible and beyond was the objective. The model war time housewife darned holes, mended tears, unravelled old sweaters and re-knitted them – in fact, with much ingenuity she repaired, adapted and reused just about everything for the war effort.'

It wasn't all plaudits for our local women during the war. The Leamington Spa Courier dated 29th November 1940 carried the following: - '**Midland Red - Ladies, Ladies, Ladies!!!** - Some of you are not playing the game. We have repeatedly asked you NOT TO TRAVEL on the buses DURING PEAK HOURS. Will you please avoid travelling between 4.30 and 7pm in order to give the workers a chance to get a ride home without waiting about. Will you please do your shopping and visiting AFTER 10am, AND BE HOME AGAIN by 4.30pm.

We know it is difficult especially for you to have household duties and mid-day meals to get. Most of us have had to alter our old-time habits and we ask you to do the same! We really cannot increase our services any more at peak hours as all our omnibuses are already at work. To cater for the early and late workers some of our buses start at 3.10am and work on until 12.20 midnight. Every day throughout the year our drivers and conductors - men and women - have to work early mornings and late nights; Saturday afternoons and Sundays; in the black-out and during the "Alerts". All we ask you to do is to avoid the peak hours and help us to help the workers keep good time and increase output! **DO NOT LET US ASK IN VAIN!**'

In December 1939, the following letter from a Mrs. Smallwood was read to the A.R.P. Committee: - "There seems to be a certain amount of local feeling on the subject of paid personnel in the A.R.P. Ambulance Service, and I think it is time something was said in their defence, though I consider it deplorable that any defence should be necessary."

"It appears that the objection is that some of the personnel receive £2 a week for their full-time services, although they were not wage earners before the war. This is entirely beside the point. The ambulance drivers enrolled a year or more ago for voluntary service, before there was a suggestion of payment. They gave up their time to training classes and night driving practises to fit themselves for what they all expected to be a difficult and perhaps dangerous job."

"Then, last February, the Home Office issued a circular stating that a certain percentage of the full-time personnel would be required in the A.R.P. services [including ambulance drivers] and that these should and would be paid. In the nature of things, it was mainly the women of so-called leisure, whose home-ties in fact prevented them from enrolling in any military or mobile units, who could give the necessary full-time required, i.e., service in eight-hour shifts, day or night."

"The payment of A.R.P. personnel was not intended to give employment to those needing the money, but to ensure that there should be a sufficient and efficient service. Presumably the Government regard this as a form of insurance on Civil Defence, and for so long as this continues to be Government policy, I consider it should be the most capable who should be paid, irrespective of financial status. As full-timers were to be the backbone of the service, it is necessary that they should be those likely to prove the most efficient and reliable drivers. The fact that these in some cases did not happen to be in need of the pay that the Government proposed to give them is surely quite irrelevant." The report was adopted.

The Leamington Spa Courier [Warwickshire at War] dated 1st September 1989 reported: - 'In 1941, women without children were required, by Act of Parliament, to register for war work in the factories, on the land or in one of the services. Registration of women continued until the autumn of 1943 when all without a valid exemption between the ages of 18 and 50 had been registered. Initially, women tended to be allotted the most straightforward of tasks but gradually, as they proved their worth, and particularly in the armed services, moves were made to train some of them for more senior positions, releasing more men for active service. The Second World War presented new challenges to women from all walks of life. It offered them a totally new range of opportunities. Women drove trucks and ambulances. They put on tin hats and they put out fires. They worked on the line in munitions factories; they ploughed the fields and harvested the crops. The collective female responsibility – to keep the home fires burning and the plane parts rolling off the track – widened women's horizons and gave them the confidence they needed to break the traditional mould.'

Ladies at the Lockheed factory. The lady third from the right is thought to be Iola Fox.

Adverts appeared in the press – one in the Leamington Spa Courier dated 21st November 1941 showed four women encouraging others to join them under the heading – '**We four women ask you urgently to join us in vital war work** with the strap-line - **Come on Women – Man the Factories!** Even the men have to admit that the war can't be won without us. There are jobs that only a woman can do. Vital jobs that need a woman's clever fingers and nimble brain. But there are not enough women doing them. Within easy reach of you, in Coventry, there are factories crying out for women to man them. They make guns, bombs and planes. But they can make two or three times as many if you come in with us, roll up your sleeves and get down to the job. Don't say you'll see about it next week. It's what we do today that can win the war. German women are working in ***their*** factories. ***They're forced to***. Let ***us*** go of our own free will, just because we don't ever want to be driven by the Nazi slave-drivers.'

The Morning News dated Tuesday 6th October 1942 reported: - '**To Release Men for the Offensive – ATS, WAAF and WRNS Need Every Woman Who is not in Vital Work** – General Sir Ronald Adam said in his recent broadcast: - "To assume the offensive on the greatest possible scale and at the earliest possible moment is the wish of each fighting service. To do this successfully we want every fit man in the fighting line. To free these men for the offensive, the fighting forces require more and more women to step into their places." That is why every woman, married or single, who is not already doing work that is vitally important for the war, is urged to volunteer for the ATS, the WAAF or the WRNS. Married women are reminded that there are not enough single women and girls available to make up the huge numbers needed now by the services.'

By September 1943, 46% of all women aged between 14 and 59 and 90% of all able bodied single women between the ages of 18 and 40 were engaged in some form of National Service.

By the end of December 1944, a number of workers, particularly part-time workers, had visited the employment exchange to ask if they could leave their jobs as it appeared that the war was coming to an end and they had heard that changes to production were taking place. They were informed that they were mistaken. "From time to time there will always be changes to production, and the war effort must continue. Vast supplies of material are being used on European fronts and the Country is preparing for the intensification of war in the Pacific. Civilian life must be kept going, hospitals are functioning at full pressure. Transport must be manned to take workers to their jobs and in some areas services are being increased. Laundries are still doing a great deal of work for the Forces. The maintenance of street lighting is a new job - for war time, the preparation of food and fuel absorbs large numbers of workers. Meanwhile men are still being called to the Forces, and not many are yet returning, and those that do return are disabled."

"In the Leamington area men are needed for engineering jobs, loco fitting and on the railways. The gas works have a variety of vacancies. There are vacancies on the food production side including several jobs in the preparation of flour, and maltsters are needed for the preparation of beer. The engineering firms need men for munitions production and one firm is urgently wanting woodworkers for an aircraft job."

"Women also are needed in numbers. Hospitals have pressing demands for domestic staff, so pressing that the offer made last summer to Midlands girls that they might transfer from their present jobs to hospital work still stands. Women with domestic interests who would like to try hospital life will receive good training for the time when they have a home of their own, and will, if they want them, find that jobs will last after the war. There are six hospitals in the Leamington and Warwick area."

"Laundries also have urgent labour problems in the district. More than 20 full time women workers are needed. Part time workers are welcomed, but that of course means larger numbers. Then there is the recruiting need for bus conductresses. Transfers from their present jobs will be arranged for bus conductress volunteers as well as for hospital volunteers. Large numbers of Midland girls are coming forward for transport service, and are enjoying the change from an indoor job, but 'wastage' in the work - for family and health reasons, continues all the time, and so new volunteers are still needed."

"There remain all the direct war jobs for women, including one of great urgency at the moment - the machining of heavy waterproof canvas sheeting for our Forces. Untrained women will be accepted for this and trained. It is obvious that there must not yet be any relaxing of the war effort in the area. Not fewer but more workers are needed."

Women's Voluntary Service

Nationally the Women's Voluntary Service [W.V.S.] was established by the Dowager Marchioness of Reading G.B.E. [Dame Grand Cross of the Most Excellent Order of the British Empire] to provide support on the Home Front in the event of future air attacks. It was officially launched on 18th June 1938, although it was 7th November before a badge was issued. A uniform, initially consisting of an overcoat and hat was not launched until 28th June 1939. By the time war broke out the W.V.S. had 165,000 members. As well as giving support to people following air raids, they quickly became involved in many other areas of Home Front activities. They organised the evacuation of children, staffed sick bays and rest centres, organised communal feeding centres and promoted 'Make Do and Mend'. Eventually, the W.V.S. controlled the activities of over a million war-time voluntary women workers.

Photo: - This W.V.S. uniform, which was on display at the Leamington Spa Art Gallery and Museum from 22nd July until 16th October 2016, is the one worn by Ruth Gibbs when she was on duty. She served in the W.V.S. during the war and by October 1945 she was Centre Organiser for Warwick Rural District. Ruth was awarded the defence medal for non-operational service. Locally, Miss Shorto was the W.V.S. Centre Organiser.

The Leamington Spa Courier [Warwickshire at War] dated 1st September 1989 reported: '**Women's Voluntary Service** – The voluntary spirit was high. By the time the war broke out every community was doing something. The Women's Voluntary Service, started in Warwickshire in 1938, enrolled over 4,000 members in its first year. A public meeting had been held at the Shire Hall in November 1938 at which the Lord Lieutenant, Lord Henry Seymour, took the chair and the Dowager Marchioness of Reading, chairman of the W.V.S was the speaker. This was followed by the setting up of centres in every borough, with the exception of Warwick, and the appointment of representatives in every village. The W.V.S was the idea of the Home Secretary and its first work was enrolment for the Air Raid Protection Service, the forerunner of the Civil

Defence. Priority work was to obtain equipment for the 81 official First Aid Points, to augment equipment provided by the Government. Unofficial F.A.P.s were established by the W.V.S in more than 100 villages, all the equipment being provided by local effort.'

The Morning News dated Monday 23rd October 1939 reported: - '**Leamington Centre For Evacuated Children – Lady Reading to Make Visit of Inspection** – The Welfare Centre and Sick Bay for evacuated children, at 25, Warwick Place, Leamington, is to be visited this week by the Dowager Marchioness of Reading, who is coming to Warwickshire as National Chairman of the Women's Volunteer Services, to personally inspect the great war-time tasks which thousands of women are undertaking freely and efficiently in the county. Lady Reading intends to spend two days in the Midlands, and she will spend a short time in Leamington, during which she will inspect the centre. The idea of sick bays emanated from W.V.S. headquarters as early as April last, and Miss Brotherton, the local W.V.S. evacuation assistant, has been actively connected with the opening and equipment of 25, Warwick Place.'

LADY READING INSPECTS AMBULANCE DRIVERS

The Dowager Marchioness of Reading also inspected the ambulance drivers based at the Brewery Headquarters, Lillington Avenue.

In week commencing 11th December 1939, W.V.S. Centres throughout the County were a hive of activity as they dealt with the collection of plum puddings for the Warwickshire Home Defence Units. The aim was to ensure that every unit received enough puddings for every man on duty on Christmas Day.

Mrs. Dorothy Riley had been a member of the W.V.S. since its inauguration. She organised the clothing section for 30 years, but her first task was to help in making camouflage nets. She said, "In June 1940 I spent many hours on Leamington station giving cups of tea and emergency food to men returning from Dunkirk. The men were exhausted, distressed and dirty, and were glad of the refreshments we passed in. The men did not leave the trains which were waiting for signals to travel on to Birmingham."

"When bombing started in Coventry we opened rest centres in Lillington and Dale Street. We had been prepared for this and trained in First Aid and emergency feeding. When we knew A.R.P. Wardens were bringing people in, teams could be called upon and gathered quickly. Most of the people were shocked in varying degrees and needed rest, tea or a meal. Some were given a bed for the night and breakfast in the morning before going back to work."

Women's Land Army

The idea for a land army scheme came about two years before the outbreak of the war. As in the First World War the Women's Land Army would come to the rescue of the nation's farms.

The Women's Land Army, colloquially known as Land Girls, came into being on 1st June 1939, although the actual employment of land girls didn't start until war had been declared. It was part of the Ministry of Agriculture and Fisheries. Scotland had its own Land Army which was run by the Department of Agriculture for Scotland.

Initially, women were asked to volunteer but the National Service Act of 1941 allowed conscription of women into the armed forces or for vital war work. One essential condition placed upon the girls, in order to satisfy a shortage of labour in another county, was a requirement that they had to be mobile, and had to go where they were sent, without protest.

In Warwickshire, there was a good response and women normally employed in shops, businesses, offices and factories took to land work with a will, doing everything from harvesting to milking, and later some of the heavier work.

On joining, the Land Army girls were given green armlets. After every six months of satisfactory service they would receive a half-diamond which was sewn onto the armlet. After two years' service, they were given a special armlet with the badges woven in. They then collected four more over the next two years upon which they would receive a scarlet armlet to replace the two-year one. This continued until the Land Army was disbanded in 1950.

Once things had settled down and uniform was available, every Land Army girl was issued with the following: - 2 green jerseys, 2 pairs of brown breeches, 2 overall coats, 2 pairs of dungarees, 6 pairs of stockings, 3 shirts, 1 pair of ankle boots, 1 pair of shoes, 1 pair of black gumboots or boots with leggings, 1 brown felt hat, 1 overcoat, 1 oilskin or mackintosh, 2 towels, an oilskin sou'wester, a green armlet and a metal badge, although as they were not in the military it was not compulsory to wear the uniform.

They even had their own song: -

Women's Land Army Song

Back to the land, we must all lend a hand.
To the farms and the fields we must go.

There's a job to be done,
Though we can't fire a gun
We can still do our bit with the hoe.

When your muscles are strong
You will soon get along.
And you'll think that a country life's grand.

We're all needed now,
We must all speed the plough,
So come with us - Back to the land.

Back to the Land, with its clay and its sand,
Its granite and gravel and grit,
You grow barley and wheat
And potatoes to eat
To make sure that the nation keeps fit.

Remember the rest
All doing their best,
To achieve the results they have planned
We will tell you once more
You can help win the war
If you come with us - Back to the Land.

In Warwickshire, there were 103 Land Army girls at the end of December 1939, rising to 187 by December 1940, 412 by December 1941, 1,351 by December 1942, 1,814 by July 1943 and 1,762 by December 1943.

Roberta 'Bob' Gunn at Gooseberry Hall Farm, Barford.

In winter, the working week was 48 hours and in the summer, it was 50 hours. A girl aged 18 years of age or over would earn not less than 22 shillings and 6 pence after deductions for board and lodging.

The first winter [1939-1940] was a particularly hard winter and the girls had to deal with many unfamiliar difficulties. As well as working in the cold for much of the day, there were the problems of driving rain, blizzards, sleet and ice and breaking through the frozen water on the drinking troughs. There was no protection on the tractors in those days. It could also be a lonely existence with a number suffering from homesickness.

Roberta 'Bob' Gunn at Gooseberry Hall Farm, Barford.

A report published in January 1940 on the first year's work by the Women's Land Army concluded that two out of three Land Army girls made good even after only one month's training. Training was either carried out at a farm with the farmer, where the girls gained a lot of practical experience, or at a college where they were given a broader view of agriculture but gained less practical experience. Skill, adaptability and a quick brain counted for more than brute strength. Many who had become successful Land Army girls were slim and under 5ft. 4in. in height.

The Fordson tractor, which was used by many a Land Army girl, was named after Henry Ford and Son who developed the range.

The training was a testing time, especially for those who had only known office work and regular hours. The working day was long, and even after they had finished for the day, they were on call for emergencies. One Land Army girl commented, "At first I found the work hard, strenuous and fatiguing but exhilarating. All the work is helped and made easier for you if you have a good boss who will consider you and encourage you." Another mentioned her glow of pride knowing that she was helping to win the war.

A Ministry of Agriculture report in January 1941 stating that tens of thousands of farmworkers were to be called up for the fighting services caused uproar in the Midlands. It was described as a "bombshell" by the Warwickshire Farmers' Union. In their opinion, the substitution of Land Girls, even if the right type could be guaranteed, would simply not be able to make up for the loss of skilled and seasoned male workers.

That same month, the Leamington Courier ran a headline: - "A Land Girl tells her story" - Gladys Wildman [LA No. 3461] of Leamington who had earlier trained at Studley College for a month, described her training as marvellous. She recounted how she had gradually grown used to the cold of winter and was thrilled by haymaking and having her tea brought out to the field and being able to carry on "as though your very life depended on getting that last load in that night." Gladys had many experiences which she could later look back on with much amusement - the first day she drove a horse and cart. The day the farmer asked her to take a horse to the blacksmith's five miles away when she had never ridden a horse before. However, she managed to ride there *and* back.

Her first job was on a mixed farm with a large poultry unit. She lived in with the farmer and his wife. She said, "I had a very pleasant bedroom but unfortunately it was adjoining the barn and it was some time before I could get used to the noise of the rats running around the barn during the night."

"In the winter months, the mud was quite a problem. I remember once having to leave one of my Wellington boots behind stuck fast in the mud. An Italian prisoner working with me at the time was most upset and when he left he said in broken English, "Whenever I see mud I shall think of you!" My day started by catching a pony in a field, which I discovered was quite a tricky business. Although I went armed with a bridle and a bowl of oats, he would often snatch a mouthful and before I could grab him he was away to the far end of the field. Then I had to harness him to a float, load up with poultry food and drive around feeding and watering the stock, which was spread over several fields. All the adult stock were on free range, battery cages had not taken over then. The afternoon work consisted of feeding again, collecting eggs, then cleaning and packing them."

"After a time poultry food became very difficult to obtain so it was found necessary to reduce the stock and I went on to milking the cows. This meant an early rise and although we milked by machine it entailed quite a lot of heavy work. About 20 buckets of water had to be pumped by hand and then lifted into a tank for cooling the milk. A fire had to be lit underneath the steriliser for sterilising all the equipment. The milk had to be put into churns before 8.00am when the milk lorry arrived to collect it. I soon realised that farm work was not such a leisurely business as I had imagined!"

"Farm work was much harder in those days, especially at harvest time without the combine harvester. After the corn was cut there was the job of stooking [*a number of sheaves set upright in a field to dry with their heads together*] and later collecting it and putting it into a rick to await the visit of the threshing machine."

"I was asked among other Warwickshire girls to form a guard of honour to the Queen in Cannon Hill Park. I remember standing for hours in the cold awaiting her arrival. Our uniforms were far from complete at this time and no coats had been issued. No one could decide whether we should wear our pullovers inside our baggy breeches or outside. I'm afraid we did not look exactly smart and it was amazing what some girls did with the regulation felt hat."

Gladys went on to say that because of the number of Land Army girls in the district, an association was formed so that they could meet once a fortnight in different locations, to discuss topics of interest, - not only "ploughing up schemes and shortage of animal food stuffs, [but] things of a more frivolous nature too."

At the end of January 1941, thanks to the kindness and patience of many farmers and their wives, there were 200 Land Army girls in Warwickshire. Mrs. Dora Fielden, chairman of the local branch of the W.L.A., wrote to the Courier appealing for still more recruits amongst all able-bodied women between the ages of 18 and 40. Women from all walks of life responded. In the same year, the Queen became Patron of the W.L.A.

This machine is a two-string sewing machine, called a 'harvest saver'. It was mounted on a trailer and came complete with its own power unit.

During the 'bumper' harvest of 1941, the labours of the old-fashioned skilled workwomen were supplemented by machinery. The land army girls lived in a caravan which was attached to a tractor together with the thatching machine. The caravan, which could travel at around 15 m.p.h., was a four-berth model with three rooms, one for sleeping accommodation, one to act as a living room and the third for cooking.

By November 1941, the number of land army girls in Warwickshire had doubled to 400, and a W.L.A. hostel [*a series of linked prefabricated huts*] was opened in December 1941 in Greatheed Road, close to Milverton Primary School. These hostels were springing up across the country. Girls would normally sleep in dormitories in beds or double bunks. They were supposed to have a wardrobe and a lockable drawer for personal possessions. There was to be a dining room, a recreation room and possibly a quiet room. An allowance was made to hostels out of which a piano, wireless set, sewing machine and items such as sports equipment could be bought. However, the facilities at Greatheed Road hostel comprised of a dining room and a piano which had been donated.

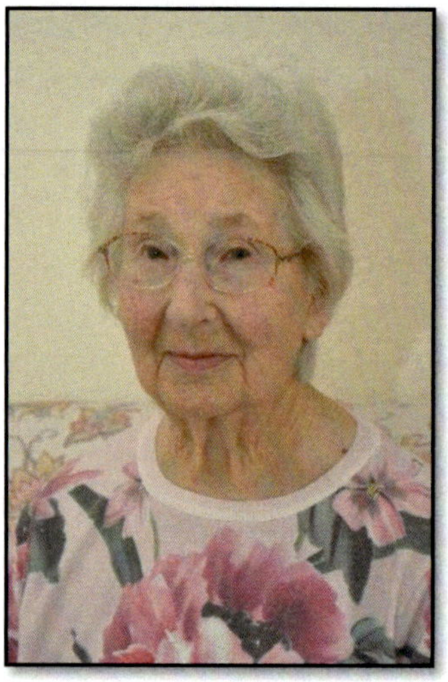

Hazel Davis née Parkes was one of the girls who was billeted at Greatheed Road. Hazel was born in 1922 and lived at Old Hill in the Black Country, then part of Staffordshire, until she was five years old. In 1927, her father had a house built in Worcester Road Hagley where the family lived until the early 1930s. Unfortunately her father died suddenly and the family had to move back to Old Hill. Their house was only nine miles from the centre of Birmingham and Hazel remembers the blitz on Birmingham. The first air raid on the city was on 9th August 1940 and that was followed by 76 other raids until April 1943. Hazel's family didn't have an Anderson shelter so they shared their neighbours'. She remembers watching the planes bombing Birmingham and the distant fires.

Her first job was in the Halford's Head Office in Birmingham. One sunny spring morning her friend Natalie, who worked in the same office, said, "Wouldn't it be a good idea to be outside all of the time – shall we join the Women's Land Army?" On 7th April 1942 at 19 years of age, they went to the office in the centre of Birmingham and joined up. Hazel required 'a medical' with her own doctor. He just asked her if she felt alright and what was she going to do. When told that she wanted to join the Land Army, he just said, "Well, go and do it then" – and that was her 'medical'!

One Friday evening they travelled by train to Leamington Spa, a town she hadn't been to before. They asked the way to the Land Army hostel in Greatheed Road and set off. As they walked in, the residents were finishing off their evening meal, so they sat down and waited. As they sat there, in walked Douglas Davis, a young 17-year-old who lived in Greatheed Road and who had recently left Leamington Boys College. While waiting to join the Royal Air Force he was working for the Ministry of Agriculture, also in Greatheed Road. His job included paying the girls their £1 per week wages. Douglas was already a member of the R.A.F.V.R, the Royal Air Force Volunteer Reserve. He was one of 250 boys that went to Coventry to be assessed for a job in the R.A.F. Only five boys passed the exam, Douglas being one of them.

On walking into the hostel, he spotted Hazel and said, "That's the girl I am going to marry!" Three years later in 1945 they were married. In November 1940 schoolboy Doug had avoided death on the Parade in Leamington during a bombing raid as recorded in the following report. Unfortunately, two soldiers were not so lucky.

The Leamington Spa Courier dated 6th May 2011 reported on the events of that night 71 years ago: - 'The German pilot who bombed Lipton's on that fateful night didn't get 17-

year-old Douglas Davis, who took cover in Lipton's doorway as the sirens went off. It was 14th November, 1940, and Coventry was already in flames as the Leamington College schoolboy dodged into the shop doorway. It was a Thursday night and Douglas was on his way back from the pictures [*cinema*] when a local policeman spotted him taking shelter.

After hearing he only needed to get as far as Greatheed Road, the policemen advised, "I'd just get on home if I was you lad". The teenager was still making his way up the road when he was deafened by the series of explosions – one of them a direct hit on Lipton's. Two years later Douglas would himself be in the R.A.F. He went on to survive 30 missions as a rear gunner with Bomber Command where the operational life expectancy was expected to be just 11 hours. He died in 2010 at the age of 86.'

Hazel goes on, "There were 42 girls who all lived in the one hut. It was an army hut but was less spacious than the normal ones, and was very cramped. We were split into areas; the Birmingham and local girls were at one end of the hut and girls from Lancashire and the north were at the other end. There were no single beds only bunk beds along both sides of the hut. My friend Natalie slept in the bottom bunk and I had the top bunk. There was a large dining room with two long tables similar to a girls boarding school. We had a very basic ablution block, it only had two baths and two showers for 42 girls. The only heating we had was an oil heater in the hut and another in the dining room."

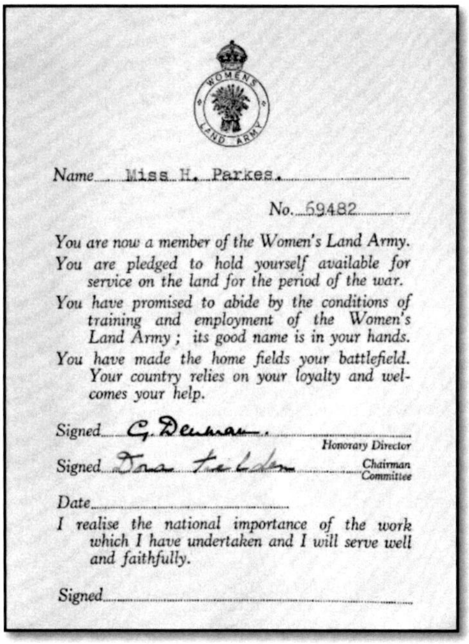
WOMENS LAND ARMY

Name Miss H. Parkes.

No. 59482

You are now a member of the Women's Land Army.
You are pledged to hold yourself available for service on the land for the period of the war.
You have promised to abide by the conditions of training and employment of the Women's Land Army; its good name is in your hands.
You have made the home fields your battlefield. Your country relies on your loyalty and welcomes your help.

Signed G. Denman. Honorary Director

Signed Chairman Committee

Date

I realise the national importance of the work which I have undertaken and I will serve well and faithfully.

Signed

"Our uniforms were issued by Mrs Siddeley who lived in Northumberland Road. There was a doctor that the girls could see, Dr. Crawford, he also lived in Northumberland Road. The hostel had lady wardens who were generally wives of serving soldiers who slept in and also brought their children. One of the girls, Sylvia from Port Sunlight, was made foreman and it was her responsibility to make sure that all of the girls were in by 10.00pm."

"We were fed very well in the hostel at breakfast and dinner time, there was a hatch at the far end of the hut which led to the kitchen. We never had to do the washing up as the volunteers always did it. Sandwiches were provided for our lunch, but they were always made the previous day by ladies from the Women's Institute; they were always cheese and always hard and curling up at the edges by the time we ate them. No drink was provided for us to drink during the day, not even water, and more often than not neither the farmer nor the farmer's wife would give us a drink either."

"We had no idea what we were letting ourselves in for and in many cases girls had to work in awful conditions. Often girls had to work all day, digging ditches, sowing seeds and harvesting crops without a break and of course there were no toilet facilities. Before the hostels were provided girls were allocated to farmers. Some had terrible experiences and some awful conditions to live in. There were good farmers but there were plenty of bad ones as well – and farmer's wives were often nasty to the girls, especially if they thought their husband was getting a little too friendly with the girls. Lady Gertrude Denman, the Director of the Land Army arranged the hostels which improved the situation."

"We had to work a five-and-a-half-day week, finishing at 1.00pm on a Saturday. It could be very tiring because don't forget as well as our farm work we also had to do A.R.P duties. We would be fire watching throughout the night about three times a week. As soon as Saturday lunchtime arrived though it was off to the railway station as quickly as possible to catch a train back to Birmingham. Unfortunately, we had to travel back to Leamington on Sunday evenings, but the short break was still very welcome. We used to enjoy dancing at the Palais de Danse and at the Town Hall. We would also have dances in the dining room at the hostel. The tables were taken out and someone would bring in a gramophone. Sometimes Canadian airmen from Wellesbourne would come over to the hostel for one of the dances. They were on operations with Wellington bombers but later they were moved to Gaydon and converted to Lancasters."

"We covered farms over quite a distance. To reach farms in a five-mile radius we had to bike there and back. The bikes, not new ones, were allocated to us when we started. One girl was allocated an army utility van to transport girls to any farms that were over five miles away. Farmers would telephone and ask for a certain number of girls. Usually he'd ask for at least four or five and then the gang of us would travel together for particular jobs. We could be at a different farm every day. There was a notice board in the hostel and every Monday morning we would check the board to see where we were going and what we had to do."

"Sometimes we were sent to totally unsuitable jobs. On one occasion a group of us was sent to learn thatching at a cottage, but thatching takes years to learn so we just had to sit there while the thatcher got on with his work. The cottage was more than five miles away so we went by van which on this occasion was driven by Bert Stowe from the transport depot at Wathen Road. On the way back Bert was just talking casually and asked if I would like to learn driving. I knew nothing about driving but two days later I was told to report to the transport depot. That conversation changed my Land Army life – no longer did I have to do the hard farm work."

"The vehicle was a very basic green utility vehicle and it certainly didn't have any heating. On the first day, I had to drive around Leamington with a mechanic then that was it, I was on my own. I was then told to go to the Hillman works in Coventry for some spares even though I said I had only one days training and didn't know Coventry or the roads to Coventry. I was just told 'to get on with it', - and don't forget all of the road signs had been taken down because of the war."

"After that I had to drive all over Warwickshire so I got to know the area well. During day time I didn't have much to do with the girls, although I still lived at the hostel. I was allocated two vehicles in the end and it was only me that used them. The green one was for everyday tasks and the gold one was for special occasions. I would take officers out and about to various farms and drive Ministry of War Agricultural Committee members from London around to the farms so that they could see what was happening. There were farm walks with farmers, where farmers were invited to visit other farms for a get together and see what was happening elsewhere and discuss issues. Also, if there was a victory parade down the Parade, and there were a few, I had to lead it. Sound equipment was put in the van and it would play 'To be a farmer's boy' or something similar."

"I married Doug at St. Mark's Church Rugby Road in January 1945. I always tell people that Lord Nuffield paid for our honeymoon. He was a philanthropist who put money into a fund for airmen who had been on a lot of missions. It paid for them to have a holiday and a good rest, so we used it for our honeymoon in the Lake District."

"As I was now a married woman, in August 1945 I left the Land Army and went home to live with my mother. However, being used to living with 41 other girls, I soon became very bored at home so I returned to my old job. I finally left the Land Army a little while later in November 1945. My daughter Lesley was born in July 1946."

"Douglas left the Royal Air Force around 1947 or 1948 and we went to live at Major Julius Bonniksen's bungalow at Harbury Lane airfield. We had a large bedroom, a sitting room, a large kitchen and we shared a bathroom with the Bonniksen's. Douglas went back to work for the Ministry of Agriculture in the accounts department and later he became an executive field officer dealing with subsidies to farmers."

"Since then, we have lived in a flat at 24 Newbold Terrace, a house in Beaufort Avenue, Cubbington and I now live in Ledbrook Road, Cubbington."

"In July 2008, 63 years after the end of the war we were awarded a certificate and a medal by the government. It took them some time, didn't it?"

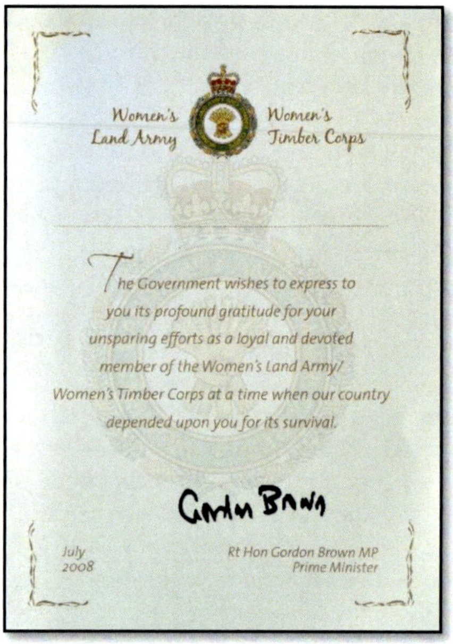
Women's Land Army

Women's Timber Corps

The Government wishes to express to you its profound gratitude for your unsparing efforts as a loyal and devoted member of the Women's Land Army/ Women's Timber Corps at a time when our country depended upon you for its survival.

July 2008

Rt Hon Gordon Brown MP
Prime Minister

Hazel Davis' Women's Land Army medal and certificate. The awards included the Women's Timber Corps who were also known as Lumber Jills. They worked tirelessly in the forests to provide timber for the war effort, felling trees, sawing timber and sharpening saws.

David Goulding remembers witnessing the demolition of the camp around 1955 or 1956 and the start of the building in the area around 1962 or 1963. This photo taken in May 2016 shows where the camp was situated, on the far side of the camper van. The area has since been developed for housing.

Prior to a well-advertised rally at Leamington Town Hall in February 1942, the warden of the hostel gave an interview to the Courier, where she described the accommodation and the W.L.A. girls' timetable. The hostel held 40 Land Army girls aged between the late teens to early 30s, with an average age of 22. The girls slept in a dormitory in "double-decker [bunk] beds". Breakfast was at 7:30am. Armed with a packed lunch the girls then left for work either by bicycle if they worked within five miles or by small van if they had to go further afield. They returned at 5.30pm for a hot meal prepared by volunteers and took turns on the washing-up rota. Conditions were fairly spartan but the warden praised the girls for their commitment and their willingness to share, right down to baths and second helpings of pudding! After supper, the girls had free time until lights out at 10.00pm except on Tuesdays and Saturdays which were 'late' nights. Someone kindly donated a piano for the common room, which gave great pleasure to many. The girls also enjoyed ballroom dancing.

On Saturday 28th February 1942, over 450 members of the Warwickshire Women's Land Army took part in the rally in Leamington. The girls, "a sturdy and happy company, aroused much interest and admiration" as they marched in procession [headed by a Royal Warwickshire Regiment band] from the W.L.A. Hostel in Greathead Road to the Town Hall. They were welcomed by the Mayor and Mayoress and addressed by Lady Denman, Honorary Director of the W.L.A. Her Ladyship congratulated the county on their success. Warwickshire had doubled its members in a year and was now approaching the 600 mark. Good Service awards were presented by Lady Denman to 36 Land Girls with two years' service, 57 with 18 months' service, 22 with 12 months' service and 117 with six months' service.

Following the rally there was a further plea for more recruits. They were putting in exceptionally good work and were being praised by farmers. However, it was not all plain sailing as W.L.A. girls were not free to take or leave a job without permission. The fact that the press printed regulations requiring W.L.A. girls to notify the W.L.A. in the event of a change of employment gives an inkling that things did not always run as smoothly as was hoped. For some, the work was physically too taxing or simply too stressful. One Birmingham girl was found drowned in the river at Evesham, and there were other sad stories too. The Women's Land Army Benevolent Fund was set up, with the local chairman Mrs. Fielden writing regularly to the Leamington Spa Courier appealing for donations.

In November 1942, when Warwickshire boasted a total of 1300 Land Army girls [out of the national total of 51,000], Mrs. Roosevelt, wife of the President of the United States of America visited Land Army girls at work at Oldbury Court Farm near Henley in Arden. She was taken on a morale-raising trip around the farm by tractor and trailer.

Leamington had become by this time the home of the oldest Land Army Hostel in Warwickshire. As a result of the successful harvest that year, residents and volunteers at Greatheed Road were treated to a Harvest Supper. This became the trigger for a new Y.W.C.A. [Young Women's Christian Association] venture, the introduction of a club with organised activities including language classes, lectures, drama, dances and occasional Saturday matinées at Stratford on Avon. The club cost 3d per week.

By August 1943 the Land Army had reached its peak membership with just over 80,000 girls employed in England and Wales. At the same time there were 26 hostels in Warwickshire, many of them requisitioned houses, but more accommodation was needed. A plea went out for volunteer domestic staff to cook and clean the hostels for a minimum of two hours a day. The situation was so desperate that "even women with children" were considered.

In 1943 there was a desperate need for women to work in other fields of industry, so much so that the Government restricted and for a time suspended recruitment to the W.L.A.

On 17th September 1943, the Leamington Spa Courier carried the following article: '**Women's Land Army - Recruiting Suspended Until Spring - Disappointment in Warwickshire** - Recruiting for the Women's Land Army has been suspended until the spring. Miss Diana Hunter, the Warwickshire County Secretary, informs us that all girls who have been waiting to be called up have now been placed in employment.

At the end of August, 1,843 girls had been enrolled as members of the W.L.A. in Warwickshire, and they are all at work. "We shall definitely not increase the number," said Miss Hunter. "There has been considerable disappointment at the suspension of recruiting but for some time past we have been restricted in this county owing to the heavy demands of local industries."

"Thirty hostels are now functioning in Warwickshire but in the changed circumstances, the work of adapting 12 additional centres has been suspended by the Ministry of Works."

Miss Hunter called attention to the new W.L.A. Proficiency Tests. Examinations both practical and oral will be arranged in the following branches of land work: - Milking and dairy work, general farm work, poultry, tractor driving, field work, outdoor garden and glasshouse work, fruit work and pest destruction. A Land Army member may enter for one branch of work only. A member failing in her examination may enter again in the same branch of work after a six months' interval as and when a further test can be arranged. No member will be permitted to enter for an examination unless she has been in Land Army employment for one year or more and has obtained permission to enter from her Land Army County Secretary who will take into account her record of service, including good time keeping. A successful candidate will be entitled to wear the Women's Land Army Proficiency Badge.'

Also in September 1943, Dora Fielden, Chairman of the Women's Land Army wrote a letter to the Leamington Spa Courier: - "Sir, - In this war our Land Girls have tackled all kinds of tough and lonely jobs. Most of them have flourished. But some of them have tried too hard and have had bad luck - and that's why the Land Army Benevolent Fund has been set up. Land Girls, of course, come under the National Health and Unemployment Schemes and Workmen's Compensation. But in a hard world that does not cover everything. The Navy, the Army and the Air Force have Benevolent Funds to deal with problems that arise. But the Women's Land Army is a new service - and that is why the Benevolent Fund is so urgently needed."

"It must be remembered, too, that Land Girls have their lives before them - they join from 17 years old upwards. The end of the war will mean the beginning of a greater need than ever before. If a Land Girl wants to make a career on the land, it means specialized training and training means money to send girls to agricultural colleges, money to help to give them a start, either in this country or in the Dominions."

"Many Land Girls will want to return to their pre-war occupations or will have to find new openings. For these also, help and training will often be essential. To meet these needs £100,000 is needed. I appeal confidently to Warwickshire folk for their quota. I shall be glad to receive subscriptions which should be sent to me at 21 Regent Grove, Leamington."

On Saturday 2nd October 1943, to celebrate the anniversary of its being called into being, the Warwickshire W.L.A. held a rally for its members when over 600 attended from various parts of the county. Tents were erected in the Mill Meadow and tea was served by the Women's Voluntary Service. Various little side-shows were run in aid of the W.L.A. Benevolent Fund and there was a programme of music by the Standard Motors British Legion Band. The strength of the W.L.A. in the county was 2,000 and there were 29 residential hostels, in addition to which several hundred resided at farm houses where they were employed. Mrs. Fielden [Chairman] welcomed the girls in the Jephson Gardens Pavilion and said they very much appreciated the good work they were doing in helping the War effort. A party of ENSA [Entertainments National Service Association] artistes gave an hour's entertainment, and the proceedings were concluded with the National Anthem.

By January 1944 there were 696 hostels throughout England, 475 were run by the Women's Land Army, 146 by the Young Women's Christian Association and 75 by the War Agricultural Executive Committees.

Fund-raising rallies continued to be held and in 1944 Lady Willoughby de Broke, wife of the Lord-Lieutenant of the county, opened a summer fair in aid of the Warwickshire Women's Land Army benevolent fund at the Regent Hotel. She paid warm tributes to "the town-bred girls who had taken up agricultural work", in what had been dubbed the Cinderella of the Services. In appealing for support Lady Willoughby de Broke hoped that the Cinderella's would have the well-deserved fairy-tale ending saying, "but for the women, Britain's enormous agricultural programme could not have been carried out during the war period. It was said that women were more adaptable than men but [she] was amazed how city-bred girls had cast aside the high heels, got into gumboots and made a real job of it."

The total raised by Warwickshire for the fund eventually reached £7,266, some of which was used to help 50 Warwickshire Land Army girls during illness. Mrs. Fielden was awarded the O.B.E. Warwickshire was so successful at recruiting that by mid-1946, a Courier headline claimed that the county was "exporting" Land Army girls to other counties. The chief labour officer for Warwickshire commented that only a few weeks earlier there had been concerns about the number of vacancies in hostels but a successful recruiting campaign had remedied the situation and he was therefore much impressed by the type of new entrant. He felt that the fresh blood would be a great asset to agriculture, alleviating the concerns of the labour office about the likely forthcoming lack of German prisoner of war labour. He rejected the assertions of Warwickshire farmers that the prisoners of war often arrived with inadequate rations for the work they had to complete. He was confident that the prisoners of war were exaggerating the situation and that their rations were as substantial as those of the civilian population.

The reward of the Land Army girls, apart from knowing how much they had contributed to the war effort, came in a public ceremony in 1946, when the Marchioness of Northampton presented some of the girls with armlets marking their service, 30 received the six years' service award and 32 received the four years' award.

At the Farewell Parade of the Women's Land Army at Buckingham Palace on 21st October 1950, Her Majesty the Queen said, "I am so very pleased to have this opportunity of speaking to the Women's Land Army, whose patron I have been for the past nine years."

Farewell Parade, Buckingham Palace, October 21st, 1950

"A Farewell Parade always has something about it that is sad, but when it comes to the culmination of a long and honourable history, our feelings are chiefly of pride and gratitude. This is certainly so today."

"The story of the Land Army has been one of a great response by the women of our country to the call of duty in the nation's hour of danger and need."

"They could not have done more for their country than they did. By their efforts they helped to ensure that our country contributed its utmost towards its food supplies, and for this the nation owes them an everlasting debt."

"The Women's Land Army has always been recruited from volunteers, and I like to think that its greatest strength lay in the free spirit which has always inspired the people of these Islands to their greatest achievements."

"The Land Army attracted girls from every kind of different occupation, and I have always admired their courage in responding so readily to a call which they knew must bring them not only hardship and sometimes loneliness, but often danger."

"By their hard work and patient endurance they earned a noble share of the immense effort which carried our country to victory. Yet their task did not end when the war was over, for they stayed at their posts through the difficult years that followed."

"Five thousand of those who served in the Land Army have decided to remain on the land. There can be no greater tribute than this to the happiness with which their work rewarded them."

"Now the time has come to say good-bye, because the job has been done but the sadness which many will feel at the parting should be outweighed by pride in the achievement. Moreover, the Land Army will not in any case be only an affectionate memory since it will live still in the shape of the thousands of members who have settled down in the countryside as the wives of farmers and farm workers or who are themselves continuing to work in agriculture when the organisation itself comes to an end."

"I thank you all for the splendid service you have given your country. In field and forest, garden, orchard and dairy, the work of the Women's Land Army has always been worthy of the ageless traditions of those who have toiled for the land they loved."

"I know that the whole nation will join with me in wishing you all good fortune for the future."

On Sunday 7th December 2008, a service in recognition of the contribution made by the Warwickshire members of the Women's Land Army and Timber Corps during the Second World War and its aftermath was held at the Collegiate Church of St. Mary, Northgate Street, Warwick.

On 21st October 2014, a memorial to the Women's Land Army and the Women's Timber Corps was unveiled at the National Memorial Arboretum at Alrewas in Staffordshire by HRH the Countess of Wessex GCVO.

Mrs. M. M. Maitland Fowler O.B.E. – Red Cross

During the Second World War, Dr. E. R. Gilmore was the Area First-Aid Commandant from 1939 until February 1944 when the role was taken on by Dr. L. Gerard Clayton. Dr. Clayton had also been appointed the Medical Officer in charge of decontamination and cleansing arrangements for the Borough in April 1942.

However, it was Mrs. Margaret Mary Maitland Fowler O.B.E., one of the best-known workers for the Red Cross in Warwickshire, who was the most prominent local person. During the First World War, she had worked as Red Cross Commandant at a hospital near Nuneaton.

As well as her work for the Red Cross and St. John's Ambulance Association, she was Vice President of the Caravan Club and the legendary owner of Leamington's Blue Café – [more about that in the later chapter on Recreation and Entertainment].

Mrs. Fowler lived in a large detached house at 21 Newbold Terrace, a house which has since been demolished.

She had four luxury blue caravans that she used for her Red Cross and St. John's work, each van being self-contained and able to be used independently of the others. Mrs. Fowler said, "When I first started using caravans for Red Cross work it was considered an extraordinary thing to do. Caravans, apart from the gypsy species, were very rare in those days, that was about 1928." In 1940, the small Winchester No.2 caravan was reserved for air-raids and was ready for use with first aid equipment, blankets, hot water bottles and tea. The large Eccles No.1 caravan and the No.3 covered wagon stood by at Newbold Terrace in case of serious air raids whilst the No.4 caravan was based at Nuneaton and stood outside of the Red Cross building. It was used as an office where the typing was carried out.

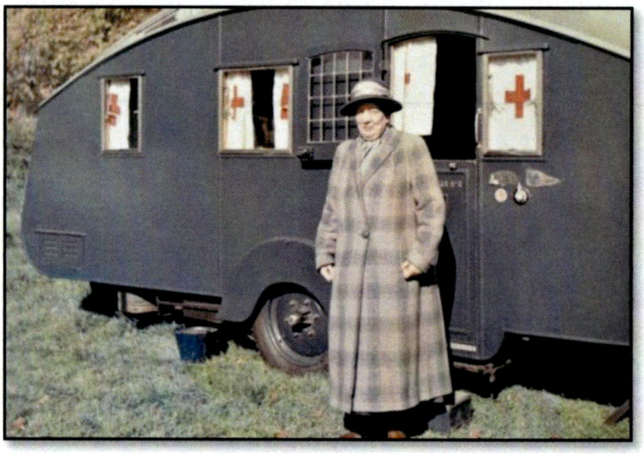

Mrs. Fowler outside her No.2 caravan.

The caravans were even inspected by the Queen. In the war years, the caravans could be seen in 'battledress' – curtains bearing the Red Cross were hung at the windows. The caravans were fitted with stoves, book shelves, cloak rooms, desks, an ice box, a wireless, and were resplendent with soft blue leather seats, silk hangings, carpets and cushions. She converted one of her caravans into an ambulance, the drawers and cupboards being filled with first-aid equipment.

She used her four dogs as a means of collecting money for the two charities, three of them were Shetland sheepdogs and the other was a French poodle. Mrs. Fowler said, "They were doing very well until the air raids, and after that I did not like to take them out after dark. Brian, the largest sheepdog, has often been out without the other dogs, with one Red Cross box and one St. John's box strapped on either side of him. He has been annoyed when very occasionally some kind person has put paper money in his box, as he cannot hear the rattle of any coins."

With her blue caravans standing by for Red Cross work she could proceed to the scene of an incident within a few minutes of a call and deal with the bombed, the injured and the homeless. The doctor on call would advise her of the best place to park and within a few minutes water was boiling on the gas stove and she was ready for action. During air-raids and on the night of the Coventry Blitz, people who had lost homes were treated by Mrs. Fowler and her helpers for shock and for cuts from flying glass. Afterwards they were taken in the caravan to the homes of friends. The caravan was also used to serve hot drinks to relatives who had gone to search for missing relatives and to firemen and to the homeless who were trying to collect their things.

Mrs. Fowler even used her own house and other premises owned by her to raise funds for various charities. She started exhibitions and sales of goods made by disabled ex-servicemen in 1934. For six years, they were held at her premises at 19 Parade and from 1940 they were held at her home at 21 Newbold Terrace. One of these events was held on Saturday 26th July 1941. It was opened by Lady Seymour and a collection was taken in aid of providing funds for outings for disabled ex-servicemen.

DISABLED MEN'S HANDICRAFTS LIMITED

Mrs M. M. M. Fowler, O. B. E.

requests the pleasure of the company of

and friends

at an Exhibition and Sale of Goods made by Disabled Ex-Service Men

On SATURDAY, JULY 26th, 1941.

At 21, NEWBOLD TERRACE, LEAMINGTON SPA.

The Exhibition will be opened at 3-0 p.m. by

LADY HELEN SEYMOUR

The Blue Caravans will be on view, when a collection will be taken in aid of providing Outings for Disabled Ex-Service Men

R.S.V.P.—21. Newbold Terrace, Leamington Spa

3-0 p.m. till 5-30 p.m.

She held another on Saturday 15th August 1942 which was opened by the famous stage star and Shakespearian actor Jay Laurier. Mr. Ernest C. Thomas, general manager of the Disabled Men's Handicraft's said that 120 badly disabled men from the last war were being helped by the organization. Its object was to provide the men with something to occupy their minds in their own homes as doctors had said that this was the very best medicine they could receive. Those who were shell-shocked found solace from such work in which they took great pride. He added that no fewer than 76 Mayor's parlours in all parts of the country contained rugs which had been made by men belonging to this organization. Some £110 was taken at the exhibition with further donations and orders expected.

The Mayor, Councillor R. S. Salt and Mayoress of Leamington Spa invited a number of people to attend the Council Chamber at 2.00pm on Tuesday 18th May 1943 to inspect a wool rug which was made by disabled ex-serviceman Frank Bull and contained 48,000 pieces of wool. One of Frank's duties in the First World War had been to drive the Prince of Wales over the battlefields. It would become a gift from the British Red Cross Society and Order of St. John to American President Franklin Delano Roosevelt.

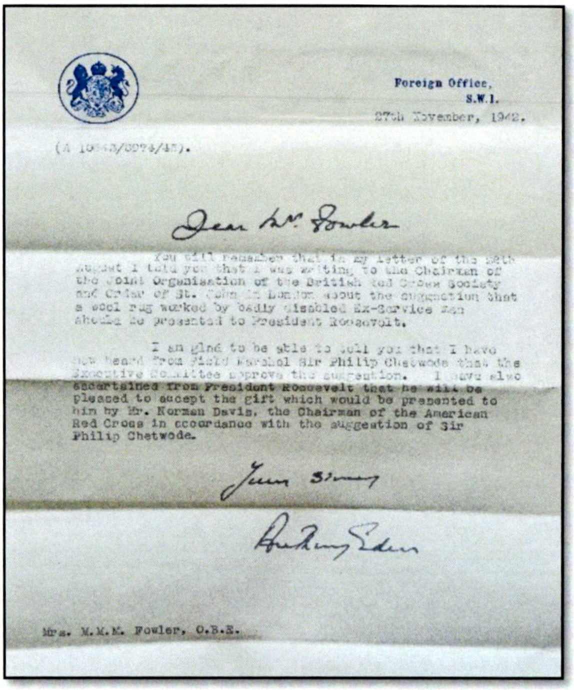

Foreign Office,
S.W.1.
27th November, 1942.

(A [illegible]/42).

Dear Mrs Fowler

You will remember that in my letter of the [illegible] August I told you that I was writing to the Chairman of the Joint Organisation of the British Red Cross Society and Order of St. John in London about the suggestion that a wool rug worked by badly disabled Ex-Service men should be presented to President Roosevelt.

I am glad to be able to tell you that I have now heard from Field Marshal Sir Philip Chetwode that the Executive Committee approve the suggestion. I have also ascertained from President Roosevelt that he will be pleased to accept the gift which would be presented to him by Mr. Norman Davis, the Chairman of the American Red Cross in accordance with the suggestion of Sir Philip Chetwode.

Yours sincerely

Anthony Eden

Mrs. M.M.M. Fowler, O.B.E.

Local M.P and Foreign Secretary Anthony Eden became involved in the proposal. He wrote to the Chairman of the Joint Organization of the British Red Cross and Order of St. John. A reply came from Field Marshall Sir Philip Chetwode to say the executive committee had approved the suggestion and that he had ascertained that President Roosevelt would be pleased to accept the gift and that it would be presented to the President by Mr. Norman Davis, Chairman of the American Red Cross.

Mrs. Fowler also raised funds for prisoners of war charities and the Red Cross 'Aid to Russia' Fund that was set up by Clementine Churchill, wife of Prime Minister Sir Winston Churchill. Mrs. Churchill took the trouble to write to Mrs. Fowler on 7th January 1943 to thank her for her kindness and help.

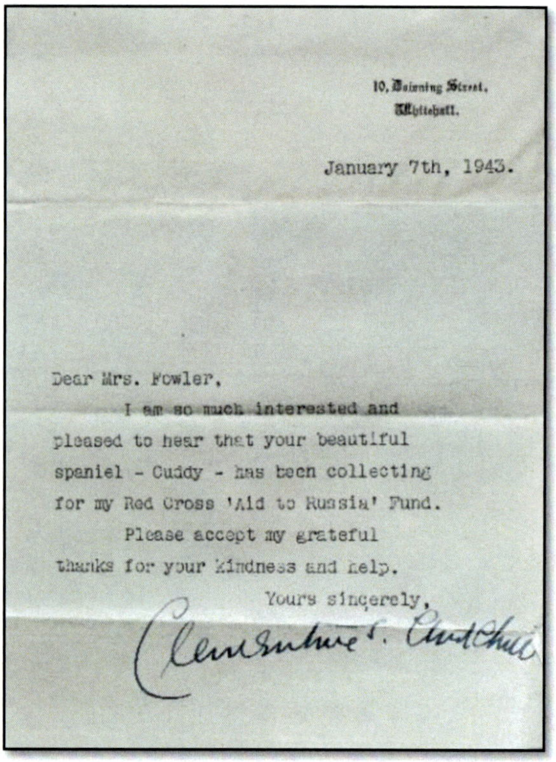

10, Downing Street,
Whitehall.

January 7th, 1943.

Dear Mrs. Fowler,

I am so much interested and pleased to hear that your beautiful spaniel - Cuddy - has been collecting for my Red Cross 'Aid to Russia' Fund.

Please accept my grateful thanks for your kindness and help.

Yours sincerely,

Clementine S. Churchill

Warwickshire War Supplies Service

By November 1939, the Warwickshire War Supplies Service had despatched the following goods to a battalion of the Royal Warwickshire Regiment serving overseas: - 430 pairs of socks, 135 scarves, 45 pairs of mittens, 30 pairs of cuffs, 10 body belts, 4 pullovers, 7 pairs of gloves, 40 balaclava helmets and 5 tin hat linings.

The Leamington Spa Courier dated 22nd August 1941 reported: - "It is no doubt a truism that there are more varieties of war-work going on now than ever before; but few of us realise quite how much valuable service is being contributed freely and without ostentation. It was a revelation to me when I looked in this week at No.18, The Parade, the Leamington depot of the Warwickshire War Supplies Service. I found it a perfect hive of industry, some 20 or more women being busily engaged in sewing, cutting-out, finishing and planning, under the direction of Mrs. Hilder. And then I learned from the Leader [the Hon. C. H. Siddeley] something of the work that is carried on there."

"The depot was opened in the very month war was declared, being founded by Lady Higgins. She, however, left Leamington about a month later, and was succeeded by Lady Siddeley. Some 70 women meet at the depot, which is open three times a week on Mondays, Wednesdays and Fridays. There are also working parties in connection with Holy Trinity Church, St. Mark's Church, Spencer Street Congregational Church, and the Catholic Women's Guild. In addition, there are quite a number of private working parties and many who sew or knit in their own homes."

"And what has all this activity produced? The record is most impressive, especially when one appreciates the quality of the work. There is nothing "shoddy"; everything is well finished and under the expert leadership of Mrs. Hemingway assisted by Mrs. Mitchell, well and economically cut. There is no doubt about the usefulness of the work. Hearing that the depot had provided garments and marked linen for the Warneford Hospital, I asked what they thought of the work and found unqualified and enthusiastic appreciation. "It was invaluable – and they were so nice about it" was the comment."

"And now for the figures. Since the depot was opened, 16,751 hospital requisites and 3,005 comforts have been made and over five miles of material have been used. The work done consists of all kinds of bandages and dressings, hospital linen, such as blankets, cot covers, pillow-cases, hospital clothing, including dressing-gowns, pyjamas, bed-jackets, helpless-case shirts, men's day shirts, bedroom slippers, sisters' coats, etc., clothing for refugees and bomb victims, women's and children's nightgowns, girls' dresses and women's tailored coats, every sort of comfort for H.M. Forces, gas-mask box-covers for recruits, sleeping-bags for first-aid post workers, grenade bags for the Home Guard [400 of these were asked for in 24 hours, and 403 were completed in that time] and overalls for the new Nursery Centre."

"Since last March, 900 dressing-gowns, 600 clothes bags, and 1,700 personal-belongings bags have been made for the County Council Decontamination Stations, in addition to other work. Another valuable piece of service is the provision of an emergency accouchement set *[for women giving birth]* for every public air-raid shelter in Leamington and Warwick. All "bits" are used to make patch-work blankets, most efficiently designed and executed. I don't think an inch of material is wasted."

"But what about finance? Most people would no doubt share my happy conclusion that a grateful Government provided a generous grant which covered all expenses. I was soon disillusioned. Nowt o' t' sort! The Red Cross certainly provides material but that is all and even that does not include the buttons and sewing cotton. The expenses of rent, rates, heating and light – these are borne, incredibly as it may seem, by the workers themselves. They form no light burden for a conservative estimate places the total at something like £120 a year. For this reason an effort is to be made next month in the form of a concert in the Jephson Gardens to raise funds. Meanwhile there are several things the depot needs. At least two more sewing machines are required and can anyone make good button-holes?"

Make Do and Mend

With so many men going away to war, women were left to fight the battle on the home front. Some women enlisted in the forces, some went into the factories or joined the Land Army but for many the battle was fought over the sink, the stove and the sewing machine. There was also a constant stream of government information poured out to remind the nation's housewives that theirs was a war against waste. Rationing and short supply was only part of the story. Stretching what you were able to get as far as possible and beyond was the objective. The make do and mend mission was meant to save valuable resources for the war effort and Britain's women took the cause to their hearts and made it work. From 1941 each person received 66 clothing coupons a year.

A Make Do and Mend scheme was given official support by the Board of Trade in autumn of 1942. A Make Do and Mend pamphlet was issued by the British Ministry of Information alongside promotional posters and a series of instructional leaflets featuring the character 'Mrs Sew and Sew' explaining sewing tips. The intention was

to provide housewives with useful tips for mending or recycling old clothes during the period of rationing. People were encouraged to improve their sewing skills. They were even encouraged to knit items of clothing for members of the armed forces.

The model wartime housewife darned holes, mended tears, unravelled old sweaters and re-knitted them with much ingenuity. She repaired, adapted and reused just about everything. Sleeves of jumpers could be re-knitted in stripes using oddments of brightly coloured wool and a striped pocket to match could be added to the jumper.

One of the booklets advised mothers to exchange their children's outgrown shoes. The ABC of mending explained how to repair every conceivable garment. Under 'C' came collars, cuffs and corsets, "Now that rubber is so scarce, your corset is one of your most precious possessions... Don't pull or stretch your corset more than you must... Watch for the first signs of cracking threads and mend at once." Clothing exchanges were set up by the Women's Voluntary Service [W.V.S.] to help parents clothe their growing children. Women could take their children's outgrown clothes and were given points for the clothes handed in which could be 'spent' on other clothes at the exchange.

The wool companies entered into the spirit of things producing patterns for almost every garment imaginable including swimsuits and underwear. One of their slogans was, "If you can knit, you can do your bit". Rationing forced women to take up their needles and pins for the war effort otherwise their families would go without.

Play Centres and Nurseries - By June 1944 there were two Play Centres in Leamington available for the free use of women worker's children - one at Shrubland Street Schools and the other at St. Peter's School, Augusta Place, each being supervised and managed by experienced staff. It was said that the women workers in the Shrubland Street School area had taken full advantage of the helpful and beneficial facilities offered by the Leamington Education Authority and a large and very happy gathering of children appeared to have found it "a home from home".

There were at least three war-time nurseries in Leamington. Nursery No.1 was at Victoria Lodge, Milverton Hill, No.2 was on Tachbrook Road and No.3 was in Pound Lane.

Recognition for Women

It took a very long time before a thank you to women in the form of a monument was erected and unveiled. Sixty years after the war ended a 22-feet high bronze cenotaph to the Women of World War Two was unveiled in London. Sculpted by John W. Mills the sculpture depicts 17 uniforms representing the different services performed by women during the war, including the Women's Land Army, ladies canteen overalls, a Wren's uniform, a nursing cape, a welder's helmet and a police overcoat. It is situated on Whitehall in London very close to Downing Street. The cenotaph was unveiled by Queen Elizabeth II on 9th July 2005 as part of the 60th anniversary of the end of the war.

Former Speaker of the House of Commons Baroness Betty Boothroyd is the patron of the Women of World War II Trust.

In dedicating the monument to the contribution of seven million women in the war she said, "This monument is dedicated to all the women who served our country and the cause of freedom, in uniform and on the home front."

"It is not by its nature purely a military memorial. It depicts the uniforms of women in the forces alongside the working clothes of those who worked in the factories, the hospitals, the emergency services and the farms."

"I hope that future generations who pass this way will ask themselves, "What sort of women were they?" and look at our history for the answer."

A.R.P Trenches and Air Raid Shelters

The 1937 Air Raid Precautions Act resulted in a statutory requirement for local governments to provide protection for the civilian population. In Leamington Spa that consisted of communal shelters for factories, offices, schools and hospitals and domestic shelters for civilians. The Corporation earmarked basements in the town centre for the protection of civilians against bomb attacks.

A.R.P. instructor Mr. A. J. Smith said whilst talking at a public meeting in 1938 that, "Householders would help themselves to avoid danger by having a protected room in a house or making a garden shelter surrounded by soft soil into which splinters would sink. Anderson shelters were highly recommended, but if a bomb fell nearer than 50 feet away there was little that could be done." He continued, "Should there be an air raid, it was always the safest course to lie down, whether in a building or in the open. Ear plugs were useful, gazing up into the sky is not a good idea - if possible face a wall and protect the back of the head with some soft material."

A.R.P. Trenches

The Morning News dated Wednesday 15th March 1939 reported: - **A.R.P. Trenches in Eagle Recreation Ground – Being Made Water-Tight by Concrete** – Workmen engaged on the A.R.P. trenches in the Eagle Recreation Ground [Shrubland Street] have struck seven springs, according to Councillor R. Wright, who, at the meeting of Leamington Town Council, asked for a statement on the position. He said each morning the men had to pump water out of the trenches before they could start work. It seemed that when the trenches were finished they would be full of water. "Is this the way to spend public money?" he enquired. Councillor G. L. Pain, Chairman of the A.R.P. Committee, said the trenches were being concreted, and would be concreted up to a point above the water level, and water would be kept out. He promised to enquire into the position regarding the trenches which Messrs. Flavel's commenced to dig during the crisis.

The Morning News dated Thursday 27th July 1939 reported that **Warwickshire was to spend £75,000 on Air Raid Trenches** – The A.R.P. Committee's report stated that the provision of A.R.P. shelters by means of trenches was preferable, where possible, to the means of basement-strengthening. The committee made a total of £75,000 available for public shelters.

On 8th September 1939, the Borough Engineer J. Sutcliffe recommended, and it was approved, that two air raid trenches each to accommodate 50 persons should be constructed in Euston Place Gardens for the use of people caught in the street during air raids.

Plans were drawn up in October 1939 for air-raid trenches at Lillington School. The trenches were installed at the rear of the school and playground.

On 12th July 1940, J. A Carter, Vicar of Lillington wrote to the Leamington Spa Courier: - "Sir, on two occasions I have reported the unsatisfactory condition of the air raid shelters at the Lillington Schools, owing to the influx of water into the shelters. The only remedies proposed were periodic pumping and the placing of old desks on the ground, both of which are utterly futile, as is proved this [Thursday] morning when after one day's rain the Headmistress reports that it is impossible for her to enter the shelter even to switch on the electric light, let alone allow small children to enter."

"I have been told, in answer to my complaints, that this condition of affairs only exists after rain; but the ground has been covered with water in the dry weather we have been having. In any case, it is absurd to think that the Germans will only choose a fine day after a prolonged dry spell to drop a bomb on the school during school hours."

"As Chairman of the Managers I consider I have a grave responsibility in this matter, and I feel my only alternative will be to call a meeting of all parents and, after explaining matters to them, close the schools until the Borough Council see fit to take some adequate measures to remedy what has up to now been a waste of the ratepayers' money."

A reply was printed on the 26th July: - Two correspondents have written to us regarding the air raid shelters at Lillington C.E. School. It should be understood that delay in completing the work has been due to the difficulty in obtaining the necessary materials; "priority" is not granted for schemes of this kind. Nor does the government allow timber for seating purposes. However, we are informed that special material which will remedy the dampness of the shelters has just arrived, and as soon as this work has been completed it will be possible to introduce seating of a temporary kind."

Communal Air Raid Shelters

Communal air raid shelters were installed in many places across the town. The most common types were surface built single storey shelters constructed with brick walls and reinforced concrete roofs. By 23rd February 1940 Leamington had public shelter and trench accommodation for 1,559 persons. By 21st June 1940 they could accommodate 2,320 persons. By 25th October 1940, it was reported that 'all trenches and shelters in the Borough were now substantially complete and that there is accommodation for 2,946 persons'. By 21st November 1941, 35 shelters had been approved by the Ministry of Home Security, 25 x 50-person shelters had been completed and there was accommodation for 4,340 persons.

On 5th December 1941, it was reported that 50-person surface type air raid shelters had been locally approved for Lansdowne Crescent, Villiers Street, Somers Place and Prince's Drive. However, the Prince's Drive shelter did not go on to be approved by the Ministry of Home Security.

By 2nd January 1942 there were five more 50-person shelters giving shelter accommodation for 4,590 persons; approval had been received to install electric lighting in 20 of the public shelters. By 24th April 1942, 40 x 50-person shelters had been authorised and 34 had been completed.

These numbers appear to show that plans changed over time regarding how many shelters would be required, because in January 1941 it was reported at the A.R.P. Committee that the public shelters were all now completed - eight of them already had electric mains supply and electric light had recently been installed into the Satchwell Street shelter. Approval had also been received to install a surface type shelter in the grounds of the Regent Hotel.

The Morning News dated Tuesday 24th October 1939 reported: - **School Air Raid Shelters – Warwickshire's £78,000 Scheme for Protection – Provides for Approximately 26,000 Children** – Warwickshire County Council, at their meeting in May, placed the sum of £20,000 at the disposal of the County Education Committee for the provision of air raid shelters for school children. It was thought that this sum would cover the cost of all the work which could be done during the summer holidays, and that it would provide for about 6,000 children. The outbreak of hostilities made it necessary to accelerate the work, and it soon became evident that a much larger number of children must be protected if their parents were to send them to school with confidence. When the £20,000 was nearly exhausted the Emergency Committee for

Civil Defence was consulted, and it was decided to extend the programme of construction and to allow the County Architect to let contracts amounting to not more than £50,000. What it is hoped may now be a final survey has been made, and this discloses that the Higher Education Committee will need to provide protection for approximately 6,000 children at an estimated cost of £18,000, and the number of children attending elementary schools for whom protection is considered necessary is estimated at 20,000 out of a total of about 30,000. This will involve expenditure amounting to approximately £60,000, and at yesterday's meeting of the County Education Committee it was decided to ask the Finance Committee to recommend the County Council to increase the sums placed at their disposal to the following amounts - Higher Education, £18,000; Elementary Education, £60,000.

A letter was received by the A.R.P. Committee from the Secretary of the Royal Leamington Spa Improvement Association in March 1940 suggesting that the Air Raid Shelters in Euston Place should be covered by flower beds instead of only turf. It is not known whether the suggestion was acted upon.

The lamp post on the right of this photo of the Parade has a sign affixed directing people to the nearest air raid shelter. Interesting to see the Midland Bank, International Stores, Haunch of Venison Inn and the Cadena Café and there is only one car.

On 21st March 1940, the A.R.P. Officer reported that he had been in touch with Sidney Flavel & Co. Ltd regarding the trenches dug in the Eagle Recreation Ground by the company in September 1938 and that they promised to fill in the trenches by the end of May 1940.

On 21st June 1940, the A.R.P. Committee resolved that adequate first aid boxes would be supplied for all air raid shelters.

It wasn't only the Town Council and the A.R.P. authorities that were providing shelters for use by the public. In 1940, the Chamber of Trade was anxious to proceed with a scheme to provide cellar accommodation for the shopping public in the event of being caught in the street or the shops during an air raid. Many of the shops on the Parade and surrounding streets have cellars.

Notices were provided which stated: - These premises have cellar accommodation sufficient for --- persons which is available in the event of an air raid during business hours. The shelter offered to the public does not purport to be in any way bomb-proof, but it is felt that some protection will be given against splinters and flying glass.

Members of the public availing themselves of the shelter accommodation do so at their own risk.

On 26th July 1940, the Borough Engineer reported the approval of the Parks and Gardens Committee to the construction of an air raid shelter under Adelaide Road Bridge at a total cost of approximately £23 - work to commence forthwith. Also in July 1940, the Board of Education gave permission for the construction of above ground shelters to be built at St. Paul's School in substitution for trenches. The surface shelter at Beech Lawn was complete except for the earth covering and provided accommodation for 86 persons. However, a shortage of cement was delaying construction of the Satchwell Street shelters.

On 13th August 1940, it was recommended that a railway arch in Bath Place be adapted as a shelter in order to accommodate approximately 160 children from Bath Place Church of England School - and also to substitute a brick built shelter for trenches for the remainder of the children.

On 27th September 1940, it was reported that surface shelters at Beech Lawn and Adelaide Road had been completed.

In October 1940, the County Council approved construction of a shelter in Mill Walk. Messrs. Clarke Bros. of Whitnash put in a tender for £34. 10s. which was accepted. The installation of electric light in the Windsor Street / Warwick Street shelter was also approved.

The Morning News dated Thursday 14th November 1940 reported: - **A.R.P. in Leamington – Domestic Shelters Scheme – Macs for Wardens: Committee Powerless** – Leamington now has air raid shelter accommodation for 2,946 persons. Approval has been given for a shelter in Mill Walk, for which a tender of £34. 10s. has been accepted [from Messrs. Clark Bros of Whitnash]. The A.R.P. Committee reported to the Town Council this week that the preliminary work regarding domestic shelters in the Borough was proceeding satisfactorily, and that tenders had been received for the constructional work and were being considered in conjunction with the County Council.

Councillor Charles W. Gardner asked that air raid wardens should be equipped with mackintoshes for use on duty, but Councillor George Pain said the committee had no authority to supply any costumes for this work at the expense of the County Council or the Government. The Committee would be sympathetic if the Town Council would agree to bear the cost. Alderman C. Davis said, "We have no power to do that."

At the A.R.P. committee meeting on 27th December 1940, it was reported that 24 surface type shelters had been constructed and 5 were in progress of construction. 23 houses had been supplied with blast walls.

In January 1941, an order was received [S.R. & O. 2210/40] making Leamington a 'specified area under the Civil Defence Act 1939' thus requiring the provision of air raid shelter accommodation in commercial buildings employing more than 50 persons.

On 1st July 1941 plans were passed by the Highways and Town Planning Committee for two air raid shelters at the laundry in Hitchman Road for the Leamington Spa Laundry Ltd. The erection of an air raid shelter in Church Street was approved subject to satisfactory arrangements with the church authorities.

On 1st September 1941, it was reported to the A.R.P. Emergency Sub-Committee that Warwickshire County Council had approved the installation of electric lighting in the Cashmore Avenue air-raid shelter.

In 1941, a public Air Raid Shelter was installed in the grounds of St. John's Church in Tachbrook Road. The Vicar described the site as, "A grass plot comprising the southern portion of the churchyard and lying between the south wall of the church and the north boundary of the grounds of the vicarage". Formal notice that the Council had given up possession of the land on which the air raid shelter had been built was given on 26th

April 1946. The shelter was removed later in the year but was still causing the vicar problems in November 1947 when the Borough Engineer wrote to inform him that he regretted that the reinstatement of the site had not yet been completed - he went on to say that he had asked the Parks and Gardens Engineer to proceed with the work as soon as possible.

The Morning News dated 10th February 1942 reported: - **Leamington Air Raid Shelters – Check to the Provision of Further Accommodation** – With reference to Leamington's air raid shelter scheme, inclement weather has meant that no increase in accommodation has been made over the past month. However, work on the installation of electric lighting in 20 shelters is now proceeding. These details were contained in the report of the Air Raid Precautions Committee submitted to the meeting of the Town Council yesterday. The report further stated that the Ministry of Home Security had not approved the proposal for the erection of a shelter in Prince's Drive, and requested the reconsideration of the siting of the shelter. Approval had been granted for the strengthening of school air raid shelters used by the general public, and in this direction work is to be carried out at Augusta Place and Leicester Street Schools.

It was reported at the A.R.P. Committee meeting on 27th March 1942 that there was constant theft of keys from the glass cases affixed to the public air raid shelters in the town. It was resolved that the glass frames and keys would be removed and that suitable arrangements would be made for the keys to be made available when required.

The Morning News dated 10th April 1942 reported: - **Boys Damage Air Raid Shelters – Could Not Have Been Used Had Sirens Sounded** – Three local boys were before the magistrates at Leamington Juvenile Court, yesterday, for wilfully damaging air-raid shelters. Two boys, aged 12, were accused of committing damage to the extent of 10/6 to air-raid shelters in Tachbrook Road and St. John's Churchyard, and it was stated that the glass key container had been smashed in each case and the key removed. In the event of an "alert" the shelters could not have been opened. The parents of both boys were ordered to pay one guinea, with costs of 10/6 to cover the damage. In the case of the third boy, aged 11, it was stated that the key to a shelter in Prospect Road had been removed. A fine of 5/-, with 10/6 costs for the damage, was imposed.

Margaret Slater née Sargent recalled, "My father was the verger at St. John's Church. He was an Air Raid Warden before War was declared. The Warden's post in our District was in the Home for Incurables, just above us in Tachbrook Road. In air-raids, my brother and I were wrapped in blankets and taken to the Air-Raid shelter there. I can't remember much about it. It was dark when we went and we went to sleep and were there all night. Mother stayed with us, but father was in and out doing Warden's duties."

On 29th May 1945, the Highways and Planning Committee were advised that the removal of surface type air-raid shelters was already being discussed with the County Surveyor.

Advert: - Leamington Spa Courier dated 8th September 1939.

Leamington History Group member Jeff Clarke attended Bath Place School after the war had ended. He says, "There were still air-raid shelters on the playground behind the school, stretching from the back wall to Lower Avenue and there were black-out curtains on a metal pole, fastened to the inside of the wooden doors."

Millicent Plester, a teacher at Clapham Terrace School said in 1980, "Mr. E. A. Baxter was the headmaster. He was also the Air Raid Warden for the Clapham Terrace District. During the war, we had brick air-raid shelters at the back of the school, on land that belongs to Warneford Hospital now. We had to practise going in."

This September 2008 photo shows the sealed off entrance to an underground air raid shelter which was located in the corner of the playground to the former Leamington College for Girls in York Road [NGR317654]. It has since been demolished.

A number of books and people state that two shelters existed in the Great Western railway goods yard in Old Warwick Road, Leamington [NGR315652]. They were supposedly positioned side by side, one being covered in earth, the other a rectangular surface shelter built of brick and concrete with brick blast walls at the entrances.

It was thought that this photo shows the remnants of what appears to be a Stanton air raid shelter that were quite numerous at R.A.F airfields.

However, a few years ago, a retired railway man informed local historian Derek Billings that it was not a shelter but a steamer for bending planks; it seems that the site was a timber yard years ago. Another alternative to consider is that it was originally built as an air raid shelter and then modified for use as a steamer after WW2? Both were demolished in the early 1990s when the yard was sold off.

The Stanton AR50 air-raid shelters were manufactured by the Stanton Ironworks Co. Ltd. in Derbyshire.

They were built of pre-cast concrete and had arch-shaped sides. They could be built in any length but generally consisted of 18 sections that were bolted together to form a standard Air Ministry shelter for 50 people. The entrance could be bricked lined and with concrete steps [if required] with an emergency escape hatch at the rear. They were often above ground or semi-sunk, but for added protection and concealment purposes, further blast walls were added and all covered with soil and turf.

The Air Raid shelter at Brandon Parade in November 1939, with Elmley Lodge in the background.

Brandon Parade taken on 11th December 2012. Marlborough House has replaced Elmley Lodge.

Domestic Air Raid Shelters

Anderson Shelter - The standard external type of air raid shelter was the 'sectional steel shelter' known as the Anderson Shelter, which was named after Sir John Anderson, a member of Churchill's war-time Cabinet. They were delivered in sections and constructed by the householder. Anderson Shelters were offered at a cost of £7, to men earning more than £5 per week, or were given free to households earning less than £5 per week. 1½ million were distributed before the war started and in total 3½ million were produced. Distribution started in February 1939 and those households that were in possession of one were required by law to have them constructed and earthed by 11th June 1939.

Anderson Shelters were surface mounted or partially underground. The construction was of curved corrugated sheeting and covered over with soil or sandbags to provide bomb blast protection - which did make a difference. People would sit on benches on opposite sides of the shelter. The floor was generally just earth, unless some enterprising builder had concreted it, but that was rare. They were said to be, "cold, dark and horrible - we huddled together for warmth, and the ground would shake when a bomb dropped close by. In wet weather, they would often become waterlogged. It was scary, there was such relief when the 'all clear' sounded."

Some people, both adults and children, wore a one-piece siren suit to keep them warm in the air raid shelters - these days we would probably say that it was combination of a 'onesie', a boiler suit and a track suit. It appears that Churchill invented it in the 1930s as a leisure suit and in a number of photographs he can be seen wearing one. It gained its name due to the sirens sounding when there was an air raid.

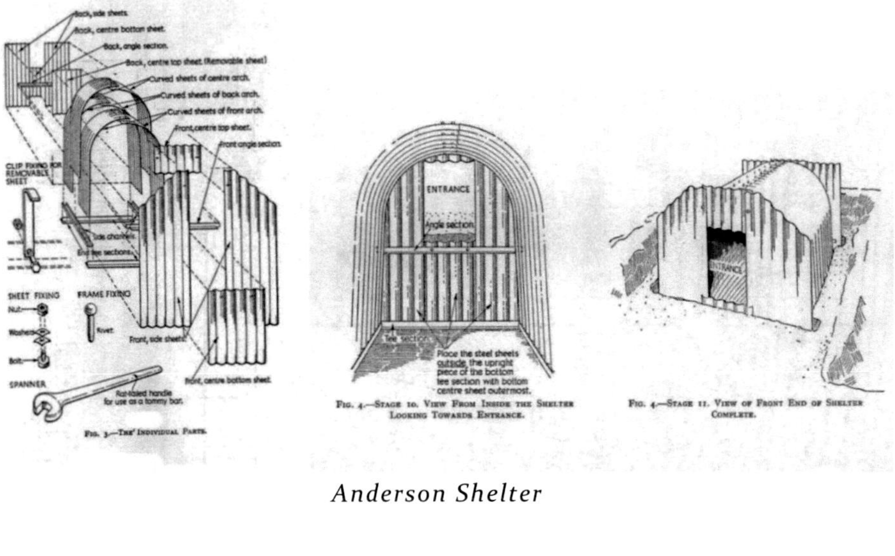

Anderson Shelter

Morrison Shelter - Self-assembly Morrison shelters were introduced in March 1941. They were designed by John Fleetwood Baker and named after Herbert Morrison, a British Labour politician and member of the war-time coalition Government. The shelter, whose purpose was to absorb the impact of falling debris during an air-raid, was a sort of cage made from heavy steel with welded wire mesh sides on a metal lath floor. It was designed for indoor use and was favoured by many families who preferred to shelter within their homes, although they were really for people without gardens. The Morrison shelter was around 6ft 6in. in length [2m], 4ft wide [1.2m] and 2ft 6in. high [0.75m] and often they would be covered with a table cloth and would double up as a table. One side could be lifted up allowing enough space for 2 or 3 people to crawl inside. By November 1941 more than 500,000 shelters had been distributed free of charge. Other proprietary designs were steel Consol shelters and pre-cast concrete Raidsafe shelters.

Leamington businesses were obviously quick to spot a business opportunity as the following advert in the Morning News dated Friday 15th September 1939 shows: - **A.R.P. Shelters** – The Clayton Fireplace Co. Ltd., Clarendon Avenue [opposite Oxford Street] - A Demonstration shelter will be open for public inspection tomorrow [Saturday], September 16 until further notice – Open every day, including Sundays – Shelters fitted complete with wireless, electric light and heating – Prices on application.

Perhaps this is a good time to ask you to consider what it would have been like to experience a bombing raid; how frightened would you be for yourself and your family? What would you be thinking? How would you cope? At night, it would be worse, maybe cold, damp and even very wet, and certainly noisy.

Getting to an Anderson shelter in the back yard, in the dark, in the middle of the night, listening to the awful wailing of the siren - and then waiting! And there could have been a few inches of water on the floor. We also have to consider that in the 1940s the chances are that it would be mothers that would look after babies. Imagine how tiring it would be holding a baby for hours on end?

This very scenario resulted in the Mayoress putting the following in the Morning News dated 22nd November 1940: - **Can You Help?** – The Mayoress of Leamington [Mrs. M. S. Moore] yesterday issued an appeal for cradles or any type of baskets suitable for babies and small children to sleep in. An inspection of air-raid shelters following the sounding of the "Alert" has shown that many mothers have been obliged to stand, perhaps for long periods, with their babies in their arms, and naturally this sort of thing proves a great strain. Those able to provide such articles [and clothes baskets would serve the purpose] are asked to deposit them at the Mayoress's Parlour, Town Hall, where they will be gratefully received.

The Morning News dated Monday 9th September 1940 reported: - '**Make Your Own Air Raid Shelter – And Protect Your Windows** – A considerable degree of air raid protection can be attained by putting into effect the suggestions contained in the Ministry of Home Security booklet, "Your Home as an Air-Raid Shelter," which was issued recently and is available at any Post Office, price 3d.

It is emphasised that the average well-built dwelling-house offers a considerable degree of protection against blast and splinters – as well as, of course, aerial machine gun fire and splinters from anti-aircraft shells. There are several ways in which shelter can be provided for members of a household. A brick and concrete shelter may be built in the garden or attached to the house. If this is not practicable, householders should turn at once to the preparation of a refuge room inside the house.

Protection of Windows – In view of the very large proportion of injuries in recent raids which has been due to flying glass it is of the utmost importance that immediate attention should be paid to the treatment of windows. The scattering of splinters of glass is best prevented by: - [1] Net fabric, like lace curtains, or transparent film stuck to the whole surface and to a margin of the window frame. [2] Strips of lace curtain or fabric of any kind or transparent film or really stout paper stuck on in strips at intervals which leave not more than 6 square inches of glass clear. A suitable adhesive can be made in the following way: 2 level tablespoonsful of plain or self-raising flour should be mixed with 3 tablespoonsful of cold water to make a smooth paste; then mix in a piece of washing soda about the size of a large almond. Add half-pint boiling water to mixture and stir briskly. Heat in a double saucepan for 10 to 15 minutes. Use when fairly fresh.'

The Morning News dated Tuesday 29th October 1940 reported: - '**Household Shelters – What to do to Prevent Flooding** – Householders are advised to take immediate measures to see that their steel shelters are not made uninhabitable by flooding during the forthcoming winter. This matter is of great importance, in view of the possibility that people may have to spend frequent and prolonged spells in their shelters at night.

The experience of last winter should have shown clearly enough which are the cases where flooding is temporary only and those where, on account of the winter rise of the subsoil water level above the bed of the shelter, major measures are required. The most obvious measure is to provide a sump into which the water can drain; and, in this connection, a useful tip is to place a bucket in a cavity in a corner of the shelter. The bucket can be lifted out and emptied as occasion requires. Householders may help themselves in this matter by seeing that the floor of the shelter slopes in the direction of the bucket.

To help keep the floor dry, it will help greatly if a course of bricks is laid down, and some rough flooring – linoleum, planking, or other suitable material – placed on top. Duckboards, if they can be obtained, would be most useful. Externally, much may be done to keep the shelter water-tight. The first thing is to see that there is the proper amount of earth over the shelter, and that it is thoroughly packed. This will prevent any water coming in from above. Another measure that might well be taken is the digging of a channel around the outside of the shelter and seeing that the ground slopes away from the shelter entrance.

Keeping warm in shelters during the winter nights is something about which people will have to exercise their ingenuity. Hot bricks, wrapped in a rug or a cloth, would provide much comfort. Shelter owners, however are warned against burning fuels which might give off dangerous fumes.'

Rationing and Food

Before the Second World War the country had been importing around 60% of its food, much of it from America and Canada. The loss of ships through enemy action forced a rethink that included rationing and using as much land as possible for food production. The population was urged to 'Dig for Victory'. This was a government campaign that encouraged people to grow their own food by transforming their gardens into allotments to grow vegetables, as well as encouraging councils to do the same with sports pitches, parks and gardens.

As the prospect of war grew more likely, the Government restarted the Women's Land Army in June 1939 - it had been an idea that was was used during the First World War. It started off as a voluntary organisation, but later women were conscripted by the Ministry of Labour and sent to help farmers cultivate their land, assist with the animals and maintain farm equipment such as tractors.

Public Information Leaflet No.1 dated July 1939 stated: - "It is very important that at the outset of an emergency people should not buy larger quantities of foodstuffs than they normally buy and normally require. The Government are making arrangements to ensure that there will be sufficient supplies of food, and that every person will be able to obtain regularly his or her fair share; and they will take steps to prevent any sudden rise in prices. But if some people try to buy abnormal quantities, before the full scheme of control is working, they will be taking food which should be available for others."

"If you wish, and are able to lay in a small extra store of non-perishable foodstuffs, there is no reason why you should not do so. They will be an additional insurance. But you should collect them now and not when an emergency arises."

In December 1939, the Ministry of Food requested that the Town Council appoint a specially authorised officer to deal with foodstuffs which might be affected by poison gas. Mr. Arthur J. Smith, the Sanitary Inspector was appointed as Decontamination Officer. *[Note: On 30th May 1945, the Medical Officer reported that the Ministry of Food had disbanded the Food Decontamination Service].*

Very early in the war, people started to drink more coffee and cocoa in order to eke out their favourite drink - tea. Before the days of smoking bans in public places and government health warnings, smoking had a different image and was seen as being quite acceptable. Wherever people lived there were long queues for popular brands such as Senior Service, Woodbines and Players Weights.

Wednesday 21st February 1940 saw the official opening of the Soldiers canteen near the railway bridges in High Street. The Leamington and Warwick Soroptimist Club undertook the main responsibility for establishing the canteen. Dr. Agnes Young [President] said that one of the Soroptimist aims was service, and they believed that in tackling the canteen they were meeting a very real need. The idea of the canteen was due to the Mayoress and Mrs. Councillor Bragg. Mr. G. H. Bailey provided the linoleum and also spent many hours helping to prepare the canteen. The Leamington Priors Gas Co. had generously provided the gas fittings free of charge, and Mr. Sims had lent a wireless set.

Dr. Young said, "There is a host of others whom I can't mention individually, but I should like to thank the various organisations who have promised to co-operate in running the canteen – the Inner Wheel, the Women's Voluntary Services, the Women's Section of the British Legion, and the British Women's Temperance Association." The Mayor [Alderman Martin S. Moore] said, "We know that the troops are catered for very well at the top end of the town by the Y.M.C.A.; but waiting for buses naturally entails a lot of waiting, and some of the soldiers have taken refuge at the Police Station. Games and darts will fill in the time here while they are waiting for the 'bus'. It gives me very great pleasure to declare the canteen open."

Colonel J. L. Mellor who is in charge of the welfare arrangements for the troops in Warwickshire said that he came to Leamington every week to see his mother, and he had been very much struck with the need of some place to which the troops could go while waiting for buses to return to their quarters. "I do look upon this enterprise as a very great move in the right direction, and one which will be greatly appreciated by the troops stationed in the locality. I am sure it will be a great success." On Saturday 16th March, no fewer than 300 soldiers used the canteen, with "the Mayor and Mayoress being two of the busiest helpers".

Many readers of this book will be aware of the terrible bombing of Coventry on 14th November 1940 during operation Moonlight Sonata, which caused over 500 fatalities, over 400 serious injuries and left buildings in the City of Coventry almost totally destroyed. Leamington had its own problems as it was also bombed on the same night also with loss of life but it didn't stop the people of Leamington helping where they could, as reported in the Morning News dated Tuesday 19th November 1940: -

'Coventry Bombed get their Sunday Dinners – How Spa Answered City's S.O.S. – Splendid Work of Voluntary Helpers – During the weekend Leamington was called on to give succour to a large number of Coventry people who were bombed out of their homes during Thursday night's devastating raid on the city. A large fleet of motor coaches brought several hundreds of these hapless but nevertheless courageous people to the Spa, where they were provided with sleeping accommodation in various church halls in the town. There were many offers of voluntary assistance at this end, and some exceptionally valuable help was accorded the authorities by the Leamington Priors Gas Company who, in response to an S.O.S. received late on Saturday night, undertook the heavy task of cooking over 150 meals at their Regent Street Showrooms.

W.V.S. Members as Cooks – So thorough were the arrangements, especially having regard to the short notice, that this particular party were assured of excellently prepared Sunday dinners, and the catering arrangements made at other centres in the town were no less efficient. The food served at the Gas Showrooms was provided by the Public Assistance authorities, and was cooked by members of the Women's Voluntary Service under the supervision of Miss Zita Fitzgerald, the Company's Home Service Advisor, who was also able to rely on the co-operation of other members of the Company from the General Manager downwards. On all sides the evacuees expressed warm gratitude for what had been done for them, and no praise can be too high for the manner in which the voluntary workers tackled the task of ensuring that nothing which would make for the comfort of those in need was left undone. One and all worked with splendid spirit.'

Rationing and Food

In September 1939, a Food Control Committee was established at Leamington Spa to oversee all aspects of the imminent food rationing programme. It consisted of 15 members, five of whom were representatives of the retail food trade in the Borough, the remainder being representatives of the consumers. Representatives of the food trade were: - Mr. Francis Warner [grocers], Mr. George Purcell [butchers], Mr. W. H. Lickorish [Co-operative Society], Mr. B. V. Bishop and Mr. H. C. Newton [nominated by the Chamber of Trade]. Consumer representatives were: - The Mayor, Alderman Dickinson, Councillors Mrs. Bragg, H. J. Pratt, R. Wright, the Rev. F. A. Bunn, Mr. H. J. Dawson and Mr. Leslie Overall. At this early stage there were two vacancies still to be filled.

The Mayor was elected chairman, with Mr. Dawson vice-chairman. The Town Clerk became the Food Executive Officer and Mr. W. E. Owen [the Borough Librarian] became his deputy. [On 12th August 1940, most of the existing members were re-elected. Mr. A. H. Swadling became the Trade Union representative and Alderman Davis and Mrs. Pollock were added to the names already mentioned].

Although rationing had not yet begun, people were reminded that hoarding food was illegal, and that shopkeepers should not sell excessive supplies to individuals.

By 20th October 1939, after two weeks of frantic work, the preparation of ration books for every resident of Leamington was almost complete.

Working in the Town Hall, under the guidance of the Food Control Committee, the task was carried out by shifts of up to 32 volunteers.

Petrol was the first item to be rationed in September 1939. Food rationing began on 8th January 1940, with butter, bacon and sugar. Meat, tea, cheese and other groceries followed on later that year. Clothes were rationed between 1941 and 1949, soap 1942-1950 and petrol 1939-1950. Chocolates and sweets were rationed from 26th July 1942. The first attempt to de-ration sweets came in April 1949, but demand outstripped supply and so after four months they were put back on ration. They were finally de-rationed by Minister of Food, Gwilym Lloyd George, on the first week of February 1953, although sugar wasn't de-rationed until September 1953. Food rationing ended completely in July 1954 when cheese and meat came off the ration.

The rationing of food had less of an impact on farmers and rural folk than it did on town folk. Many rural families grew vegetables in gardens and allotments, kept chickens and pigs and could collect nature's harvest from the fields and hedgerows without worrying about vouchers. The villages still had their queues, but there was usually enough bread to go around.

The weekly ration *per person, per week* for bacon and ham was 4oz, [113 grams], sugar 8oz, [227 grams], tea 2oz, [57 grams], milk 3 pints [1,800 ml], which sometimes dropped to 2 pints, [1,200 ml], cheese 2oz, [57 grams] which sometimes rose to 4oz [113 grams], and even up to 8oz. [227 grams]. Cooking fat started at 2oz, [57 grams], and although it went to 4oz, [113 grams], it often dropped back to 2oz, [57 grams], margarine 4oz, [113 grams], and butter 2oz, [57 grams]. Jam and marmalade was 1lb, [454 grams] every 2 months.

In addition to the above, as from Monday 11th March 1940, you were entitled to 1s. 11d. [9p], worth of meat a week. Offal was originally unrationed, but at times formed part of the meat ration. One egg a week, if available, sometimes dropping to one every two weeks, and one packet of dried eggs every four weeks. The amount of sweets allowed fluctuated between a high of 16oz [454 grams] per month and a low of 8oz [227 grams] per month, but as the war continued and shortages intensified, having a ration book didn't guarantee that sweets could be found and bought. In 1945 it was 12oz [340 grams] of sweets every four weeks. Fish, tripe and sausages were available, if you were prepared to wait for some time in a queue - but even then, you may not get any.

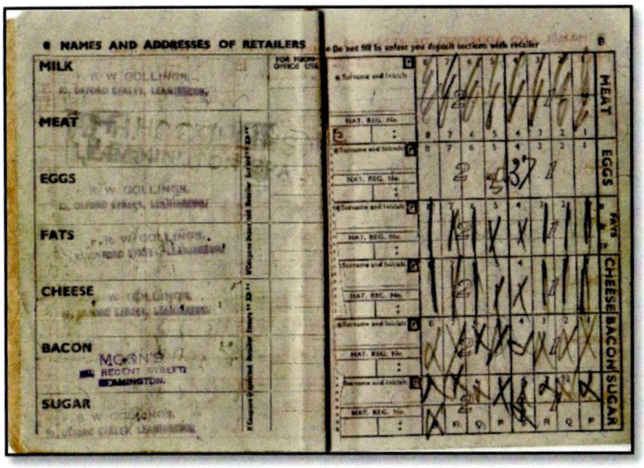

There was also a monthly points system; for example, 12 points allowed you to buy one can of fish or meat, or 2lb. [907 grams] of dried fruit or 8lb. [3.6kg] of split peas. Vegetables and salad were not rationed but were in such short supply that for many people they might as well have been.

As from 1st October 1941 there was a 100% Government grant to provide milk for schoolchildren. By Christmas 1941 some 85% of all school children were receiving the free milk.

In 1943 new ration books and identity cards [for those over 16 years of age] were issued from the Food Office at 3 Regent Grove. Adults received a general [buff] book and children a child's [green] one. This time the ration books and clothing ration books were bound together, although they were detachable. Everything was issued in one visit according to the person's surname. As an example, people with surnames beginning with the letter 'F' had to visit on Monday 7th June 1943, 'Ga-Gi on Tuesday 8th and Go-Gy on Wednesday 9th. The office was open from 9.30am until 1.30pm and 2.30pm until 6.00pm.

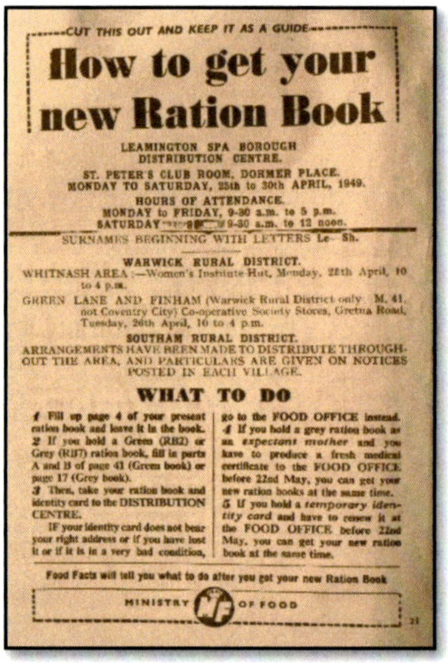

CUT THIS OUT AND KEEP IT AS A GUIDE

How to get your new Ration Book

LEAMINGTON SPA BOROUGH DISTRIBUTION CENTRE.

ST. PETER'S CLUB ROOM, DORMER PLACE.
MONDAY TO SATURDAY, 25th to 30th APRIL, 1949.

HOURS OF ATTENDANCE.
MONDAY to FRIDAY, 9-30 a.m. to 5 p.m.
SATURDAY 9-30 a.m. to 12 noon.

SURNAMES BEGINNING WITH LETTERS Le—Sh.

WARWICK RURAL DISTRICT.

WHITNASH AREA:—Women's Institute Hut, Monday, 25th April, 10 to 4 p.m.

GREEN LANE AND FINHAM (Warwick Rural District only M. 41, not Coventry City) Co-operative Society Stores, Gretna Road, Tuesday, 26th April, 10 to 4 p.m.

SOUTHAM RURAL DISTRICT.

ARRANGEMENTS HAVE BEEN MADE TO DISTRIBUTE THROUGHOUT THE AREA, AND PARTICULARS ARE GIVEN ON NOTICES POSTED IN EACH VILLAGE.

WHAT TO DO

1 Fill up page 4 of your present ration book and leave it in the book.
2 If you hold a Green (RB2) or Grey (RB7) ration book, fill in parts A and B of page 41 (Green book) or page 17 (Grey book).
3 Then, take your ration book and identity card to the DISTRIBUTION CENTRE.

IF your identity card does not bear your right address or if you have lost it or if it is in a very bad condition, go to the FOOD OFFICE instead.
4 If you hold a grey ration book as an *expectant mother* and you have to produce a fresh medical certificate to the FOOD OFFICE before 22nd May, you can get your new ration books at the same time.
5 If you hold a *temporary identity card* and have to renew it at the FOOD OFFICE before 22nd May, you can get your new ration book at the same time.

Food Facts will tell you what to do after you get your new Ration Book

MINISTRY OF FOOD

New ration books were issued in 1949, but this time had to be collected from St. Peter's Club Room at Dormer Place. This reminder was printed in the Morning News dated 21st April 1949.

Shops Opening Hours

On Thursday 24th October 1940, at a meeting of Leamington Chamber of Trade, it was decided to ask members to close their shops during the winter at black-out time. They also agreed to ask the Borough Council to make a closing order for all shops to close at 6.00pm each day.

In November 1940, the Borough Council issued an Order affecting the hours of closure for shops between 17th November 1940 and 2nd March 1941. Briefly, the Order gave the general hours of closing for shops in the Borough as 7.30pm on Saturdays and 6.00pm on other days. In the case of barbers and hairdressers it was 8.00pm on Saturdays and 7.00pm on other days. Half days remained at 1.00pm. This Order did not affect the sales of newspapers and periodicals, tobacco and smokers' requisites nor sweets etc.

The Morning News dated Monday 18th November 1940 reported: - '**Early Closing of Shops** – The shopping public are reminded that the Defence Regulation 60A, made by the Secretary of State, Home Department, brings earlier closing of shops into operation under the shops [Early Closing] Act, 1928, from 17th November until 2nd March. On and after today the general closing hour will be 6.00pm.'

In mid-July 1941, the Mayor said that because of the food position, the tea room at the Pump Room was to be closed daily between 1.00pm and 3.00pm, which included the busy lunch time period. The Mayor told the Leamington Town Council that the committee had been reluctant to take this step. The tea room was originally opened to provide morning coffee and afternoon tea and they thought those services should continue. The staff problem was also difficult but when conditions permitted the committee would be glad to revert to the old system.

Warwickshire War Agricultural Executive Committee

The Leamington Spa Courier dated 22nd September 1939 reported the: - '**Ploughing up of 25,000 acres of Warwickshire grassland** – The National Campaign for an increase in the production of food is being carried out in the County of Warwick by the Warwickshire War Agricultural Executive Committee, with the assistance of six District Committees. The Executive Committee, which has already held three meetings since the War began and is now meeting weekly, consists of the following: - Col. C. J. H. Wheatley, Berkswell Hall [Chairman], Mr. F. Cattell, Falcon Lodge, Sutton Coldfield, Mrs. Fielden O.B.E. Kineton House, [Chairman of the Women's Land Army in Warwickshire], Mr. R. H. A. Holbech, Farnborough Hall [Chairman of the Cultivation and Finance Committee], Mr. A. Roden, District Organiser of the Transport and General Workers Union, Captain H. V. Terry, Ragley Estate office, Captain George L. Pain, formerly County Land Agent, whose headquarters have been established at No.2, Market Place, Warwick, has been appointed Executive Officer of the Committee, and Mr. L. Edgar Stephens, [Clerk of the County Council] its secretary.'

Each of the six districts had a District Committee, assisted by a District Officer; these committees also met weekly. Leamington Borough came under 'D' District. Mr. R. Richmond was the chairman and Mr. J. Milne Redhead the District Officer.

Each District Committee served as the 'eyes and ears' of the Executive Committee [to which the Ministry of Agriculture and Fisheries had delegated wide powers] in respect of all matters affecting food production. Advisors were appointed in each parish, or group of parishes, to give advice to the committees as to which land should be ploughed up, what land was not being properly cultivated, labour shortages etc. The principal task of each committee was to decide how much of the total apportionment for the county [25,000 acres] should be ploughed up, and to see that it was ploughed up and sown with a suitable crop. The first priority was to devote as much of the newly ploughed land as possible to the growing of cereals and potatoes.

In addition, they assisted farmers to obtain a good supply of labour, supplies of seed, fertilisers, spraying materials, machinery and implements. They also facilitated the use of any tractors and steam tackle in the District and organised measures for the destruction of rabbits, rats, rooks, sparrows and other pests.

In December 1940, a letter was received by the Town Clerk from the Ministry of Agriculture suggesting the establishment, in districts of more than 20,000 population, of a Horticultural Committee to encourage food production in allotments and private gardens. It was recommended that this new committee be constituted. Mr. Allsopp, the Hon. Secretary of the newly formed Leamington Horticultural Society said that his organisation would be glad to co-operate with the new committee.

In 1980, Grace Meadow recalled her time with the 'War-Ag' [Warwickshire War Agricultural Executive Committee]. "When I joined the War-Ag the offices had moved from Warwick to Nos. 6 and 12 Guy's Cliffe Avenue, Leamington, and the 100 or so staff filled every available space, - bathrooms and attics included. The bath was covered with a trestle table top to hold piles of forms and files."

"There was no central heating and the upper rooms had very small gas fires, usually with several broken elements so consequently we often worked in coats and woollen gloves. If anyone complained of the cold they were told to put on more clothes. I remember one occasion when one of the girls asked if we would be paid extra for working on Sunday and the answer was, "The troops don't get paid extra for fighting on Sunday so why should you for working on Sunday?" There was no answer to that."

"Departments were many and varied - horticulture, drainage, lands, feeding stuffs, and fertilisers to name but a few, and labour, which included the call-up and farm workers and hostels for P.O.W's and displaced persons from Estonia, Latvia, Lithuania and Poland."

"Camps were set up where parties of children with their teachers came from 60 schools in all parts of the county to help with the Warwickshire corn and potato harvests."

"Training schemes in agriculture and horticulture were organised for the rehabilitation of men invalided out of the forces. Holiday camps were situated mainly in fruit picking areas - oh! - those endless warrants that had to be made out authorising cheap rail travel for campers and their bicycles - a necessary piece of equipment for reaching the farms."

"It was an interesting job where we learned that growing food is much more than just sowing and reaping and that animals need constant care. I shall never forget how surprised one new girl was when told that milk had to be cooled."

In December 1939, the Town Clerk referred to the importance attached to allotments by the Ministry of Agriculture and Fisheries in view of war conditions. It appeared that the number of vacant plots available would for the time being be likely to meet the demand in Leamington. The Town Clerk also pointed out that local authorities had the powers to provide seeds etc. at cost price to allotment holders.

Jephson Gardens

It seems strange to think that the subject of vegetables in the Jephson Gardens could be described as "Revolutionary", but that is exactly the word that was used in the Morning News dated Wednesday 15th April 1942. '**Vegetables To Be Grown In Jephson Gardens – Flower Beds And Tennis Courts To Be Cultivated – Council's "Revolutionary" Measure – May Save Railings From Demolition** – By a substantial majority Leamington Town Council, at their meeting on Monday evening, adopted what Councillor R. S. Salt described as "a revolutionary measure" when they agreed to a suggestion that vegetables should be planted in beds in the Jephson Gardens and that a portion of the tennis courts should also be turned over to food production.'

The ground was ploughed in late April 1942, immediately harrowed, and was yielding a bumper crop of tomatoes from 1,000 plants by August. Root crops were also grown. Flowers were replaced by vegetables on the main lawn [except near the path]. The greenhouses were also pressed into service for growing tomatoes and lettuce, although bedding plants were not completely ousted. The produce supplied municipal establishments such as the Pump Room and the British Restaurant.

FOOD FACTS

Number 29

POTATOES help to protect you from illness. Potatoes give you warmth and energy. Potatoes are cheap and home-produced. So why stop at serving them *once* a day? Have them twice, or even three times — for breakfast, dinner and supper.

ON THE KITCHEN FRONT

Coffee Potato Scones

Sift 6 ozs. plain flour, 2 level teaspoonfuls baking powder and $\frac{1}{2}$ teaspoonful salt in a basin. Mix thoroughly with 4 ozs. mashed potato. Rub in 2 ozs. fat with the tips of the fingers. Blend to a soft dough with $\frac{1}{2}$ teacupful strong, milky, sweetened coffee. Roll out to $\frac{1}{2}$ inch thickness on a floured board and cut into rounds. Glaze the tops with a little milk. Bake on greased baking sheets in a hot oven for 15 minutes.

Potato Drop Scones

Rub 2 ozs. mashed potato into 4 ozs. flour already salted with $\frac{1}{4}$ teaspoonful salt. Make into a stiff batter with $\frac{1}{2}$ a beaten egg and 1 gill milk. Allow to stand for a time. Sift in a small teaspoonful cream of tartar, a small level teaspoonful bicarbonate of soda and $\frac{1}{2}$ oz. sugar just before cooking. Cook in spoonfuls — as for Scotch drop scones — on a greased girdle or in a heavy frying-pan. Serve with a little hot jam.

Surprise Potato Balls

Cook 1 lb. potatoes and beat well with a fork. Add a large grated carrot, 1 teaspoonful chopped parsley and some salt and pepper. Use a little milk, if necessary, to bind the mixture, but do not make it wet. Form into balls. Make a hole in each, drop in a small teaspoonful of sweet pickle and close the hole. Roll the balls in browned breadcrumbs, place on a greased baking sheet. Bake in a moderate oven for 15 to 20 minutes.

These are good for any and every meal.

Parsley Potato Cakes

Here is a new breakfast dish which you can prepare the day before.

Boil 1 lb. potatoes and mash them while hot with a very little hot milk. Season with salt and pepper to taste.

Next morning, add a tablespoonful chopped parsley. Shape the mixture into little cakes, cover well with browned breadcrumbs and pan fry in a little hot fat, or bake in the oven.

P's for Protection Potatoes afford;
O's for the Ounces of Energy stored;
T's for Tasty, and Vitamins rich in;
A's for the Art to be learnt in the Kitchen.
T's for Transport we need not demand;
O's for Old England's Own Food from the Land;
E's for the Energy eaten by you;
S's for the Spuds which will carry us through!

Experiment with your meals as much as you can. It gives variety and it does you good.

Make a point of listening to the Radio Kitchen Front at 8.15 every morning.

THE MINISTRY OF FOOD, LONDON, S.W.1

Nearly three years later and the Morning News dated Wednesday 10th January 1945 reported the discontinuation of the project: - **'Vegetable Production to Cease in Jephson Gardens – Site to be Re-established as Lawn** – It was reported at the meeting of Leamington Town Council, on Monday, that the Warwickshire War Agricultural Executive Committee had raised no objection to the discontinuation of vegetable production in the Jephson Gardens, and the Council adopted a recommendation from the Parks and Gardens Committee that the site be re-established as a lawn.'

Ministry of Food

The Ministry of Food placed articles and adverts, with imaginative ideas and recipes, in the local press to help the housewife deal with rationing.

The following was in the Leamington Spa Courier dated 29th November 1940: - **Food Facts** - One of the chief purposes of the Ministry of Food is to help the housewife to make the most of her housekeeping money, and to see that everyone can buy a fair share of the food important to health. In addition to giving news and guidance regarding foods in good supply, the Ministry subsidises certain foods so that they can be bought at a reasonable price. A list of price-controlled foods is given on the next page: -

Price-controlled Foods

Bacon, butter, canned salmon, cheese, cod fillets, condensed milk, dried fruits, eggs, ham, herrings, jam, lard, lemons, meat, milk, onions, oranges, dried peas, beans, lentils, potatoes, rabbits, sausages, sugar and tea.

Biscuit Tin oven

A little emergency oven is a sensible thing to have by you these days. One of those big square biscuit tins makes an excellent one. You can use it over an oil stove. Cut two parallel slits, one inch by four inches, in the centre of one side of the tin about one inch apart. Make the lid into a door by wiring it to the tin at one side. Balance the oven firmly on top of the stove, slit side down. Put inside an inverted baking tin or the trivit from the grill pan to support your baking tray. You can cook slow baking dishes such as milk puddings and casseroles in this way, and you'll find it useful for heating up such things as shepherd's pie.

Biscuit Tin Oven

A little emergency oven is a sensible thing to have by you these days. One of those big square biscuit tins makes an excellent one. You can use it over an oil stove.

Cut two parallel slits, one inch by four inches, in the centre of one side of the tin about one inch apart. Make

Eat the foods that give protection and you need not fear infection; but can mix on equal terms with the most outrageous germs!

It was very important that food was not wasted and so tips on how to keep food for longer were welcome. These tips were published in the Leamington Spa Courier: -

How to keep the loaf fresh - To keep bread fresh during warm weather, it should be wrapped in a clean, dry cloth and kept in a well-ventilated place, not in a cupboard. Make sure the loaf is cool before wrapping. Don't use a damp cloth. If you keep bread in a bin, be sure the bin is well ventilated and clean; even if there are ventilation holes, keep the lid tilted.

How to keep milk fresh longer - Stand the milk bottle in a basin of cold water, first removing cap. Saturate a piece of butter muslin under the cold-water tap, put it over the milk bottle, resting on the top and with both ends touching the water. Stand in a draught. The floor of the larder is cooler than an upper shelf. Never place milk in an airless cupboard.

How to preserve tomatoes in their own juice - Remove the skins; cut medium or large tomatoes in halves or quarters; leave small ones whole. Wash and drain jars and pack the tomatoes in tightly, putting a layer of salt between each layer of tomatoes [about ¼ oz. salt to each 2lbs. of tomatoes]. Fix the rubber rings [previously soaked in hot water], lids and clips or screwband. If the screwband is used, give it a half-turn back to allow for expansion. Then place the jars in a pan and completely cover with cold water. The bottom of the pan should be covered with newspaper, cloth or straw. Bring slowly to simmering point - this should take about 1½ hours - and keep at this for 30 minutes. Remove jars one at a time and place on a wooden surface. Tighten screwbands, and tighten again as jars cool. Test the seal by removing clips or screwbands. If the seal is perfect, you should be able to lift the jar gently by the lid.

How to have fresh garden beans this winter - Preserve runner beans for the winter by salting. Choose young, fresh beans. Wash, dry, and string them thoroughly, breaking large beans into two or three pieces. Put a deep layer of dry salt into a dry crock, then press in a layer of beans. Continue alternately with a layer of salt and a layer of beans, pressing well down until the jar is full. The top layer should be of salt, at least an inch thick. Use at least 1lb. of cooking salt to each 3lbs. of beans. Cover the jar securely. After a few days examine for shrinkage. If the beans have shrunk, fill up with more layers, finishing with salt, and re-cover.

By 19th January 1940 there were reports of local hoarding – With bacon, ham, butter and sugar having been rationed for eleven days, local traders reported that customers were accepting the situation in a philosophical manner and with the minimal amount of grumbling. However, it was assumed that people were utilising hoarded supplies.

The following week the headline was: - '**Don't blame your local butcher** – If you failed to get the meat you required last weekend, don't take it out on your local butcher. Like everyone else in these turbulent times, he is having to adjust to changes outside his control. Last week the Leamington and District Masters Butchers Association gave details of the problems they have been faced with recently. On the 15th January, the Government closed down all livestock markets and inaugurated a new system of meat distribution. Retail butchers in Warwick and Leamington can now only obtain meat from the central abattoir in Coventry.

Prior to this move, local butchers made use of the 18 licensed slaughter houses in Leamington and, through personal contact with livestock traders, were able to buy exactly what their customers demanded.

To avoid duplication of effort, the newly formed Retail Buying Group transfers meat from Coventry to the distribution depot in Kenilworth Street. From here the meat is sorted and delivered to the local shops. With this new depot taking shop staff away from their usual duties, Leamington butchers have appealed to customers to place their orders, preferably by telephone, at least a day before delivery is required.

Although this new centralised distribution scheme enables meat supplies to be more easily regulated, much of the cost has fallen on the butchers. They have had to pay £200 to establish the depot; transport costs of £50 a week are only partly borne by the Government, and the Leamington and Warwick group has had to deposit with the Ministry, as a guarantee for future payments, the sum of £5,000, the value of one week's supply of meat.

Customers will also have noticed the lack of English meat offered for sale recently. Last week this amounted to only 2oz. per person, the remainder of the portion being made up with imported meat. Butchers are saying this situation has arisen because farmers have not delivered the usual amount of livestock to the official collecting centres. What is happening to the remainder of the animals that usually reach the market is uncertain. However, if you should be offered some prime English beef ....'

Ten months later and meat was still hitting the local headlines as the Leamington Spa Courier dated 15th November 1940 shows: - **Leamington Meat Supply – Points for the Housewife** – If Leamington housewives are not able to get the joint they had desired this weekend they will find the explanation in the following statement issued to the Courier yesterday by Mr. George Purcell, President of the Masters Butchers' Association: - "Up to the present, the public, and particularly the public of Leamington, have been very fortunate in respect of their meat supplies. As regards meat, in fact, the war has so far not made itself felt. The position is changing rapidly, however, and there is likely to be a shortage, particularly of English meat."

"The farmers have now disposed of practically all of their grass-fed cattle, and there is only a small supply of stall-fed cattle likely to come forward weekly. Of this supply, it is possible that only a fraction will be available in Leamington, owing to transport and other difficulties. Regarding the supply of imported meat, here again we have our special difficulties owing to the war. The position in Leamington this week-end is that there is practically no English meat available, but there is a good supply of imported lamb of first-rate quality, and also a lesser quantity of best imported beef. Housewives who find their butchers are unable to supply joints as desired are asked to appreciate these points."

Another way to win the war was to feed your old scraps of food to pigs. As the poem said...

Because of the pail, the scraps were saved,
Because of the scraps, the pigs were saved,
Because of the pigs, the rations were saved,
Because of the rations, the ships were saved,
Because of the ships, the island was saved,
Because of the island, the Empire was saved,
And all because of the housewife's pail.

Here is one of the Ministry of Food recipes for you to have a go at: -

Woolton Pie

Woolton pie was originally named Lord Woolton pie. It was named after Frederick Marquis, 1st Earl of Woolton [1883-1964], who became the Minister of Food in 1940.

It was created at the Savoy Hotel in London by its then Maître Chef de Cuisine, Francis Latry. It was one of a number of recipes suggested to the British public by the Ministry of Food during the Second World War to enable a nutritional diet to be maintained despite shortages and rationing of many types of food, especially meat.

This 'vegetable pie' recipe involved dicing and cooking potatoes [or parsnips], cauliflower, swede, carrots and, possibly turnip. Rolled oats and chopped spring onions were added to the thickened vegetable water which was poured over the vegetables themselves. The dish was topped with potato pastry and grated cheese and served with vegetable gravy. The recipe could be adapted to reflect the availability and seasonality of ingredients.

Ingredients:	
1lb diced potatoes	3 spring onions
1lb cauliflower	1 teaspoon vegetable extract
1lb diced carrots	1 tablespoon oatmeal
1lb diced swede	A little chopped parsley

Method: Cook everything together with just enough water to cover, stirring often to prevent it sticking to the pan. Let the mixture cool. Spoon into a pie dish, sprinkle with chopped parsley. Cover with a crust of potatoes or wholemeal pastry. Bake in a moderate oven until golden brown.

Egg Rationing

Fresh eggs were rationed in June 1942 and dried egg was the Government's response to the wartime shortage of fresh eggs. Dried egg powder became available in the same year, and it was used to supplement the egg allowance while rationing was in place.

The tins of egg powder, which came from America, contained the equivalent of a dozen eggs and was extra to the regular egg ration; the cost was 1s. 9d. It was advertised as pure fresh egg with no additions, and nothing but the moisture taken away. "It is pure egg, spray dried. Dried eggs are just as good as fresh eggs, and should be used in the same way. Keep the egg powder in a tin with a tight-fitting lid, and store in a dark place." The powder needed to be reconstituted prior to use and then needed to be used immediately. One level tablespoon of egg powder and two level tablespoons of water equalled one egg. The powder and the water were mixed and then allowed to stand for about 5 minutes. Any lumps were removed with a wooden spoon and finally the mixture was beaten with a fork or a whisk.

The Government tried to sell the idea of powdered eggs and suggested that they could be used for such things as scrambled eggs, cakes and big creamy omelettes, but the majority of the public were not convinced. They were probably right!

Potato Picking

Early in the war there were concerns about the potato harvest as the Morning News dated Tuesday 23rd January 1940 reported: - **The Potato Harvest in Warwickshire – Danger of Labour Shortage – School Children To Assist In The Work** – Warwickshire Elementary Education Committee have had some negotiations with the War Agricultural Executive Committee regarding assistance which can be rendered to farmers by children of school age at the time of the potato harvest. A serious shortage of labour is expected next autumn and there is some danger of loss unless the crop can be harvested at the proper time. We have therefore authorised the Director of Education to arrange that schools may assist in securing the potato and other harvests of 1940 where he is satisfied that other labour is not available. *[Part report].*

Schools closing to allow school children to assist with potato picking became the norm and it didn't stop when the war ended. In October 1953, over 2,000 Warwickshire children were released by schools to assist with the potato harvest. In 1953 they did five full days or 10 half days working six hours a day and were paid 1s. 1d. per day.

The Leamington Spa Courier dated 14th November 1941 reported on the activities of Clapham Terrace School: - **Potato Picking by Leamington Children** - Clapham Terrace Senior School has closed for a fortnight in order that the children may assist in potato picking. Each day buses call at the school and parties have been taken to Charlecote, Walton, Alveston, Hatton and Stareton. When conditions are good the children thoroughly enjoy the work and they have rendered invaluable assistance to a number of farmers who were beginning to fear that this year's crop of potatoes would remain unlifted. Generally speaking, the crop is satisfactory.

This 1942 photo of children collecting the potato harvest, was taken at Sydenham Farm, close to the top of what is now Sydenham Drive. Ken Aitken is on the left with Rosie Cox and Cyril Reading - Olga Fahey is on the far right of the photo. Arthur Tickle farmed Sydenham Farm and also had 'Land Girls' [Women's Land Army] helping him on the farm. His brother John Tickle farmed at Grove Farm, near to Harbury Lane crossroads, and had a couple of German prisoners of war who 'lived in'. Close by at Highdown Farm, just off the Harbury Lane, there were a number of German prisoners of war held.

On 26th October 1942, the parks and gardens superintendent reported on the success of the potato crop grown on the Campion Hills.

Fruit Rationing

Fruit was very much in short supply during the war. Many children did not know what a banana was until long after the end of the war. On 6th August 1942, the Morning

News carried the story that oranges were now available in the shops and were reserved at the rate of 1lb per head to children in possession of a green ration book. The following day they could be sold to other customers, but priority was to children, schools, hospitals and invalids.

The following article from the Morning News dated Tuesday 16th February 1943 shows just how scarce oranges were: - **S.O.S. Oranges** – The Mayor of Leamington [Councillor R. S. Salt] would be most grateful for the gift of an orange for a little boy aged four years who is desperately ill. His Worship spent some hours on Friday searching the town for oranges, and was successful in obtaining three. More are urgently required, however, and an appeal is made to the generosity of those who may have some fruit in their possession. Gifts should be forwarded to the Mayor at the Mayor's Parlour, Town Hall.

The Leamington Spa Courier dated 14th May 1943 reported: - **Story of Two Lemons - Five-year old girl who "wants her daddy home".** On the afternoon of Saturday 8th May 1943, two lemons made £1,050 during the Wings for Victory lunch in the Town Hall. Mayor, Rowland Salt had that morning received a curious shaped parcel which he opened immediately. He found inside two 'splendid' lemons and a note which said, "Dear Mr. Mayor - My daddy sent me these lemons. Would you please get some money for 'Wings for Victory' for I want my daddy home?" The reporter subsequently interviewed the sender of the letter, a five-year-old girl. On the previous day, the Mayor had auctioned a banana which raised £500.

The Leamington Spa Courier dated 3rd September 1943 reported: - **Red Cross Prisoners of War Fund** - £2. 5s. has been received by Mrs. M. Ratcliff for the above fund from Mrs. Key, 4, Newbold Place, from a competition for a lemon. Mrs. Ratcliff has also handed into Headquarters for the same fund £162. 10s. from the sale of prisoner of war parcel booklets. This ingenious idea of representing articles - margarine, tea, apple pudding etc. - which help to make up a prisoner's parcel [and allowing the donor of 6d to feel responsible for having supplied a prisoner with an article of his choice] has proved very popular. Each booklet contained 20 such articles, and 325 entire copies have been sold.

Cooking Fats Rationing

The Ministry of Food announced **Rationing of Cooking Fats – Immediate Registration Essential** on 17th July 1940. Everyone must register at once for cooking fats. Rationing – 2oz a person a week – comes into force next Monday. After that date, cooking fats and margarine can be supplied only by retailers with whom the consumer is registered.

Wartime Christmases

On 8th December 1939, the Leamington Spa Courier carried the following: - **Plum Puddings for the Troops – 4,000 wanted.** The collection of Christmas puddings for Warwickshire troops, which is being organised by the Women's Voluntary Services, is arousing great interest. The Lord Lieutenant of Warwickshire [Squadron Leader Lord Willoughby de Broke] and Lady Willoughby de Broke have consented to send a message of greetings to be included in each batch of puddings sent. Four thousand puddings in all are required. All gifts will be most gratefully received. The collecting depot at Leamington has been changed to 19, The Parade [by kind permission of Mrs. M. M. M. Fowler, O.B.E.,] and will be open daily from 10.00am to 4.00pm from Monday to Saturday of next week.

A Christmas party at the Ranelagh Tavern in 1940. Notice that there are only women in the photo as most of the men are at war. The landlady Mrs. Green is far left on the front row. [Mrs. Green's husband George Green played football 8 times for England and over 400 times for Sheffield United].

Mrs. Fletcher is in the back row wearing the top hat, Mary Jane Tew [aka 'Polly Gabriel'], from St. Georges Road, is top left-hand corner holding the fan. Mrs. Gough is the lady with the two spots on her face in the front row and Bella from Clarence Street is the lady in the checked outfit on the far right in the second row from front.

In many ways, Christmas 1940 was the first wartime Christmas. Austerity had kicked in, and there were many shortages. Rationing would have an effect on families Christmases until 1954. In 1940 the town had been bombed, people had died, the full effects of rationing were now well known, the men were away at war – some had been killed or were in concentration camps, many children had been evacuated and were away from their families and shelters had been built in back gardens and were being used. Some families were mourning the loss of loved ones either at home or in combat overseas. We were certainly at war and the people of Leamington knew it – but whatever the problems, they were going to make the best of it.

Rationing made the Christmas dinner a real challenge, but it was still the main event of the day, and housewives across the country came up with some ingenious, but not always appetising ideas. For months before Christmas they scrimped and saved small amounts of their normal rations of sugar and tea so there would be more on the day. During the week before Christmas, rations were increased by 1½ lb. of sugar, 8d. worth of meat and ½ lb. sweets.

Turkey and chicken were unaffordable and unavailable – the weekly meat ration for a family of four wouldn't cover a small chicken. The alternative was to use offal, or even rabbit – if you could get one. Even in the late 1950s, my family only had a chicken once a year, and that was on Christmas Day.

Very little fruit was imported into the country and nuts were costly. Christmas puddings, mince pies and cakes didn't contain dried fruit and marzipan – the housewife looked for alternatives – and she found them by substituting carrot and potato. They were certainly adaptable and imaginative! One piece of good news was that sherry was off the ration.

As this advert from the Morning News dated Thursday 21st November 1940 shows, war-time cookery demonstrations were held at the Gas showrooms in Regent Street. As it was close to Christmas, such delicacies as Christmas pudding without eggs and mock apricot tart, are likely to have been some examples of what could be achieved without the normal ingredients.

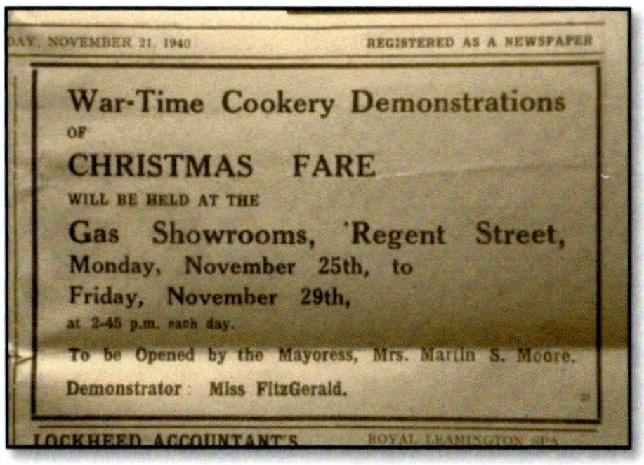
DAY, NOVEMBER 21, 1940 REGISTERED AS A NEWSPAPER

War-Time Cookery Demonstrations
OF
CHRISTMAS FARE
WILL BE HELD AT THE
Gas Showrooms, 'Regent Street,
Monday, November 25th, to
Friday, November 29th,
at 2-45 p.m. each day.
To be Opened by the Mayoress, Mrs. Martin S. Moore.
Demonstrator: Miss FitzGerald.

LOCKHEED ACCOUNTANT'S ROYAL LEAMINGTON SPA

The Ministry of Food gave more ideas to the housewife - War Time Queen of Puddings. Queen of puddings has always been a favourite. Try this war time recipe without eggs. Make a pint of sweetened vanilla custard, using about three-quarters of the usual amount of custard powder to a pint of milk and water. Put a dessertspoon of cocoa into a bowl with a heaped breakfast cup of breadcrumbs. Beat the custard well in with a fork - the mixture should be nice and wet. If you can spare a small nut of margarine add it to the custard too. Spread a layer of jam - any kind will do - on the bottom of a greased pie dish, pour the custard mixture over the jam and bake for about 20 minutes in a brisk oven. [Enough for four people].

Christmas pudding without eggs	
1 cup flour	1 tsp sweet spice
1 cup breadcrumbs	1 cup raw grated potato
1 cup sugar	1 cup raw grated carrot
½ cup suet	1 tsp bicarbonate of soda dissolved in 2 tablespoons milk
1 cup dried mixed fruit	
Combine all ingredients and place in a greased pudding bowl. Cover and steam or boil for 4 hours.	

Mock Apricot Tart	
Potato pastry	4oz cold mashed potato
4oz self-raising flour	A little water
Pinch salt	
1½ - 2oz lard	
Rub fat into flour, stir in potato and form into a ball using water to mix. Line a 7-inch pie plate and bake in a moderate oven 180°c for 20 minutes.	
Filling	
1lb grated carrots cooked till soft	Few drops almond essence
4 tblsp jam sauce [boil equal quantity of jam and water together and allow to cool]	
Fill the pastry case with the carrot mixture and save a little of the jam to spread on top of the filling. Note: the carrots really do taste like apricots!	

Christmas Cake	
8oz self-raising flour	4oz dark brown sugar
2 eggs	1 tsp baking powder
1 jar mincemeat	
Mix all ingredients together, place in a greased and lined 7-inch round tin and bake at 160°c for 1 hour.	

Mincemeat	
1½ chopped apples	4oz golden syrup
4oz suet	1 tsp ginger
3oz chopped nuts	1 tsp mixed spice
3oz dried fruit	Lemon flavouring [or lemon rind]
Mince the apples, mix all ingredients together and it is ready to use. [This does not keep well].	

Christmas trees were scarce as there was a lack of manpower to cut them down due to the men being away. Not only that, space on trains was limited as it was needed for troops and munitions. Some families bought small, sparse, very basic artificial trees and some even made a tree from oddments of wood. The artificial ones were around two feet in length and had very few branches. Even when they were dressed they had very few baubles and decorations on them – and most of those were handmade such as paper stars. Decorations for the house were also in short supply. Paper chains were popular, and many children have made these in school using a mixture of flour and water as glue. In wartime, they would be made from odd scraps of paper, sometimes coloured paper if it could be found, or just plain old newspapers. Foraging for holly and pine cones was certainly useful in brightening up the living room.

The public were discouraged from giving presents, although they were encouraged to give to the war effort, and many did by buying war bonds, if they could afford them. Toy factories had been requisitioned for the war effort, so it was all about make do and mend. Dads would make wooden toys such as spinning tops, aeroplanes or farm implements for their sons using odd bits of recycled wood, and mums would be knitting dolls and the like for their daughters using spare bits of wool. Children, and adults for that matter, would have small stockings, possibly attached to the mantelpiece, that would contain the handmade items and perhaps even an orange - if you were lucky, an apple, a few nuts and possible a coin like a 6d. [tanner] or even a thre'penny bit. However, more likely than not, instead of being given a coin each, a sixpence would be put into the Christmas pudding mix and one lucky person would find it – as long as they didn't swallow it! The presents would be wrapped in brown paper, or even newspaper, and string, which could be used again afterwards.

In 1941, the Ministry of Supply decided that 'no retailer shall provide any paper for the packing or wrapping of goods except food stuffs or articles which the shop keeper has agreed to deliver.'

After the presents, church services were very popular, followed by Christmas lunch, or dinner if you like, then it would be the King's Speech *[King George VI]* on the radio with everyone huddling around to listen. The Christmas hats that people would have worn were probably made from newspaper. In the evening, singing carols and singing songs was popular, in fact you could say it was a ritual, especially if someone could play the piano that many families had, or another instrument such as the ukulele – or it may have been card games or charades. Christmas didn't stop one's duties and responsibilities though - so the Wardens still checked the streets, the Home Guard still went on duty - as did all other Civil Defence personnel, the Fire Brigade, Police and ambulance staff.

Petrol Rationing

Petrol, or the lack of it, was a particular problem, and as this scarce resource required conserving as much as possible, the Government introduced a number of special measures, one of them being rationing which started on 16th September 1939. This was the first commodity to be rationed. However, as most working class people didn't have cars anyway, it tended to affect the middle and upper classes more. Nevertheless, there was a noticable increase in bicycles on the roads.

Ration coupons in the form of a Motor Spirit Ration Book became available but only for people using their cars for war work and doctors. Petrol could only be dispensed into the tank of the vehicle mentioned on the ration book and not into any other vehicle or container. As the petrol allowance only allowed people such as doctors, a petrol allowance to do their job, they were unable to do other voluntary work. This was one reason why in July 1942 the Ministry for Homeland Security asked the Women's Voluntary Service [W.V.S.] to run the Volunteer Car Pool [VCP] scheme. The Government would requisition or even buy cars for essential civil defence use. The W.V.S. provided drivers, all unpaid and voluntary, although it was open to all volunteers, men and women, that could guarantee to produce a car in an emergency. By 1944, there were over 570 VCP schemes across Britain, involving transporting people to hospital, carrying evacuees, Land Army girls, service personnel, delivering or collecting official papers, food or clothing supplies as well as other duties. The rationing of petrol continued until 1950.

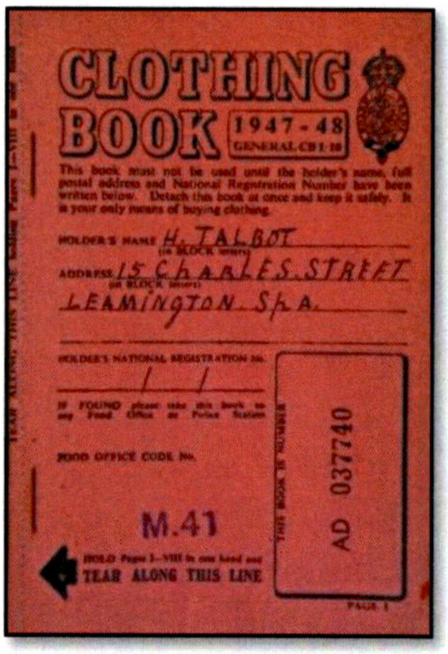

Clothes Rationing

Clothes rationing was announced on 1st June 1941 and came into force immediately. To start with spare coupons in existing ration books were utilised until 1st June 1942 when specific red covered ration books were introduced. Each item of clothing was given a points value. Adults were allocated 66 points which had to last them a year, although the number allocated was reduced as the war progressed. Eleven coupons were needed for a woman's dress and eight coupons for a man's shirt or trousers. A new pair of women's shoes required five coupons, but for some reason a pair for a man required seven coupons. From 1942, children received an extra 10 coupons.

Soap Rationing

In February 1942, the Ministry of Food advised that as from Monday 9th February, soap may be bought only against a coupon or buying permit. The oils and fats used in soap manufacture occupy much shipping space, and some of this must be saved for food.

"You will have 4 coupons in each 4-weekly period, and will be able to use these how and when you like within the period. There will be no registration and you may buy from any shop stocking the kind you require."

"Each of the four coupons which make up a four-weeks' ration will entitle you to any one of the following: -

Either 4 ounces of hard soap [common household soap in bars or pieces], or 3 ounces of toilet soap, or 3 ounces soap flakes or chips, or 6 ounces soap powder No.1, or 12 ounces soap powder No.2, or 6 ounces of soft soap."

"Rationing will not apply to shaving soaps or dental soaps, shampoo powders, liquid soap, or scourers. The coupons to be used are those in the frame at the top of page 15 of the Yellow Book [RB9], the book you use for jam. Coupon numbers and periods will be the same as for sugar and tea, so that you will start with coupons 29 to 32 for the first period - February 9th to March 8th. Coupons 1-28 are of no value. Coupons will not be cut out, but must be cancelled by the shopkeeper in ink or indelible pencil."

Coal Rationing

Despite being a coal producing country, coal was put on ration in July 1941. This had a major effect on most families as it was the main source of energy for cooking and heating. Meals were cooked on a coal range in the kitchen, hot water was heated by a coal boiler or in a pan on the range, and coal was used in the living room grates which is likely to have been the only source of heat in the house. On 11th June 1958, the welcome news came that coal rationing and price control was to end the following month. The statement was made in the House of Lords by Lord Mills, the Minister of Power and in the House of Commons by Paymaster General Reginald Maudling. After 17 years of coal restrictions, it was the last of the war-time rationing restrictions to be lifted.

British Restaurant and Schools Canteen Scheme

British Restaurants were a World War II Government initiative set up by the Ministry of Food to provide low cost 'off ration' communal eating for the needy, and were run by local government on a non-profit basis. Eventually there were over 1,000 of them, including the one in Leamington Spa which was in Regent Grove.

The following is the summary report of the initial planning meetings held in 1941 that would subsequently lead to the opening of Leamington's 'British Restaurant' on 22nd August 1941.

At the inaugural meeting of the British Restaurant Committee [BRC] on 16th April 1941, the town clerk reported that it was expected that a considerable number of special workmen would be billeted in the Borough during the next few weeks, and the Chief Billeting Officer reported on the accommodation available, with particular reference to the question of feeding. After discussion, it was recommended that: -

(1) The original scheme for a British Restaurant, located in the municipality of Leamington Spa, is proceeded with as rapidly as possible.
(2) A Special Sub-Committee, comprising the Chairman, Alderman Benison and Davis, Councillors Mrs. Bragg and Purcell, and Mr. H. Kelly is appointed to discuss the details of the scheme with the Borough Engineer, and to report.
(3) In the event of an emergency arising prior to the scheme being in operation, the downstairs room of the Liberal Club be used as a dining room for the service of meals, to be cooked in the town hall kitchen.
(4) That an Emergency Sub-Committee, comprising the Chairman, the Mayoress, Councillor Mrs. Bragg and Mr. H. Kelly be appointed, with authority to make all necessary arrangements in the event of the emergency scheme being required and to engage the necessary staff.
(5) That the following retailers are appointed to supply the British Restaurant: -
Butcher: - Messrs. J. Hall & Sons, High Street.
Supplier of Manufactured Meat: - Mr. G. T. Higginson, 71 Clarendon Street.
Grocer: - Grimbly Hughes & Co. Ltd.
Supplier of Milk: - Hygienic Dairies Ltd.
Baker: - Mr. C. Pearson, 118, Shrubland Street.
Greengrocer: - Griffin & Steel Ltd. and Tarver & Sidwell Ltd.

At the follow-up meeting of the BRC on 19th April, the Borough Engineer reported on the steps being taken to prepare the downstairs room of the Liberal Club with a view to it being available, if required, by the evening of Wednesday 23rd April. Mr. Kelly was asked to obtain, forthwith, an adequate store of non-perishable foodstuffs from suppliers. He was also asked to peruse the applications for manager/manageress and to select a limited number of candidates to attend for interview at 3.30pm on Monday 21st April. The Mayoress and Councillor Mrs. Bragg were asked to have a preliminary interview with a local candidate with a view to her appointment as cook.

At a Special Sub-Committee meeting on 23rd April, the Borough Engineer submitted plans for the scheme – which were approved – and he was instructed to carry out the work by direct administration with all possible speed. The quotes from [a] Wilson and Mathiesons Ltd for two 2-oven enamel finished solid fuel ranges with fire back boilers, one fitted with a hot closet and one for steamer pans, were recommended for acceptance; [b] John Wright & Co. Ltd for gas cooking equipment, including a 40-gallon water heater, single steamer, bain-marie, etc. [c] Midland Electric Light and Power Co. Ltd for a refrigerator. Linoleum would be laid in the kitchen, dining room, etc., on the first floor and on the wooden exit stairs. The Borough Engineer also submitted estimates amounting to £500 for crockery and small pieces of equipment and £1,750 for the remaining equipment and works.

On 16th May 1941, the Town Clerk again reported to the BRC on the imminent arrival, and billeting, of a large number of special workmen in the town, and that the chief billeting officer was concerned where they would be fed. It was agreed that the Committee would hasten the opening of the Restaurant by using the Liberal Club in Denby Buildings, Regent Grove. A week later the Chief Billeting Officer again emphasised the ever-increasing need for communal feeding in Leamington – adding that the number of remaining voluntary lodgings, where food could be provided, was very few. On 30th May it was recommended that a draft lease be submitted to the Liberal Club for their approval. This was duly prepared by the Town Clerk in June as the Liberal Club wanted a legal agreement with the Council.

By mid-June, following the interviewing of three candidates, [Mr.] J. W. McNab of Coventry was installed as Manager of the Restaurant on a salary of £350 per annum and given the task of employing a cook, assistant cooks, general kitchen helpers, a store-keeper clerk and a labourer. At the subsequent meeting, a week later, the go-ahead was given to purchase the necessary equipment for the Manager's office, order a fish fryer from the Ministry's equipment pool for installation in the kitchen and obtain quotes for the provision of two ticket machines.

At the meeting on 24th June 1941, it was agreed that a proposal be prepared for a joint scheme named 'Communal Feeding and School Canteen', as being operated at Stoke-on-Trent, to facilitate the preparation of school children's meals at the Restaurant. They would then be conveyed to the school feeding centres, with the Local Education Authority bearing a realistic proportion of the cost. At the Elementary Education Committee meeting held on 22nd July, it was proposed that – in the event of the scheme being approved by the Town Council – the actual cost to the Restaurant of providing the cooked meals be charged to the parents of the schoolchildren receiving the meals, subject to individual cases of exceptional circumstances. Furthermore, that the chairman [Councillor Smith], Councillor Durham and the Director of Education be authorised to purchase equipment and take the necessary steps to implement the scheme.

At the 8th August meeting the Restaurant Manager recommended that its opening hours be from noon to 2.30pm for the time being, but be reassessed in the light of experience. Also that prices be charged in accordance with a proposed scale and be reassessed at the next meeting. It was also agreed that although some furniture was on loan from the Liberal Club, the manager be authorised to purchase 50 x 8-person tables as well as the two ticket issuing machines at a cost of £16. 17s. 6d. An electric steamer and a potato peeler was due for delivery in the next few days. It was also recommended that the cooking equipment be converted from solid fuel to gas at an approximate cost of £25. Should gas supplies be cut off it could be re-adapted to solid fuel within half an hour.

The British Restaurant was formerly opened by the Mayor [Alderman M. S. Moore] on 20th August 1941 and opened to the public on the 21st. It would serve 2,416 meals in its first week of operation. It was hoped to obtain vegetables from the Jephson Gardens cultivated area. Meal prices were: - Soup and Bread 2d., Meat and Vegetables 8d., Plum Tart 2d., Tea 1d. and Coffee 2d. Colonel Pemberton, representing the Divisional Food Officer, congratulated Mr. McNab [manager] on the meals served.

The following provides an insight into the development and evolution of the British Restaurant, referred to as 'the Restaurant' – during its eight-year duration.

5th September 1941: - The personnel of the Royal Armoured Corps lunched with the Mayor at the Restaurant, following the display of tanks throughout the town in the presence of Anthony Eden, War Minister. The Mayor noted that Leamington's population had increased from 29,000 to 45,000. Also on 5th September it was decided to erect a two-way hanging board above the archway leading from Regent Grove to indicate the whereabouts of the restaurant.

17th October 1941: - Decision made to serve food upstairs as well as downstairs in the Restaurant. Consideration was being given to providing school meals.

6th January 1942: - Mr. Henry Ford and his son Edsel generously offered the Council the free use of two vans to support the Council's wartime 'feeding arrangements'. Also on 6th January 1942, it was reported that the school's canteen scheme had been approved by the Board of Education and that school canteens would be established during the year.

9th January 1942: - The Restaurant was doing tremendous business and from its opening in August 1941 to the end of the year it served an average of 3,600+ meals per week. It was soon feeding the 600-700 school children as requested by the Board of Education. However, the BRC thinks it will struggle to cope with this volume and that a new cooking facility would be needed.

16th January 1942: - Decision taken to increase meal prices by 2d. The Directorate of Camouflage has offered to paint murals in the Restaurant and a meeting will be held with their representatives.

23rd January 1942: - A site was being sought for a Central Kitchen to provide additional cooking facilities to enable the Restaurant to cope with additional meals for school children.

16th February 1942: - Messrs. Hall and Ladell of the Directorate of Camouflage attended the Municipal Restaurant Committee meeting and explained their proposals for mural decorations at the Restaurant. The go ahead was given and the Borough Engineer was authorised to supply the necessary materials.

23rd February 1942: - The Superintendent of Parks and Gardens was authorised to plough up and cultivate a suitable area of land at the top of Campion Hills which was in the possession of the Corporation under an agreement with William Willes, subject to a portion being available for allotments.

6th March 1942: - The two vans handed over via the Ford Emergency Food Vans Trust have the capacity to carry 640 portions of food in the four insulated containers within each van and will be ideal to transport the school meals from the Central Kitchen. They will be driven by the Women's Voluntary Service [W.V.S.] and be maintained by Soans the local Ford dealer. Teas were also now available between 6.00pm and 8.00pm, at a cost of 1s.

13th March 1942: - Since the beginning of the year 41,000 meals had been served at an average of 4,000 per week.

13th April 1942: - The Town Clerk was requested to requisition a piece of ground fronting Brunswick Street for the erection of a Central Kitchen at an approximate cost of £3,100 for the erection and equipping of the kitchen.

17th April 1942: - Tennis lawns to be ploughed up to grow vegetables. The Restaurant was to open nightly for dinner, 6.00pm to 8.30pm and it is open to all citizens.

20th April 1942: - The provision of meals for school children under the school's canteen scheme commenced on 20th April 1942.

12th June 1942: - The Central Kitchen to be built in Brunswick Street by Messrs. Grooms of Leamington, at a cost of £1,359. 16s. 6d. Meanwhile, the Restaurant was now serving 5,000 lunches, 900 teas and 3,000 school meals weekly.

17th July 1942: - The erection of the Central Kitchen was progressing and should open at the end of August.

28th August 1942: - The British Restaurant was just over a year old. When the Central Kitchen opens, it is hoped to operate it on a 'cash and carry' basis. The murals for the restaurant were being prepared on the top floor of the Town Hall and are progressing well.

16th October 1942: - During the summer, 1.5 tons of tomatoes were grown in the Jephson Gardens, with takings of £1,512.

18th December 1942: - The Education Department to be asked to pay 7d, an increase of 1d, for the school meals provided. The Town Clerk reported that the mural decorations were complete, and on the proposed visit of Clive Gardiner – Art Advisor to the Ministry of Food – and Colonel Pemberton to inspect them. It was recommended that a suitable personage be invited to the formal presentation of the murals. The Central Kitchen in Brunswick Street will be open in 3 to 4 weeks' time under the management of the Restaurant.

1st January 1943: - Over Christmas the local disabled ex-servicemen from the 1914-1918 war were given dinner and tea at the Restaurant.

18th January 1943: - £500 of vegetables sold from the Jephson Gardens during the festive season. Since its opening in August 1941, 245,000 meals have been served in the Restaurant and 80,000 school meals provided.

12th February 1943: - It was hoped the Restaurant would open on Sundays to provide meals for transferred war workers.

12th March 1943: - It was proposed to add 6d. to the meal prices on Sundays, when it will open from noon to 1.45pm.

19th March 1943: - The glasshouses in the Jephson Gardens, currently growing lettuces for the Pump Room Restaurant, would soon supply the British Restaurant.

21st March 1943: - First Sunday opening of the British Restaurant. The hours were 12.00 noon until 1.45pm. An additional charge of 6d. was made for Sunday service.

26th March 1943: - It was reported that the new Central Kitchen would be open from 12.00 noon to 2.00pm daily, [except Sundays], for the sale of cooked meals under the Cash and Carry Service. The object of this service was to assist housewives in general by providing cooked meals which they could serve in their own homes. In this way, a considerable saving in shopping time and fuel could be effected. Customers would be expected to bring their own containers. The prices would be, meat and vegetables 9d., sweet or pudding 3d.

Mr. W. Mabane, Secretary to the Minister for Food, was at the British Restaurant on 9th April 1943 to formally accept the murals from artists Dorothy Annan and Trevor Tennant. Photo courtesy of Sebastian Tennant.

Warm praise was given to the artists, Dorothy Annan, Trevor Tennant, Colin Sealy, Thomas R. Rathmell ARCA, Arthur C. Shipman and Edwin La Dell ARCA, who were the producers of the work in the Upper Dining Room, and Eric Hall ARCA for the Lower Dining Room. Mr. Mabane also visited the recently opened Central Kitchen where 700 school meals were provided daily. The mural in the background is 'Home Guard Manoeuvres and the use of Camouflage' by Eric Hall.

This mural by Eric Hall titled 'Home Guard Manoeuvres and the use of Camouflage' was displayed in the ground floor dining room and shows a scene with uniformed figures practicing an ambush and children running alongside a canal.

Image courtesy of Leeds Museums and Galleries [Henry Moore Institute Archive].

This mural by Dorothy Annan, which was displayed above the serving area, titled 'Leamington Life' measured 16 feet x 8 feet and occupied the east wall.

Image courtesy of Leeds Museums and Galleries [Henry Moore Institute Archive].

This mural by Edwin La Dell titled 'Scene on a Trainer Aerodrome' measured 20 feet x 10 feet and occupied the west wall of the restaurant. It depicts a camouflaged aircraft, a lookout post, and camouflage netting being installed at an airfield.

Image courtesy of Leeds Museums and Galleries [Henry Moore Institute Archive].

This mural by Colin Sealy titled 'Street Scene', measured 10 feet x 8 feet, is a stylized image of architectural elements derived from the town.

Image courtesy of Leeds Museums and Galleries [Henry Moore Institute Archive].

This mural by Arthur Shipman is titled 'By the River Leam', measured 10 feet x 8 feet, combined elements from the town's bridges and included the figure of a sailor flirting with a girl, and a child going for a walk escorted by her mother and a nun.

Image courtesy of Leeds Museums and Galleries [Henry Moore Institute Archive].

During his time as a 'camoufleur' working for the Camouflage Directorate in Leamington, artist Thomas 'Tom' Rathmell decided to rent a house at 22 Heathcote Road, Whitnash. The mural that he was inspired to paint for the British Restaurant was titled 'Carrying on with domestic duties after an air raid'. Measuring 12 feet x 8 feet it shows children playing and women hanging out washing in a garden framed by bombed houses and a barrage balloon. The setting was apparently derived from photographs in a local newspaper of bombed buildings, together with a house in Halls Close and included a family he knew that lived at 13 Halls Close, at the rear of his rented house.

Image courtesy of Leeds Museums and Galleries [Henry Moore Institute Archive].

14th May 1943: - After a disagreement between two Leamington Borough Council committees [i.e. 'Education' and 'Restaurant'] concerning the Brunswick Street kitchen, school meals were scheduled to be done at 11.00am and 'cash and carry' meals were available at noon.

18th June 1943: - The British Restaurant Committee advised that it had acquired another property – 113, Warwick Street – as a 'cash and carry' operation.

16th July 1943: - The cost of the evening meal was increased to 1s. 6d.

17th September 1943: - One hundred American soldiers visited the town and lunched with the Mayor in the Restaurant. Mr. McNab reported that the staff worked 55 hour weeks but always volunteered to serve all servicemen.

15th October 1943: - The Restaurant will be available for community services on a Sunday evening and Sunday tea will be served from 5.00pm to 7.30pm. It was proposed to open another Central Kitchen on the old brewery site in Lillington Avenue.

17th November 1943: - The new 'cash and carry' depot, [British Restaurant No.2], was opened at 113, Warwick Street and it can accommodate 100 diners for dinner. Meals came from the Central Kitchen and on opening day 50 customers used the 'cash and carry' option and 17 were seated for dinner. It provided 1,585 'cash and carry' meals in its first 10 days.

24th December 1943: - The Mayor provided a Christmas treat for 150 children which included tea at the British Restaurant.

18th February 1944: - A social centre will open at the Restaurant from 21st February on a one-month trial, from 7.00pm to 10.00pm every night for people over 16 years old. In 1943 the Regent Grove premises served 235,826 meals, the Central Kitchen 'cash and carry' provided 51,902 meals and 120,169 school meals and the Warwick Street 'cash and carry' 7,113 meals.

A new Central Kitchen, to provide school meals is proposed for either Leicester Street or on land adjacent to the Corporation Depot, Lillington Avenue. Both sites were deemed suitable. Wherever it is built, it must be demolished when the war ends.

14th April 1944: - The responsibility for the Central Kitchen is to be transferred to the Education Committee. Use of the Town Hall's kitchen is requested by the Restaurant.

28th April 1944: - Some American guests [Armed Forces] visited Leamington and lunched in the Restaurant, they had been to Stratford-upon-Avon for the Shakespeare birthday celebrations.

14th July 1944: - Several thousand refugees who have experienced the 'flying bomb' attacks in London and the South East have arrived in Leamington and the Restaurant staff are preparing for busier times.

Meals were supplied to a party of refugees who had been housed at 'The Gables' Kenilworth Road. Another property requisitioned for housing refugees was 38, Clemens Street. The Pump Room Committee agreed to provide baths at a reduced cost of 3d. per person – the Billeting Officer was to ensure that they only had one bath per week. The Ministry of Health authorised the provision of meals at a reduced cost.

18th August 1944: - The Borough Council [hereafter referred to as Council] thanked the staff of the British Restaurant for the excellent meals they have been providing.

13th October 1944: - On 1st November the Central Kitchen will cease providing 'cash and carry' meals and the Education Committee will take over its operation. The staff will transfer to the British Restaurant which will provide the meals for the 'cash and carry' at 113, Warwick Street.

20th October 1944: - On Sundays the Restaurant will now serve lunch from noon to 1.45pm and teas between 4.00pm and 6.00pm and the new weekday opening hours will be lunch from noon to 2.00pm and teas from 4.30pm to 7.30pm.

June 1945: - The 'cash and carry' depot at 113, Warwick Street closed at the end of June 1945 due to a decline in the number of meals being served.

20th December 1945: - Three hundred children with 'special circumstances' will attend the Mayor's Christmas party and have tea at the British Restaurant. On 21st December the elderly will also eat at the Restaurant.

11th January 1946: - A party was held for the helpers who ran the Hospitality Committee's Canteen and Hostel, originally in High Street now located in Spencer Street.

1st February 1946: - Price increases at the Restaurant are from 1s. 1d to 1s. 3d, from 1s. 4d to 1s. 6d and tea from 1d to 2d.

15th February 1946: - The Social Centre has moved from the Restaurant to the Garrison Theatre at the rear of the NAAFI, 19, The Parade.

29th March 1946: - The future of the British Restaurant is in doubt as the BRC has been served with notice to quit on 29th September. The Ministry of Food has been informed. A large number of requests have been received for large parties for lunch, so the Restaurant may open from 12.30pm to 7.00pm.

3rd May 1946: - Although a notice to quit has been received from the owners of the Liberal Club, the Restaurant will remain open until at least 31st March 1947.

31st May 1946: - Self-service meals have been discontinued at the Restaurant.

January 1947: - The total number of meals provided in 1946 was 138,662.

14th February 1947: - Although the Restaurant will continue to trade during the present food crisis, the local Chamber of Trade is objecting because the Council is attempting to acquire the Liberal Club premises, possibly using Compulsory Purchase powers.

7th March 1947: - Acquiring the premises occupied by the British Restaurant is not being done by underhand methods as the Council had been intending to acquire the premises prior to the war.

14th March 1947: - The Council decides to place a Compulsory Purchase Order on the Liberal Club premises as it proposes to use it for council accommodation after the Restaurant closes.

10th October 1947: - A Ministry of Health inspector is conducting a public enquiry into an application by the Council to make a compulsory purchase of the Liberal Club premises in Regent Grove [and would find in favour of the Liberal Club]; the Council has been paying an annual rent of £155.

26th December 1947: - On four days prior to Christmas the 'Mayor's Fund' provided dinners for the elderly folk of Leamington. In addition some 500 children had tea at the Restaurant also courtesy of the 'Mayor's Fund'.

2nd April 1948: - The Council is required to pay £400 per annum for a new lease on the premises.

1st October 1948: - The District Valuer is currently negotiating the purchase price of the Liberal Club on behalf of the Council.

31st December 1948: - The Restaurant is expected to close in March 1949.

11th March 1949: - The closure of the Restaurant is rescheduled for 30th September 1949.

Footnote

Circa 1950, the Leamington Borough Council paid £8,000 for the Regent Grove site and the Liberal Club relocated to 87, Upper Holly Walk, a building designed by the renowned architect William Thomas. In 2015 the name of the club was changed to the Oak House Sports and Social Club.

The Central Kitchens in Brunswick Street were demolished circa mid-1980s.

Y.M.C.A.

The Young Men's Christian Association, more commonly known as the Y.M.C.A., was founded by Sir George Williams, a worker in the drapery trade in London in 1844. During the Second World War, the association introduced mobile canteens, taking refreshments to the troops, and supported displaced people, refugees and prisoners of war. Their presence could also be seen on the Home Front. This photo shows Anne Clarissa Eden, the wife of Anthony Eden, then Foreign Secretary, doing her 'bit' as the driver of one of the Y.M.C.A.'s local mobile 'tea cars'.

Local Defences

On 16th July 1940 Adolf Hitler issued Directive No.16, stating that an invasion was necessary 'to eliminate the English homeland as a base for carrying on the war against Germany, and, should it be necessary, to occupy completely'. The German codename for the invasion of Britain was Operation Sealion.

To counter the potential invasion, during 1940 extensive fortifications were rapidly constructed, comprising mainly coastal defences and inland stop lines. The stop lines consisted of natural and artificial barriers, particularly rivers and canals, backed up by defences of anti-tank ditches, barbed wire entanglements, roadblocks, weapon positions, pillboxes and other obstacles. Across the country there were 28,000 pillboxes, but only 6,000 still survive today.

The Southern Command Oxford Canal Stop Line followed the course of the River Thames to Oxford, then along the Oxford Canal via Banbury to Napton on the Hill, then west along the Grand Union Canal to the River Avon between Leamington Spa and Warwick.

Anti-aircraft defences for Leamington Spa were coordinated from a headquarters located in a former house, The Gables, at the north of Kenilworth Road. Light Anti-Aircraft Artillery [LAA] guns were deployed in Warwickshire to protect towns, factories and railways. The primary purpose of these guns was to engage low flying enemy aircraft. Many different types of LAA guns were used during the Second World War, including Lewis guns, Bren guns, 20mm Oerlikon guns, two pounder pom-pom guns and 40mm Bofors guns. The gun emplacements were generally insubstantial, comprising little more than circular earthworks, sandbags and occasionally earth-protected blockwork walls. Portable ammunition lockers would have been provided and at some sites there was a basic shelter for the gun crew.

Whitnash resident Len Shurvinton remembers a Bofors anti-aircraft gun being towed across the fields at Sydenham Farm on a wheeled platform. It was situated on what is now Campion School car park and was known as Able Site. It was manned by returning soldiers from Egypt. There are no known photos of the gun but this particular photo [previous page] is of a 40mm Bofors light anti-aircraft gun displayed at Coalhouse Fort, East Tilbury in Essex.

The photo on the right shows a 40mm Bofors anti-aircraft gun. This particular one was stationed at Sheerness in Kent. It had a crew of six and could fire up to 120 shells every minute.

The Lockheed factory at Tachbrook Road was protected by LAA guns located on the office and factory roofs. Lockheed was known as Baker Site. There are no known visible remains of LAA batteries in Leamington Spa.

Most of the artificial defences have long since been removed. However, there are still some examples of pillboxes and anti-tank concrete blocks in the local area.

Pillboxes

The main types of pillbox constructed at Warwickshire stop lines were Standard Types 22 and 24. These were two of seven designs supplied during June and July 1940 by the FW3 branch of the Directorate of Fortifications and Works at the War Office.

Adjacent to the Oxford Canal near Napton several 'Stent' prefabricated concrete pillboxes are still in existence as shown in this photograph. This type of pillbox is square in plan and based on the design of the FW3 branch Type 26 pillbox.

One pillbox of brick and concrete construction, located on top of the railway embankment, just north of the viaduct, alongside Prince's Drive [SP307656] was demolished in the 1960s.

One local pillbox that still remains is a Type 24 pillbox near the Bottom Lock on the Grand Union Canal at Radford Semele. It is on land owned by farmer Henry Marriott. This pillbox protected the Grand Union Canal locks and the former London, Midland, Scottish [LMS] railway viaduct crossing the canal. The pillbox is positioned on the dismantled railway line with the main embrasures facing the canal locks and viaduct.

The pillbox is of a Standard Type 24 irregular hexagon design. The entrance door face has two rifle embrasures and the other five wall faces each have one embrasure. The wall construction is brickwork shuttering with concrete infill and an overall wall thickness of 450mm. The roof is of a reinforced concrete construction. Internally there is a 225mm thick brickwork Y-shaped blast/anti-ricochet wall. Post World War Two this pillbox was modified to create a bat hibernaculum by modifying the entrance and fitting wall boarding inside.

Radford Semele Pillbox photographed on 16th April 2013.

This December 2001 photo is of the Type 22 pillbox that protected the railway viaduct crossing the River Avon at Warwick [SP298654]. It was demolished in 2002.

Anti-Tank Islands and Anti-Tank Obstacles

The planning and construction of stop lines was generally abandoned during late 1940 when the defence strategy was changed to defence in depth and a more aggressive and mobile form of counter attack. Mobile forces were located close to the coastal defences, and fortified inland towns and villages were created. The fortified towns and villages were given various designations such as anti-tank islands, nodal points, centres of resistance and defended localities. The Warwickshire towns of Henley-in-Arden, Stratford-Upon-Avon, Warwick and Leamington Spa, Rugby and the City of Coventry were proposed as anti-tank islands and were defended by the Home Guard.

Some of the main artificial defences for both anti-tank islands and anti-tank stop lines were anti-tank obstacles. The purpose of the anti-tank obstacles was to obstruct the progress of a tank, or, should it attempt to cross the obstacle, expose the tank's vulnerable underside to fire. There were six main types of obstacles; one of which being anti-tank concrete blocks. They were constructed to various designs, for example cube, coffin, pimple, cylinder and octagonal. Positioned in lines or groups they formed a continuous anti-tank barrier, with rubble spread about to stop the cylinders being overturned and rolled by the enemy. There are still examples locally of these blocks, but they have a different function today!

This photo taken by Derek Billings in April 2009 shows cylinders that were unearthed when the old Whitnash School was refurbished and extended as the St. Margaret's Centre, Community Centre.

Some cylinders are a garden feature for a house in Brunswick Street, Leamington Spa as shown in this photo taken on 28th November 2015.

A number of the cylinders from the old Whitnash School were rescued by the Ashdown Camp, Badsey near Evesham where they are now displayed.

Octagonal concrete blocks were located at road bridges crossing the Grand Union Canal at Leamington Spa. The blocks were located adjacent to several bridges for many years after WW2. Blocks adjacent to the bridge opposite the old Ford's Foundry site at Old Warwick Road were removed when the new bridge was constructed. Octagonal blocks are still in existence at several bridges by the Oxford Canal near Napton and at several bridges by the dismantled Leamington to Rugby railway line.

The Morning News dated Thursday 14th December 1944 reported: -
Removal of Road Blocks – Replying to Councillor R. S. Salt, at the meeting of Leamington Town Council, this week, Alderman A. Ashton [Chairman of the Highways and Town Planning Committee] said the work of removing road blocks in the Borough was being carried out as speedily as the labour situation would allow.

This is not an anti-tank concrete cylinder from Leamington Spa, it was photographed in March 2016 in Cathiron near Rugby.

However, it shows the ingenuity of people in that they can come up with a simple idea to use the old blocks in a useful way.

Recreation and Entertainment

It may seem strange to have an entertainment heading in a book about the war. However, entertainment was very important to people, and those in Leamington Spa were no different. In 1939 the impending political crisis did not prevent people from enjoying themselves. One of the highlights of the sporting year was a Festival of Fitness in Victoria Park, the first large scale event to boost the government's keep fit plan. The main attraction was a demonstration by S. C. Wooderson who had just returned from running in America.

As soon as war broke out all cinemas were ordered to close at 10.00pm so the evening performances started at 5.45pm.

On 1st September 1939, the service to the 20,000 televisions in Britain was stopped and it wasn't started again until BBC broadcasts resumed on 7th June 1946. Seven years without the TV! However, the average family didn't have TV, they listened to the wireless, or as we say now, the radio. When war started the national and regional radio programmes combined to form the Home Service.

The Morning News dated Tuesday 27th February 1940 reported: - '**Sunday Opening of Cinemas – Leamington Innovation Welcomed** – Any doubts which may have existed regarding the demand for Sunday cinemas at Leamington were dispelled on the introduction of this war time innovation. Three cinemas, the Regal, Regent, and Clifton, were open for the first time on a Sunday and though capacity business was not experienced, the size of the audiences at all three houses suggested that the facilities provided by Sunday opening are likely to prove popular with the public. Mr. E. Wilmot Carlton, supervisor of the Leamington cinemas, told the Morning News that he was very satisfied with the support accorded the opening performances, particularly as the arrangements had been completed at such short notice. The attendances were such as to justify the company's action in applying for permission to open on Sundays and a number of soldiers were among those who expressed pleasure that the application had been granted.'

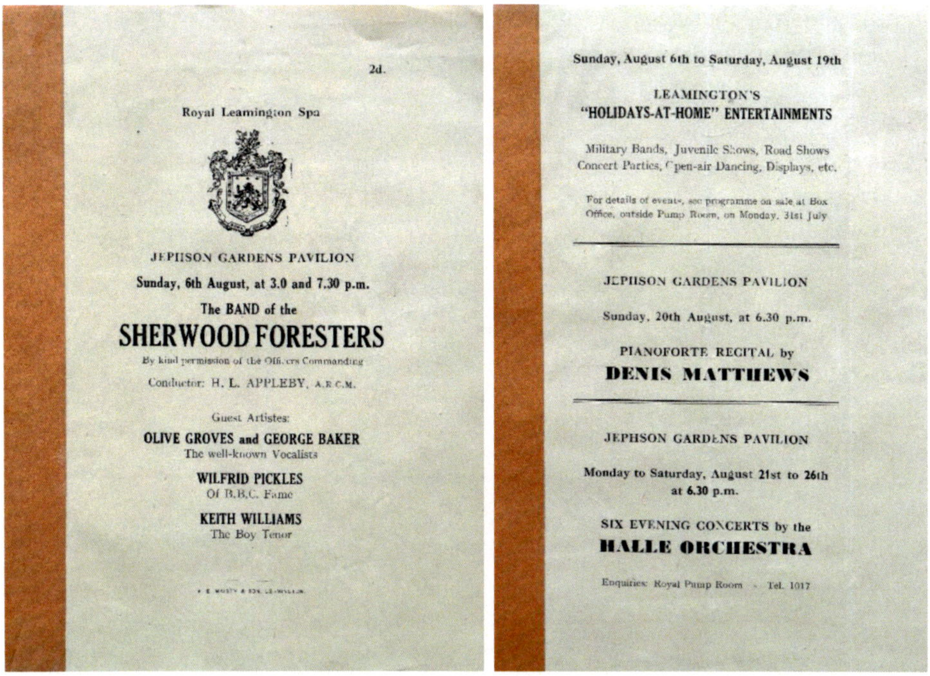

2d.

Royal Leamington Spa

JEPHSON GARDENS PAVILION

Sunday, 6th August, at 3.0 and 7.30 p.m.

The BAND of the

SHERWOOD FORESTERS

By kind permission of the Officers Commanding

Conductor: H. L. APPLEBY, A.R.C.M.

Guest Artistes:

OLIVE GROVES and GEORGE BAKER

The well-known Vocalists

WILFRID PICKLES

Of B.B.C. Fame

KEITH WILLIAMS

The Boy Tenor

Sunday, August 6th to Saturday, August 19th

LEAMINGTON'S

"HOLIDAYS-AT-HOME" ENTERTAINMENTS

Military Bands, Juvenile Shows, Road Shows

Concert Parties, Open-air Dancing, Displays, etc.

For details of events, see programme on sale at Box Office, outside Pump Room, on Monday, 31st July

JEPHSON GARDENS PAVILION

Sunday, 20th August, at 6.30 p.m.

PIANOFORTE RECITAL by

DENIS MATTHEWS

JEPHSON GARDENS PAVILION

Monday to Saturday, August 21st to 26th at 6.30 p.m.

SIX EVENING CONCERTS by the

HALLE ORCHESTRA

Enquiries: Royal Pump Room - Tel. 1017

Leamington's 'Holiday's at Home' Programme for August 1939.

The Morning News dated Wednesday 15th May 1940 reported: - '**7,000 in the Gardens on Monday** – Despite the cancellation of the Whitsun Bank Holiday, Leamington had a fair number of visitors on Monday and no fewer than 7,000 persons paid for admission to the Jephson Gardens during the day. This was about half the number that entered the gardens on Whit Monday, 1939. Nevertheless, having regard to the exceptional circumstances, it was a striking and encouraging attendance.

The Band of the Grenadier Guards proved a popular attraction in the Pump Room Gardens, and the total number of people who took chairs for the three performances was 2,000. The "Roosters" Concert Party were also well supported with a total of nearly 1,000 patrons for their two performances. Nearly 1,000 meals were served in the Pump Room Tea Room and there were 500 attendances at the swimming bath.'

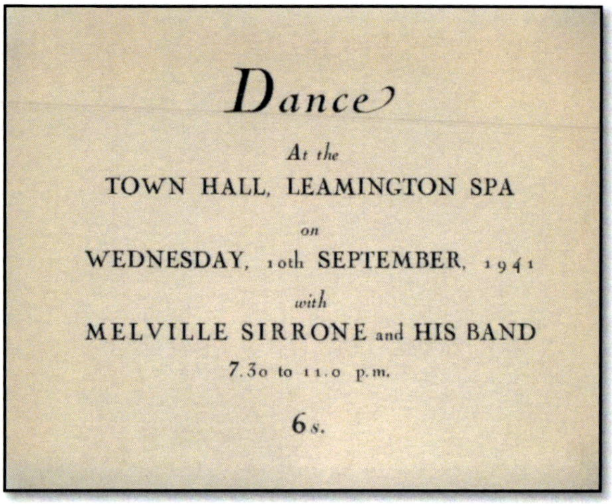
Dance

At the

TOWN HALL, LEAMINGTON SPA

on

WEDNESDAY, 10th SEPTEMBER, 1941

with

MELVILLE SIRRONE and HIS BAND

7.30 to 11.0 p.m.

6s.

There were four cinemas in Leamington at the time, Regal, Regent, Clifton and the Scala. On Thursday 21st November 1940 Clive Brook was starring in 'Convoy' at the Regal, 'Dr. Cyclops' was on at the Regent in gorgeous technicolor and the Clifton was showing 'The Briggs Family' with Edward Chapman and Laraine Day in 'And one was Beautiful' and the Scala had Louise Platt in 'Forgotten Girls' and Johnny Mack Brown in 'West of Carson City'.

Jephson Gardens · Leamington Spa

Saturday, August 14th, at 6-15 p.m.

A "FRIENDS OF MUSIC"

Concert

(under the auspices of the Leamington Corporation)

THE BOYD NEEL STRING ORCHESTRA

(Leader: FREDERICK GRINKE)

Conductor: BOYD NEEL

WITH

JAN VAN DER GUCHT

Tenor

At the Piano:

FRANZ HOLMAN

Concert Direction:
W. H. Priestley & Sons Ltd.

Programme
Price 6d.

A concert by the Boyd Neel String Orchestra was given at the Jephson Gardens Pavilion on Saturday 14th August 1943.

Pauline Zwicker née Wilson said, "Films seemed to be so good in those days and it was nice to be able to book a seat at the Regal Cinema. The Palais on Saturday afternoons for tea dances was a good place to learn to dance and the floor was beautifully sprung. To miss a Friday night dance at the Town Hall would have been a great disappointment. There was no need to go with a partner, all your friends went and there was usually someone nice to escort you home. The men on leave, the mixture of nationalities and uniforms all made for an exciting time. Ballroom dancing schools were popular. Gilbert and Enid Wright had a school on the Parade and Eric Hancox had one somewhere down the Willes Road."

It wasn't only the foreign troops and the men on leave that came into town for the dances and the cinema. Another group was the men and women of 91 Bomber Command who were based at Wellesbourne. This circa 1942 photo shows them with a Wellington Bomber. It has Hercules side valve engines and Rotol propellers.

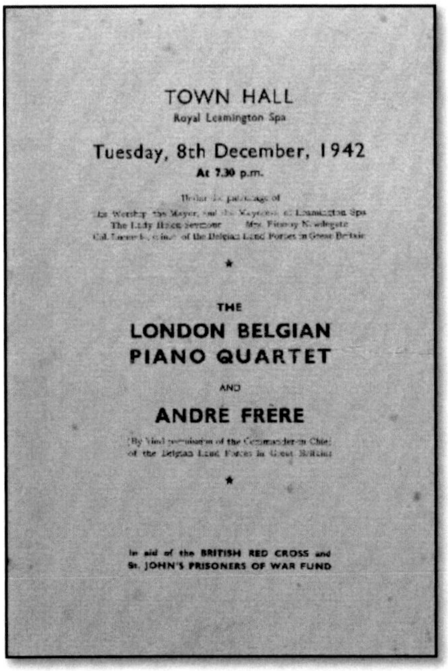

Dances were extremely popular. There were "Ye Olde Tyme Dances" at the Blue Café in Bath Street and dances and concerts at the Town Hall and in the Jephson Gardens Pavilion.

In November 1940, the Royal Air Force Station Orchestra with BBC Entertainer Chick Fowler played afternoon and evening concerts at the Town Hall.

On 8th December 1942, the London Belgian Piano Quartet and Andrè Frère performed at the Town Hall. André Frère was a Corporal in the Belgian Army and so permission from the Commander-in-Chief of the Belgian Land Forces in Great Britain was required for him to play.

The Blue Café - The Blue Café and Dance Hall at 52 Bath Street has been advertised since 1924 and continued to be listed in local directories until 1945. The proprietor was Mrs. Margaret Mary Maitland Fowler OBE.

The entrance was on the right-hand side of the Parthenon building. The rest of the ground floor was Blackburn's the men's outfitters. There were about five stone steps leading up to the entrance door through which was a steep staircase leading to a landing, to the right was a large room that was used for the ballroom and dancing area. It had blue cork/lino flooring and included a stage on the right-hand side of the room for the band. Around the walls were a great many large flags. Turning left from the landing took you to the café area which was over the outfitters shop and looked out onto Bath Street.

In the Blue Café, everything was blue, from the paint on the walls to the curtains and table cloths, and Mrs. Fowler herself wore blue. Leamington History Group member, the late Noreen Connolly had fond memories of pre-war autumn evenings spent there. She said, "We used to go dancing quite a lot with the girls. Occasionally we would go to the Blue Café. It was upholstered everywhere in blue velvet and Mrs. Fowler who owned the premises never wore anything else but royal blue with silver fox. Her Rolls Royce was royal blue and her chauffeur whose name was Morgan, was dressed in a royal blue coat and boots." The Blue Café hosted some of the most famous dance bands of the day.

In the 'Memory Lane' column of the Leamington Courier dated 16th October 1992, Bee Blackwell, recalled the excitement of visiting the Blue Café as a young girl before the war. One year, just before Christmas, Bee and her friends were allowed to attend one of the celebrated Blue Café Tea Dances. Each clutching a canvas bag holding their dancing shoes and 1s. 3d for their tickets, they rushed up the steep steps of the Blue Café to the cloakroom on the top floor. They were overwhelmed by the ballroom, the décor, the size of the stage and the shining floor, surrounded by small blue-clothed tables, but not so much that they didn't take to the floor along with everyone else when the Black Satin Orchestra played 'Painting the Clouds with Sunshine'. Waitresses wearing blue fluted aprons served thin slices of bread and butter, fish paste sandwiches, small iced cakes and trifle with cream. Balloons and streamers were thrown from the stage as the last waltz was played, leaving them to make their way home through the late afternoon gas-lit streets.

In October 1939, the Leamington Courier reported that, 'a happy company of old time dancers attended the opening session of Ye Old Time Dance Club at the Blue Café'. Despite the wartime black-out, transport and other restrictions, people came from as far away as Moreton-in-Marsh. Only one young lady had to be turned away, having forgotten her gas mask. Local musician Frank Rawlings and his Band played favourites such as the Old-Time Waltz, the Empress Tango, Jazz Twinkle, the Palais Glide, the Veleta and the Boston. In October the following year the Dance Club opened their ninth season with a programme by the Rawlings Band, and an audience of close on 200 made up of local devotees and Allied Military personnel. The popular programme was followed the next week by a skate dancing demonstration. Like the Windmill in London, the Blue Café never closed, continuing to promote musical and other events throughout the war. It was well-known that young women who worked at Lockheed liked to go dancing there on their days off, some of them calling in at the Bath Hotel further up the street, for a bit of 'Dutch Courage' beforehand.

A Blue Café dance admission ticket for Wednesday 11th December 1940.

On a number of occasions wounded soldiers were entertained at the Blue Café. On one occasion 'a large party from a Midlands Canadian Hospital were brought in motor coaches to Leamington as guests of the Alexandra Musical Society. On the way, they saw Warwick Castle, Guy's Cliffe, and other places of interest, and at Leamington they visited the Jephson Gardens. Tea was served at the Blue Café through the kindness of Mrs. M. M. M. Fowler, O.B.E., the Hon. Treasurer. Mr. Ernest C. Thomas, the founder of the Alexandra Musical Society thanked Mrs. Fowler for the kindness and help always given to him in his work for the wounded and disabled men.

He stated that already this year over 32,000 hospital patients and disabled ex-servicemen of 1914-1918 and of the present war had been entertained by the means of garden parties, visits to the Shakespeare Country, weekly visits to theatres and weekly whist drives in some 20 Midland hospitals and convalescent homes. Thousands of hospital patients visiting Birmingham had also been provided with tea at local cafes.

On Christmas day, this year, funds permitting, the Society hoped to be able to give a parcel to some 5,000 hospital patients, and badly disabled ex-servicemen, and to give a number of Christmas parties.'

The Frank Rawlings Band.

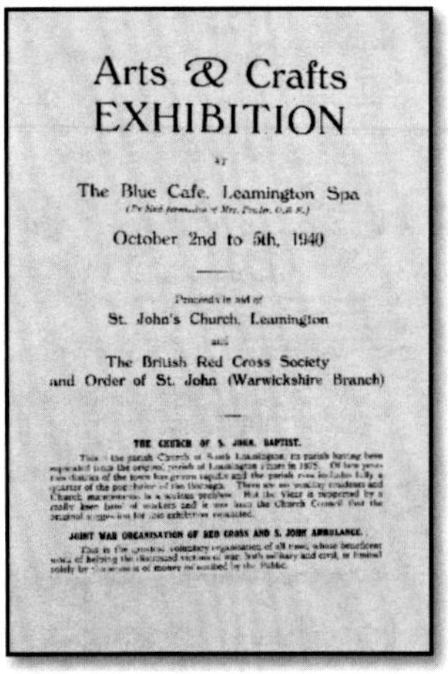

It wasn't only bands and dancing at the Blue Café as this flyer for an Arts and Crafts exhibition between 2nd – 5th October 1940 shows. This particular one was in aid of St. John's Church in Tachbrook Street, the British Red Cross and St. John Ambulance.

Not all requests for support turned out successfully though. Mrs. Fowler wrote to Gracie Fields, the actress and singer who did a great deal of work for the war effort. Gracie Fields signed up for E.N.S.A., the Entertainments National Service Association and travelled to France and other countries to entertain the troops. She had been made a C.B.E for her services to entertainment in 1938. Mrs. Fowler received a reply from her manager Bert Aza – "It's quite impossible dear lady. Every minute of Gracie's stay here is booked up with E.N.S.A. I have hundreds of requests to attend to. All have to be turned down. It's gratifying to know Gracie's popularity is as great as ever."

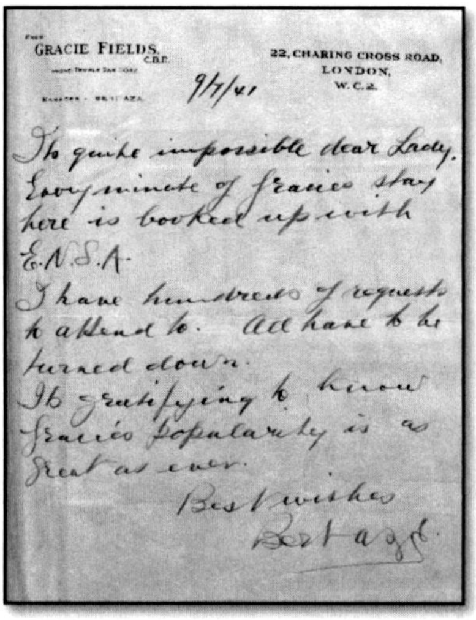

Mrs. Fowler's lease on the Blue Café expired on 25th March 1945. She remained in Leamington until her death in 1957 aged 76.

Some Polish Officers visited the Parade and although there was a Polish Festival at the Royal Pump Room on Thursday 13th February 1941, the Polish Army did not arrive in the country until 1946-1948.

Pauline Wilson said, "During 1943, 'Stay-at-Home' holidays were arranged in Leamington from July 26th to August 7th. The winner of a 'Miss Leamington Spa' competition was to preside at most of the functions during the holiday fortnight. The finals of the competition were held on the stage of the Regal Cinema."

"Miss Gladys Goss, of the Civil Service Social Club was the winner and Miss Eleanor Murdock, from the Imperial Foundry and I were her attendants. Councillor R. Wright briefly addressed the audience on the importance of "staying put" during the holiday season, and said that Leamington's programme of attractions was intended to keep people at home in order to avoid unnecessary travelling. An open-air theatre was erected in the Pump Room Gardens and variety shows, children's matinees, clowns and talent competitions were held daily and the evenings finished with open air dancing from 9.00pm."

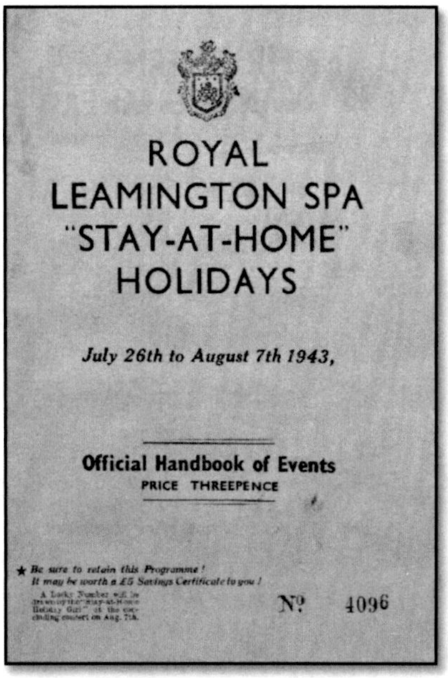

"Special entertainments were arranged during the fortnight. On the last Friday and Saturday of the holiday the famous Russian Cossack riders gave displays in the Victoria Park. These amazing riders fought in the First World War and later banded together and became well-known for their fearless demonstrations of horsemanship."

The Pump Room had Van Der Venn and his Trio playing on weekdays at 11.00am and 3.00pm.

In November 1940, there was a celebrity concert by Bratza, the celebrated violinist and Dushko Yovanovitch the pianist.

Jan Berenska and his orchestra rehearsing at the Royal Pump Room.

It was agreed in March 1941 that as from Sunday 9th June the Jan Berenska Quartet would be engaged to play in the tea room of the Pump Rooms on Sunday afternoons at a fee of £6 per performance.

Jan Berenska was very busy at various venues during the war. The Leamington Spa Courier dated Friday 19th November 1943 reported: - On Sundays at 3.30pm Jan Berenska and the Royal Spa Quartet will be at the Royal Pump Room where admission is 1s. On Fridays from 8.00pm until 11.00pm he is at the Town Hall with his dance orchestra, admission costs 2s. 6d.

On Sunday 21st November, he again played at the Town Hall with his orchestra, this time accompanied by the famous English Prima Donna Laelia Finneberg; admission was 1s. and 1s. 6d. or could be reserved for 2s.

On Tuesday 30th November, he did another dance at the Town Hall this time for the National Fire Service whose operational station was at Adelaide Road. Tickets cost 5s. and the proceeds were in aid of Warneford Hospital.

LEAMINGTON SPA MUSIC COMMITTEE
in association with
C·E·M·A
TOWN HALL
LEAMINGTON SPA.
Monday, September 27th
at 7-0 p.m.
JACQUES STRING ORCHESTRA
Conductor:
Dr. REGINALD JACQUES
Leader:
RUTH PEARL
with
LEYLAND WHITE
Baritone
Programme will include: Suite for Strings, Handel arr. Jacques. Concerto Grosso in E minor, Vivaldi. Divertimento, Mozart. Fugal Concerto, Holst, etc.; and Songs with Orchestra
TICKETS: 5/-, 3/6, & 2/6 reserved
2/- unreserved
Tickets and all information from the Royal Pump Room
Telephone: Leamington 1017
Council for the Encouragement of Music and the Arts

On Monday 27th September 1943, the Jacques String Orchestra was at the Town Hall. This was a CEMA concert – Council for the Encouragement of Music and the Arts. The council administered a treasury grant "to maintain the highest standard of art in war-time, and to bring people everywhere all the refreshment and recreation which music, drama and painting can give".

Many readers of this book will remember the brilliant annual pantomimes performed by members of the Lockheed Sports and Social Club in the 1950s and 1960s. However, the show had started many years earlier and went on through the war years.

Popular comedian Tommy Trinder visited the Lockheed munitions factory on 21st June 1940 as he launched the first War Savings ballot.

During the new year of 1942 the cast performed 'Babes in the Wood' to packed houses. It was so popular, and demand so great, that extra performances were put on. The profits from the show were divided between the Denville Home for Aged Actors and the local Sunshine Home for Blind Babies.

Also in 1942, Leamington decided to co-operate with the "Stay-at-Home" holiday plan. A Committee was appointed to make arrangements for a continuous round of entertainment for the August Bank Holiday week for the Pump Room Gardens which resembled a large open-air theatre. On Monday 3rd August, there was a horticultural show at 1.30pm, folk dancing at 2.30pm, beekeeping demonstration at 3.00pm and 6.00pm, Band of the Duke of Wellington's Regiment at 3.00pm and 8.00pm, open-air dancing at 4.00pm, talk to allotment holders at 4.30pm, open-air theatre at 7.00pm and "Civvy Farm" demonstrations, sideshows and competitions throughout the afternoon. Further events took place for adults and children each day during the week.

The Radio show 'Workers Playtime' would be broadcast from various workplaces throughout the country and on 19th May 1942 they broadcast from Lockheed. There was even a football match played at the Windmill Ground when a Czechoslovak Army XI beat a Norwegian Army XI by 2 goals to 1.

There were a number of these types of football match. Another took place on Saturday 8th May 1943 when a Belgium XI met "D" [Lockheed] Company, 1st Warwick Battalion Home Guard at the Windmill Ground, Tachbrook Road. The game, which was said to be very clean and enjoyable, resulted in a decisive victory for the Home Guard, the score being 7-1.

Another popular venue was the Palais de Danse in Spencer Street at which the following two photographs were taken in the 1940s. Neither are dated and in all likelihood, they were taken after the war ended. Slightly to the right of centre on the front row of the second photo is local Member of Parliament Anthony Eden.

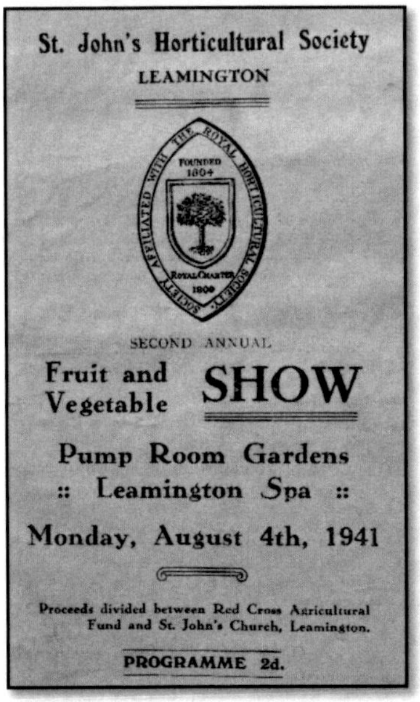

St. John's Horticultural Society
LEAMINGTON

SECOND ANNUAL
Fruit and Vegetable SHOW
Pump Room Gardens :: Leamington Spa ::
Monday, August 4th, 1941

Proceeds divided between Red Cross Agricultural Fund and St. John's Church, Leamington.

PROGRAMME 2d.

The programme cover for the 2nd St. John's Horticultural show held on Monday 4th August 1941.

The Holidays-At-Home programme for 1944 started on Saturday 5th August 1944 and ended on Saturday 19th August. Thousands of holiday makers came in each day from Coventry, and the town's entertainments did good business. One of those doing 'good business' in the Jephson Gardens was Mr. S. L. Whittington Wickes, described as "The Amazing Chang". With the aid of his assistant he presented the headless lady. Later, while the lady is presumably in a cabinet, a number of daggers were inserted to form a torture collar. The lady later emerged completely unscathed. In the King of the Magic Rings trick he obtained three rings from the audience and after they were apparently smashed with a hammer, they were found concealed in a small box encased by other boxes each one attached to a floral buttonhole. It was said that he was equally good with a bullet catching trick. He even managed to produce an R.A.F officer from an "empty chest".

On Sunday 6th August the band of the Sherwood Foresters gave two performances in the Pavilion. Wilfred Pickles, Miss. Olive Graves and George Baker were the guest artists. On Bank Holiday Monday, the day's events in the Pump Room Gardens included the 5th show of the St. John's Horticultural Society, the band of the Sherwood Foresters, a cabaret circus and open-air dancing. In the Jephson Gardens Pavilion there was children's entertainment and at Victoria Park there was a bowls tournament.

British Welcome Club - Rear of 19 The Parade
The Leamington Spa Courier dated 2nd June 1944 reported that: - a British Welcome Club is to be opened in Leamington at premises offered by the N.A.A.F.I [Navy, Army and Air Force Institutes] at the rear of 19, The Parade. The club will serve as a meeting place for American and other Allied troops with British troops and civilians. There were however no American troops actually stationed in Leamington itself although there were some a few miles away at Stareton.

The idea behind Welcome Clubs was to enable visiting Allied troops, particularly American troops, to socialise in a safe and genial atmosphere with local people. The first Welcome Club was set up in Sunbury in 1942 and there were eventually around 200 across the country. Efforts had been made to start a Welcome Club in Leamington since February 1944 but suitable premises could not be found.

At a meeting called by the Mayor at the Town Hall on the evening of Wednesday 31st May 1944, Mrs. T. H. Ryland, County Organiser of the Women's Voluntary services [which was responsible for the scheme] stated that the first British Welcome Club had been so successful under the W.V.S. that the Ministry of Information had asked them to go ahead in opening other clubs throughout the country. More than a hundred were already in existence, with three already operating in Warwickshire - at Atherstone, Alcester and Nuneaton.

It was very difficult for the many thousands of American troops stationed all over England to make social contacts. The Welcome Clubs were usually opened one or two nights a week with the object of providing somewhere for them to socialise in a safe and genial atmosphere and to provide introductions to local residents, leading to invitations to their homes.

It was recommended that girls, civilians, Services and Land Army personnel, etc. should be invited into membership, but, generally speaking no girl under 17 should be admitted. Girls put up for membership would have to be approved by the Committee. Each American Unit would be issued with a certain number of membership tickets. When started, members of the Club would be asked to form a Junior Committee.

Mrs. Ryland explained that clubs varied greatly in character, some liked games, others dancing, whilst some went in for serious debates. Ping pong, however, was invariably popular and when the Americans were present the racquets were usually in action.

There would she said be more difficulty in getting the Club going in Leamington than in many other places because the troops were not stationed in the town and transport would be a problem. However she believed this problem would be surmounted.

Replying to a question as to whether the Clubs were intended merely to provide opportunities for Americans to meet English girls, Mrs. Ryland said, "We find that the Americans are not always meeting our best type of girls. Too often they meet girls at the street corners. This Club will give a chance for the best type of American to meet the best type of English girl. Further, the Americans are interested in meeting Englishmen of similar professions to their own."

Lady Coventry spoke warmly in praise of the proposal to start the Club and support came from several of the American officers' present. In moving the formal resolution to inaugurate the Club, Mr. Alan Pollock said it was a shame that the Americans should be left to wander aimlessly about the town, with nothing to do. The Club would supply a very definite need.

The Mayor was elected President, with Mr. Pollock as Chairman, Mrs. Berger [12a Lillington Avenue], Hon Secretary, and Mr. R. A. Bellerby Hon. Treasurer. They would form the executive committee, with the addition of Miss Shorto and Councillor Davidson.

Admission was free to all members of the Services [including the Women's Land Army and the National Fire Service] in uniform. Members of the Forces on leave were also welcome to use the club. The only 'passport' required for admission was for them to wear their uniform. Civilians' admission was confined to club members who had paid a quarterly subscription of 3s. Application could be made to the W.V.S office in Warwick Street. Regular club nights consisting of dancing, ping pong and darts were held on Tuesdays and Saturdays between 7.30pm to 10.30pm in the Garrison Theatre behind the N.A.A.F.I.

By August 1944, members of the Armed Forces were beginning to know of the existence of the Club and Mr. J. Lucas of 76 Northumberland Road had become the Hon. Secretary. Regular weekly social evenings were taking place and the American members returned the hospitality by inviting the hostesses and members of the Committee to a camp 'in the Midlands'.

On Sunday 8th October 1944, 40 of the hostesses of the club entertained 20 British and 20 American wounded soldiers, and on Thursday 5th there was a special dance to the music of the 77th Station Hospital Band of the U.S Army.

On Saturday 23rd December 1944, the club organised a Christmas Party for around 200 guests. The club was decorated with Christmas decorations, a large Christmas tree was put up, beer was provided and Servicemen and women were entertained by club hostesses. The Town Clerk [Mr. A. F. Greenwood] acted as Santa and distributed presents to everyone. The evening included dancing and carol singing and the party broke up around midnight to the strains of 'Auld Land Syne'.

At the end of 1944 the club was six months old and had 50 club nights to its credit. Thanks were passed on to the military authorities who lent the hall, the W.V.S who assisted with the supervision, the parties of ladies who looked after the catering, the various voluntary service dance bands, and the civilian members and junior committee who took charge of the entertainment.

In January 1945, the Junior Committee suggested that on each evening there should be a Belgian host who could make announcements in French.

By January 1946, club nights were cancelled due to poor attendance and the increasing difficulty of getting dance bands. The club officially closed on 26th March 1946 due to the lack of support and poor attendances by members of the forces, quite understandable as the troops had returned home. The club had served a very useful purpose for a short time but was no longer required.

The Executive Committee of the British Welcome Club held their final meeting at the end of April 1946, bringing a formal close to the Club. Most other Welcome Clubs were also brought to a close during 1946.

After payment of all outstanding liabilities their accounts showed a surplus of £74. 4s. 3d. A donation of £50 was made to the Army Benevolent Fund and the balance of £24. 4s. 3d. was sent to the District Bank in Chester to pay for a summer party in aid of troops and ex-servicemen from the Dominions and Colonies.

Allied Services Club – 7 Bertie Terrace
The Allied Services Club was opened on the afternoon of Saturday 11th January 1941 by Brigadier Blakesdon Houston in the presence of a number of leading townspeople including the Mayor and Mayoress, Alderman and Mrs. M. S. Moore, as well as members of the armed forces. Through the efforts of the Leamington Rotary Club £500 was raised for the adaptation and equipment of the premises. The club closed on 6th July 1945.

Leamington Officers Club – 8 Newbold Terrace

The Leamington Officers Club was first registered on 3rd September 1943. The Secretary was Major Walford Barnes and the Steward was Arthur Meredith Collier. On Sunday 19th September 1943, a representative gathering of townsfolk and military officers from various parts of the Midlands assembled at 'Rossmore' 8, Newbold Terrace, the occasion being the opening of the Club by Group Captain Lord Willoughby de Broke, M.C; A.F.C; Lord Lieutenant of the County. The leased premises [renovated by Messrs. Stowe and Co. Ltd.] comprised a dining room, lounge and cocktail bar [rear of lounge] on the ground floor, and a room on the first floor with a full size billiard table.

By February 1944, membership numbered 250. The subscription for officers residing in Leamington was £3 per annum and for "country members" residing outside Leamington, 30s. per annum. There were 10 beds and the nightly charge for bed and breakfast [including bath] was 8s. This fully licensed club had a short life, closing on 1st June 1946.

Pubs and Beer - Pubs and beer have always been important to many in our country and the fact that there was a war on wasn't going to change that. However, there were times when pubs were unable to obtain beer for a number of reasons. This resulted in different pubs closing on different days and/or at different times with little or no notice. The customer didn't know what was going on or whether his 'local' was going to be open, so much so that the Licensing Justices became involved and issued some guidance.

The Swan Inn 73 Clarendon Street taken on 6th February 1940. The landlord at the time was Ernest Felton.

In July 1941, the Leamington Spa Courier reported that: - "The Justices are much concerned about the present state of confusion caused by licensed premises opening for sale only during certain varied hours of the day," said Mr. A. H. Swadling, Chairman of the Leamington Licensing Justices. "They suggest that licensees should make their own arrangements whereby each licensed house is open every day during the same hours only. They strongly recommend that such hours be from 12 noon till 2 p.m. and from 8 till 10 p.m. The Chief Constable is in agreement with this suggestion."

Shortages in wartime meant that a number of products became more expensive as some unscrupulous suppliers saw an opportunity to make more profit. Breweries were anxious to ensure that customers were not overcharged for their products. An advert in the Leamington Spa Courier dated 19th November 1943 states: "FOR YOUR PROTECTION - the price of Ansells THE BETTER BEER is displayed in all of Ansells houses. Just as you can rely upon the quality of all Ansells beverages, so you can be assured that no increase in our authorised prices is permitted." Official spirit prices were also displayed in all licensed rooms.

In December 1943 Ansells, who supplied many of the local pubs, brought out a new brand, 'Strong SS Stout'. Their marketing in the Leamington Spa Courier stated, "Here is a name new to you - which represents Ansells greatest achievement in providing all who need a fine strong Stout in wartime. Ansells Strong Stout is also intended to replace Ansells Milk Stout which, as soon as present stocks are exhausted, will no longer be available, due to the use of milk products being prohibited for the purpose. At all Ansells houses [price in public bars 9½d. per half pint] or from off-licenses 1/6d. per pint bottle."

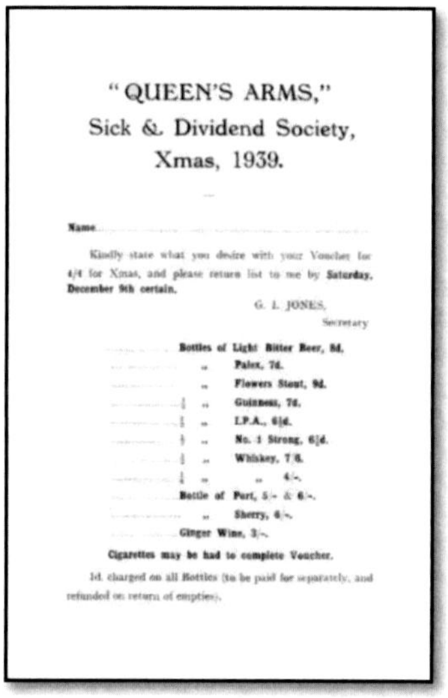

"QUEEN'S ARMS,"
Sick & Dividend Society,
Xmas, 1939.

Name..

Kindly state what you desire with your Voucher for 4/4 for Xmas, and please return list to me by **Saturday, December 9th certain.**

G. L. JONES,
Secretary

.... **Bottles of Light Bitter Beer, 8d.**
.... **" Palex, 7d.**
.... **" Flowers Stout, 9d.**
.... **" Guinness, 7d.**
.... **" I.P.A., 6½d.**
.... **" No. 1 Strong, 6½d.**
.... **" Whiskey, 7/6.**
.... **" " 4/-.**
.... **Bottle of Port, 5/- & 6/-.**
.... **" Sherry, 6/-.**
.... **Ginger Wine, 3/-.**

Cigarettes may be had to complete Voucher.

1d. charged on all Bottles (to be paid for separately, and refunded on return of empties).

A Christmas 1939 order form for members of the Queen's Arms, Queen Street, Sick and Dividend Society.

The Leamington Spa Courier dated 25th July 1945 carried the following article supplied by the Brewery Society: - 'WHAT NO BEER? – When the landlord of your local tells you that he has 'sold the last drop', you naturally think that less is being brewed today than in the past. Actually, the reverse is the case. Apart from all the beer which is being sent to our forces overseas, the amount of beer brewed for consumption in this country has risen by several million barrels per year since before the war. This increase has been achieved in spite of innumerable difficulties. Today, there is a limit to which Brewers can increase their output because malt, hops and other brewing materials, casks and bottles, and labour are all in short supply. The truth about the 'beer shortage' is in fact quite simple; beer has never been as popular as it is today and even with greatly increased production, supply cannot keep pace with public demand.'

Correspondence with loved ones

As anyone who has lived away from home will be aware, hearing from or about loved ones and family is very important. Letters are always anticipated, and there is a sense of disappointment if one doesn't arrive. The same applies if a member of the family is away from home, letters and even the occasional photograph are always anticipated and welcome. During the war they played a vital role as far as morale was concerned. These days if a soldier is in a conflict zone, they can rely on technology such as Skype, Facebook and Viber.

But during the war contact relied on the Post Office and the British Forces Post Office to pass on letters and postcards and it could be months before someone heard from their loved ones. Radio broadcasts could give a sense of what was happening abroad, but that didn't necessarily give the truth of a situation besides which it was information about family that was required. Once news had been received at home it was often passed onto the Leamington Spa Courier or the Morning News as a way of keeping the public informed.

The authorities realised the importance of mail to both the servicemen serving abroad and the family members at home, but in war time delivery of mail is especially difficult as space on aircraft is limited. In the early part of the war the Ministry of Transport was having serious problems maintaining a postal service to servicemen in the Middle East. The Post Office suddenly realised that the solution to their problems was a microfilm system invented by Kodak back in the early 1930s - and so the 'Airgraph' service came into being.

The idea itself was simple, photograph the letter at the sender's end, have the censor check them, give them a serial number, put them onto 16mm film, fly the roll of negatives to the destination end, print out the letters and deliver them. That way a huge quantity of letters could be sent at relatively little cost and with a massive saving in aircraft space. It is estimated that 1,600 letters weighed around 50lbs, but a reel of negatives only weighed 5oz.

Fortunately, the Kodak office in Cairo already had the capability to photograph letters and so the service from Cairo to London started quite quickly. The first Airgraph service comprising of around 70,000 letters commenced on 21st April 1941.

This system was a huge success, in the first month alone around 350,000 letters were sent and in the second month this figure rose to over 500,000. However, the service in the opposite direction took a while longer to start. It was August 1941 before the first Airgraph, sent by Queen Elizabeth to General Auchinleck, and with the serial number 'one' was sent. In the UK the printing on a roll, was done by Kodak at Wealdstone before being passed on to the Post Office for cutting, folding, enveloping and delivering. The Airgraph service was extended to other parts of the world and by the end of the war over 330 million Airgraphs had been processed.

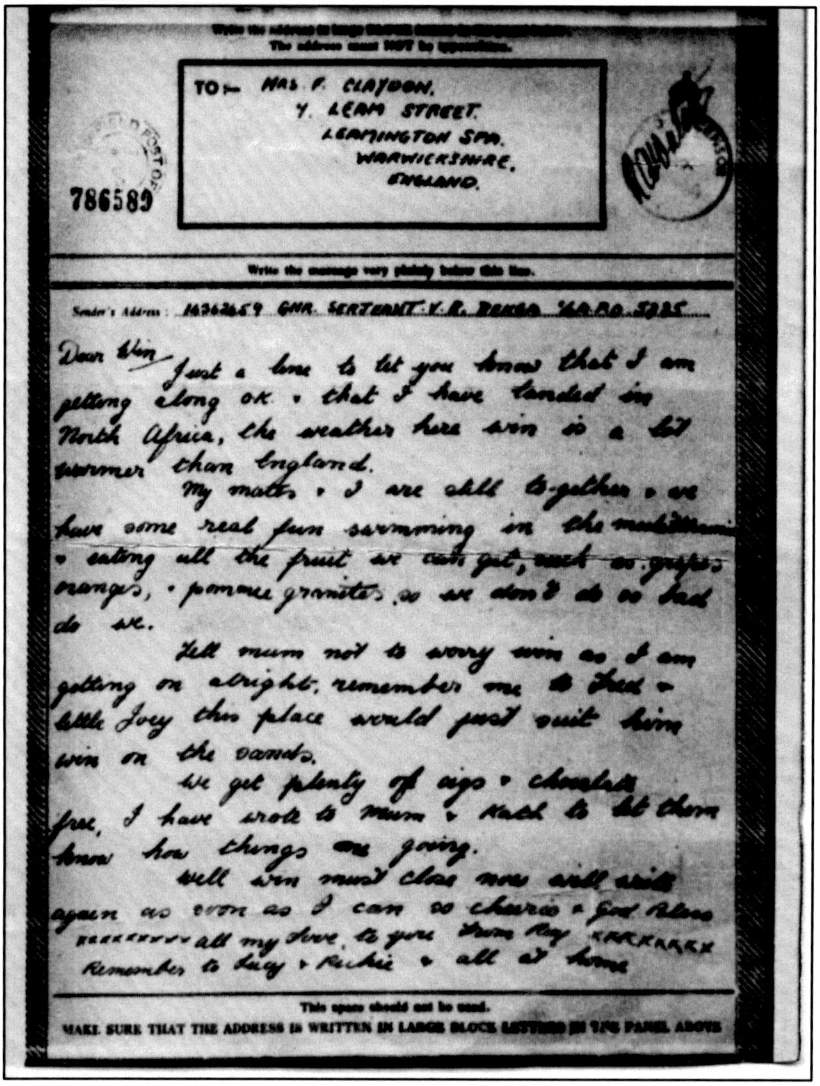

TO:- MRS. F. CLAYDON.
7. LEAM STREET.
LEAMINGTON SPA.
WARWICKSHIRE.
ENGLAND.

786589

Write the message very plainly below this line.

Sender's Address: 14362659 GNR. SERJEANT V. R. DENBO [illegible]

Dear Win,
Just a line to let you know that I am getting along OK & that I have landed in North Africa, the weather here Win is a lot warmer than England.
My mates & I are still to-gether & we have some real fun swimming in the Mediterranean & eating all the fruit we can get, such as grapes, oranges, & pommee granites, so we don't do so bad do we.
Tell mum not to worry Win as I am getting on alright, remember me to Fred & little Joey this place would just suit him Win on the sands.
We get plenty of eggs & chocolate free, I have wrote to Mum & Kath to let them know how things are going.
Well Win must close now will write again as soon as I can so cheerio & God Bless xxxxxxxx all my love to you from Roy xxxxxxxx
Remember to Lucy & Richie & all at home

This space should not be used.
MAKE SURE THAT THE ADDRESS IS WRITTEN IN LARGE BLOCK LETTERS IN THE PANEL ABOVE

A copy of an airgraph, an interesting forerunner of the microfiche. It was sent to Win Claydon, the mother of Leamington History Group member Joe Claydon. The airgraph was sent by her brother. The 'Little Joey' mentioned is Joe, who is not so little anymore! Win lived at 7 Leam Street and worked for Emil Romback at Spa Fancy Bakery in Wise Street.

One of those to use the Military Airgraph Service was Sergeant Norman Southwell 271/68th Field Regiment Royal Artillery who sent airgraphs and later air letters and letter cards to his aunt Mrs. Laura Bradshaw who lived at 102 Plymouth Place. Norman spent time with the P&I Force [Persian & Iraq] and in Italy, India and Burma.

Sergeant Norman Southwell

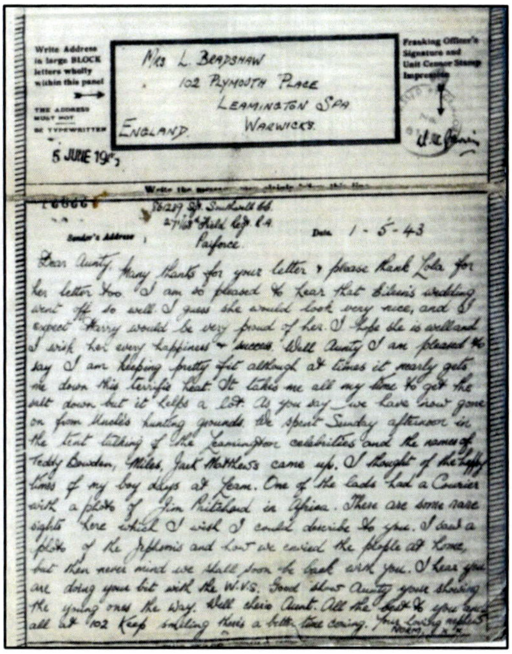

Write Address in large BLOCK letters wholly within this panel

THE ADDRESS MUST NOT BE TYPEWRITTEN

MRS L. BRADSHAW
102 PLYMOUTH PLACE
LEAMINGTON SPA
WARWICKS
ENGLAND

Franking Officer's Signature and Unit Censor Stamp Impression

5 JUNE 1943

Sender's Address: 768219 Sgt. Southwell 66. 271/68th Field Regt. R.A. Paiforce

Date 1-5-43

Dear Aunty. Many thanks for your letter & please thank Lola for her letter too. I am so pleased to hear that Eileen's wedding went off so well. I guess she would look very nice, and I expect Harry would be very proud of her. I hope she is well and I wish her every happiness & success. Well Aunty I am pleased to say I am keeping pretty fit although at times it nearly gets me down this terrific heat. It takes me all my time to get the salt down but it helps a lot. As you say we have now gone on from Uncle's hunting grounds. We spent Sunday afternoon in the tent talking of the Leamington celebrities and the names of Teddy Bowden, Miles, Jack Matthews came up. I thought of the happy times of my boy days at Leam. One of the lads had a Courier with a photo of Jim Pritchard in Africa. There are some rare sights here which I wish I could describe to you. I saw a photo of the Jephson's and how we envied the people at home, but then never mind we shall soon be back with you. I hear you are doing your bit with the W.V.S. Good show Aunty you're showing the young ones the way. Well cheerio Aunt. All the best to you and all at 102 Keep smiling there's a better time coming. Your loving nephew Norm

Much of the correspondence was about the family, 'I am alright', 'hope you and the family are alright', etc. In May 1943, he says that he is keeping pretty fit but the terrific heat gets him down - "It takes me all my time to get the salt down." It was thought necessary to keep replenishing the salt lost by sweating. Some of the messages were a little cryptic - "As you say we have now gone on from uncle's hunting grounds." Often, nostalgia crept in and there were references to Leamington - "We spent Sunday afternoon in the tent talking of the Leamington celebrities and the names of Terry Bowden, Miles and Jack Matthews came up." He continues, "I thought of the happy times of my boy days at Leam" and "One of the lads had a Courier with a photo of Jim Pritchard in Africa." "There are some rare sights here which I wish I could describe to you." No doubt the censor would have had something to say if he had. "I saw a photo of the Jephson's and how we envied the people at home, but then never mind we shall soon be back with you. I hear you are doing your bit with the W.V.S. Good show aunty, you showing the young ones the way."

Later in the month he says that he is ok and is settling down a bit on dry land for which he is truly grateful. Reading between the lines becomes the norm, in this case he has been at sea and suffered with sea sickness. "We are in a canvas camp in the middle of nowhere, completely desert for miles around. The heat of the day is pretty strong but at times very cold at night. We are fairly well fed here but mostly tinned stuff. We had a most interesting trip but of course I am not allowed to describe it - I thoroughly enjoyed the different sights we met on our way, it was an education to be sure."

In June 1943 he continues, "We were talking of Gill and uncle last night as we sat on our beds in the tent. A Sgt from Leam who knows Gill well and myself, his name is Cooper. Well aunt the weather steadily increases in temperature and has now reached 109°, it is hell about midday. We shall soon be melted away when it gets really hot. We have now been issued with a civi radio and everyone now sits round it in the lines with great pleasure, and it relieves the boredom. We are all waiting for the day to get moving towards the end and hoping it won't be long now, what a day aunty when we meet again."

In July 1943, the nostalgia continues, "I should like to be having one at the "George" with Boz in his new job." The "George" refers to having a pint in the George Hotel, an M&B pub in High Street. He continues, "Fancy Peter being in Malta, I hear Jim is in Africa now. What grand news of Sicily aunty? We had a NAAFI show visit the camp which was very good, one fellow was from Whitnash funny enough. There is nothing I want aunty except a pipe. One cannot get a pipe for love or money in the East. I started out with 3 but lost 2 on the boats and then I broke one in a vehicle so now I have to smoke fags. If any of the men folk should see one I should be greatly obliged. The food and water situation is good and the health bill is pretty good on the whole. We get a morning and evening [church] service each Sunday - voluntary, which is well attended. It just makes Sunday a bit different from week days which are so much alike here. Well aunty I will close now, wishing you and all at 102 all the very best for the coming months and hoping we shall see big changes in the war towards a very peaceful end when we can re-unite and make up for this life. Don't worry about me aunty for I have never felt better and very confident of success when our turn comes along."

Later that month he writes, "I am ok and keeping pretty fit in spite of the troubles and trials of this Army life. Since I wrote last we have made a good move for the better. The move was rather trying for our day chosen for moving was the hottest of the year being 124° shade temperature and then of course there was the dust encountered. However, we made it and are now 4,000 feet above sea level in the hills which is a very pleasant change with a noonday temp round about a 100° and quite cool night and morning. Three nights ago we actually had a shower of rain which was well appreciated by all for it reminded one of an English evening. Entertainment is much better here for there is a town 20 miles away where one can visit pictures and a hotel. We have got a very good canteen organised now where one can obtain almost anything including whisky so you may guess we are very well satisfied at 8/6d a bottle. Altogether we are very well satisfied with the move and are contenting ourselves to settle here until called to a more active theatre which we hope will not be very long. All the boys talk of Leam and what they will do when this lot is over."

In November 1943 and part of the Middle East Force [MEF] he writes, "I have tonight received your parcel quite safe and sound. Thank you ever so much aunty for the grand pipe and cigarettes. I am thrilled with it honestly. It is a godsend out here, for it is terribly difficult to obtain an English pipe and if you can they cost over two pounds sterling. Tobacco is much easier to come by than cigs so really I am set up now. Please thank Lola for her letter aunty. I am looking forward now to the photo which she has promised me for my collection. I like plenty of photos around for they brighten one up a little when feeling a bit depressed. Did you receive my letters from the leave camp and snaps? We have been spending our time lately on a Battery Concert. We got together a small party of players, some band instruments etc. and produced a very decent concert for the boys. We did two shows at 6 and 8pm. We have sent an account of it to the Spa Courier so you may see it referred to in some future edition. We are anxious to put on a straight one - act, play or Shakespeare so thought that perhaps, the old Courier could help us a bit. As you know it has always been a hobby of mine and having been appointed stage manager I am anxious to get things going. It helps to pass the monotonous evenings away and is good fun for all. I don't think it will be too long before the end do you? Thank God when it arrives."

In December 1943, he writes, "I am glad you enjoyed reading my epistle and that the photo got through ok. As you say, we have seen a bit of the world which we may not have seen otherwise, but as yet nothing to beat old England. We are looking forward to Xmas now but of course it will be pretty tame compared to the good times we had at home, but we must not complain for we are all looking forward to being at home for the next one."

In January 1944, he writes, "Just a line to let you know that I am ok except for being in the fashion with a cold. The weather is now very cold and wet which I think accounts for it after the heat. Things are pretty quiet with us and there is very little news. I got down to the town last night to see an opera "Madame Butterfly" which was very good though not up to an English production as the words could not be understood of course. We get to the pictures [cinema] twice a week now, which brightens the situation a bit though they are very old pictures."

By June 1945, he writes, "Just a few lines as promised to let you know that I am ok and arrived back with the unit again after a cross country trek across Italy. We are now just outside Trieste at a place called Udine. We were put here of course in case of any trouble with Tito but that is now settled up and everyone here is having a real holiday I can tell you. The weather is scorching hot and everyone here is a dark brown copper colour. I had a very good sea voyage back which took about 10 days as we came back via Algiers and Malta. The sea was very calm so I really enjoyed it and it was my first voyage without sea sickness. Time is spent here now mainly with sport which consists of swimming classes under Les James, yachting, cricket, horse riding, dancing in the evening with our own dance band led by Reg Ball. Also in the neighbouring village the Coldstream Guards run a dance and have invited our Bty. Time passes rather well for me as I am in a new job now acting Quarter Master as our QSM is in release group and may have to leave us any day. My release group is low and I think we shall get reinforcements for I think the Regt. will be made up and go to India."

Checking the post each day for good news became a ritual. However, not all news was good news and as much as letters and postcards were very much anticipated, the folded telegram in the small brown envelope delivered by a young boy on a bicycle or motor cycle, or the knock on the door by someone in uniform was dreaded. Words cannot express the feeling when either a telegram boy or an officer walks up the path.

The Leamington Spa Courier dated 27th August 1943 carried the following: - **Prisoners of War** - Last Saturday - for the first time since the fall of Singapore, in February, 1942 - Mrs Kathleen Wall, of Lillington, received tidings of her husband, Pte. Gordon Wall, of the Royal Ordnance Corps. A postcard then came to hand from him saying, "I am a prisoner of war, and being quite well treated. Am fit and well, so don't worry. Keep smiling."

Also, in the same Courier edition another item reads: - Mrs. G. Hopkins, of 76, Waverley Road, Leamington, on Monday received a postcard from her son, Dvr. G. Hopkins, now in Japanese hands. He says he is in the best of health, and adds, "don't worry." Dvr. Hopkins volunteered for service in H. M. Forces on October 30th, 1939, whilst working at the Lockheed. From India, he went to Malaya, and was taken prisoner at Singapore on February 11th, 1942.

The Leamington Spa Courier dated 3rd September 1943 reported: - **Died on Active Service** - We regret to record the death, on active service, of Frederick John Victor Hitchman, of 26, New Street, Leamington. News has been received by his wife that he died on August 23rd from asphyxia due to drowning. Tpr. Hitchman, who served in the 3rd [King's Own] Hussars, was the elder son of Mr. and Mrs. E. Hitchman, of Radford

Semele. He was 24 years of age, and besides attending the Church of England day and Sunday school of his native village, he was for six years a member of the Church choir. Before the war he was employed by Miss Shaw, of Guy's Cliffe Avenue. He was married to Miss Ethel Doughty, of 26, New Street, in July, 1940. They have a daughter aged eight months.

In the same edition of the Courier it was announced that Captain Bernard Bishop, the eldest son of Mr. and Mrs. B. V. Bishop, of Warwick Street, Leamington, had been awarded the D.S.O for gallantry and devotion to duty during the fighting in Tunisia.

There was also news of a letter from the commanding officer of H.M.S. Leamington to the Deputy Mayor [Alderman Martin S. Moore]. In it he says, "With reference to your kind offer of a gift for the coming Christmas, we are well equipped with warm clothing; but indoor games, perhaps a football or boxing gloves, newspapers and periodicals from home are the things most appreciated by the ship's company, if you would care to select from these. Alternatively, they would be delighted to receive cash. Please extend the sincere thanks and very best wishes of H.M.S. Leamington to the citizens of Leamington Spa."

The Leamington Spa Courier dated 17th September 1943 carried the following announcement: - **Wing Commander P. Olver - A Prisoner of War.** Mr. and Mrs. Percy Olver, of Gulistan Road, Leamington, this morning received a postcard from their son, Wing Commander Peter Olver, stating that he is a prisoner of war in Germany. He was reported missing early in July.

The Leamington Spa Courier dated 22nd October 1943 reported: - 'On Tuesday 19th October 1943, at 42 Warwick Street, the thousandth package for prisoners-of-war of the Royal Warwickshire Regiment, was made up by the Comforts Fund of the War Activities Committee in the presence of Brigadier C. T. Tomes, O.B.E., D.S.O., M.C. [Colonel of the Regiment], Lt.-Col. M. H. V. Kendall, M.C. [Commanding Officer at Budbrooke], and Major Cubberley [Secretary of the Regimental Association]. This bundle was made up by Mrs. Matthews, one of the ladies who has been working with the Comforts Fund since the early days of the war, it is addressed to Pte. John Moore.

The idea of sending packages to prisoners of war as from next-of-kin and the Regimental Association originated with Brigadier Tomes in 1941, when the Regimental Association undertook to establish a special fund for the purpose. The Comforts Fund, whose pleasure it has been, since the beginning of hostilities, to supply woollen comforts for all battalions of the Royal Warwickshire Regiment, was asked to provide the necessary organisation, and Miss Dorothy Mellor [who is in charge of the supply department] took on the extra work of buying and superintending the packing and despatching. Mrs. Roland Hollick acts as Secretary for this part of the work, and has been the recipient of many grateful letters from both the prisoners of war and their next-of-kin. These show that the packages are reaching their destination regularly, and are greatly appreciated.

It is interesting to hear that 58 parcels were sent out in 1941, 489 in 1942, and this year 432 are already on their way to lighten the lives of the men in the prison camps in Germany. In the 432 parcels, which the committee have packed this year, there have been 8,356 separate articles – an average of 19 in each bundle. Though the thousandth parcel is special because of the little celebration connected with its despatch, the contents are similar to its fellows which are ready for the next shipment. Each parcel includes a vest, shirt, towel, pillow-case, two handkerchiefs, pair of gloves, cap comforter, hair-brush, comb, hone, two packets dentifrice, pencil, cake of soap, metal polish, 1lb. chocolate, and a pair of shoulder titles.'

The Leamington Spa Courier dated 2nd June 1944 reported: - **D.S.M for Leamington Seaman** "For outstanding courage leadership and skill in light coastal craft in many daring attacks on enemy shipping in enemy waters." Able Seaman Reginald Percy Taplin of 44 Windmill Road, Leamington has been awarded the D.S.M.

People long to be at home at Christmas time - it must have been even more difficult during war time. This circa 1943 Christmas card was sent by Len Reading to his wife Margaret [Marg] at 97 Queen Street.

It wasn't only letters and postcards that were sent home. Below is the 1943 Christmas menu card for H.M.S. Manatee. Breakfast consisted of coffee, shredded wheat, bacon and eggs. Lunch was tomato soup, roast turkey, boiled ham, sprouts and peas, roast potatoes, Yorkshire pudding, Christmas pudding and fresh fruit. There was cake for tea time and for supper it was cold roast pork, sauce, presumably apple, cheese and mince pies. I am sure that the people on ration at home would have appreciated knowing how the matelot's [sailors] were not struggling for food.

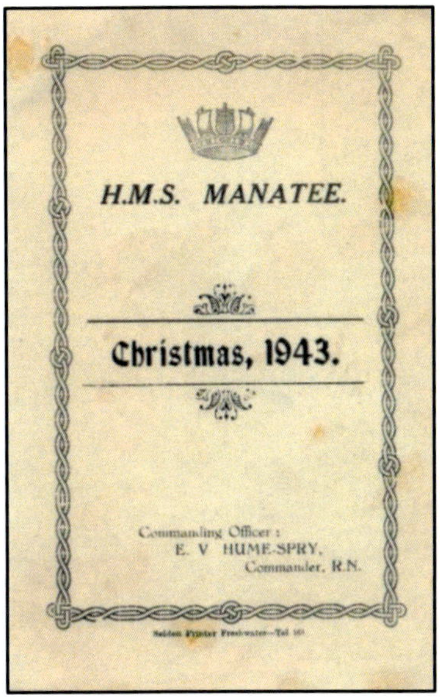

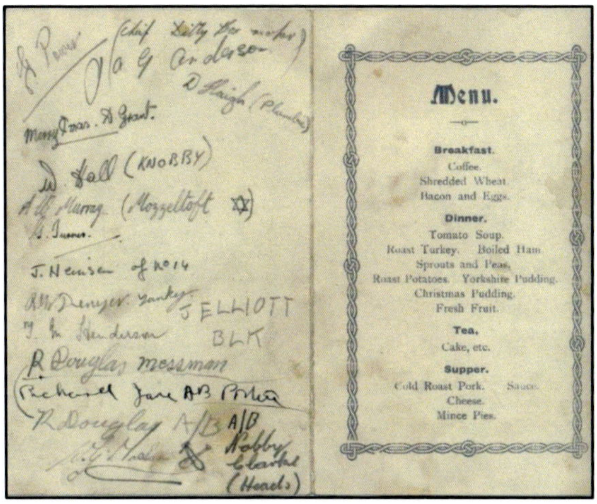

This letter was posted in 1944 by Len Reading to his wife Margaret. It was forwarded via H.M. Ships with an inland second class stamp due to a concession to forces. Under the date of 16th June 1944 it is stamped 'passed censor'.

It wasn't only mail from oversees that was opened and examined as this envelope posted in 1942 from Queen Street to Heath Terrace shows.

Lance Corporal Harry Bradshaw, Royal Engineers, Middle East Forces, posted this card to his mother Clara Barnett [remarried] on 29th July 1942.

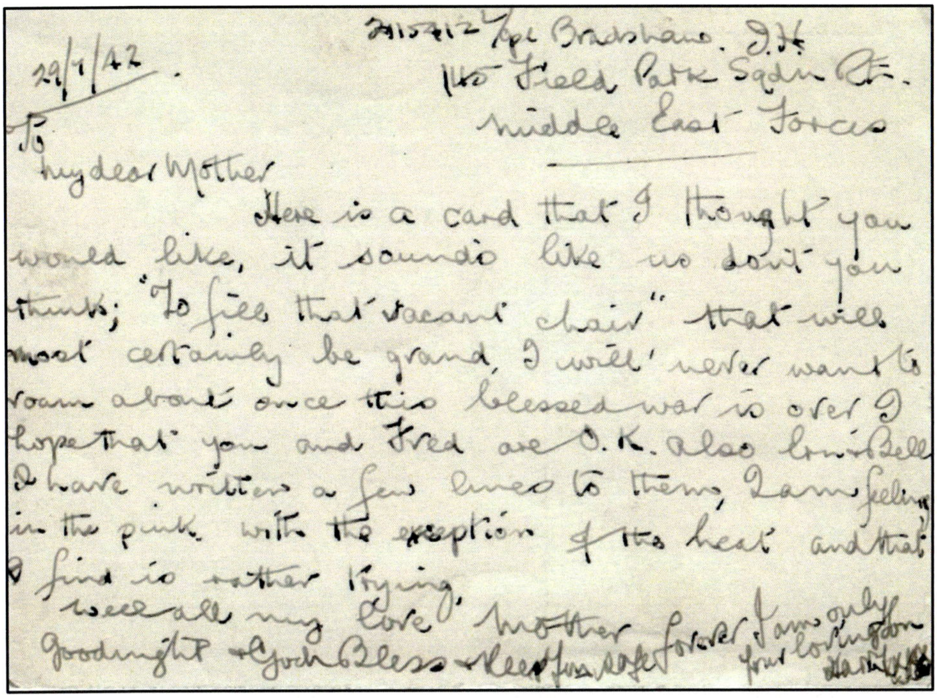

29/7/42.

2115412 Cpl Bradshaw. J.H.
146 Field Park Sqdn R.E.
Middle East Forces

To
My dear Mother

Here is a card that I thought you would like, it sounds like us don't you think; "To fill that vacant chair" that will most certainly be grand, I will never want to roam about once this blessed war is over. I hope that you and Fred are O.K. also Ern & Bell I have written a few lines to them, I am feeling in the pink with the exception of the heat and that I find is rather trying.

Well all my love Mother forever I am only
Goodnight & God Bless & Keep you safe forever
Your loving son
[illegible]

Embroidered postcards were also very popular.

Sometimes a coincidence happened and it provided an opportunity to send something home. This was the case with Arthur and Len Frost [above] who lived with their parents at 51 Waterloo Street. Arthur Frost, [right], had been granted two weeks embarkation leave before being sent to join the British Pacific Fleet in 1944. He had been stationed at the Royal Naval Air Station at Abbotsinch, Paisley in Scotland, which is now Glasgow International Airport. He was assigned to the MONAB'S, this was the Mobile Operating

Naval Air Base intended for the Pacific war. His brother Len, [left], was granted two weeks embarkation leave before being sent to the Indian Ocean, to be based at Basra, in Iraq. He was a DEMS gunner, which was a Royal Naval rating operating the main armament on merchant ships, hence DEMS, Defence Equipped Merchant Ship. He had previously been on Atlantic convoys. Len spotted Arthur on Birmingham New Street Station and they both decided to have a photo taken to send to their parents as it was the first time they had met since 1941.

In his youth, Gordon Evans lived in Avon Road Whitnash where his mother kept an Off Licence. At the tender age of eight his father treated him to a flight in a DH60 Gypsy Moth and from that day the flying bug bit.

On leaving school in the 1930s, he spent two years in an engineering tool room at Lockheed, before being offered the chance to work as a trainee ground engineer at the Leamington, Warwick & District Aero Club – Bonniksen's Aerodrome at Harbury Lane. He assisted with the day to day maintenance and repair of the club's four Gypsy Moth's. His salary was 10 shillings per week and his hours were from 8.00am until the light went.

During 1938/1939 Gordon was one of two resident engineers at the aerodrome. Major Bonniksen [the owner] was a friend of his father and on occasion he would give Gordon the occasional instruction while they were on air tests.

Gordon eventually learned to fly properly under the Civil Air Guard Scheme which was announced by Sir Kingsley Wood, the Secretary of State for Air, on 23rd September 1938 before the outbreak of war. However, as Gordon was 'on the staff' his turn didn't come until late in the day in 1939. The scheme was civilian in nature, and established in conjunction with local flying clubs to encourage and subsidise pilot training in exchange for an 'honourable undertaking' that in times of emergency, members would serve in the Royal Air Force Reserve.

The Second World War started and Gordon volunteered for the Volunteer Reserve and went off to serve in the forces. Gordon was never very forthcoming about his wartime career, but from hints and snippits his family deduced that he had been in Burma, associated with RAF Dakotas and Typhoons. He sketched and painted the image on the previous page of Basha-on-the-Hill in Kuala Lumpur, Malaya and posted it home in April 1946.

It wasn't only on our side that postcards were being sent – the Germans were doing exactly the same thing as the following postcards from 1942 show. An album of these postcards subsequently ended up in Leamington. How it did so is something of a mystery.

Dresden, König Georg Kaserne

DRESDEN N 25
4.9.42.-16
Feldpost
Paul Schulze, Dresden N 6
M/1294
c 4450

Factories

Lockheed, and the other local factories, that were making munitions were always going to be targets for German bombers. In Old Warwick Road, even tin hats were being made – and looking at this photo, that includes Ede Rourke, it appears that it was a very dirty job.

Lockheed made retractable aircraft undercarriages and hydraulic brakes. They had their own fire brigade with a fire engine which had a detachable ladder and the words 'Lockheed Borg & Beck Fire Brigade' on the side. The workers proudly called the engine "The Red Indian", because "this scarlet painted monster with its brightly polished lamps, bell and radiator does in some ways remind the onlooker of the wild and woolly west." This was the mainstay of the Lockheed Fire Brigade from 1938 when it was bought from Leamington Fire Station.

Shadow Factories - As well as 'normal' factories there were also 'shadow' factories around the country that were built by the Government during the late 1930s. Shadow was not to do with secrecy - but was to indicate that the factory was shadowing a similar type of factory. The 'Shadow Scheme' was set up by the Government to increase aircraft production by using the skills from the motor industry. Coventry is a good example as its shadow factories mainly built aeroplanes and aeroplane engines. Other factories were built so that there would not be a total collapse of production if a major facility was bombed and destroyed. With many of the men away at war, thousands of women worked in the shadow factories. Butlin's Farm at Cubbington 'shadowed' the Lockheed factory and even had its own canteen as shown on one of the following photographs.

Mike Wardle says, "My grandparents farmed Newbold Comyn Farm and I know some of the farm buildings were requisitioned by Lockheed during the war as a machine shop and for storage."

Butlins Shadow Factory on 15th September 1942. Photo courtesy of Warwickshire County Record Office Ref: CR3581a,1735 (1of6).

Butlins Shadow Factory on 15th September 1942. Photo courtesy of Warwickshire County Record Office Ref: CR3581a,1735 (2of6).

Butlins Shadow Factory on 15th September 1942. Photo courtesy of Warwickshire County Record Office Ref: CR3581a,1735 (3of6).

Butlins Shadow Factory on 15th September 1942. Photo courtesy of Warwickshire County Record Office Ref: CR3581a,1735 (4of6).

Butlins Shadow Factory on 15th September 1942. Photo courtesy of Warwickshire County Record Office Ref: CR3581a,1735 (60f6).

Ford's acquired the Imperial Foundry site on the Old Warwick Road on 23rd August 1940, it having been previously owned by Flavel's, the well-known Leamington stove maker until 1939. A steel making facility was installed which consisted of two cupolas, three converters, an overhead crane, and an arc furnace with a mechanised mould line.

The company were then able to make Bren gun carrier track links in steel and several other war related components including bomb casings. By the end of the war the company had produced enough tank tracks to supply more than 360,000 armoured vehicles and tanks, as well as 163,244 high explosive bomb casings, around half a million smoke bomb casings and also practise bombs.

Kigass in Chapel Street manufactured the primer pump for Spitfire aircraft which are in use today in working aircraft.

Henry Griffith & Sons Ltd was a jewellery factory in Tachbrook Road; they produced ailerons, or hinged wing flaps for Lancaster bombers as well as parts for smoke bombs and other military devices.

A photo of the Henry Griffith's factory but not during war time.

This 1943-1944 photo shows technicians and staff with the ailerons, or hinged wing flaps, which were made for Lancaster bombers.

C. H. Soans & Son Ltd. At the outbreak of war C. H. Soans Ltd. the automobile engineers and motor vehicle dealership in Dormer Place was turned over to the reconditioning of military vehicles for the Ministry of Defence. The vehicles were generally collected from the large army depot at

Ashchurch near Tewkesbury. Just collecting the vehicles from the depot and getting them back to Leamington often took a full day as conditions there were chaotic. Most were Ford built War Office Transport 1 or 2 [WOT1 or WOT2] trucks. Following the blitz on Coventry the car showroom area was requisitioned for Rotheram & Sons, makers of precision instruments, who had been bombed out of their Coventry premises. The two distinctive towers at each end of the building were used for A.R.P fire-watching duties each night.

Sidney Flavel & Co.

Just before the war broke out, Flavel's installed some very large presses which came in useful when the Government started looking for factories which could be used for making and reconditioning ammunition boxes.

Ammunition boxes being painted at Flavel's.

Flavel's went on to produce millions of ammunition boxes during the war. Day and night working was introduced, with three people at each press working continuously throughout the day. Many of the workers were called up into the armed forces but some remained at the factory their jobs being considered to be 'reserved occupations'.

Bill Box was one such person and helped to solve the problem of how to move the ammunition boxes from their delivery point at the rear entrance of the factory to the storage facility at the other end. He suggested an overhead roller conveyor track and lift to pass the boxes over the top of the Drilling Shop. Various sizes and shapes of ammunition boxes were reconditioned, repainted, inners installed and fitted with long straps.

During the first week of September 1943 production far exceeded the monthly target of 30,000 watertight ammunition boxes.

Ammunition boxes being tested in a water tank at Flavel's.

Flavel's also made some 'secret' products from what was at the time a special metal. This metal was duralumin, a kind of aluminium alloy which arrived at Flavel's in various diameters. A government inspector from the Aeronautical Inspection Department would check that no metal was missing.

Even during the First World War, Flavel's was involved in munitions work. They had contracts for the manufacture of trench bombs and other munitions. Fuse caps for the protection of the fuse and propeller were made for 20lb aerial bombs and cases were also made for the trench Howitzer and trench mortar bombs. Immediately after the First World War, having bomb cases surplus to requirements, Flavel's sold some as souvenirs to the general public. Cases for the trench mortar bombs [approx. 9 inches in diameter by 12 inches high] were advertised as being "eminently suitable for a palm vase, price 10s. 6d" and for the smaller cases [4½ inches by 4¾ inches high], it was claimed "Can be used for a fern pot, price 2s. 6d".

Lid assembly of ammunition boxes at Flavel's.

Gladys Maclaren who lived in Radford Road went to work in the accounts department at Flavel's in 1924. She said, "The office moved to the Social Club and we worked in the billiard room. The Club was an old house in Ranelagh Street. We were there during the war. At the side of the billiard room, there was a room where we kept old records and this was our air-raid shelter. I remember one tea-time a plane came over just as I was having a cup of tea, and we all had to get into the side room and shelter. We had several lunchtime raids and we could see the swastikas on the planes. We were in the Social Club all through the war. I remember VE Day in the billiard room."

Women in the Flavel's Staff Canteen in 1942. Photo courtesy of Warwickshire County Record Office. Ref: PH,919/1.

Throughout the war the A.R.P. Committee would issue advice to factories and businesses about the consequences of air raids. They were advised to duplicate and keep copies of their records in a suitable location away from their own district, where the possibility of damage from air raids was remote.

Examples of records to be copied were an inventory of assets including equipment and vehicles, an inventory of stock, balance sheet and profit and loss account, leases and insurance policies, customer and prospective customer lists, special drawings and blue prints, lists of debtors, supplier's invoices, lists of orders received and cash received. A small reserve of all stationery and other miscellaneous items used in the office should also be kept as it would be difficult to obtain these items at short notice.

Scientific instruments, tools and equipment in everyday use should be stored in a safe or underground vault where they would escape damage from blast caused by bombs or by fire.

Flavel's children's Christmas party in 1943. It was held in the canteen at the suggestion of Mrs. Isobel Flavel, then Chairman of the Board and was the first such party in modern times. Back row L-R: Len Harbour, Peggy Harris, Nurse Roberts, Mrs. Flavel, nine girls from St. Ann's Home at Warwick Place Leamington, a party entertainer, Bill Box and Teddy Roberts, the foundry manager, on the far right. The second row is made up of five mistresses from the home, plus Mrs. Roberts who is in front of the entertainer. Director Duncan Wright is on the left of the group of younger children and Fred Rogers is on the right. Local author, the late Jean Field, aged five, in a dress with a white collar is sitting next to Fred Rogers.

Lockheed Hydraulic Brake Co. Ltd - Automotive Products

By 1937 Lockheed's Aircraft Hydraulic Division was fully established and produced the first ever retractable undercarriage operated by hydraulics for the Armstrong Whitworth 'Ensign' commercial passenger airliner. Military as well as civil aircraft were being fitted with hydraulic equipment. In 1938 prior to the start of the war Lockheed celebrated the production of the millionth set of hydraulic brakes for cars and aircraft produced at the Tachbrook Road site.

Even before war was declared, the Leamington factory had taken air raid precautions installing sand bagging and camouflaging. Plane spotter patrols and later the Home Guard were initiated. Air raid shelters were also built, some underground in the fields behind the factory, and gas decontamination areas were established. Air raid drill was compulsory. Inside the factory glass was removed from office partitions and black-out material was erected, with the factory working by electric light. In September 1939 women workers at Lockheed helped to apply camouflage paint to various buildings and many exterior surfaces, doors and windows.

Poster courtesy of Leamington Spa Art Gallery and Museum [Warwick District Council] M4736.2012.4.

Also prior to the war starting, the Lockheed Sports and Social Club was developing well, they had all of the amenities they required in place, with one exception - a 'really fine' sports field. The company directors with their usual generosity presented them with a site of 27 acres. This was in the course of being laid out on a scale that would have made it one of the finest sports fields in the Midlands, and was about half completed when war broke out. It wasn't until the end of the war that it was finally completed.

The war years made the Club the hub of the company's social activities. Membership grew by leaps and bounds with it being open to the personnel of army units who were stationed nearby on defence duties.

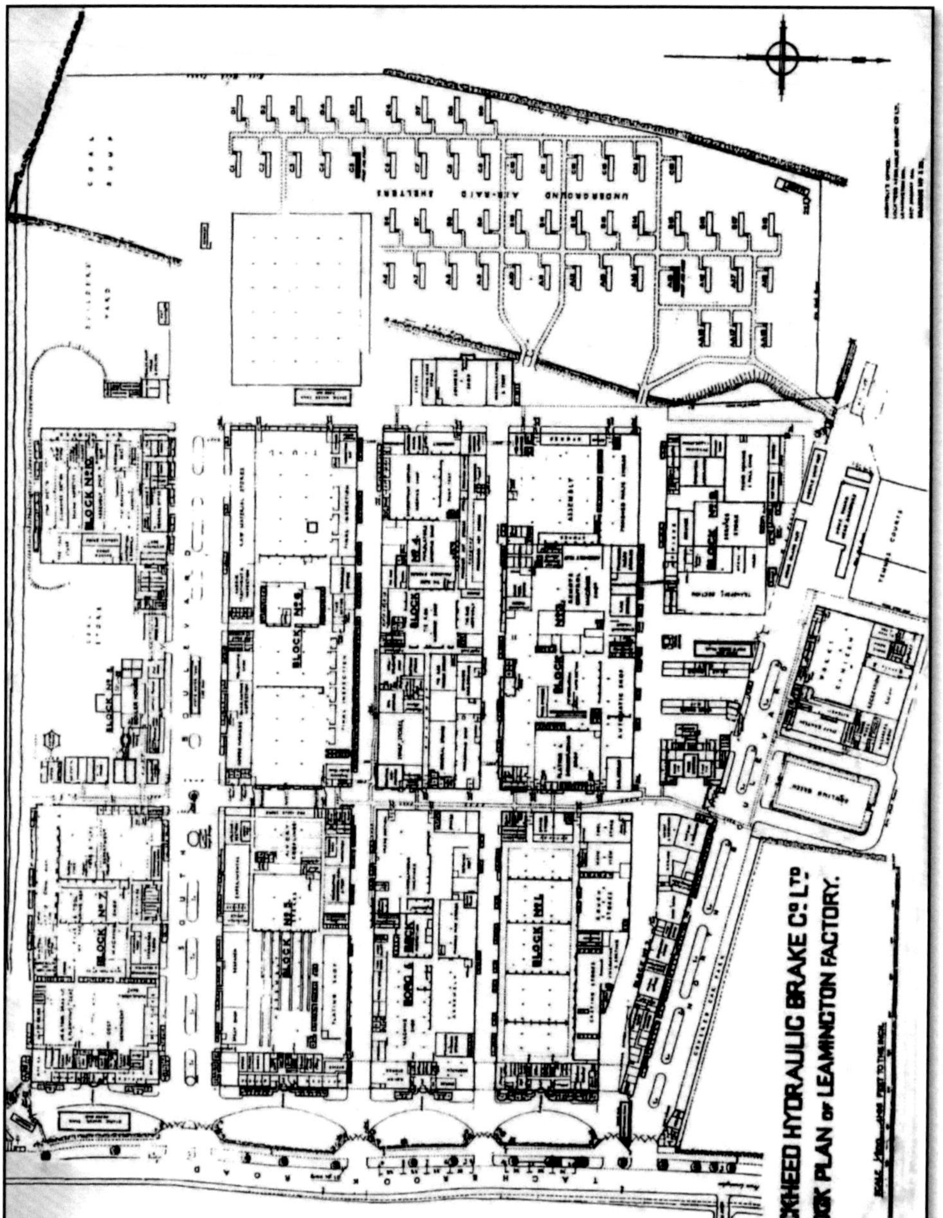

This block plan of Lockheed has Tachbrook Road at the bottom. Although it is a little difficult to read in detail, it is interesting to see the large number of underground air raid shelters at the top of the plan.

Churchill and Cromwell tanks amongst others used Borg & Beck clutches.

It was fortunate that Lockheed had moved into the aircraft industry because 1939 was getting ominously closer and the rantings of Hitler dangerously louder. As war started, the workforce increased to around 10,000, many were local men and women, but others were drafted in from across the country. Having already established its aircraft hydraulic division, they were soon ready and able to produce more than two million aircraft parts for the war effort. Borg and Beck clutches were used extensively on Cromwell and Churchill tanks and many other armoured vehicles. All supply vehicles supporting the armed forces also utilised Automotive Products components. The newly formed Lockheed Industrial Hydraulics Division produced the hydraulic actuation for the steering of virtually every motor torpedo boat launched by the Navy during the war.

In February 1941 women workers from Lockheed's Leicester factory were evacuated to Leamington.

Early in 1941, British Red Cross workers were presented with two ambulances by members of the Lockheed Borg and Beck Sports and Social Club. It was originally intended to supply just one, but owing to the restrictions imposed by the Ministry of Supply, the purchase of a new chassis was not possible. Having decided to convert a second-hand chassis, it was found that there was enough money to provide two such ambulances.

The first of them was handed over on Wednesday 22nd January 1941 and the other a few weeks later. One was to be used in Leamington and Warwick, and the other went to Coventry. Major E. S. Phillips, D.S.O., took the opportunity of thanking the Lockheed workers. He said that he could vouch as to the value of the ambulances in recent weeks. He had been responsible for the ambulances in Coventry on the night of 14th - 15th November 1940, the night of the Coventry Blitz. All of them turned out and every ambulance returned damaged, some almost beyond repair. He was glad to say that among the ambulance drivers there were no casualties of note although they were working among high explosive shells the whole night.

In November 1940 the Lockheed Hydraulic Brake Company asked the 'Watch Committee' for permission to use St. Helens Road for additional staff car parking. The application was granted.

Lockheed suffered from German bombing on two occasions although they may well have been the target on two other occasions, when bombs dropped on Ranelagh Terrace and when a stick of bombs dropped over the town.

[Full details can be found in my book, "The Bombing of Royal Leamington Spa"].

Poster courtesy of Leamington Art Gallery and Museum [Warwick District Council] M.4736.2012.5.

Bernard Griffin was a wartime fireman at Lockheed, having joined the firm in 1941. As the war ended the factory fire and police services were amalgamated under the leadership of Column Officer Gammon. By then Bernard had police duties and was also the Chief Officer's deputy on the Works Fire Brigade.

Throughout the factory there were 240 fire extinguishers, 750 buckets, and 150 lengths of hose of varying sizes as well as 60 hydrants. On 25th November 1960, the Volunteer Fire Service held their 21st Anniversary Dinner and presentations were made to Mr. S. Guice, the longest serving member, Mr. W. Bloxham and Mr. C. Smith, all of whom had completed 21 years as volunteers.

Referring to page 73 of "The Bombing of Royal Leamington Spa", details are given of Leutnant Wilhelm Schmitter, the German pilot who was responsible for both bombing raids on the Lockheed factory. The first raid was on Saturday 13th June 1942 and the second on Thursday 16th July 1942. It is interesting to read in the spotter's report that fire from the Quad Lewis gun was seen entering his plane and then reading in the German records that from mid-July until mid-August 1942 Schmitter was given leave to recuperate from his wounds and a 'well deserved rest' from his front-line flights, confirming that the Lockheed gunner did indeed hit him.

Between 14th February 1942 and 16th July 1942 Schmitter had flown over 45 missions against Great Britain. As well as the photo above he is also on the left of this photograph in front of his Dornier Do.217 aeroplane with Unteroffizier Wagner, Feldwebel Krohn and Feldwebel Gräbel.

The first bombing raid on Lockheed caused the death of Walter Williams and injury to two others. The incident happened at 13.06pm but the alert wasn't sounded until 13.10pm. It caused damage to three workshops, the Borg and Beck, the Aircraft Experimental and the Aircraft Plating. At 13.30pm Stratford Upon Avon Sub Fire Station reported that they had sent two large Home Office fire engines and one Home Office self-propelled engine to the works. The all clear was sounded at 13.37pm.

Damage covered an area of some 10,000 square feet affecting roofs, walls and services. It caused a small fire which was brought quickly under control by the factory brigade. The enemy plane was reported to have released his bombs at 80 feet and machine-gunned personnel on the factory premises. Fifty-nine-year-old Lockheed worker Walter Herbert Williams lived at 14, Ash Grove Place, Leamington Spa. He was one of the injured during the bombing raid and unfortunately died at Warneford hospital from shock and serious injuries to his legs, at 01.15am on 14th June. Two bomb splinters were found some time after the incident, one measuring 4 inches long and 1¼ inches thick at Ford's Imperial Foundry some 1,330 yards from the site of the incident. The second splinter, 3½ inches long and 1 inch thick penetrated the roof of a house at 72 Bury Road, a distance of 1,150 yards from the site of the incident. A fin from one of the 500kg bombs was found in the factory. By 16th June production was already back to 85% and by the following night it was back to 100%.

Besides the three bombs that fell on the factory, a high explosive bomb landed in a field south of the factory, formerly known as Home Farm but was then part of the Lockheed Works. It landed near a gun site about 100 yards from the junction with Heathcote Road. The bomb exploded and blew out the end of a War Department hut. It also caused some damage to nearby windows in Tachbrook Road but fortunately there were no casualties.

Poster courtesy of Leamington Art Gallery and Museum [Warwick District Council] M.4736.2012.6.

Pauline Wilson who worked in the Tool Control department said, "Because of the hours we worked, which made shopping for clothes difficult, the clothes would sometimes come to us. Logan's on the Parade displayed their merchandise in the Work's Canteen during the evening, and we were able to go shopping there after work." This photograph was taken around 1940 at a Christmas party in the staff canteen at Lockheed and includes Pauline Wilson, Rosalie Fennel and Jack Fahey. Pauline is 4th left on the inside of the left-hand table.

During the war, William Henry Allcock was a setter and an A.R.P. Warden at Lockheed. On the night of the Coventry Blitz, 14th November 1940, a number of people were asked to go to Coventry to assist in the rescue and William was one of them. Towards the end of the war William saw service in Borneo. He wrote a book about his wartime experiences which is now in the Imperial War Museum.

The two photos above are the last that were taken of the gun position at Lockheed before it was dismantled in 1997. They were taken on a Sunday afternoon by William's son Anthony Allcock, who is now the New Projects Manager at A.P Racing.

The demolition of the block started at 8.30am the following morning. The photo on the left shows William Allcock, he had been taken back by Anthony to have a final look before the gun was dismantled and the block demolished. The photo on the right shows Graham Allcock, William's grandson.

Bonniksen's - Leamington Spa Aerodrome

In January 1932 Major Julius Bonniksen of 171 Tachbrook Road Leamington Spa purchased 62 acres of land at Harbury Lane between Leamington Spa and Bishops Tachbrook for the purposes of starting an aeroplane service for Leamington and district and also for starting a flying club.

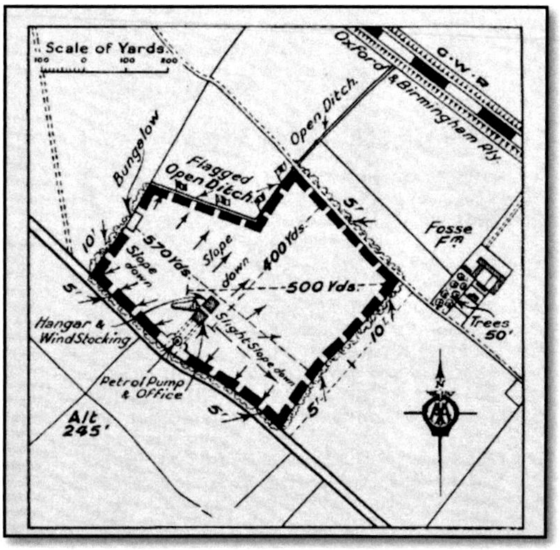

In the early part of the Second World War, the airport at Baginton, Coventry was involved in air defence and was the base for various fighter squadrons. Alongside the airport, on a 25-acre site, was the huge factory of Armstrong Whitworth Aircraft [AWA]. Many of its prototype aircraft were test flown from the airport during the war years.

The twin-engined mid-wing Armstrong Whitworth Whitley heavy bomber was reaching the point of obsolescence by the start of the war but in May 1940 it suddenly became one of five aircraft types given overriding production priority by the new Ministry of Aircraft Production. The Whitley subsequently bore the brunt of the early night raids on Germany, until more modern aircraft were developed. Other types of aircraft were the Argosy, a pre-war design aircraft and the Ensign which was a large four-engine passenger aircraft.

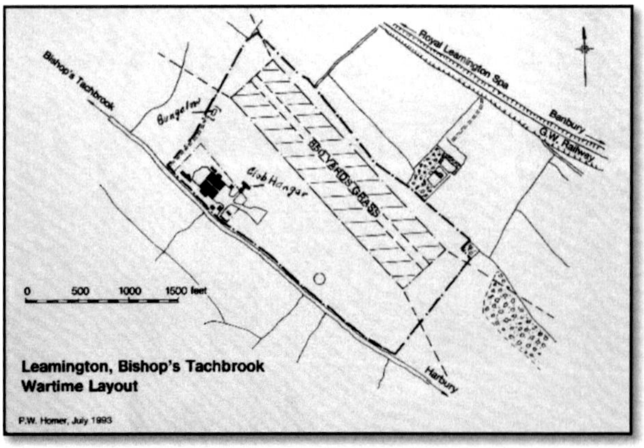

Leamington, Bishop's Tachbrook Wartime Layout
P.W. Homer, July 1993

The outbreak of the war brought an end to civil flying at Leamington and the Armstrong Whitworth Aircraft Company of Coventry took over the aerodrome. It was used extensively by the company both as a base for the assembly, service and repair of a number of aeroplanes, particularly the Whitley bombers. Two Bellman type hangers and outbuildings were erected during the early war years for use by the Company.

On 1st September 1939 seven AW27 Ensign aircraft were sent from Whitchurch in Bristol to Baginton. Later, on 15th December 1939 one of these aircraft - G-ADSU named "Euterpe" overshot at Leamington during an emergency landing ending up across Harbury Lane with its underside damaged.

Following the Luftwaffe Blitz on Coventry on 14th November 1940, serviceable aircraft were dispersed to Bonniksen's Leamington aerodrome in Harbury Lane. The Whitley's flying from the grass field were a regular feature for the remainder of the war. Armstrong Whitworth's chief test pilot, Charles Turner-Hughes lived in Leamington and was a regular visitor to the aerodrome.

J.E.B with pupils and visitors. 1939.

The De Havilland 60G Gypsy Moth [G-AAFI] pictured above was first registered on 15th May 1929, by Francis E. N. St. Barbe. S. P. Jackson purchased it in 1930 followed by Major Bonniksen in 1931. At the outbreak of war it was impressed into the R.A.F. as DG.579 and delivered to No.20 M.U. [Maintenance Unit] at Ternhill for storage, later being released to No.2 School of Navigation at R.A.F. Cranage on 7th August 1941. On 4th June 1942 it was transferred to No.10 Air Gunners School at Barrow, then to No.5 M.U. Kemble on 25th February 1943. It was later delivered to No.2034 A.T.C. Squadron at Boscombe with serial No.4033M. Its subsequent fate is not known.

On 17th September 1939, Major Bonniksen entered the R.A.F. Volunteer Reserve being posted to 'The Central Flying School' at Upavon on 18th September. He took the first War Course, which was his 60th Flying Instructors Course. As a Pilot Officer, he flew the Avro Tutor, Hart, Harvard, Oxford and Anson. On 28th October 1939, he was assessed as "Above the average".

On 3rd November, he was posted to No.10 Bombing and Gunnery School at R.A.F. Warmwell. His job classification was Flying Instructor and Armament Liaison Officer. He was responsible for Gunnery Organisation and Serviceability of Squadron Armaments. In March 1940, he was posted to No.9 E.F.T.S. [Elementary and Reserve Flying Training School] at Ansty Aerodrome as a Pilot Officer flying Tiger Moths.

The Armstrong Whitworth 'Whitley' Bomber. *This twin engine heavy bomber had a crew of five and was powered by two Rolls Royce Merlin 12-cylinder engines. It could fly at 245 miles per hour. The photo, courtesy of Jock McVarish, was taken on 6th December 1944 to commemorate the last Whitley to be assembled at Bonniksen's Aerodrome. Everyone in the photo was given a copy.*

In August 1986 Mrs. Huntley of Bush Heath Lane, Harbury was photographed for a 'memories article' in the Leamington Spa Courier with a copy of the photograph in which she is present. She said that the aerodrome was now used by BRS Midlands for storing tractors. When the photograph was taken, Mrs Huntley's maiden name was Biddle. She remembers working there as a young girl in the canteen along with Mrs. Enid Bayliss of Dovehouse Lane. She said, "About 250 people employed by S&S Cars, [the forerunner of Jaguar] worked there assembling." Larry Sheasby also worked there prior to service with the R.A.F. in 1946. He recalls that between six and seven Whitley's were built each month and that Bill Brown used to come from Rolls Royce to test the Merlin engines.

Troops from other Countries

Czechoslovak Troops - Leamington Spa was a base for a number of allied troops, particularly the Free Czechoslovak Army.

Following the fall of France in 1940, Czechoslovak troops were evacuated from the south of France to England. The troops were initially based in a tented camp in Cheshire.

In September 1940, they were moved to Mid-Warwickshire, where they were based until relocation to Dorset in 1942. Local historian Alan Griffin tells of Czech soldiers in Leamington Spa: -

"In September 1940 several specially chartered trains pulled into Leamington station. On board were almost 4,000 men of the Free Czech Army, who were to spend the next two years in Mid-Warwickshire. Many of the group were mere teenagers who had trekked across occupied Europe to reach the assembly point at Agde in the south of France."

The Czechoslovak Brigade headquarters were at Harrington House, a large Victorian villa in Newbold Terrace. The troops were billeted in Leamington Spa, Warwick and some of the villages in south Warwickshire such as Moreton Morrell, Moreton Paddox, Kineton and Wellesbourne. In Leamington Spa they were billeted at the Masonic Rooms in Willes Road, the Lachine Hotel in Newbold Terrace and the Y.M.C.A. on the Parade.

The Czechs were made welcome in Leamington Spa and made every effort to become part of the community as well as demonstrating aspects of their culture to the locals. They organised choirs, orchestras, cooking exhibitions, art demonstrations, sporting competitions and put on plays. On 10th November 1940, they performed a concert at the Regent Cinema in aid of the Mayoress' War Relief Fund and the Rotary Club Services' Fund.

Their football team was of a high standard and played against many of the Midlands first division sides. A number of international matches were played at the Lockheed F.C ground in Tachbrook Road against army teams from other European countries.

A postcard sent to London from the Czechoslovak Field Post Leamington Spa on 28th May 1941.

The town can be grateful to one of the Czech officers for saving the life of a local child. The Leamington Spa Courier dated 18th July 1941 reported that, "at 11 o'clock last Saturday morning I was motoring up Tachbrook Road behind a saloon car which was driving slowly, close to the pavement when, without warning and without there being any time for the driver to alter course or apply brakes, a small child dashed across the pavement in front of several Czech soldiers and right in front of the car ahead of us. Instantly, without there being time to think, a Czech officer dashed into the road, grasped the little child by the neck of her dress and, literally, threw her back towards the pavement where she fell full length; her feet easily within inches of the wheels of the car. It was all over in a split second but beyond any possible question the lightning action of the officer saved the child's life. He and his comrades went laughing on their way as the child rose weeping from the ground. My wife and I smiled at them and clapped our hands in appreciation as we passed."

The same Leamington Spa Courier reported: - 'Czech Army Display in Midland Town. On the football field of a Midland town on Saturday afternoon, members of the Czechoslovak Army gave a sports display before a large and appreciative company. If the magnificent physical condition of the Czechs seen on Saturday is a fair sample of the whole army, the conclusion to be arrived at is that one day the Germans, to their surprise, will find themselves up against an army of super-athletes.

What little the people of our land have seen of the Czechs has confirmed their first impressions, that these men represent one of the foremost races of Europe, intellectually as well as physically; while their patriotic fervour burns with a zeal that one day will effect a relentless sweep of the enemy from their land. And so British people welcome the presence of members of this gallant nation, and are pleased to witness examples of their prowess, whether as athletes or as vocalists.

Speaking on Saturday, it was to us an unforgettable spectacle. Never before have we seen soldiers in full fighting kit tearing over the ground at 20 miles per hour - with the lightning burst of speed associated with the 100 yards sprint. But so it was in their machine-gun relay race. The speed, too, at which the runners raced in the 880 yards race was good to watch.

The army games were an inspiration, and the various gymnastic displays - acrobatic, parallel and horizontal bar exercises, with pyramid building were evidence that no body of men could possibly surpass the Czechs. Spread out over the arena the various "gym" exercises were given with superb precision. The Czechs' final display, in which the entire company took part, brought into the arena about 400 men, moving with mathematical precision, the whole presenting a spectacle but rarely seen on our shores. Such colourful gymnastic spectacles will be copied, doubtless, in the future curricula of our schools and colleges, to the advantage of the future citizens of our land and the welfare of the Empire.'

During Christmas 1943 a number of Czech soldiers visited Warwick hospital and presented wooden toys to young patients in the children's ward.

The Czechoslovak Memorial Fountain.

The Czechoslovak Memorial Fountain in the Jephson Gardens commemorates the seven volunteers from the free Czechoslovak forces stationed in Leamington Spa who parachuted into their homeland to assassinate SS General Reinhard Heydrich, "The Butcher of Prague" during Operation Anthropoid. The memorial represents a falling parachute with streams of water forming the parachute strings.

Further information can be obtained from Alan Griffin's 2004 book 'Leamington's Czech Patriots & the Heydrich Assassination' or his 2012 book 'Leamington Lives Remembered'.

On Saturday 20th April 1940, a party of 150 Canadian troops visited Leamington. The troops were entertained for three days by the Birmingham Hospitality Committee. Saturday's programme of events included a tour of Shakespeare country visiting Stratford Upon Avon and Warwick Castle. Afterwards they called at the home of Mrs. M.M.M. Fowler at 21 Newbold Terrace and inspected her celebrated Red Cross blue caravans. Later in the afternoon they visited Kenilworth Castle.

On 6th July 1940, Wise Hall in Tachbrook Street and part of St. John's Church was requisitioned by the military, the letter being signed by a Major Lovett. The formal agreement was signed on 26th August 1940 recording a rental payment of £80 per annum. The basement which was used to store furniture was not requisitioned until 5th April 1944.

Wise Hall is the building to the right of St. John's Church.

The Leamington Spa Courier reported that during the Second World War Wise Hall was used as a military detention centre. However, the father of local historian Tessa Whitehouse told her that it was used to billet Czechoslovak troops. It is fair to say that the Hall was used for a number of military purposes over the period of requisition. Certainly, in the early part of the war it was used by 213 A.F. Company Royal Engineers attached to 95th H.A.A. Regiment Royal Engineers, but they 'marched out' on 28th March 1941.

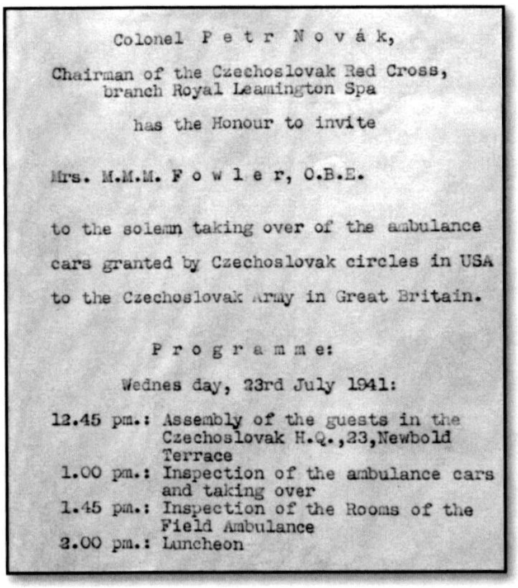
Colonel P e t r N o v á k,

Chairman of the Czechoslovak Red Cross,
branch Royal Leamington Spa

has the Honour to invite

Mrs. M.M.M. F o w l e r, O.B.E.

to the solemn taking over of the ambulance cars granted by Czechoslovak circles in USA to the Czechoslovak Army in Great Britain.

P r o g r a m m e:

Wednes day, 23rd July 1941:

12.45 pm.: Assembly of the guests in the Czechoslovak H.Q.,23,Newbold Terrace
1.00 pm.: Inspection of the ambulance cars and taking over
1.45 pm.: Inspection of the Rooms of the Field Ambulance
2.00 pm.: Luncheon

On 23rd July 1941 Colonel Petr Novák, Chairman of the Leamington Spa branch of the Czechoslovak Red Cross invited a number of guests to 23 Newbold Terrace to attend the take-over and inspection for a number of ambulance cars.

In November 1942, a reunion of Czech and British friends took place one Friday evening at the Blue Café in Bath Street, when a dance was held under the auspices of the Czechoslovak British Friendship Club. By permission of the Officer Commanding of the Czechoslovak Independent Brigade, nine first-class performers of the band came to play. "The Czechs were great dancers and their dance music was equally good", said an impressed Chairman and Secretary of the 'Stay-at-Home Holidays' Committee. He continued, "An augmented Czech band was being invited to play for dancing during the holiday season and was responsible for a variety show. A great deal of the success of the evening is due to the catering arrangements which, considering war-time rationing, shows an ingenuity and artistic taste which is truly continental. The Czech visitors are hospitably housed and fed by their friends in Leamington, who looked forward to seeing them again during their 'Stay-at Home Holidays'".

Belgian Troops - It is known that Belgian military police were billeted at Wise Hall and that there was a Belgian army camp at the "bottom of Campion Hills".

A letter dated 1st March 1946 from Capt. D. L. Milner, on behalf of Lt. Col. T. M. Lovett, Quartering Commandant for Leamington, who was based at 14 Newbold Terrace, said that he was making an application for authority to surrender the Wise Hall on 29th August 1946. Following 'de-requisition' various works took place to bring the hall back up to standard which included replacing the stage in time for Christmas 1946. The remainder of the effects were returned in March 1947. Mr. H. Wilson-Wood, a Chartered Architect and Surveyor of 26 Northumberland Road was employed to negotiate with the War Office for 'rehabilitation'. He recommended that an amount of £502.17s.5d. be accepted from the War Department.

American Troops - There were a few American troops stationed in Leamington Spa. Local historian Derek Billings attended Milverton school during the latter years of the war and walked to and from school in Rugby Road from his home in Victoria Street.

He said, "Sometimes when passing by a house in Clarendon Square at the top of Binswood Street, American soldiers would be leaving or coming out of the house. The word soon spread amongst the local children that they would give you chewing gum! It seems like only yesterday but I do remember the gum was in strips wrapped in silver foil and was pink in colour. I was too young to find out why the Americans were there though. Clarkes, the grocers shop in Binswood Street are the same family who now have a greengrocer's shop in Warwick Street. You could, if you had any coppers, buy penny and halfpenny glasses of pop! which they poured out of screw topped bottles. The first ice creams available after the war were from the dairy lower down Binswood Street where they gave you a circle of ice cream with a paper wrapper."

However, the majority of Americans were based at a United States Military Hospital in the hamlet of Stareton, near Stoneleigh, four miles to the north of Leamington, where injured airmen were brought for rehabilitation. Passing through Stareton from the Stoneleigh Road it was about ½ mile further on, on the left-hand side.

Photo taken by Steve Carvell on 8th June 2006.

The British built 1,000 bed general hospital site was set up on land belonging to Lord Leigh located in Stoneleigh Park. Rehabilitation Center Number One [Plant No.4167] was run by the 8th Convalescent Hospital Unit. It opened for patients on 5th October 1943 under the command of Major Frank Stinchfield.

The patients as well as the staff were given passes out and were often seen in Leamington Spa due to the nature of the rehabilitation hospital. Leonard McDermott, a postal clerk and Jerry Kloehr the mail orderly visited Kenilworth and Leamington. Leonard wrote about Leamington, "My first impression of this town was very favourable. The parks, gardens and wide streets are typical of a resort town. I had tea and sandwiches at a YMCA canteen, enjoying a chat with a young Irish worker. The ride back to camp was really lovely.... the setting sun casting long shadows over the rolling hills. Then just as I came back to camp a brilliant moon rise."

In December 1943, the 8th Convalescent Hospital received orders that it was to be reassigned to a field army. It was replaced at Stoneleigh by the 307th Station Hospital. A large number of personnel from the 8th Convalescent Hospital remained with the new unit including Major Stinchfield who continued as Commanding Officer.

Photo taken by Steve Carvell on 8th June 2006.

Having the Americans so close did cause a few problems. The Coventry Evening Telegraph dated 6th February 1945 reported that: - a 24-year-old married woman, of Tachbrook Street, Leamington was sent to jail for a month at Leamington yesterday for concealing an American soldier who had been posted as a deserter. For aiding and abetting, her 23-year-old married friend, of North Villiers Street was similarly sentenced. Both defendants pleaded "Guilty". The soldier was traced to the woman's house, but when the American military police called she denied his presence. After a search, he was arrested in a bedroom. The 2nd defendant admitted providing the soldier with civilian clothing and the defendant confessed to burning his uniform in the copper. "My husband is in the forces and I have a child twelve months old", the defendant told the Bench. The 2nd defendant pleaded that she also had a child which was eighteen months old. "But for your domestic circumstances we should have taken a more serious view and the sentences would have been more severe", the Mayor told the defendants, *[Note: I have omitted the names of the defendants].*

Also in 1945, a 17-year-old woman, who was lodging in Leicester Street, was charged with frequenting an American Army camp. She was sentenced to three months' imprisonment.

Following D-Day the number of patients at the rehabilitation centres increased as injured soldiers from the continent were sent there for treatment. The hospital's capacity had now been increased to 3,700 because of extra land it had acquired.

Photo taken by Steve Carvell on 8th June 2006.

On 22nd November 1944 the rehabilitation center was re-designated the 826th Convalescent Center with the now Colonel Stinchfield retained as Commanding Officer. On 25th February 1945 Colonel Stinchfield was appointed Supervisor of Convalescent Rehabilitation in the United Kingdom.

Following V. E. Day on 8th May 1945 an open day was held by the hospital on 10th May. Allied servicemen and civilians were invited and buses were put on for the local people from Leamington Spa. At the end of the day some of the visitors were transported home on the bus that had been used for transporting patients. Unfortunately, before it arrived at Leamington Spa it veered off the road, mounted a steep bank on the opposite side and came to a halt. Several people were slightly injured with sprains and cuts. After a short while an American ambulance pulled up with medical staff on board who gave first aid to those who had been hurt and then returned them home in the ambulance. Later the passengers found out that their driver was a hospital patient who wasn't authorised to drive the bus.

The Convalescent Center was closed on 18th May 1945 although Stoneleigh Park continued to have a military presence after the war offering training facilities for the British Forces. The M.O.D. vacated the premises in the early 1950s. The low level single storey buildings are still, in 2017, part of the redeveloped Abbey Park Estate at Kenilworth, although it is understood that they are due to be demolished in the next couple of years.

A small information booklet on Warwick and Leamington was produced for members of the United States Armed Forces. The Leamington section of the booklet was introduced by Leamington Mayor Arthur Ashton who wrote, "On behalf of the townspeople of Royal Leamington Spa it gives me much pleasure to offer a warm welcome to the members of the United States Armed Forces in the United Kingdom to this beautiful Spa in the green heart of England and to express the hope that this booklet will be of interest to them when they visit us. We are glad to offer hospitality now and trust we may see you and your families on future occasions when, together with our Allies, we have won the World peace."

Besides containing a potted history of the town there was advice and suggestions on where to eat and sleep, hospitality and accommodation, useful addresses, entertainment, sport, recreation, transportation, shopping and worship along with places of interest in the town and the district.

They were advised that licensing hours were on weekdays from 10.00am to 2.00pm and 6.00pm to 10.00pm; but on Sundays, noon to 2.00pm and 7.00pm to 10.00pm.

Suggestions for bed and breakfast at local hotels were: - 'Alkerton', 31 Binswood Avenue, 8s. 6d; 'Armathwaite', 52 Holly Walk, 12s. 6d; 'Desmond', Kenilworth Road, 12s. 6d; 'Lachine', Newbold Terrace, 10s. 6d; 'Spa', Holly Walk, 12s. 6d; 'St. Columb', 5 Milverton Hill, 3½ to 5 guineas per week; 'Central Hotel', Euston Place, 10s. 6d; and the Crown Hotel High Street, 12s. 6d.

Cafés and restaurants included the British Restaurant at Regent Grove; Blue Café Victoria Terrace, although it was actually in Bath Street; Burgis and Colbourne, The Parade; Bobby & Co., The Parade; Café Colette, 25 Bath Street; Cadena Café, 134 The Parade; Gaiety Café, 146 The Parade; Polka Dot Café, 57 Warwick Street; Pattison's Café, 20 Victoria Terrace; Crown Hotel, High Street; Pump Rooms, The Parade, and Little Kitchen, Euston Place.

Salisbury Hall, Windsor Street taken by Colin Jennings on 22nd April 2007.

Canteens were at the Y.M.C.A., The Parade; Y.M.C.A., Salisbury Hall, Windsor Street; Soldiers' Canteen, High Street [sleeping accommodation]; N.A.A.F.I., The Parade [sleeping accommodation]; Allied Services Club, Bertie Terrace, Union Road [sleeping accommodation]; Y.M.C.A. Girls Hostel and Club, 28 Leam Terrace [sleeping accommodation] and the Officers' Club, 8 Newbold Terrace [sleeping accommodation].

One of the Americans who spent time in Leamington Spa was John Buccellato. In October 1940, as a fresh-faced young American, just out of his teens, he enlisted in the United States Army infantry. His parents who were middle-class Sicillian immigrants lived in an apartment block facing Central Park in New York City. Within two years 'Butch' Buccellato found himself in Italy and North Africa alongside his colleagues fighting against the Nazis. In 1944 he arrived in England on board the Queen Mary which had been requisitioned as a troop ship. By the early summer of 1944, 'Butch' and a large number of military personnel of many nationalities were in Leamington awaiting orders for their departure for *Operation Overlord,* the allied invasion of Europe.

The GI's found the Spa town very much to their liking and they enjoyed their strolls in the Jephson Gardens where on one occasion they found their Australian infantry counterparts honing their marksmanship skills by shooting the ducks on the ornamental pond. The Aussies plucked and dressed the ducks and roasted them over fires fuelled by smashed up wooden park benches that they had 'liberated'.

At a dance in the Palais de Danse in Spencer Street, 'Butch' met a good-looking girl named Elsie Stanley who lodged with her sister Kit in rooms at 31 Willes Road [Lansdowne Crescent]. In due course 'Butch' packed his kitbag for the uncertainties of Omaha Beach on the French channel coast leaving behind Royal Leamington Spa and Elsie, who was soon to realise that she was pregnant. On 18th March 1945 Elsie gave birth to a daughter, christened Pamela Ann.

Elsie Stanley with baby Pamela.

Some sixty-five years later on a particularly cold March morning, local historian Alan Griffin was cleaning in the Parish Church, broom in hand, when he was approached by a lady, who introduced herself as Mrs. Pamela Birch, and her husband Terry. He says, "They were quite obviously on a quest, their enquiry centred around any baptismal record we might have for Pamela. She had been born at 31 Willes Road in 1945 and had brought with her a Birth Certificate which bore the name of her mother Elsie Stanley. The space for the name of the father was blank and had a line drawn through it."

'Butch' Buccellato [right] with Pamela and her half-brother Paul Buccellato at 31 Lansdowne Crescent in 1999.

Pamela now picks up the story. "My mum, of course knew my father's name and she made several attempts over the years to find out what had happened to John Buccellato but all her efforts came to nothing. As I got older, I too became keen to find out what had become of my father but as the years passed I began to think that even had he survived the slaughter on Omaha Beach he must surely have succumbed to old age."

"It was the personal computer my daughter Sally-Anne acquired, and her access to the internet, that ultimately helped us to unravel the story in 1998. The service records of former U.S Army personnel have been available online for some time under the USA Freedom of Information legislation. It didn't take long to access the records and to establish that not only did 'Butch' survive Omaha Beach but he was also alive and well and living on the Hudson River north of New York."

Within a matter of hours Pamela had spoken to her father on the phone. The following year, daughter and father met for the first time when 'Butch' came over to England. They came to Leamington where the former GI posed on the steps of the house in Willes Road where Pamela had been born and together they walked in the Jephson Gardens and admired the ducks!

Pamela told Alan Griffin in 2010 that Butch was still going strong at the grand old age of 90. He had never forgotten his brief wartime stay in Royal Leamington Spa during the long and eventful journey from Central Park, New York to the battle on Omaha Beach in 1944.

Canadian Troops - The bonds between Leamington Ontario and Leamington England were considerably strengthened at a ceremony outside the Town Hall one Saturday afternoon in 1942 when the gift of a Utilicon vehicle was formerly received by the Mayor [Alderman M. S. Moore] from Mr. J. A. Langley, representing the High Commissioner for Canada.

The Utilicon was used both as an ambulance and for carrying stores, and was operated by the local Civil Defence services. Mr. Langley said, "The people of Leamington Canada appreciate the spirit their kinsmen here have shown in this struggle for freedom, and the noble and heroic efforts they have made to safeguard the heart of the British Empire, so they welcomed this opportunity of showing their admiration by sending to you this 'Utilicon'."

The Utilicon vehicle being formerly received by the Mayor.

He continued, "Leamington, Canada has a population of only 5,000 people, but is allied to Leamington, England, in more ways than name. As I understand it the first settlers came from these parts and their early influence is still noticeable there today. In presenting this gift to your Worship, I might describe it as a token of the affection and admiration felt by those who, while they cannot engage in actual fighting, can at least take the opportunity of helping those who daily risk their lives."

Lady Helen Seymour thanked the Canadians for their generosity and said that although we were going through dark days the unity of the Empire had never been stronger than after 2½ years of war.

'Cloister Crofts' Prisoner of War Camp

Prisoner of War camps were built throughout the British Isles during the Second World War to accommodate military prisoners captured by the Allies. Until 1942 the number of prisoners captured was relatively small and consisted mainly of Luftwaffe aircrews and naval personnel. From 1942 onwards, following the North Africa campaign, the POW numbers steadily increased.

To cope with this influx contracts were placed with various major building contractors to construct camps of standard designs. A typical POW camp would have consisted of a guard's complex and prisoners compound. The guards' complex would have typically comprised of officers' and soldiers' accommodation, administration offices, storage buildings and an elevated water storage tank. The prisoners' compound typically consisted of accommodation huts, dining and recreation huts, workshops, ablution huts and a camp reception station [CRS]. The CRS consisted of sick bay rooms, medical officer's facilities, offices, stores, ablutions and a kitchen.

These camps were built quickly and were intended to be temporary short life structures. Many of the buildings were prefabricated huts built out of standard panels produced in factories. Examples of these huts are Nissen huts, timber huts, British Concrete Federation [BCF] huts, Orlit huts and Ministry of Works [MoW] standard huts.

Records show that Prisoner of War Camp 25 was located in Cloister Crofts. Access to the camp was by gates on Kenilworth Road although there may have been a larger entrance for vehicles in Cloister Way.

Pauline Mullis who now lives out of the area, recalled moving into one of six huts at the end of the Second World War. She recalls them being long wooden huts with no insulation, minimal facilities with baths being taken in front of the fire.

She and her mother moved into one of the huts in March 1945 whilst her father was still in the Services. One of the things she remembers him doing when he came home was sub-dividing the hut into bedrooms and a living room. He lined the walls to reduce the heat loss, and in order to carry out these 'improvements', enlisted the help of neighbours. The family remained at the former camp until 1953.

It is thought that the previous occupants were Italian prisoners of war who carried out a variety of tasks in the locality, including the building of a 'new' road to Leamington at the top of the present Gresham Avenue. Sources suggest that they would go round the streets offering such items as little dolls and beaded bracelets in return for cigarettes. They were not allowed to receive money in exchange for their goods.

Local historian Joe Claydon remembers the Italian prisoners selling homemade crafts to local families. He still has the bracelet bought by his family.

Mike Wardle says, "My grandparents farmed Newbold Comyn Farm and they were helped on the farm by POWs. They must, obviously, have been billeted locally. They made me a wooden toy parrot, which I kept for many years."

An 86-year-old resident from Dereham Court also remembers the Italian contingent in Leamington Spa. His son Stan relates that his father used to see the men regularly being driven by civilians to the farms around Golf Lane, Whitnash, where he grew up. They helped on farms, digging turnips and so on, and sometimes gave a turnip to the children. Civilian transport was provided by the Markham family, who later set up one of the local taxi firms.

Memories

It wasn't only the adults that were affected by the war as the memories of Tom Williams and these entries from the Shrubland Street School Logbook show: -

Tom Williams - "Leamingtonians will have vivid memories of the outbreak of War in 1939. The broadcast by the Prime Minister, Neville Chamberlain, that we were at war was heard in a crowded Shrubland Street School on, I think, a Sunday morning. Other teaching colleagues and I had gathered to receive coachloads of children who were being evacuated from Coventry. The outbreak of war had been anticipated and children were being removed from large cities to escape from the dangers of the expected bombing, an action which subsequent events proved to be wise. Having registered each child we took groups of the somewhat bewildered youngsters along the neighbouring streets knocking on doors and eventually finding 'homes' where they could stay. The innate kindness of the good folk of Leamington was demonstrated by the finding of a place of refuge for all."

Shrubland Street School Logbook

21st July 1939 - "Children brought gas masks to school to do gas mask drill."

31st August 1939 - "School closed at 4.15pm for the reception of evacuated children until further notice."

1st September 1939 – "School closed by order for International crisis."

25th September 1939 - "School reopened after being closed for 3 weeks for the receiving of children evacuated from Birmingham and Coventry. No Shrubland Street child admitted to school unless he/she brought with him/her the necessary form of permission signed by the parent and issued by the Local Education Authority. The double shift system commenced, the Shrubland Street 'A' School occupying the morning session from 8.45am to 12.15pm daily."

9th October 1939 – "Consequent upon an amalgamation of the four Coventry evacuated schools to use the Shrubland Street "J" School, this, the Shrubland Street "A" school commenced full time, children attending morning and afternoon, and carrying their gas masks on every visit to school."

12th March 1940 - "31s. [shillings] contributed by children and staff for The Teachers World Lightning Penny Fund for Finnish Children destitute through the war. The following articles made by the children were sent to the Women's Voluntary Services for Civil Defence: - 5 blankets, 1 small blanket, 11 helmets, 8 scarves, 2 pairs of socks, 6 pairs of mittens, 6 pairs of cuffs."

22nd May 1940 - "Trenches drill done daily - children march into trenches and take up defensive position."

12th June 1940 - "Adhesive paper sent from the Education Office to fix on all outside windows in case of air raids."

14th June 1940 - "Mr. Davies left school to join the RAF."

8th July 1940 - "From today onwards, the timetable of the school will be upset. All the classes in turn will visit the air-raid trenches each morning at 9.10a.m. immediately the registers are opened, to take down all apparatus needed if a raid took place. Then at 4.00pm. in the afternoon, all classes will again visit the trenches to regain their things as the trenches are open to the public in the evening."

23rd August 1940 - "German plane came over and dropped bombs near to school 11.30am. Children took shelter in the trenches until 12.10pm. Attendance dropped from 300 to 242 in the afternoon."

15th November and 20th November - "Both recorded violent air raids."

The school was reorganized again in 1941 into Juniors and Infants.

22nd April 1941 – "During the holidays, Mr. Williams received his order to join the AOC on the clerical staff, and leaves us on Thursday."

22nd October 1941 – "Notified this morning that the school is to close on October 23rd, 24th, 27th, 28th in order for the senior boys to go potato picking."

29th April 1942 - "Dinner for the children commenced in the school hall. 26 children and 2 teachers from the Infants Department stayed. Dinners were cold and there was not sufficient food."

In 1944, a book drive was held to collect books for the men in the forces to read. "Forty sacks of books altogether taken away, making a total of 9,176 books for the book drive. Timothy Hirons collected the most books - 339. For his efforts he received a certificate of merit and had to attend the Town Hall at 4.05pm."

12th July 1944 – "Notified by Mr. Greenwood, the Town Clerk, that the school has to close tomorrow on Friday 13th July on account of the evacuation of children from London as a result of the attacks by flying bombs. The school to be used as a rest centre."

17th July 1944 – "Received a letter from the Town Clerk extending the closure until Monday 24th July."

24th July 1944 - "Reopened."

8th and 9th May 1945 – "Closed today for the celebrations of Victory in Europe Day."

10th May 1945 – "A great many children are absent today on account, I presume, of late celebrations."

25th June 1945 - "School closed promptly at 12 noon today to allow anyone who wished to see and hear the Prime Minister, the Right Honorable Winston Churchill speak in the Pump Room Gardens."

Gwendoline Millward neé Atkins. In 2004 Gwen wrote her memories of the war. Gwen died in February 2009. Her 'Story' is as follows: -

Photo of Gwen taken in 1962.

CHAPTER 1 - PEACE

"On August 14th 1945 the Second World War ended. Japan had surrendered after receiving two devastating blows. Atom bombs had been dropped on Hiroshima and Nagasaki."

"I was 13 years old and had another few months of school to go before I left at 14. I went to Milverton School in Rugby Road, Leamington Spa, having failed my 11-plus by one mark. My parents were so upset at my failure that they went and had a chat with my headmistress and she told them about the one mark. Thinking back over the exam after the papers had been collected I suddenly realised I had made a stupid mistake on one of the questions. So, I never had the opportunity go to the Leamington College for Girls with my friend Shirley Harper."

"The day after the war ended, August 15th, was declared VJ Day, Victory in Japan Day. Previously when the Germans had surrendered and the war in Europe had ended May 8th 1945 had been declared VE Day, Victory in Europe Day. I remember I was up very early on the morning of VJ day and I slipped out of the house where I lived at 14 Woodbine Street. It was a beautiful day weather-wise, brilliant sunshine and blue skies, and I walked along the street and stood at the top of Church Hill. Even now, some 50 years later, I have never forgotten how I felt that day as I stood there."

"Everywhere was so quiet. I looked down the hill and there was no-one about, with no cars to be seen. Not many people had them in those days and anyway there was no petrol to be had, unless you used a vehicle for war work. Everything seemed to be at peace. "Yes", I told myself, "we really are at peace". I kept repeating to myself, "Peace,

Peace", and I couldn't take it in. The war had gone on for six years minus two weeks, tearing my life and millions of other families apart. On that sunny morning I likened the world to one of those glass paper weights that release a snowstorm when turned upside down."

"For years the world had been turned upside down and instead of snow there had been planes, bombs, bullets and bodies in the air but this had been righted and everything had settled and was calm again. At least that's how it seemed to me as I stood at the top of Church Hill that morning, and how apt that name was. Churchill was the name of the man who had been our Prime Minister during the war. He had given us, in England, and other people around the world, the fortitude and courage when things looked really bad to soldier on and give our all to help our country and win the war. My family had certainly done their bit. My father worked in munitions and was a Special Constable."

"My mother, well my mother worked so hard at keeping a large house spotless. A house that contained her family, soldiers billeted on us, and evacuees. She fed us well, I don't know how on wartime rations. My elder brother Frank was in the army in The Royal Signals and spent a large amount of the war with the 1st Army in North Africa and then Italy. His fiancé, Marjorie, worked in the food office before going into the ATS. My sister Mollie worked at the Lockheed Aircraft Factory and so did her fiancée Idris before he was called up into the army. My brother Bob also worked at the Lockheed, in the Jig and Tool drawing office, and was also an ardent member of the Home Guard. I was in the Brownies."

CHAPTER II - WAR BEGINNING

"I was seven years old and on holiday in Weston-Super-Mare with my parents when war was declared on September 3rd 1939. I remember looking out of the windows of the coach that took us home the next day. It was a grey day, in keeping with everyone's mood and there were soldiers drilling on the beach. The tide was right up to the beach for the first time since we had been there instead of stopping a mile or so out. Back home I found to my delight, the schools had been closed but that didn't last long. No time at all in fact."

"All the apprehension and the fear of the grown-ups went unnoticed by me. Life changed so gradually that I didn't notice it at first. I was more interested in playing in the street with all the other kids, going over the Guys Cliffe fields and making paper boats to sail in a pond we found over there. I founded the Black Hand Gang with me as their leader."

"That didn't last long. The boys said I was too bossy! I was the only girl in the street by the way until another two, Valerie and Pam, arrived during the war. Before I had Valerie and Pam to play with, my best friend in the street was Michael Cooke. He used to walk to school with me on Sundays when we went to Sunday School at St. Mark's. I also used to swap my Tiger Tim comic with Mickey as we called him, for one of his racier ones, such as Beano or Dandy."

"Life got a bit cumbersome when we had to take our gas masks everywhere we went. They were supplied in a cardboard box with a long loop of string to hang on your shoulder, but you can imagine how long that lasted. Most people ended up carrying them in a bag specially shaped to hold them, made up of what I seem to remember looked like imitation leather. We had gas mask drill at school. We used to climb down into the school air raid shelter, which was under allotments by the school grounds. The entrance was a round manhole in the ground and we climbed backwards down a wooden ladder into a long narrow shelter. By the time we were all down there, the noise was indescribable. The headmaster soon put a stop to that by telling us to put on our gas masks. We sat on wooden forms that lined the walls and I remember the smell of damp wood and concrete and an even more peculiar smell that came from the nozzle of my gas mask."

CHAPTER III - OUR HOUSE 14 WOODBINE STREET

"When you look back on your life you can remember the highs and lows, but not the middle of the road days. Same with the weather. I can remember very hot summers and freezing cold winters. Our house didn't have central heating, not many did in those days. There were fireplaces in all our bedrooms but the only time my mother ever lit a fire in one was if you were ill in bed and you had to be pretty poorly even then."

14 Woodbine Street [blue door] taken on 4th January 2015.

"It was a tall narrow house. A front door led off the street, but we didn't use it much. We usually went down the steps off the pavement into the basement area, and in through the kitchen door. When you looked up to the street from the kitchen window all you could see of people walking by was their bottom half. My family and I got quite good at recognising people's legs. Off the kitchen was a larder with shelves, and that was as large as the kitchen."

The tin bath in the photo is not the family's bath.

"The kitchen was also our bathroom, as it contained a bath with a hinged lid that my mother used as a long worktop on which to bake and do the ironing. When the bath was in use the lid was held up against the wall by a wooden peg. It was filled with hot water, heated in a gas copper that stood in a corner of the kitchen. This was all a great improvement on bath time previously. Then we used to bathe in front of the fire in our living room in a tin bath that was kept hung on a hook in the larder."

"Five inches was the depth of water suggested for a bath during the war. I have read that King George VI had a black line painted at this height around the inside of the baths in Buckingham Palace. I don't know how true that is. To economise, my mother used to bath me, and then get into the same water herself. I would have done it the other way around if I'd been her. She didn't have some of the Guys Cliffe fields attached to her person."

"Going down a step from the kitchen towards the back of the house you entered a room where we spent most of our lives. It was always referred to as 'the room'. Ask where someone or something was and the answer was invariably in 'the room'. There was always a lovely fire in winter. We ate around a scrubbed table that was usually covered by a fringed cloth. A snowy white linen one was used at meal times."

"My brother Bob did his homework from Technical College on that table. We played board games on it and on weekend evenings the whole family played cards around it. We would usually play Rummy or Newmarket and have a little gamble, only a penny a hand but it made playing more interesting."

"The window in 'the room' looked onto the back garden. My father grew flowers and vegetables. There was a very old cooking apple tree and gooseberry bushes - without babies under them! In the garden was a very tall pole with a wireless aerial attached to it. I often had to take the wireless accumulators to a shop along Regent Street to have them recharged. I hardly ever played in the garden. I was usually out in the street with the other kids, Michael Cooke, George Newey from next door and others, including a boy called John Rodenhurst whom the others called Enoch. I've never worked out why."

"My parents had the front bedroom at street level. The room at the back was my bedroom that I often shared with my grandmothers when either of them came to stay.

There were three more bedrooms on the top floor and above them was one flight of stairs leading to a lavatory and another flight leading to an attic. My mother scrubbed this out and I had it as a playroom. The cistern of the upstairs lavatory protruded in a box-like affair into this attic and my friends and I thought it great fun to flush this lavatory while someone was actually sitting on it! You just had to lift the lid and push the ball-cock down and wait for the invective to float up through the floor."

CHAPTER IV - DAILY LIFE

"I have mentioned the freezing winters and the scarcity of the cars during the war. These two facts meant that when it snowed, and we had a lot of snow in the winters during the war, people swept the snow from their fronts and off the pavement into the gutter. Consequently there were piles of snow at least three feet high in places, sometimes along the whole length of the street. We used to try to walk to school on these piles of snow without touching the pavement. Most of the piles were quite firm and held but occasionally your wellington clad leg would go through. You ended up with a wellie full of snow, not to mention a soaking wet black woolly stocking, which was precariously fixed to your liberty bodice with a button pushed through a loop."

"I never stayed for school dinner. My mother cooked at dinner time. There would be me, brother Bob who cycled home for dinner from the Lockheed, my Dad before he went to 'munitions', Marjorie when she worked at the food office, perhaps grandmother, a soldier who was billeted on us, or an evacuee. I'll tell you about the soldiers and evacuees later. I used to walk home from school every dinner time and my mother gave me three jobs to do each day. That's how I earned my pocket money. First of all I had to go to Miss Stokes' bread shop, which was just around the corner in Warwick Place. I always bought a large tin loaf price fourpence halfpenny."

"To a little girl Miss Stokes seemed very old. She was a spinster who wore old fashioned long dresses and her hair was parted in the middle and plaited. The plaits were then wound round into "earphones" over each ear. In retrospect she could have been no more than in her early thirties."

"I suspect she was dominated by her mother who was never seen but you knew she was keeping tabs on everything that was going on through the open door that led from the shop into their living room. I used to gaze with fascination at Miss Stokes, I wondered what her christian name was. She never actually looked anyone in the eye, and only spoke to say how much things were and to say 'thank you' when you paid her."

"When her mother died her hair was cut and her skirts went shorter. She got married and had a baby rather quickly, but then her husband deserted her. Listening to the grown-ups talking I gathered he had also ran off with her money. She had sold the shop after her mother died. I thought it all really sad!"

"When I came back from the bread shop, my mother gave me the household scraps to take to the 'pig bin' as we called it. Dotted around everywhere were dustbins, our nearest one being on Church Hill under a big tree. Everyone used to put their scraps, potato peelings and such like in these bins which was then used to feed livestock."

"My other dinner time job was to dust 'the room'. My mother had done the fireplace, run the carpet sweeper over the carpet and then left me to dust round. By the time I had finished these jobs the others had all come home and we all sat down to eat. I hated the days when we had tapioca for pudding, it seemed to look like the frog spawn that Mickey and I brought back from Guys Cliffe fields."

"During one dinner time the air-raid siren sounded. Bob, my mum and me went up to one of the top bedrooms at the back of the house because we were sure we heard a bomb drop. We could see smoke rising from the direction of the Lockheed. Bob cycled off to work again and when he came home that evening he said a bomb had been dropped. No one had been hurt but there was quite a bit of damage."

"Leamington Spa wasn't a prime target for the German bombers but when the raids on Coventry were at their height we had a stick of bombs across the bottom half of the town. A vegetable shop in Bath Street and a house in York Road were two of the buildings hit. One bomb fell not far from the Town Hall on the Parade. There is a plaque on the statue of Queen Victoria that stands just by the Town Hall. It reads: - 'A German bomb moved this statue one inch on its plinth on the 14th. November 1940'. She was never put back in place and if you care to climb up and look you can see the mark on the plinth."

"A lone German plane actually machine-gunned the Parade one afternoon and people dived into Woolworths and other shops to take cover."

"Left on my own I would probably have slept on after the siren sounded at night, but my parents would carry me down three flights of stairs, by the light of a torch held by my mother. I was put to sleep on the settee in 'the room'. I was more frightened of my father losing his footing in the dark and dropping me than of the air-raid. After a while we got to know the sound of the German aeroplane engines. They had sort of throbbing sound, quite distinctive from ours. When he heard them, my father used say "Jerry" in a warning sort of voice."

"Later in the war, the remains of the house in York Road was the scene of a Civil Defence competition between two teams of firemen and ARP workers. ARP stands for Air Raid Precautions. They had to rescue a little girl - me - trapped in an upstairs room while her distraught mother - a neighbour of ours by the name of Mrs. Wright - pleaded with them to save her little girl. I had to lean out of the window and call for my 'mother' and then wait to be rescued. One team lowered me down on a sort of seat on a rope and the second team carried me down fireman's lift on a man's back. Miss Ellen Wilkinson, who was in the coalition government during the war, presented a prize to the winning team. She said that my make believe mother and I were as good at acting as film stars."

CHAPTER V - THE FILMS AND RADIO

"Frank and Marjorie used to give me presents of the Film Review annuals at Christmas. I read them avidly, and there wasn't much I didn't know about the film stars of that time. There were Shirley Temple, Sonja Henie, Tyrone Power, John Payne, Bing Crosby, Deanna Durbin as well as our British favourites such as Stewart Grainger, James Mason, Dennis Price, Margaret Lockwood, Patricia Roc, Jean Kent and husband and wife team Michael Dennison and Dulcie Grey. I could go on and on."

"Before he went into 'munitions', my father was manager of Freeman Hardy and Willis, the shoe shop in Regent Street. Thursday was early closing day and he always took my mum and me to the pictures first house every Thursday evening. We usually went to the Regal. There was the Regent Cinema and Scala Cinema in Leamington Spa, but I don't remember going to them much. In fact I don't think we went to the Scala at all. It was generally known as the 'Flea Pit'. We always sat in the 1/9's and usually row F or one in front or back of it on the left-hand side of the cinema as you faced the screen. I used to sit by the aisle, then my mum and then my dad. I would sit lost in a dream world, soaking up the music and dancing of the Hollywood musicals and as young as I was I appreciated the superb acting of our British stars. I was quite good at imitating some of the people I saw on the screen and my family would roll the carpet back at one end of 'the room', and I would entertain them. I got applause too. I can still do a passable Carmen Miranda to this day."

"I have always loved dancing, and perhaps this stems from the fact that I used to go to the Linden School of Dancing every Saturday afternoon. I learnt tap and ballet and what was called 'Musical Comedy'. I used to do the splits for that."

"I used to like the start of the newsreel at the cinema. Loud stirring music was followed by Geoffrey Summers sensuous voice announcing, "This is the Gaumont British News bringing the truth to the free peoples of the world". Whatever was shown about the war, it always included a clip of British Tommie's grinning at the camera and giving the thumbs up, just to show us they weren't downhearted, I suppose. The war was on Pathe News as well, and that started with the words 'Pathe News' over a large cockerel crowing, accompanied by more stirring music."

"The radio was the main source of entertainment for people during the war. I especially remember Tommy Handley in ITMA [It's That Man Again] - In Town Tonight, Paul Temple thrillers, Uncle Mac on Children's Hour with Toy Town and Larry the Lamb, and Monday Night at Eight. I can still sing the signature tune to that one. I loved the beginning of In Town Tonight. It was a Friday night programme and would start with the sound of traffic, then a man's voice would shout "Stop" and all would be quiet. Then the announcer would say, "Once again we stop the roar of London's traffic to bring you ..." and he would go on to tell us the names of the stars on the programme that evening."

"People working in factories had non-stop music played to them to keep their spirits up and to help the long day's toil. Twice a day there was a programme called 'Music While You Work' when popular songs were played so the workers could sing along. My friend and I made up a couple of lines to sing to the signature tune - it went: "Music while you work for workers, Hurry up, you blinkin' shirkers," and these are the words we made up to the song that the seven dwarfs sang in Snow White: - "Whistle while you work, Mussolini is a twerp, Hitler's barmy, so's his army, Whistle while you work"."

"People in factories were also entertained in their canteens during the dinner break. Entertainers toured the factories, and these half hour entertainments broadcast by the BBC, were called 'Workers' Playtime'. You didn't know which factory it was being broadcast from. We were only told it was coming from a factory in the North of England or wherever. Most of the performers belonged to ENSA – [Entertainment National Services Association]. They also went to the front line and entertained the troops. A young girl by the name of Vera Lynn became everyone's favourite. She sang songs whose words conveyed all our feelings during those dark days. She also went abroad and sang to the troops often coming under fire herself. She became known as 'The Forces Sweetheart', and some years after was made a Dame."

"The BBC also broadcast tips on how to keep healthy by the Radio Doctor whose name was Charles Hill. So called experts told us how to 'Make Do and Mend'. Most of all I liked Mabel Constanduras who played both parts in a sketch where an exasperated woman was trying to explain to a very tetchy 'Grandma' the finer points of wartime recipes along with handy hints."

CHAPTER VI - HOLIDAYS AT HOME

"People didn't go away for the summer holidays during the war. It wouldn't have been any use going to the seaside anyway. Most of the beaches around the coast had fortifications on them and trippers were banned. In Leamington we had what were called 'Holidays at Home'."

"There were two or three marquees erected on the Pump Room Gardens, and the area outside the biggest one was part fenced off with an open-air stage and seats for the audience. There you could sit and be entertained by such stars as Leslie Hutchinson, better known as Hutch, Ivy Benson and her All Girls Band, and comics, one of whom was Rob Wilton. He took great delight in telling us what his missus said to him the day war broke out. There were talent contests and children's shows, you name it they had it, all to keep us entertained and at home during the summer."

"My mum was so busy looking after us all at home. I used to drive her up the wall I know, from asking if I could go down to the Pump Room Gardens to see what was happening. To shut me up she would say, "Oh go on then, but don't be long". I would hang over the wooden fence watching the couples dancing on the grass to record music and, sometimes a live band. I studied their steps and then went home and practised them in 'the room' and that is how I learnt ballroom dancing."

CHAPTER VII - MY TWO FRIENDS

"I had to walk along Strathearn Road on my way to school and my friend Christine lived at number 27. We were about the same age, give or take a month or two. Her mother and mine used to go and sit in the park of an afternoon when Christine and I were babies in our prams. They sat on the same bench one afternoon and got talking and a firm friendship developed between them. At that time Christine and I were too small to talk, but we made up for it though as we became friends. We used to stay over at each other's houses."

"Mrs. Gosling, Christine's mum, had to go into hospital once and so Christine stayed with us. On our way home from school each day we stopped off at her house, made Mr. Goslings bed and did any washing up or tidying that needed doing, so that things would be nice when he came home from working on the tobacconist's counter at Burgis and Colbourne's."

"We are still friends sixty years later. She lives in Kent now and is a grandmother several times over. We meet only occasionally but when we do we carry on chatting as if we had never been apart. My other friend, Shirley Harper, the one who passed her 11 plus and went to college - lived at the bottom of Church Hill with her parents John and Margaret Harper, her brother Tony and younger sister Jennifer."

"Mr. and Mrs. Harper kept a grocer's shop and sold the creamiest ice-cream you have ever tasted, made on the premises. They also had a milk round and delivered to our house. They were a close-knit and loving family. John Harper was enlisted into the RAF. His wife kept the business going and he used to help with the milk round when he came home on leave. On his last leave he said "Goodbye" to all his customers as he had the feeling he wouldn't come home again - and he didn't. He was a navigator on a bomber and was shot down during a raid over Dusseldorf."

"Margaret Harper died two or three years ago and like our Queen Mother was a widow for much longer than she was a wife. That was also the fate of thousands of other women. Margaret Harper brought up her three children and ran the business. Tony grew up to be the spitting image of his father. It was as if John Harper was living through his son."

CHAPTER VIII - MY DAD

"My dad, Francis Harold Atkins, was a special constable. He used to get dressed up in his uniform in the evenings and go out on the beat around Leamington Spa. Another special used to come and call for him, his name was Mr. Fuller. He had lost his toes through frostbite during the First World War. I used to gaze at his feet encased in shiny black boots and wonder what happened in the spaces at the toes of his boots, or were there spaces? Did he buy boots three sizes smaller than he would have done had his toes been there?"

"I used to see my dad when he was on duty at the 'Holidays at Home'. I thought that it was great to be seen on such friendly terms with the law. I have his Civil Defence medal, and his medal for Faithful Service in the Special Constabulary awarded to him by the Secretary of State in 1949 for long service. I have a lovely photo of him and his colleagues on parade for the Mayor's Sunday in November 1947 along with a letter from the then Mayor, Councillor Purcell, to the Police Superintendent, J. C. Gardner asking him to convey his keen appreciation of the 'specials' efficient services when they escorted him on that Sunday. Dad was very patriotic. Whenever the National Anthem was played on the radio at home he insisted we all stood to attention. Even though he wasn't usually demonstrative he got quite emotional one Christmas when he was toasting 'absent friends', and his voice broke so he couldn't go on when he toasted my brother Frank, who was then in North Africa."

"Dad was well into his fifties during the war and what with working in munitions and being a special constable, he must have felt weary but I never heard him complain. Come to think of it I never heard much complaining from anyone during the war years. Everyone seemed to buckle down and get on with things. If anyone did moan about the lack of something you would more than likely hear the person they were moaning to say, "Don't you know there's a war on?" Another thing I noticed when anyone met someone they knew on leave from the forces they would most likely say, "Hello, when are you going back?" and the answer would most likely be, "Blimey mate, I've only just got here!""

CHAPTER IX - MY MUM

"Now we come to my Mum. What can I say? How can I get across how hard she worked during the war? She and millions of housewives like her were the unsung heroes of the war. They didn't actually take up arms. They wrote letters and sent parcels to the men and women away from home and kept their families warm and fed as best they could. In the words of the old song they 'Kept the Home Fires Burning'. My Mum kept a large house with numerous rooms and staircases spotlessly clean without electricity or running hot water. We had gas lights in all of the rooms, but no light at all on the stairs."

"The gas copper in the kitchen did for the very large weekly wash as well as to fill the bath in the kitchen. We ironed with a gas iron that had a long metal flex that fitted onto a gas jet. I used to turn the handle of the big mangle that stood in the larder while my mother fed sheets and towels and other articles through it after she had washed them by hand, or boiled them in the copper. She used to look after about eight of us at times. It would depend on how many soldiers we had billeted on us or if we had an evacuee. Then there was the shopping, it all had to be carried home from town - no delivery boys or car boots to be filled in those days. Looking back I suppose the more people you had in the house the more food coupons you had so you could do more with what each person was allowed."

"When she was older Mum's right shoulder was much lower than her left. She said she reckoned that it was from carrying a heavy shopping basket home for all those years."

"Talking to my brother Bob and sister Mollie about how hard Mum worked during those years, Bob said he knows he never went hungry and Mollie said she just doesn't know how Mum did it all."

"Life was so upside down in those days. Mealtimes were disorganised with the family and soldiers all working different times. Then when the raids on Coventry were at their height there were nights when the sirens went and Mum didn't get a lot of sleep. I am ashamed to say now I took her for granted. She was my Mum and that's what mums did."

CHAPTER X - FRANK

"Frank was the eldest of us four children. He was born in January 1916, so he was 23 when the war was declared. He worked at Courts the builders in Leamington Spa, and was a quantity surveyor. He joined the Royal Signals in 1940 and was in North Africa with the 1st Army and later went to Italy where he was posted to Milan. He actually saw some opera at the Opera House."

"Frank was very good looking. He looked very much like Tyrone Power or John Payne the film stars. He had lots of girlfriends and used to claim a hanky off each one or perhaps pinched one, I don't know. When he and Marjorie were married she had a long length of hankies tied corner to corner."

"When I was nineteen, I went to work at Leamington Spa telephone exchange. That was in the days when it was manual working. In fact it was so manual you actually had to pull a key back on your switchboard to ring the bell in the subscribers house. One of the telephonists said to me, "Ooh, are you Frank Atkins sister?", and when I said I was she told me that she used to work at a salon where Frank had his hair cut. She and the other girls used to go weak at the knees when he walked in. That was a ladies' hairdressers as well. Perhaps it was one of the first unisex salons?"

"Mum used to write to Frank every Monday afternoon after she had finished her mammoth wash day and cooked dinner. It was, I should think, a chance to rest her legs before the influx of people for the next meal. We always had cold meat, mashed spuds and pickles and rice pudding on washdays. Nice and easy. I also used to write to him occasionally and Mum enclosed my letter with hers."

"I even thought of a ruse to get me out of going to Sunday School on Sunday afternoons. Well I had already been to the Children's Service in the morning and I thought that religion in the afternoon as well was a bit much. Mind you, afternoon Sunday School was one way of getting rid of the offspring while parents had their afternoon 'nap'. I decided I was going to write to Frank every Sunday afternoon and I went to my attic playroom, sat at my desk and wrote a long letter to Frank. I told him what us kids would like to do to Hitler if we ever got our hands on him. Things like tying him up and sticking pins in him all over and covering him with honey and letting bees sting him. Well that idea lasted just one Sunday. I gave the letter to my mum and she wanted to know when I had written it. It turned out I had been so quiet she thought I was at Sunday School, so that was it, a good telling off, and packed off to St. Mark's the next Sunday under the guardianship of Mickey Cooke."

"Frank wrote home regularly and he used to pop the occasional note in for me. He would write a few words of Italian and tell me what they meant, and I used to brag to the kids in the street that I could speak Italian. Frank was a sergeant by the time the war ended. He came home on a month's leave and was married to Marjorie in October 1945. I was their bridesmaid. They had a short honeymoon in Malvern and then Frank went back to Italy until he was demobbed in June 1946."

"He went back to Courts until he retired after working there for 50 years. He died of cancer the day after his 73rd birthday."

"As you know the family name is Atkins. I thought that very apt for Frank, him being in the Army, as the first British soldier has been called Tommy Atkins ever since the First World War. Frank's second name is Thomas after Uncle Tommy who was a Tommie in the First World War."

"When I was at school, Mr. Parker our history teacher looked up the origin of our surnames. An Atkins apparently was a serf on the baron's land and we were in bondage."

CHAPTER XI - MARJORIE

"Marjorie was living in Kenilworth when she met Frank in 1937. She was introduced to him on a train by a mutual friend and she said, "That was that". They got engaged before Frank went into the Army and Marjorie went to work at the food office, issuing ration books and clothing coupons. She said it was a real eye opener on how devious people can be. People who came in for ration books had all of a sudden acquired lots of relatives. Despite the world situation she says she quite enjoyed it and was even seen fleetingly in a film called, 'The Gentle Sex' in which Rex Harrison and his then wife, Lili Palmer, starred. She was in a crowd scene with other ATS [Auxiliary Territorial Service]. The whole family trooped to the pictures to see that."

"During May 1944, the Ministry of Defence had a 'Salute The Soldier Week', and also weeks to salute the sailors and airmen. Marjorie and other ATS helped at exhibitions showing aspects of army life and the weapons used, including tanks. Marjorie had her picture in the paper sitting on a mini motorbike that could be dropped by parachute. The exhibition was at Bobby's store in Eastbourne."

"It was a very warm May that year and when the girls were off duty they went up on to the roof of Bobby's to sunbathe. They took off their uniforms and lounged around in their underwear. Marjorie said no one wore the standard issue of army knickers, they were so frightful that they bought their own. Whilst they were sunning themselves they heard laughter and they walked around the balustrade that encircled the roof to see where it was coming from. They couldn't see anything until one girl noticed a window in a building opposite and they realised to their horror that they were just across the road from the NAAFI, where there were quite a few servicemen at the window having a good eyeful. Needless to say, Marjorie and the other girls blushingly retired off the roof to more private quarters downstairs."

"Marjorie went back to the ATS after she and Frank were married and he went back to Italy but being a married woman she was automatically released after six months. She went home to Kenilworth to live with her parents and Frank joined her when he was demobbed. In January 1947, they moved into their first home, a flat opposite Courts where Frank worked, and raised a family, a daughter Susan and a son David."

CHAPTER XII - MOLLIE AND IDRIS

"Mollie was the second eldest born in 1918. During the war, she worked in the copper hose and tube shop at Lockheed. She was engaged to Idris Sparrow from Tonypandy in Glamorgan. He also worked at the Lockheed and had come to Leamington Spa to find work as a tool maker, there being no work in the Rhondda except mining. Mollie worked with a lot of Welsh girls who had come to the Lockheed for the same reason. She said they kept her laughing all day long, they were having the time of their lives in England. Women weren't allowed in pubs in Wales and so they were never out of the pubs in Leamington Spa."

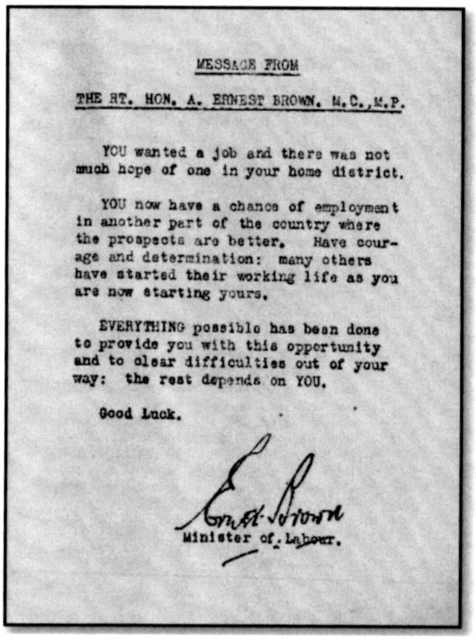

MESSAGE FROM

THE RT. HON. A. ERNEST BROWN, M.C.,M.P.

YOU wanted a job and there was not much hope of one in your home district.

YOU now have a chance of employment in another part of the country where the prospects are better. Have courage and determination: many others have started their working life as you are now starting yours.

EVERYTHING possible has been done to provide you with this opportunity and to clear difficulties out of your way: the rest depends on YOU.

Good Luck.

Ernest Brown

Minister of Labour.

Youngsters in Wales were issued with a 'Juvenile Transference Scheme' booklet giving information about living and working in other parts of the country.

"People in munitions worked a twelve-hour day, seven days a week, but whenever Mollie and Idris talk about those days, it is all about the laughs they had."

"On 26th May 1939, a government minister by the name of Leslie Hore-Belisha was successful in passing the Military Training Act, the first peacetime conscription law. Anyone over 21 years of age had to sign on for six months' service. They were called 'militia men' or 'Hore-Belisha's boys'. There were rumblings of war and in June of that year Idris was called up into the militia, and was sent to a new camp at Hereford, It is now the headquarters of the SAS."

"He had just passed his apprenticeship exams at the Lockheed and had to take more exams at Hereford. He passed them and was called an Artificer in the Royal Artillery. War was declared in September and instead of being released after just six months, Idris stayed on until 1941 when he was finally released to go back to the Lockheed for production work on aircraft."

"Mollie and Idris were married at Warwick Registry Office on March 1st 1941. If you marry a Welshman you simply have to do it on St. David's Day. It was a quiet wedding. That evening they celebrated with friends at the local Palais de Dance, and Mollie moved in with Idris at his digs."

"In 1943 preparations were being made for D-Day, and Idris was called back into the Army. He was a Craftsman 1st Class in the Royal Electrical Mechanical Engineers [REME]. Mollie moved back home to Woodbine Street and shared a bedroom with me. I can remember her getting up early to start her long day at the factory and putting on her turban. She had dark hair, like Frank, and wore it in a pageboy. Long hair was the vogue during the war, especially the 'Veronica Lake' hairdo. Veronica Lake was an American film star and was reckoned to be the ultimate in glamour. She had long blond hair that she wore combed over one side of her face. From behind she "smouldered provocatively"."

"Unfortunately some women who copied her style and who worked in munitions had terrible accidents in which they had their hair torn off after getting it caught in the machinery. Thereafter all hair had to be covered. Most people turned their head squares into turbans - a-la Hilda Ogden of Coronation Street, but then another item of hair fashion came into being. It was called The Snood. It was just a large crocheted hair net really. You rolled your front hair, as was the fashion in those days, and tucked your long flowing locks into this Snood that hung down the back. It sounds a peculiar fashion I know, but it did look slightly better than the turban. Snoods were all colours, you could match them to your outfit and there were even twinkly ones for evening wear."

"Towards the end of the war, a new hair fashion came out. Hair was cut short to about two inches all over and worn curly. Because it did not require Kirby grips or combs to hold it in place it was called the Liberty Cut. I went for it straight away. It was just the style for my naturally curly hair."

"To return to Idris. Towards the end of the war he was stationed at LAD Kineton. LAD stands for Light Air Detachment. He was very near Leamington Spa, so when he had leave he used to cycle home. He palled up with an army cook at that camp, I don't know what his name was. Idris always referred to him as Jock. One weekend on leave in the summer Idris cycled home carrying some delicious beef dripping that Jock had given him on the quiet. He carried it in a valise strapped on his back and what with the warm weather and his exertions on the bike he found to his dismay that the dripping had melted in the valise and soaked right through his uniform. As you can imagine, the weekend leave was spent boiling and cleaning his uniform and valise, and getting them ready for parade on Monday morning."

"When that weekend leave is mentioned we say, "Ooh, do you remember when..? Wasn't it awful? Wasn't he a mess?" and then proceed to fall about laughing. Idris was demobbed in 1946, and he and Mollie had the back room on the first floor of our house as their own sitting room, so they could have some privacy. That was usually my bedroom and so I moved up to one of the bedrooms on the top floor at the front of the house. Mollie and Idris eventually bought a house in Lillington and moved there with their daughter Mary."

CHAPTER XIII - BOB

"Bob was born next. He is ten years older than me, so that made him 17 years old when war was declared. He is quite different from Frank in looks. Whereas Frank had black hair and brown eyes, Bob had auburn hair and freckles. When he grinned he looked really cheeky and a lot like Mickey Rooney. As I have mentioned, he too worked at the Lockheed, in the Jig and Tool Drawing Office. It was a reserved occupation and so in 1940 he joined the LDV [Local Defence Volunteers] until eventually the 2nd Company Home Guard was formed."

"They really did have to drill with broom sticks and wore arm bands until rifles and uniforms were issued. The first uniforms were made of waxed denim to make them waterproof. They were eventually issued with standard army uniform. Like everyone else Bob worked a 12-hour shift at the Lockheed then three nights a week he was at the drill hall with the Home Guard."

"They did guard duty at night on a rota. Six of them at a time and it worked out to a duty every 10th night. They guarded the underground reservoir on the Campion Hills. Strangely enough it was never guarded during the day. Perhaps the powers that be decided Jerry wouldn't poison the water or blow it up during broad daylight."

"Bob used to be on guard at night, go home for breakfast and then go to another days work at the office and just to keep him up to scratch, the office manager made him do physical jerks at ten o' clock in the morning. One day a week Bob went on day release to technical college. He did homework at night when he didn't go down to the drill hall. He turned out to be a first-class draughtsman and was Head Draughtsman in later life at Dunlop in Coventry."

"Bob followed the war on a map of the world that was hung on a wall in 'the room'. It was quite big, I should think a yard square. There were flags of all the countries fighting the war. The Union flag for the British forces, the Swastika for the Germans, Rising Sun for the Japs and the Stars and Stripes for the Americans or to call it by its proper name, The Star-Spangled Banner. With these flags pinned on the map, you could follow the advances and retreats of the different armies. It was wonderful to see our march across Europe as the war was coming to a close."

"Bob also took the magazine 'War Illustrated', he kept them all and had them bound. They ran into several volumes and are all in his bookcase to this day. I have seen photographs of Bob and his Home Guard Company. He became a sergeant, and his commanding officer was Captain Gates. Bob says he was exactly like Captain Mainwaring in Dad's Army. He had his manner and spoke like him. There was also a spiv in the company who always had a bit of 'under the counter' dealing going on."

"When I looked at the man in the back row of one of Bob's Home Guard photos I couldn't believe my eyes. There was a young man who could have easily been Ian Lavender, who played the part of Private Frank Pike. There was also a man who, Bob says, was always a bit late coming to attention - just like Corporal Jones. I can remember Bob cleaning his rifle. He also had a sten gun that he kept in the cupboard of his bedroom. He slept in the back bedroom on the top floor. It was three flights of stairs up from 'the room' and as he went up and down the stairs and around the house he always seemed to be singing. He had a good voice too."

"He used to sing Mexicali Rose quite a bit. We had a record of that and 'Begin the Beguine' was on the reverse side. These were two of Hutch's songs. I heard him sing both at the 'Holidays at Home'. We played these records on a wind-up gramophone that was enclosed in a mahogany cabinet. It was about three feet high and just under three feet square. It was a lovely piece of furniture. You lifted the lid to use the turntable. There was a space beside that to store records and there was also space for the tin of gramophone needles and the handle that fitted into a round hole in the side with which you wound the gramophone. At the front of the cabinet were two doors that opened to show the speaker, that had carved mahogany to cover some of the speaker mesh. After Mollie had been to the pictures to see Anton Walbrook in

'Dangerous Moonlight', we had strains of the Warsaw Concerto drifting through the house for hours on end."

"During the war Bob was courting a girl called Barbara who lived at Cubbington, just outside Leamington Spa. I used to go over there with my parents. Our two families got on well together. We used to sing songs in the evening around the piano whilst Barbara played. We were at Cubbington one summer evening when there was a scare that a parachutist had been seen in the sky. It turned out to be a barrage balloon that had broken free and got to a great height."

"Bob was called out one night in a panic. To call out the Home Guard, the ones who were on the 'phone were the first to be alerted. They called out the next lot, who in turn called out the others. They were all assembled at the drill hall. Bob says they were all loaded down with ammunition, bandoliers, [pocketed belt for holding ammunition], over their shoulders and grenades hung on their belts. They were finally mustered at the bridge over the River Leam. It was a false alarm of course but Bob says he often wonders how they would have fared if the Germans really had landed. Don't we all?"

"They also had night time manoeuvres. One night they went to Chesford and had to pretend to take the bridge over the river. That went well but they weren't too pleased when Captain Gates said, "Right men, we have to go back across the river, but the bridge has been blown up", so they had to wade back through the water."

"Apparently they liaised with the regular army quite a bit. One evening a sergeant came to show them how to lecture men on warfare. When he finished he picked on one of the men and said, "You, come and show us how to use a bayonet". He stepped back into the company and the private started talking and prodding at the sandbags with the bayonet and never looked up. When he had finished he found he was on his own as everyone had quietly moved away. A short sharp lesson to show you must look at people you are lecturing."

"The company went to Dover to train with the regular army on the White Cliffs. Bob says at one time he was riding at speed through Dover on a Bren gun carrier and he really felt like a proper soldier. He eventually married a girl called Sylvia who moved to Leamington Spa from Folkestone, Kent. They have a son Paul and a daughter Janet."

CHAPTER XIV - SOLDIERS AND EVACUEES

"If you lived in a big house with lots of bedrooms - as we did - and there was room to spare you had to have soldiers or evacuees billeted with you. We had both but at different times. We had soldiers by the names of Ray and Eddie to start with, and Ray became a member of the family. He was in the Royal Signals like Frank and his headquarters was in one of the big houses along Kenilworth Road."

"I can remember when he started courting a blonde girl called Ruth, my family used to tease him because he was so smitten he went off his food and couldn't sleep. He brought her home to meet us a few times but the romance ended. He then met another girl called Ruth although she was always called Red because of the colour of her hair. He married her after the war and I was one of the bridesmaids at their wedding. I wore a pale blue lace dress and carried a posy of sweet peas."

"Ray was like a brother to me. One Christmas while he was living with us he bought me a bicycle, a utility model, all black, not a bit of chrome anywhere. Who cared about chrome anyway, I had my heart's desire - a bike!! I had that bike for years until it was pinched one day because I had left its chain and padlock at home. Not long after that Christmas, Ray was sent abroad and met up with Frank in Italy, not surprising I suppose as they were in the same regiment."

"I can't remember much about Eddie, he was very quiet and came and went without causing waves. Not like Jock who came next, he was making a cigarette lighter from bits and pieces, and all he wanted in the end was a wheel to ignite the flint. Everyone he met or who came to the house he asked if they had a "wheel forra leeter" in his lovely Scots accent. It got so bad in the end that people used to joke that he would ask the same question of the German High Command if he ever came face to face with them. Another soldier was Dick, he was a dispatch rider, unmarried and came from Kettering."

"Jock also fitted in with our family. His mum used to write to my mum. She was so pleased that Jock was being looked after properly. Dick was killed in an accident whilst riding his khaki motorbike, it was awful. This was the first time death had come anywhere near me. My mum and dad and I went up to Kettering to meet Dick's family. I don't think it was for the funeral because I can't remember one. Dick's brother was very kind to me and I found myself telling him all about my books, especially my film annuals. He had some too, they dated back to the early 1930s, and he gave them to me. I have them to this day."

"During our evenings round the fire in 'the room', we were amused by another soldier we had billeted on us. I can't remember his name but he spoke fluent German. He used to do imitations of Hitler giving one of his frenzied speeches to the masses. He looked a bit like Herbert Lom, the film star of that time and he was really good fun and kept us laughing a lot. You really needed people like that during the war years."

"We must have had a bedroom free while he was staying with us, or perhaps my mother made us double up again because his mother came to live with us for a while. I remember she was quite a large lady and, wonder of wonders she had a false leg! Gosh, it did fascinate me. It had a joint at the knee that locked or unlocked for sitting and standing. One day we were all sitting round the table in 'the room' and a new leg was delivered to the front door. That leg was passed round the table from person to person and was very well inspected. It also caused considerable merriment. It was a pale pinky-beige colour, and could have been made of bakelite. It had a sort of harness, made I think, of a light webbing, with which it would have been strapped to the waist once the stump was inserted in the top of the leg."

"We had all nationalities in Leamington Spa. As well as Czech, Belgian and Polish soldiers, we had Americans - everyone called them Yanks. Girls went for them in a big way. Their uniforms were tailored in a much nicer material than our soldiers' battledress. They had more money and their accents were straight out of the 'movies', as they called them. Disgruntled people used to say they were overpaid, oversexed and over here. My Mum and Dad didn't approve of them at all and the girls who went with them were, "no better than they should be". Lots of girls married them though and went to live in America."

"My friend Pam, who came to live in the street, had an aunt who married a Czech and went to live in Czechoslovakia after the war. Not such a good choice I shouldn't think the way things turned out."

"We also had German prisoners of war in Leamington Spa, they wore brown uniforms with big round patches on their backs. I used to see lorry loads of them on their way to work on farms with just a driver and a soldier to guard them. Some of them married English girls and settled here after the war."

"We had one other evacuee beside the soldier's mother. She was a girl from London. She came to Leamington Spa with her mother but the mother had to stay elsewhere as we were a bit full at the time and I had to share with this girl whose name I can't remember. I apologise for all these names I can't remember but it was over fifty years ago! I'll tell you one thing though, my friend Christine had an evacuee at her house, and his name was George Gascoigne! We both thought it a funny name and that one has definitely stuck in my memory. Anyway, the girl staying with us was in her teens and very interested in boys. My mother was frightened to death she would 'get into trouble' while she was living under our roof."

"That was one of the main things mothers used to worry about during the war, keeping their daughters out of trouble. Nice girls didn't do it, or if you did you kept quiet about it and hoped you wouldn't get caught out - in more ways than one. You'd be surprised what little gems of knowledge young ears picked up when grown-ups were talking. Pam, Valerie and I used to wonder how babies were born. How did they get out? Out through the belly button was the best we could come up with at the time. Children were so innocent in those days."

"This girl from London turned out to be another destined to work at Lockheed. She fancied a feller she worked with there and I could see she had to smarten herself up if she wanted a chance of hooking him. Young as I was, I could see she didn't make the best of herself. Let's face it, I studied all these glamorous film stars at the pictures every Thursday night, and I didn't miss much. I got her to have her hair cut decently and pinned her front roll for her. Her clothes improved after my mother had dealt with them for a week or two, and we both worked on her make-up. She got her man in the end."

"We also had another recruit to the street gang. Next door had evacuees, and one of them was John Wadham from Deal in Kent. He was a blonde, gentle natured boy about my age and he joined in our jaunts over the fields and played in the street with us. The neighbours were Mr. and Mrs. Scott, she was known as Scotty. They had a black mongrel dog that hated all other dogs. One day he was going berserk in their basement area over another dog that was trying to get at him from the pavement above. My mother couldn't stand the noise any longer and threw a bucketful of water over him. Unfortunately Scotty was just coming out of her door to sort them out and the water went all over her. I was dying to laugh but I didn't dare. The look my mother gave me was enough, my very respectable mother couldn't bear to think that she had done something as awful as half drowning a neighbour. Scotty was a very good natured woman, not one to hold a grudge, and it all blew over. The episode was never mentioned again in our house."

Me - or Little Gwennie Atkins – "The only uniform I wore during the war was a Brownie uniform. I joined the Brownie pack at St. Albans, a church that has long since been demolished. My strongest memory of the Brownies is shivering in my brown cotton uniform while we stood for the minute's silence on Armistice Day Church Parade at which we were joined by the Girl Guides, Cubs, Scouts and Sea Cadets. I did the usual Brownie things, I worked for my badges, learnt knots and promised to, "Do my duty to God and the King, and to help other people at all times"."

"Woodbine Street was a street where most people got on well together. On VJ day we had a street party just like thousands of others in this country. Every household chipped in with something, be it a trifle, cakes or sandwiches, gallons of pop for us children and something stronger for the grown-ups, who carried their celebrations into the evening, even dancing in the street to records on someone's gramophone. I was put to bed by then. In fact my mother put me to bed early all the time, about 7.00pm-7.30pm. When I complained that other kids were playing out in the street, she used to say, "Yes, and that's why they don't do as well as you at school, they are too tired"."

"I can say with some pride I usually came second in my class in end of term exams. Top girl, but there was always this boy I couldn't get the better of. Perhaps it was because I didn't get very good marks for history and geography. Those two subjects always let me down even though I was top in arithmetic and English. It was hard to concentrate in history lessons as Mr Parker's trousers were far more of a fascination. He never wore a belt or braces and I would gaze spell bound as his trousers slid lower and lower over his hips as he paced back and forth in front of the class enthusing over the Bronze Age, Vikings, 1066 or whatever. Then all of a sudden he would put his hands in his pockets and hoist his trousers up and all would be well for a short time until they started descending again."

"Going to bed early might have made me brainier if I had gone to sleep straight away. When I slept in the top bedroom at the front I used to hang out of the window talking to Mickey and the others and dart back into bed when I heard my mother come upstairs. She had seen and heard them shouting to me. We were all really for it one summer's evening. As usual I had been put to bed early and not long after Mickey and the others returned from scrumping plums. They threw some up to me at the window. I caught a couple and then one went whizzing past me and went splat on the wall. You can imagine what my mother said when she came upstairs to tell me to get back into bed and saw ripe plum stuck on the wallpaper. I got the full brunt of her fury because as soon as the others realised what had happened they legged it off home."

"At the top of the street on the corner with Church Hill, a brick air raid shelter had been built. It was quite long and had no light. We used to dare each other to go in on our own and walk not run, through the dark and out the other end. I used to hate that but I did it. It was not only dark but also smelly."

"Looking back on those years I might just as well have been an only child. There were ten years between Bob and me. He was interested in girls but not in his little sister that's why I was out playing in the street and reading. I had a bookcase in my bedroom that Bob had made at school. Three whole shelves were full of my books. Of course there were all the film annuals, there were adventure books and a lot of books that had been handed down to me from my mother including What Katy Did, Little Women and Christie's Old Organ. I was lost to the world when I was reading, I would suddenly come to and hear my mother say, "You haven't heard a word I've said, you've got your head in that book again"."

"I have often thought about Frank, Mollie and Bob being born so close together and then me tagging along later. When I grew up I said to my mum, "I wasn't a planned baby was I mum?", and she replied with a wry grin, "No you weren't, you were an awful shock". She seemed to have got over it though. We were talking about the war one day and she said that I cheered her up during those years. The war didn't seem to touch me much and I had chattered away to her about other things, and what with my singing and dancing sessions in 'the room', it seemed I was the proverbial little ray of sunshine."

"Mollie has since told me that she got a bit fed up with me when I was very small. She said that whenever she was off out with her friends, mum would say, "Take Gwen with you". One of my earliest memories is of Mollie and her friends riding on my pram, [with me in it], down a hill on the way to the Victoria Park."

"I am like Bob in looks, I started off with golden curls and was auburn by the time I started school. When I was little, people used to say I looked, "a proper little Shirley Temple". It must have been the golden curls and pretty dresses my mother made me. My mother was a great knitter. Mrs. Gossling, my friend Christine's mother was a tailoress, so Christine used to get pretty dresses knitted by my mother and I remember Mrs. Gossling tailored me a grey coat, one just like the two young princesses, Elizabeth and Margaret Rose wore."

"My mother taught me to knit and I was very good at it. All the girls at school who could were allowed to knit for the war effort during classes, as long as their work didn't suffer. I loved this and turned out khaki gloves, balaclavas, scarves and socks by the dozen. What I loved knitting most of all were sea boot stockings for the sailors. They were knitted on big wooden needles in thick white waterproof wool. Even though they were nearly the length of a man's leg, I could knit one pair in no time at all. All the wool was provided by the school."

"I remember our school adopted a ship. We used to write to the men on it and they wrote back. In one letter, I told how our dog Rover had to be put down because of old age and his back legs had gone. I had a lovely letter from a sailor saying how very sorry he was. I often wonder now what he really thought. There he was out on the high seas, liable to be bombed or torpedoed at any time and there was I safely at home, worried as to whether Rover had gone to heaven or not."

"I fell in love for the first time during the war. One of the films I went to see on Thursday evening was called, "The Stage Door Canteen". It was about a place in America they called a canteen. Servicemen went there to dance and be entertained and to dine. Famous people from stage and screen came here to entertain them. In the film, you followed the fortunes of a group of servicemen who went into this canteen and I fell in love with one of them, a young recruit. He was so good-looking, dark eyes and a lovely smile. The others called him "California" because that was where he came from. I have never found out who played him but I have never forgotten him nor what he looked like. Well, you don't forget your first crush do you?"

CHAPTER XVI - THE END OF THE WAR

"When the war was drawing to a close, I was 13 and the Allies were liberating all the people in the concentration camps. The horrific stories and pictures in the newspapers gave me bad dreams. It all came as an awful shock to me. I had spent the war years playing with my friends and living with a loving family. I hadn't really suffered any hardship at all and yet all those millions of people in Europe and the Far East had endured horror after horror. I hadn't realised how cruel human beings can be to one another."

Gwen Atkins

"Gradually all the men in the armed forces came home. Frank came home from Italy for a month's leave when he and Marjorie were married. The day Frank came home we were expecting Marjorie to come to our house for mid-day dinner. I was as usual playing in the street when I saw her turn the corner. I knew she didn't know that Frank had arrived home, so I danced up to her chanting, "Frank's home, Frank's home". She took off down Woodbine Street like a bat out of hell - well they hadn't seen each other for two and a half years. I ran after her and we both hurtled down the steps into the basement area and in through the kitchen door. Marjorie ran past mum who was cooking the dinner and into the room where Frank was. I went to run in after her but my mum practically caught me by the scruff of my neck and said, "Oh no you don't. They don't want you in there". We all eventually sat down to dinner grinning like Cheshire cats. That was a lovely day!"

"It took years for the world to recover from the war. Devastated Europe had to be rebuilt, as well as our own cities and towns. Not only buildings but the social structure as well. Rationing went on for ages as countries with food had to feed those who hadn't any. It was the end of the war and also the end of my childhood. I left school in December 1945 and went to work at the Lockheed in the aircraft drawing office. I thought I would train as a tracer but found I wasn't keen on that and left after a few months to take up a new career."

Eva Coad said, "I was 11 years old at the outbreak of war and I don't remember feeling any sort of emotion at the time except perhaps a bit of excitement. I do remember my father who was a soldier in the First World War calling the Germans all the names under the sun, the most suitably repeatable one being "warmongers". He also said a few unkind things about Attlee too. I do remember my dad making wooden frames to fit inside all the windows and my mother covering them with blackout material and these we had to fit into the windows every night when it got dark enough to have to light the gaslight. We also were told to put sticky tape across all the panes of glass in the windows. These were placed from corner to corner usually in the form of a cross and we were told that this would prevent the glass splintering and flying into people's faces if we ever had a bomb fall in the near vicinity."

"War was declared in September and as the days shortened it was very strange to see the transport of the time, buses, cars etc. with the windows all blacked out with a sort of blue paint and the headlights had a cover over them which had just a slit to allow the minimum of light through. It was very difficult to see from a distance and especially in bad weather so I suppose there must have been quite a few accidents although I don't remember hearing of any."

"The outbreak of war also coincided with my starting at senior school, which was Clapham Terrace. Of course we always had to carry our gas masks everywhere we went. Once a week we had a "gas mask drill" which involved the whole school being taken into the hall and of taking the masks out of the box in which they were carried and then we all had to don these horrible things as quickly as we could. I didn't like them very much as I always felt I was going to suffocate. We had to hold a piece of card over the bottom of the mask and breathe in, the result being that the mask tightened around your face and that was supposed to show that it was a proper fit. The boys in the school of course loved to breathe out in such a way that they made a rather rude noise and set everybody giggling."

"In the early days of the war we weren't allowed to stay in school for lunches and so we always walked home to Rushmore Estate by way of the "ladderbridge" which crossed the canal by Flavel's Foundry. One day there were four of us going home at lunch time and as we crossed the "ladderbridge" we could see an aircraft with German markings flying down the railway line and turning towards Flavel's and as he got closer he started firing. Of course, we were frightened to death and flew down the steps and hid under the arch until he had gone. This sticks in my memory for more than one reason because one of the girls with us started screaming and crying and I thought she was hysterical. I remembered reading somewhere that if someone was hysterical the best thing to do was slap them across the face, so I did! Well it worked, but the thing was that we had a very irate mother knocking on our door telling my mother that if I hit her daughter again she would come and hit me!"

"We had very few cases of enemy activity in Leamington in comparison with places like Coventry and Birmingham but there was a time that a bomber dropped a stick of bombs across the town. One fell very close to our house, in fact there was a direct hit on a house in The Close, off Llewellyn Road. We were sitting under the stairs because that was supposed to be one of the safest places to sit in the case of an air raid and it felt as though it had dropped in our garden. My sister and her friend were just turning into Llewellyn Road on their way home from the pictures and they were blown off their feet. She rushed into the house with a face as white as a sheet."

"My mother was a wonderful manager as far as food was concerned, I don't ever remember going hungry. Mind you, I'm sure she went without very often to make sure we were okay. She was very clever because as there were six ration books in our house, she registered with two grocers and two butcher's shops - three books with each one. That way when she wanted meat she was almost sure to get a little bit extra because the butcher couldn't always weigh out the exact amount that we were allowed. The same applied to things like butter and bacon."

"We were always given some money when we went into town and if ever we saw a queue outside a shop we would stand in line and get whatever was going. Sometimes it would be sausage at the pork butchers or perhaps the greengrocer would have some rabbits. Carrots and potatoes came into their own during the war too. If what they say about carrots being good for the eyesight is true, the wartime population must have had 20-20 vision all round, as we used carrots grated up in cake and biscuit recipes and we were encouraged to drink carrot juice."

"It was the same with potatoes. We were given Woolton Tips, Mr. Woolton being the Food Minister and every week he would come on the radio with different recipes using things like carrots and potatoes in place of flour and dried fruit. Dried fruit was in very short supply because of course we had to import it from abroad but the navy and merchant ships were more concerned with getting more important things into the country. Occasionally though there would be a consignment brought into the country and the shops would ration it out to their "regular" customers. It would probably be only about a quarter of a pound of currants and so those poor girls who were going to be married and wanting to have a wedding cake had to try a bit of "black market". They would do some swapping with other people who didn't want their dried fruit and would exchange it for some sugar or a few eggs and in that way they could build up enough to make a reasonable cake for the occasion. Some mothers would make the cake which would in all probability be quite a small one, then make an artificial cake from card, decorate it to look like a wedding cake and then slip that over the real cake for the table at the reception. When the cutting of the cake time came it would be carried into the kitchen or wherever and the real cake would be cut into minute portions to be distributed among the guests and nobody was the wiser."

"Another thing that future brides would do was to try and find someone who somehow or other had got a parachute, they were obtainable but don't ask me how, then they would then use the material from that to make their wedding dresses because they were usually made from silk. As the war churned on rationing bit very deeply and sometimes the rations were cut to incredibly small amounts even to half an egg per person each week. That was a challenge to the shopkeeper."

"As I got older and was allowed to stay out with my friends a bit later in the evening we were always rather on edge on the nights of the full moon, which was called a "bombers moon". It was a fact that the air raids did increase on those nights and quite often our group meetings, which were always on a street corner somewhere, were quickly dispersed as we made a speedy head for home when the air raid sirens started."

"Clothes rationing was difficult too but as I was tall for my age and had "large" feet I always qualified for some extra clothing coupons which made it as bit easier for my Mum."

"There were some very sad times too as young men who lived in the area were sent off to war and were killed or taken prisoner. One of our close neighbours lost a younger brother in the navy and I remember a boy that I had been at school with who joined the Merchant Navy. His ship was sunk but he survived in a lifeboat before being rescued. I remember a friend whose brother was in the army and because he had been in the Territorial Army prior to war being declared had been among the first sent to France to fight. At Dunkirk he was taken prisoner by the Germans and spent the rest of the war in a prisoner of war camp."

"I remember how pleased she was when they received the very occasional letter from him. She proudly brought one of his letters to school to show everybody. How strange the address looked and sounded. If I remember it correctly it was something like "Kreigsgefangannapost", whatever that meant but she didn't see him again until he was repatriated after the war ended."

"At 14 years of age I left school and went to work at Lockheed in the "aircraft section" of the Progress Office. Unfortunately, I hadn't been there very long when I was taken to hospital with rheumatic fever, an effect my mother thought was due to sitting in very damp air raid shelters in the Eagle Recreation Ground during the nights of the bombing of Coventry. My father would insist that we went there for safety. I was in hospital from April to August 1942 and whilst there I saw a German bomber fly low over the hospital. We heard some loud explosions and later learned that he had targeted the Lockheed factory. Anyway, in August the doctor came and told me that due to the hospital having to accommodate some patients from Birmingham who had been bombed out of their hospital I would be moved to a convalescent home in Kineton. So, in about 12 hours I had to learn to get out of bed and walk because I had been kept lying flat for the previous 5 months. I was put in an ambulance and taken to Kineton."

"I think it was at the age of 16 years that everyone had to volunteer for something to aid the war effort and so I joined the Red Cross and was attached to Detachment 507 which met at Dale Street Church rooms for training. Our Commandant was Miss Irene England who much later became Mayor of Leamington. We had a very thorough training in nursing and had to do a certain number of hours work at the Warneford Hospital as part of that, my stint being on Victoria Ward. I remember Dr. Clayton was one of our examiners. We really thought we were something special when we were dressed in our uniform, very proud of the Red Cross on our aprons and our flowing headdress. We were asked to form a guard of honour on the steps of the Warneford Hospital when the Princess Royal came on a visit."

"I remember our detachment taking part in a parade in Leamington, it was probably to celebrate the end of the war. I remember having a fit of the giggles during it because our detachment was placed with an American band behind us and an English one in front of us so that the front ranks were marching to a strict military beat while those of us in the rear ranks were being treated to a Glenn Miller type march. Goodness knows what it looked like but my word didn't we feel proud!"

"We were sent as a detachment to meet the trains on Leamington Station when the repatriated troops were sent home travelling by train to their various destinations. We greeted them with cups of tea and coffee and sandwiches. I remember how tired and gaunt a lot of them looked. It made me feel very sad and made me think how futile war is. Miss England was sent to Germany and was at Auschwitz concentration camp to help with the release of the inmates. She looked so ill on her return I think it took her a long time to recover from some of the awful sights she saw."

"On a lighter side of course was the advent of the GIs. Because there was an American hospital at Stareton outside of Leamington we had quite a lot of the "walking wounded" who came into town and of course the girls thought they were wonderful. I think we all thought they lived in huge houses with swimming pools and big cars - just like the films. They certainly were attractive because their uniforms were so much smarter than the English army outfits, and of course they had that certain air about them too. At that time, I used to go about with a group of friends and we met three very nice young "Yanks" as we called them - Johnny, Clive and Willard. Johnny was my friend, he was very nice, he had a girl back home in the States and I think they just wanted to make friends. They had had a bad time in the fighting on the Second Front and having suffered injuries were being treated at Stareton before being sent back to Germany. I took Johnny home and he got on like a house on fire with my family. We were very grateful to him because he would often come to call for me with "gifts" of tinned peaches and tinned ham etc. The Americans seemed to cater for their soldiers very well. I expect it was illegal for him to bring these things to us but they tasted good. He went back to Germany and I never heard from him again - who knows what happened to him?"

"On VJ day which was in August 1945, the hospital at Stareton held an open day for anyone who wished to go and organised buses from Leamington and the surrounding areas. Of course myself and my friends went. Well it was a wonderful time because they had a rodeo and various side shows all with an American flavour and best of all they had a refreshment tent. To us people who were still rationed the sight of peaches and "real" cream, ham, sausages, burgers etc. was sensational, so we all tucked in and had a great time."

"Eventually we decided to go back home and joined the queue for the bus to Leamington. Well we waited and waited and no bus. So we asked a GI who had been cycling round the park when the bus would be coming to take us back home. He said he would go and enquire and within a matter of minutes he was back driving a military type bus and we all piled in. As we had been waiting for quite a while the queue had got very long and he crammed us all into the bus so that we were sitting on each other's laps as well as standing in the aisle. All went well at first but as we were going down the road from the camp all of a sudden the bus veered off the road, mounted a steep bank on the opposite side of the road and came to a halt."

"Well, I'd started off sitting on my friend's lap and was now sitting on the floor in the aisle with a sheet of metal across my feet. Everybody was trying to get out of the bus but because of the angle at which it had come to rest it was very difficult. One lady sprained her ankle because of the drop from the step of the bus to the ground underneath. Eventually we all got out and were sitting on the bank at the side of the road feeling a bit shocked when an American ambulance came into sight and pulled up."

"The medical staff got out and ascertained who had been injured and one of the staff came to me and said "are you alright?" I said, "Yes thank you", and he said "does your foot hurt?" When I looked down my foot was covered with blood. It appeared that the sheet of metal that had been laying across my foot had been the base of the seat that we had been sitting on and it had cut into my foot. Anyway, all the injured were taken back in an army ambulance. I was mortified when it pulled up outside our house and people in the street stared and wondered what was going on. It took quite a while to live that down. Neither of my friends were hurt fortunately and they were taken back to Leamington by the usual transport. Afterwards we found out that the driver of the coach was in hospital recovering from malaria and shouldn't have been driving at all as evidently he had an attack whilst driving the bus."

Patrick Kingston [Wartime Transport]

Patrick was two years old when the war started, having been born in August 1937 at 27 Northcote Street. In the early days of the conflict his family took in billeted war workers who were working at Lockheed. There were four women workers who stayed with the Kingston's for the duration of the war, as well as some others who were only there for a short time. The four girls were: - Doreen who was 18 years of age and came from County Durham, Joyce who came from Sheffield, Catherine Haggerty from Glasgow and Betty Jones who hailed from Tredegar in Wales. One of the others was Margaret Billingham from County Durham who is in this photograph with Patrick which was taken around 1942 in the back garden at 27 Northcote Street.

Patrick says, "As the war continued, I remember Mr. Bond, the Billeting Officer, who was based at Denby Buildings, coming to the house and providing bedding and blankets for the workers. At Christmas time the girls used to go home to their families."

Patrick started at Clapham Terrace School in September 1942 aged 5. The Head Teacher was Mr. Edgar Baxter and his first teacher was Miss Allcock who lived at Radford Road opposite the allotments. She had already retired but was brought back once the war started. Other teachers included Mrs. Lovell, Mrs. Williams, Miss Plank and Mrs. Riseland who lived at Leicester Street. He remembers the windows in the school having anti-splinter brown tape on the windows.

Patrick says, "A square brick air-raid shelter had been built between the playground and the LMS railway embankment. We used to use it for air-raid practise, although fortunately I never had to use it for the real thing. It had concrete benches and a dirt floor so it wasn't built for comfort although it did have electric lighting. The children used to stamp their feet on the floor to create dust, it wasn't very pleasant. The shelter was knocked down very soon after the war ended and the site became the school garden."

As Patrick grew up he became very interested in transport and is considered to be something of an expert on the subject, so was the ideal person to ask for some information about transport during the war.

Buses – The Midland Red Bus Company introduced an emergency timetable that started on Saturday 6th January 1940. Local bus services were reduced and even cut completely at various times during the war years. One of these times was on 16th January 1943 as a result of instructions from the Ministry of War Transport.

Midland Red Emergency Timetable courtesy of the Patrick Kingston Collection.

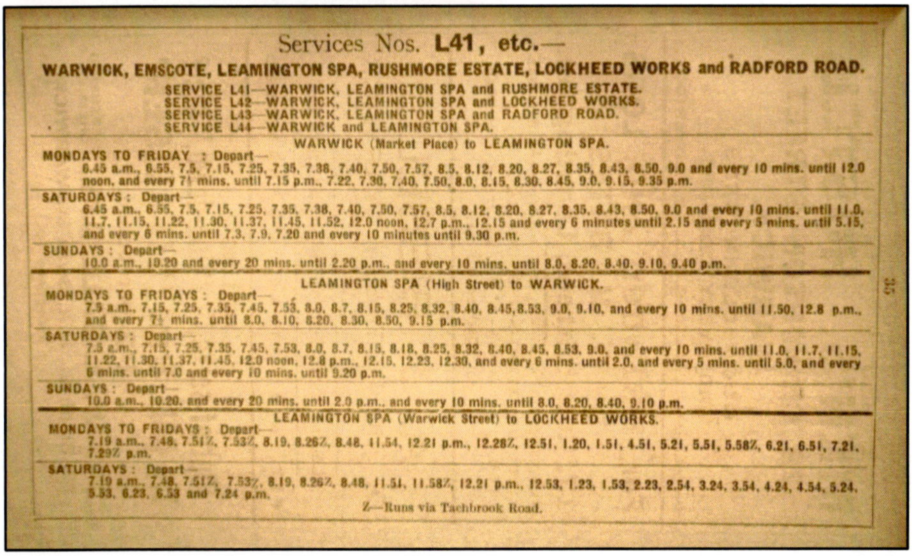

Services Nos. **L41, etc.**—

WARWICK, EMSCOTE, LEAMINGTON SPA, RUSHMORE ESTATE, LOCKHEED WORKS and RADFORD ROAD.

SERVICE L41—WARWICK, LEAMINGTON SPA and RUSHMORE ESTATE.
SERVICE L42—WARWICK, LEAMINGTON SPA and LOCKHEED WORKS.
SERVICE L43—WARWICK, LEAMINGTON SPA and RADFORD ROAD.
SERVICE L44—WARWICK and LEAMINGTON SPA.

WARWICK (Market Place) to LEAMINGTON SPA.

MONDAYS TO FRIDAY : Depart—
6.45 a.m., 6.55, 7.5, 7.15, 7.25, 7.35, 7.38, 7.40, 7.50, 7.57, 8.5, 8.12, 8.20, 8.27, 8.35, 8.43, 8.50, 9.0 and every 10 mins. until 12.0 noon, and every 7½ mins. until 7.15 p.m., 7.22, 7.30, 7.40, 7.50, 8.0, 8.15, 8.30, 8.45, 9.0, 9.15, 9.35 p.m.

SATURDAYS : Depart—
6.45 a.m., 6.55, 7.5, 7.15, 7.25, 7.35, 7.38, 7.40, 7.50, 7.57, 8.5, 8.12, 8.20, 8.27, 8.35, 8.43, 8.50, 9.0 and every 10 mins. until 11.0, 11.7, 11.15, 11.22, 11.30, 11.37, 11.45, 11.52, 12.0 noon, 12.7 p.m., 12.15 and every 6 minutes until 2.15 and every 5 mins. until 5.15, and every 6 mins. until 7.3, 7.9, 7.20 and every 10 minutes until 9.30 p.m.

SUNDAYS : Depart—
10.0 a.m., 10.20 and every 20 mins. until 2.20 p.m., and every 10 mins. until 8.0, 8.20, 8.40, 9.10, 9.40 p.m.

LEAMINGTON SPA (High Street) to WARWICK.

MONDAYS TO FRIDAYS : Depart—
7.5 a.m., 7.15, 7.25, 7.35, 7.45, 7.53, 8.0, 8.7, 8.15, 8.25, 8.32, 8.40, 8.45,8.53, 9.0, 9.10, and every 10 mins. until 11.50, 12.8 p.m., and every 7½ mins. until 8.0, 8.10, 8.20, 8.30, 8.50, 9.15 p.m.

SATURDAYS : Depart—
7.5 a.m., 7.15, 7.25, 7.35, 7.45, 7.53, 8.0, 8.7, 8.15, 8.18, 8.25, 8.32, 8.40, 8.45, 8.53, 9.0, and every 10 mins. until 11.0, 11.7, 11.15, 11.22, 11.30, 11.37, 11.45, 12.0 noon, 12.8 p.m., 12.15, 12.23, 12.30, and every 6 mins. until 2.0, and every 5 mins. until 5.0, and every 6 mins. until 7.0 and every 10 mins. until 9.20 p.m.

SUNDAYS : Depart—
10.0 a.m., 10.20, and every 20 mins. until 2.0 p.m., and every 10 mins. until 8.0, 8.20, 8.40, 9.10 p.m.

LEAMINGTON SPA (Warwick Street) to LOCKHEED WORKS.

MONDAYS TO FRIDAYS : Depart—
7.19 a.m., 7.48, 7.51Z, 7.53Z, 8.19, 8.26Z, 8.48, 11.54, 12.21 p.m., 12.28Z, 12.51, 1.20, 1.51, 4.51, 5.21, 5.51, 5.58Z, 6.21, 6.51, 7.21, 7.29Z p.m.

SATURDAYS : Depart—
7.19 a.m., 7.48, 7.51Z, 7.53Z, 8.19, 8.26Z, 8.48, 11.51, 11.58Z, 12.21 p.m., 12.53, 1.23, 1.53, 2.23, 2.54, 3.24, 3.54, 4.24, 4.54, 5.24, 5.53, 6.23, 6.53 and 7.24 p.m.

Z—Runs via Tachbrook Road.

35

Patrick says, "With so many men at war, the bus companies started to recruit women – something that they had also done during the First World War. Although I am aware of women conductors locally, I am not aware of any women drivers in Leamington."

"Two of the women conductresses at Leamington were Mollie Harrison who came from Staffordshire and Rose Turner. After the war Mollie went on to work in the canteen at Old Warwick Road. Betty Whetstone from Coventry was appointed the Welfare Conductress and after the war she continued at Leamington working on Enquiries. This particular photo [above] shows eighteen women wartime bus drivers as they pose for a photo with a new experimental S4 fleet bus at Birmingham in 1944."

"On 1st June 1939, all signposts which might be helpful to parachutists started to be removed but of course this caused problems for bus drivers and everyone else."

"Buses, including our local Midland Red ones, were blacked out so as not to be visible from the air. Headlamps had to be cowled or screened and wheel arches or mudguards were painted white as shown in this photo of two wartime Midland Red buses at Banbury."

"The number of interior lights were reduced and the remaining were covered in a form of a shroud. What light there was was directed towards the passenger. The black-out created problems for drivers, especially on foggy nights. It was also difficult for conductors trying to issue tickets, take money and hand back the correct change to customers in the dark."

"I remember being on the 517 Leamington to Coventry bus with my mother one very dark Christmas Eve around 1941 or 1942. It was a single decker CHA type with a sliding door. We were going to my grandparents who lived in a cottage off Woodcote Road. The bus was very full as they often were and we weren't standing next to each other. I should have got off at Woodcote Road but I couldn't get through the crowd to follow my mother to the sliding door. The bus started off again and a number of people were pressing the bell for me until the bus stopped at Northumberland Road, so I had to walk back on my own in the dark whilst my mother was coming the other way."

Photos: - A Clayton Harris Verometer Bus conductor's ticket machine and ticket. The Verometer was made by the Clayton Dewandre Company of Lincoln. Photos courtesy of the Patrick Kingston Collection.

On 2nd January 1942, the necessity for transport co-ordination under 'post-blitz' conditions was reported to the A.R.P. Committee. It was decided that Mr. S. Wood would take control with Mr. J. Parker, Leamington's Sub-District Officer for Transport.

During 1943 the problems that the bus drivers were having were discussed at the local Watch Committee meeting. Some of the drivers were having difficulties locating bus stops due to the obliteration of the painted signs.

Patrick says, "On V.E Day, buses into town were diverted. The ones coming into the top of town came down Upper Parade and turned left into Warwick Street, then down Willes Road, right into Leam Terrace, around the back of the Parish Church to the terminus which was at George Street, High Street by the old Police Station and Packington Place. Many buildings were lit including the Parish Church which was floodlit."

Coaches – "In some parts of the country, coaches were converted into ambulances as soon as the war started. The Black and White Company coaches passed through town on their way from Nottingham to Cheltenham. Coach services gradually became more and more restricted until around 1941-1942 when the Ministry stopped all but essential services in order to conserve fuel. Not all operators managed to resurrect their businesses after the war. However, those that did, prospered very well. Conditions were right for a great deal of expansion as many people used coaches for their annual holidays. This boom would last into the 1950s and 1960s until people started jetting off to the Costas of Spain."

Railways - Patrick continues, "At this time Leamington was covered by two railway stations, the principal station was the Great Western, the other being the L.M.S. Avenue [London, Midland, Scottish] off Avenue Road."

"The main railway companies had been working on their plans for new timetables for some time before the war started. The Great Western Railway Company became the first to introduce its new emergency timetable on 25th September 1939 and had issued a booklet on air-raid precautions back in April 1938. The railways were affected quite considerably by the war. In September 1938, the Ministry of Transport announced that they would be taken under government control through the 'Defence of the Realm Act', if and when the country was under threat from enemy aggression."

"Passenger services were reduced or cut as priority was given to evacuation trains, munitions trains, the distribution of air-raid shelters, non-stop troop trains, petrol trains, tank trains, casualty evacuation [ambulance] trains, coal trains and even prisoner of war trains. Plans had been formulated prior to the start of the war for the evacuation of children from London and other major cities which were considered to be at risk from enemy bombing. The evacuation of children started on Friday 1st September 1939. The ambulance trains ran fairly frequently and were usually 9-10 coaches long, were painted green with the usual red cross on the sides and the roof."

"Military convoys were a regular occurrence and were great for the children, especially boys, who were usually very interested in watching."

"In June 1940, the Railway Executive issued instructions for the removal of station, street and bridge signs, but due to the number of problems that this created, there was some relaxation regarding the station name signs. People may know their station when seen in daytime but at night it looks completely different and it wasn't easy to know where you were when stopping at an unfamiliar station."

"Besides there being a complete black-out at railway stations, railway excursions were stopped. The trains had a form of black-out on the windows and interior compartment bulbs were reduced in number and power. A 15-watt glass bulb was installed in each compartment and covered with a metal shroud. As the war continued and as coaches were serviced they were painted in a brown livery rather than the normal brown and cream as this made them less visible from the air, it was also an economy measure. As an aside, once black-out restrictions had been lifted in 1945, a tender of £52. 10s. was accepted for the lighting of the subway between the two railway stations at Leamington Spa."

Signs were introduced around the station – 'For your own safety and that of fellow passengers see that the blinds of your compartment are kept down during black-out hours in accordance with the notice in each carriage.

Notice to passengers – Air Raid precautions – During an air-raid: -

1. Close all windows and ventilators and pull down the blinds as a protection against flying glass.
2. If danger seems imminent, lie on the floor.
3. Never leave the train between stations unless requested to do so by a railway official.
4. Do not touch any outside part of a coach if a gas attack is suspected.

During black-out hours: -

1. Keep all blinds drawn.
2. Keep all windows shut except when necessary to lower them to open doors.
3. Make certain the train has stopped at a platform and that you alight on the platform side.
4. When leaving this compartment, close windows, lower blinds again and close the doors quickly.'

Patrick continues, "In 1941, a poster was issued across the network by the Railway Executive Committee asking, "**Is your journey Really necessary? Don't help Hitler by travelling this summer.**"

"In 1942, the Americans shipped over a few hundred big, black S160 class freight locomotives to help with the war effort. The idea was that they could be used in this country until D Day when they would be transported to Europe to help out there. I remember walking along Radford Road, just past Warneford Hospital, and my mother pointing one out to me as it crossed the bridge. They had USA on the side of them."

"At Leamington station the ticket collectors were all women. Some of them went on to become station announcers working in the telegraph office once the war was over. One of them was Ethel who later married and became Ethel Luscombe and she lived in St. Helen's Road. One would often see military personnel on the trains, mainly soldiers, but sometimes sailors and airmen, evacuated children with teachers, injured and repatriated servicemen, perhaps wearing a blue uniform or on crutches. When the Americans came into the war they would be seen around the station as there was a military hospital at Stareton."

A southbound ambulance train, near Oxford, hauled by GWR locomotive No.6965 'Thirlestaine Hall' circa 1944/1945. Taken by Roger Simpson courtesy of the Patrick Kingston Collection.

Patrick continues, "Just after V.E Day, I was taken to London for the day. We went to Buckingham Palace and saw the King and Queen with the two Princesses coming out of the Palace on one of their 'Victory Parade Drives'."

Eva Sabin née Kilby

In 2011, Eva wrote, "I grew up at Kilby's greengrocer's shop in High Street. We lived above the shop with my grandparents who owned it."

"My first recollection of the Second World War is a Sunday morning in the shop with my mother listening to the speech declaring we were at war with Germany. I was six years old and I remember mother crying and hugging me. I was sad but did not understand what it was all about. The next thing was ration books and shortages and men going off to be soldiers, gas masks which you had to take everywhere with you and the horrible smell of rubber when you put it on."

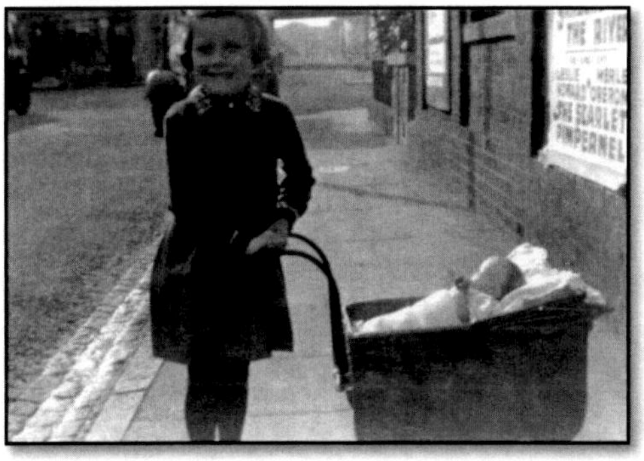

"Probably the bombs that fell on Leamington and Coventry actually brought the war home to us. The night that bombs dropped near the Parish church I was having my bath in the tin tub in front of the kitchen range. The scream of the bomb falling was enough to make me leap out of the bath, soaking wet and onto my mother's lap as it exploded."

"Another time I was in bed with ear-ache, which I had quite often and was probably glue ear, when I felt mother trying to lift me out of bed as the bomb dropped on the other side of the railway. The force threw her on top of me. I was gathered up and we rushed down stairs to join my grandparents in the sitting room."

"The night Coventry was bombed I sat on the stairs with mum and dad looking out of a north facing landing window." Dad said, "My God, Coventry is having it tonight." "The sky was a red glow for as far as I could see and the next day people from Coventry flocked to Leamington by the busload for respite and refuge. I think that apart from the bombing of Coventry, the thing that had most effect on Leamington and its people was the stick of bombs that dropped on Regent Street, at Lipton's on the Parade, [displacing Queen Victoria's statue opposite and killing two soldiers sheltering in the shop doorway], at the corner of Bedford Street, on the Pump Room Gardens and in York Road."

"We had a family evacuated from London. Their name was Coates and the daughter shared my bed. They brought a maid with them but moved on to the country quite soon. Also at this time Leamington had a lot of evacuee children from London and we had to share our time at school with them. We locals had mornings at school and the evacuees went in the afternoons. The younger teachers had left for the war and a lot of elderly teachers were brought out of retirement to fill the gap. I still think we had a good education and could put a lot of today's children to shame."

"Dad was in the Home Guard and a gun used to hang on the kitchen wall. He taught me how to fire it in case it was needed. Dad grew a lot of vegetables on the St Mary's allotments. I have a photo [previous page] of his greenhouse full of tomatoes from floor to ceiling, it even got him a write-up in the Courier. We also kept a pig which was slaughtered in October, parts of which were salted down for bacon and ham and the other bits and pieces everyone joined in to cook. Nothing was wasted."

Mary Hill née Davis - "I remember helping out at the Allied Services canteen in Bertie Terrace. The Manager of the Midland Bank and a committee ran it. It was open every night and we served hot snacks, baked beans, reconstituted eggs, sausages etc. and hot drinks. There was a rota of helpers and we did a night each. The members of the services, both men and women, just had their snacks and chatted. It was full every night. On my night, Mr. Ernest Rogers from Locke & England used to come to check the money at the end. His glasses always got steamed up owing to the heat in the kitchen."

"I remember the men coming back from Dunkirk. Trainloads of them came, all absolutely exhausted. The Leamington Golf Club was one of the receiving bases for them. Brookhurst Club House acted as a reception centre, the men were sent there, sorted and then sent to their home towns."

Betty Monica Still - Post Office Telephones - "I was born on 13th March 1921 at 4 Victoria Road Leamington Spa. When I was five, my family moved to 42 Willes Road, which was my home until I married. I left the girls' grammar school aged 16 and went to train as a telephonist at the GPO. I finished school one Friday in July 1937, and started work the following Tuesday, as Monday was a Bank Holiday. There was a six-week training course and I hated it. We covered from 8.00am to 8.00pm, working a 48-hour week, with shorter hours on Sundays and Bank Holidays."

"Intent on finding a more interesting job I enrolled in an evening class for shorthand and typing lessons but on completion realised that I had no choice but to carry on at the telephone exchange, which was then on the first floor of the old Post Office in Priory Terrace."

"There were a few surprises though. To begin with the minimum height requirement was five feet four inches, to enable operators to reach the bank of switches, working to the 24-hour clock during the war, only taking on grammar school girls and the curious 'split duties', whereby the eight-hour working day was split into two shifts, 08.00am-12.00 noon and 16.00pm–20.00pm, with the afternoon off. Although I didn't care for the original training I got on very well with the job and with my colleagues."

"At the outbreak of war, at the age of 19, I became a trainee supervisor and also carried out some training in a 'school room' set aside on the upper floor at the Post Office."

"The war brought a great influx of government departments and officials who took over the big houses on Kenilworth Road and Newbold Terrace. Officers from Canada, Czechoslovakia and Poland along with government officials and the Camouflage Unit billeted in the town meant a huge increase in the volume of work."

"As the GPO exchange could barely cope, another exchange was built on the floor above, so that there were 20 positions on each floor. No-one working there could understand why, when there was the constant threat of bombing, that something as vital as a telephone exchange should be built in such a vulnerable spot at the top of a building. This odd thinking was not confined to Leamington. It was not widely known that the Ministry of Supply, based at Warwick Castle, had an exchange built at the top of Caesar's Tower [the only tower with electricity]. Again, the workforce could not fathom the rationale of building a telephone exchange at the top of the tallest tower for miles around. The work there was highly secret and so the government brought its own operators and supervisors from London. When they were on leave Leamington supervisors had to go to Warwick to cover, 'ordinary' operators couldn't do so because of the secret nature of the work."

"During the war, telephone exchanges had become more automated to cope with the volume of traffic and were being constantly updated. When a new post-war exchange was being planned for Wise Street in Leamington, those who had been employed during the war received a letter from the government asking them to "volunteer" at the old exchange whilst the new one was being built, so enabling current staff to be trained in the latest equipment."

Pauline Zwicker née Wilson said, "I remember the railings dividing our house in Chandos Street being taken up for the war. Despite clothing coupons we all managed to look quite smart. A little bit of dyeing and ingenuity could work wonders especially where stockings were concerned. Even in offices we worked long hours, quite a bit of evening overtime and always a full Saturday or Sunday, sometimes both. Saving was easier then. With clothes rationing there was little to spend one's money on except entertainment. A session at the roller skating rink [where the Loft Theatre now stands] before the Camouflage people took over cost 9d. which would also secure quite a decent seat at the cinema. An ice cost 2d. Just about anyone could afford a cup of office tea at 1d. How busy we were having fun!"

Freda Watson recalled in 1977: - "There were many different sorts of people in Leamington during the war. There were the camouflage, they were a queer lot, long hair. The Czech Army was here for training. They were a nice crowd, billeted in the town. Canadians and Australians came here when on leave for a holiday. The Polish Air Force was here for a short time. An Allied Services Club was opened at 6 Bertie Terrace. I often went there in the evenings to help. It was run by volunteer staff and open every evening. Members of the forces could get bed and breakfast if they were really stuck. Mrs. Needham, the wife of the Midland Bank Manager, was the volunteer caterer. The Czech Army was here for a long time. They did charity concerts. After the Coventry Blitz their choir gave a concert of songs, in aid of the blitzed people, at the Theatre Royal in Regent Grove. It was on a Sunday afternoon and was packed. There was also a Czech-Dutch football match which took place on Lockheed's ground. We also had evacuees from Coventry, quite a number of them stayed here then went home after the war."

Colin Jennings lived in Windsor Street and was only four years old when the war started and just 10 when it ended. He says, "I remember being in Portland Street at night and seeing a large number of German bombers lining up and coming together in formation before making their way back to Germany."

He attended Milverton County Infants and Junior School. On his way to school he would pass Waterloo Place, the end house was used as a centre and canteen for soldiers. In the cold days of winter, he often stood under the porch for a warm as there were hot water pipes inside the porch. Sometimes one of the W.V.S. ladies would take him in and give the hungry Colin some food. Colin has in his possession this photo which it is thought was taken at Christmas 1939 or 1940. Colin says, "all of the children lived in Windsor Street and John Street. I am not in the photo and most of them are older than me. Photographers would gather together a number of local children in the streets, take a group photo before having a

number of postcard sized prints produced. They would then attempt to sell them to the children's parents. The lad in the centre of the photo with the fair hair is Eric Timms, the son of a local baker. The family lived at 14 Windsor Street."

Colin also remembers playing around the site of Beech Lawn which today is the site of the fire station. On the Grove Street / Warwick Street corner, the military used the area for storing military vehicles. He says, "Soldiers were on duty to not only guard the vehicles but also a covered-up reservoir. We would talk to the soldiers and sometimes they let us hold their rifles which were really heavy."

Whilst playing near the Saxon Mill at Guy's Cliffe, Colin and a group of his friends found a tree that had fallen across a side stream parallel to the river. He says, "Two huge branches formed a V shape, the lower one being about a foot above the surface of the water with the upper one going up at 45 degrees to the water. Three of us stood on the lower tree branch, held on to the upper branch and started bouncing up and down splashing those on the river bank. The top branch snapped off and the three of use fell into the water. My friends managed to scramble to the side and get out but I couldn't swim and started going up and down and was gradually choking with the water. A Czech soldier who was sitting on the bank nearby with his girlfriend came over and grabbed my hair trying to pull me out. I was more frightened of him than the water but I couldn't fight him off. Eventually, he managed to throw me onto the river bank like a huge wriggling fish. He saved my life without even getting a thank you, while I went home like a drowned rat. It didn't seem so important then, I wasn't old enough to appreciate what he had done."

Miscellaneous

This part of the book is for snippits of information that are a little difficult to put in a chapter of their own. For instance, part of the Oak Inn building at Radford Road was used as a mortuary during the war.

The first war wedding of a Leamington man took place on Monday 4th September 1939 when 23-year-old Sgt. Pilot Terence Frank Kennan married 22-year-old Miss Thelma Barford Ward at Warwick Register Office. They brought the wedding forward as Terence, a reservist, had been ordered to re-join the Royal Air Force.

Although the new Heathcote Inn building in Tachbrook Road was completed in 1940, it was used by the Home Guard as a base and a drill square for the duration of the war and reopened as the Heathcote in 1945.

Just under 30,000 'enemy aliens' were interned during the war the main internment camp being on the Isle of Man. Prior to going to this camp, the 'aliens' were housed in temporary camps in various locations across the country. The Leamington Spa Courier dated 30th August 1940 reported on the difficulties one of our local residents had: -

'**First Leamington Alien Freed** – Mr. E. Lemburger, of 7, Dale Street, is the first enemy alien of this district to be released from internment in accordance with the Asquith Committee's recommendations. He has held a "key" position in a dairy since prior to the outbreak of war. "I did not expect to be interned" he told the Courier, "and thought that I was taken by mistake. After passing a tribunal I thought I became a 'friendly enemy'. Sent from one camp to another, one always a bit better than the one before, I realised that it was a general round-up."

"In the last camp at Huyton we still had to sleep on the floor but we could start concerts, variety shows and lectures, which were often visited by guards in khaki, who did everything possible for us. Through an amplifier we listened to the news. A victory of the R.A.F. was enthusiastically greeted but misfortune cost us a sleepless night. I hope that the 18 points of the White Paper will be replaced by a one-point paper stating that all genuine friends of England should be set free. It is my opinion that there were some reasons behind the round-up, till now undisclosed, but once these become known the Government's action will be more understandable."

In Vienna, Mr. Lemburger [who was 30 years of age] was taken prisoner by the Gestapo as hostage to get his mother, who was also arrested, to sign a declaration handing over all her property "voluntarily" to the Nazis.'

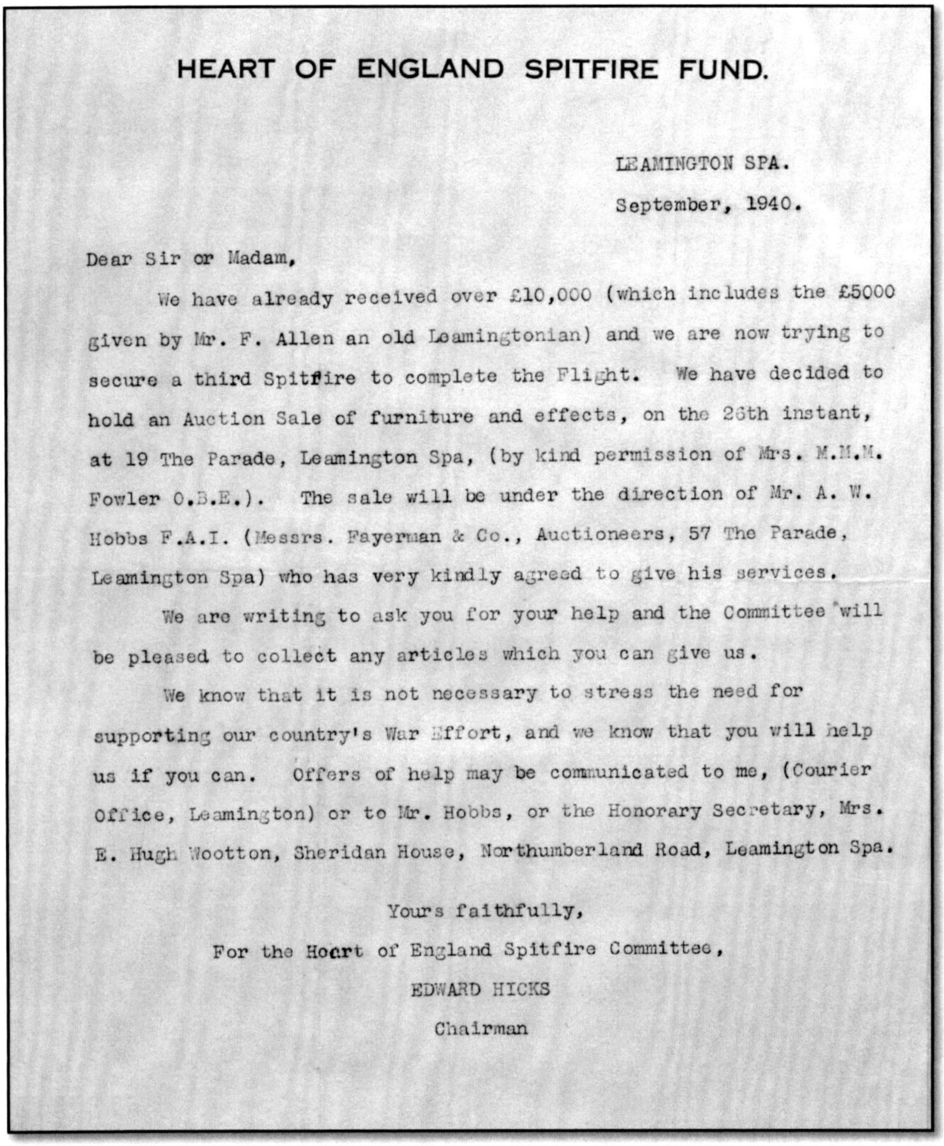

HEART OF ENGLAND SPITFIRE FUND.

LEAMINGTON SPA.

September, 1940.

Dear Sir or Madam,

We have already received over £10,000 (which includes the £5000 given by Mr. F. Allen an old Leamingtonian) and we are now trying to secure a third Spitfire to complete the Flight. We have decided to hold an Auction Sale of furniture and effects, on the 26th instant, at 19 The Parade, Leamington Spa, (by kind permission of Mrs. M.M.M. Fowler O.B.E.). The sale will be under the direction of Mr. A. W. Hobbs F.A.I. (Messrs. Fayerman & Co., Auctioneers, 57 The Parade, Leamington Spa) who has very kindly agreed to give his services.

We are writing to ask you for your help and the Committee will be pleased to collect any articles which you can give us.

We know that it is not necessary to stress the need for supporting our country's War Effort, and we know that you will help us if you can. Offers of help may be communicated to me, (Courier Office, Leamington) or to Mr. Hobbs, or the Honorary Secretary, Mrs. E. Hugh Wootton, Sheridan House, Northumberland Road, Leamington Spa.

Yours faithfully,

For the Heart of England Spitfire Committee,

EDWARD HICKS

Chairman

Washing and Bathing - During the war years, and even into the 1950s and 1960s, not all homes had built in baths or bathrooms. Many people washed at an earthenware sink in the kitchen that had one cold tap. If they were lucky they had a gas-powered Ascot water heater. Baths were taken once a week in a tin bath in front of the fire. The tin bath would be hung on a hook or a nail in the backyard and brought in once a week. Hot water would be boiled in saucepans, or possibly a gas fired copper. If saucepans were used it was a time-consuming process and by the time there was enough water, it was lukewarm. In order to save water during war years only 5 inches of water per family was allowed and so the family had to share the bath water. It is likely that dad had the first bath and children had the last one - by this time the water would be quite tepid as well as being a little 'scummy'! The toilet or lavatory was more likely to be not only in the backyard but up the backyard and some distance from the house. Sometimes they would be shared with neighbours, sometimes they were built together. A walk to the 'loo' in the middle of a cold, dark, wet night was not a pleasant experience and so a pot under the bed was the preferred option. The other problem with these facilities was that they would freeze up in winter.

Keep Calm and Carry On - We have all seen the posters, or more probably copies of posters, telling the population to keep calm and carry on. At the start of the war millions of posters were printed, they were designed to keep up morale in the event of mass bombings or poison gas attacks. However, the Keep Calm and Carry On posters were never used and in 1940 over two million of them were recycled into paper pulp.

The Morning News dated Thursday 19th December 1940 reported: - **The Duke of Kent at Leamington – Informal Visit to Y.M.C.A. Headquarters – H.R.H. Chats with Soldiers and Voluntary Workers** – The Duke of Kent, wearing the uniform of the Royal Air Force, paid a short visit to Leamington on Tuesday evening when he inspected the branch headquarters of the Y.M.C.A. His Royal Highness was able to see some of the valuable work which is being carried on twelve hours a day, for seven days a week for the comfort and well-being of members of the Forces. The visit, which was purely informal, took most of the troops by surprise. The Duke chatted freely with many of the soldiers, asking them questions about themselves and enquiring after their welfare. He took a close interest in the facilities provided for the men and expressed the conviction that they were being well catered for.

Looting - It would be good to think that scavenging and looting never happened. However, the following article in the Morning News dated 14th January 1941 shows that it did: -

Looting Charge – A labourer who looted property from houses at Lillington while engaged on repairing property damaged by enemy action was sentenced to six month's hard labour at Leamington Police Court, yesterday. "If it had not been for your good character the punishment would have been more severe," observed the Mayor [Alderman M. S. Moore]. A man from Millers Road, Warwick pleaded "Guilty, but very, very sorry" to a charge of stealing a lady's costume, valued at £2. 2s., from the house of Wilfred Horace Pendrey, 123, Kinross Road. The Chief Constable [Mr. Arthur E. Young], who reminded the Bench that the offence was punishable by death, said Mr. Pendrey and his wife were injured by enemy action, and when Mr. Pendrey returned to his house he missed a quantity of property, including the coat.

Local historian Joe Claydon's dad came across this flyer which is addressed to German soldiers. It was supposed to be one of many that was dropped over Germany, probably towards the end of the war. Unfortunately, the plane carrying this one came down in this country. It is not known whether it was shot down or crashed.

On Thursday 6th February 1941, the Morning News carried this advertisement: – **Educational – German Lessons** - Conversations given at 1, Colonnade. Terms moderate. [Ed's note: I'm not sure whether this is ironic or opportunistic!]

The Morning News dated Tuesday 25th November 1941 reported this case from the magistrate's court: - **Worked 14 Hours a Day on Munitions – Neglected Garden – Ejectment Order Granted – Magistrates Hint to Leamington Corporation** - Leamington Corporation obtained at the Petty Sessions yesterday, the first ejectment Order against a Council house tenant for failing to cultivate his garden. Mr. J. C. Staite [Chairman] expressed the magistrate's opinion that providing the Corporation were satisfied the respondent from Waverley Road, was now prepared to carry out his obligations, as promised, they should refrain from enforcing the Order. Mr. C. Peter Clarke [Deputy Town Clerk] who undertook to convey the Bench's observation to the Housing Committee, had earlier described this as a test case on the Council's policy to secure a better cultivation of their estates.

Other tenants would be watching these proceedings, and if this man, with the worst garden, obtained the discretion of the Court by digging his garden after receiving notice to quit, the Corporation would clearly have to abandon their attempt to improve cultivation of their estates. The father of five children said he was a munitions worker employed for 14 hours a day and had been unable to garden on account of ill health, having had in the last six years pneumonia twice and bronchial pneumonia. He had recently had the garden dug by casual labour and was now prepared to maintain it in a cultivated state.

The Morning News dated 12th January 1942 advised people about: - **Claiming For War Damage** – The War Damage Commission has just issued a new explanatory pamphlet which it is hoped will be of assistance to the public. Known as C.2.X, it explains the steps to be taken in making a claim on the Commission's Form C.2 for payment of the proper cost of carrying out repairs to war-damaged houses, shops, flats, tenements or office buildings. The pamphlet gives information with regard to the evidence in the form of builders' accounts, etc., required to support the claim; the authorised arrangements for the repayment of the fees of architects, surveyors or other such persons employed in a supervisory capacity; and a form of authority which may be given by the claimant if he wishes the Commission to pay the money direct to his builder.

The Morning News dated Saturday 16th January 1943 reported: - **Anti-Gas Vehicles on the L.M.S.** - The L.M.S [London Midland Scottish] Railway's organisation for defence against air raids has been further strengthened by the introduction of special anti-gas vehicles. Converted from old passenger carrying coaches, these units are attached to the regular riding van and form a permanent feature of selected breakdown trains. The units are divided into two sections - one containing A.R.P. clothing and all the stores and requisites necessary for dealing with gas, and the other section serves as a riding compartment and dressing room. The provision of these anti-gas units will enable L.M.S. breakdown gangs to deal with any wreckage occurring in a gas-infected area - and with any wreckage so contaminated - without calling in outside assistance.

The Leamington Spa Courier dated 3rd September 1943 had the following item: -
How to build 50 Lancasters: Sufficient aluminium to build 50 Lancaster bombers is lost each year through aluminium milk bottle caps being thrown away. Please don't waste this valuable metal! Save your caps and hand them in a paper bag to your milkman.

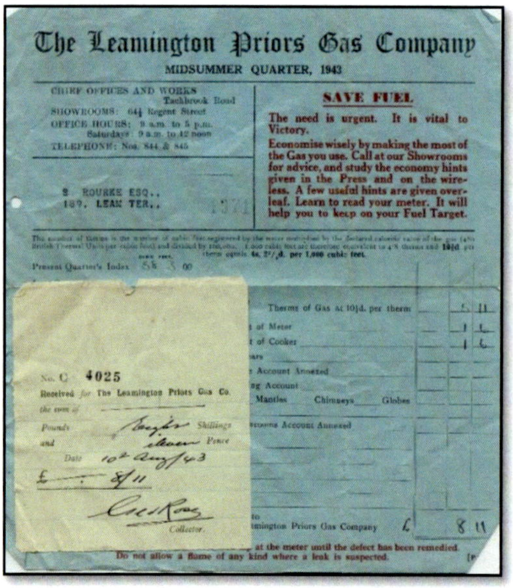

The Leamington Priors Gas Company

MIDSUMMER QUARTER, 1943

CHIEF OFFICES AND WORKS Tachbrook Road
SHOWROOMS: 64½ Regent Street
OFFICE HOURS: 9 a.m. to 5 p.m. Saturdays: 9 a.m. to 12 noon
TELEPHONE: Nos. 844 & 845

S. ROURKE ESQ.,
189, LEAM TER.,

SAVE FUEL

The need is urgent. It is vital to Victory.

Economise wisely by making the most of the Gas you use. Call at our Showrooms for advice, and study the economy hints given in the Press and on the wireless. A few useful hints are given overleaf. Learn to read your meter. It will help you to keep on your Fuel Target.

Present Quarter's Index 58 3 00

Therms of Gas at 10½d. per therm — 5 11
of Meter — 1 6
of Cooker — 1 6
Mantles Chimneys Globes
Leamington Priors Gas Company £ 8 11

No. C 4025
Received for The Leamington Priors Gas Co.
the sum of
Pounds Eight Shillings
and eleven Pence
Date 10th Aug/43
£ - : 8/11
Collector.

at the meter until the defect has been remedied.
Do not allow a flame of any kind where a leak is suspected.

This gas bill for the summer quarter of 1943 is for 189 Leam Terrace. The cost for three month's gas usage was 8s. 11d.

The Leamington Spa Courier dated 16th June 1944 reported: - **D-Day Wounded at the Warneford Hospital** - To the Warneford Hospital, Leamington, has been given the honour of caring for some of the men who sustained wounds in the landing in France on "D-Day". The Mayor, [Alderman A. Ashton], was among the first to take them comforts and assure them of the gratitude of the people of Leamington, who he said, were proud of the great feat of arms carried out on the beaches of Normandy. Marshall Stalin has declared that, "the history of wars does not know of any such undertaking, so broad in conception, so grandiose in scale, and so masterly in execution."

A 'Courier' representative who chatted with some of the men – they were mostly air-borne troops – found them in excellent spirits and anxious to get back as quickly as possible. Pte. James Stephenson, of the Parachute Regiment, whose home is in Newell, Ottley, Yorks, described the tense feelings which he experienced as the bomber in which he was being carried reached its objective. "We were all on edge, and eager to jump, because we had been so closely packed together," he said. "We could tell we were over the French coast because of the anti-aircraft fire. Then the time came to jump. As soon as I landed I became a casualty as my foot struck a German block house. As I lay injured before being picked up I watched the gliders coming in. Never shall I forget the wonderful sight."

"Neither shall I," chimed in another 22-year-old – Pte. David Lathrope, of London – who was wounded when taking part in an attack on a machine-gun nest. "It was a stupendous experience, but it was pretty rough going at the beginning. I saw four Germans drop from my rifle fire." Corporal George Burdid, R.E. of South Shields, said he thought everyone had gone mad when the landings were made. "We all knew where Jerry was, and we wanted to get at him," he said. "Unfortunately, I was wounded in the leg and back by machine-gun fire from a German 'plane. I'm fed up lying here, and I want to get back to my pals."

The Leamington Spa Courier dated 22nd September 1944 reported on a First Aid and Rescue demonstration at the Gas Works. 'The Leamington Priors Gas Company's Division of the St. John Ambulance gave a demonstration of their first-aid and rescue work before a large gathering of county officers of the Brigade. Supt. Badger gave a description and an explanation of the various appliances which were to be used. The programme arranged by him consisted of a number of incidents designed to show the use of special apparatus when working in places where there might be an accumulation of gases, or where the rescue might have to be undertaken in a gas-laden atmosphere.'

On 27th June 1945, the Watch Committee resolved that both Police War Reserve and the Women's Auxiliary Police Corp will be retained as part of the local police force.

Surrender of Firearms – The Leamington Spa Courier dated 15th March 1946 reported that the surrender of firearms must be completed by March 31st. The appeal of the Chief Constable [Mr. W. Rees] to residents of Leamington to surrender firearms to the police has met with a good response. So far one German machine gun [used in aircraft], two rifles, five automatic pistols, 15 revolvers of varying calibres, and a quantity of ammunition have been handed in. "No Morse pistols, flint locks, or other antique weapons have come to hand," said an official, "and we do not expect any, for the simple reason that we were inundated with old time firearms in 1940, following an appeal for weapons in view of the threatened invasion. What we do expect is more war souvenirs." Surrender of firearms may still be made at any police station before March 31st, after which those who still possess them and do not hold a licence will be liable to prosecution.

The Leamington Spa Courier dated 8th December 1989 reported: - '**Memories of War Time** – "I am at last putting pen to paper to let you know I was very interested in your paper Warwickshire at War. I remember the bombs from York Road to Regent Street. As a boy I remember one dropped in the Pump Room in front of the lamp post by the side of the path from the river bridge to the bottom of Bedford Street, and other bombs were dropped in a field facing the bridge at the back of Whitnash cemetery and one bomb in the middle of the field alongside the Heathcote public house."

"I was most interested in reading of the air force bases around the area, but you failed to mention the airfield that was situated at the top of Edgehill. I think it was called Shennington [I may be wrong]. I also saw the picture of an Ensign Class air-liner that belly landed at Bonniksen's airfield in Harbury Lane and went up to see it. I suppose you had not enough space to include some of the other aircraft crashes around Leamington, that is the biplane that ended upside down in Leamington Cemetery. The bomber that crashed behind the church at Bishops Tachbrook; the biplane that made a forced landing and tipped up on its nose in the playing field off Heathcote Lane; the American bomber that crashed and blew up in a field in Harbury Lane, killing the pilot and finally, the bomber that exploded in mid-air and fell on a farm cottage at Harbury Lane near Harwood's House". G. Harris Flat 5, 15 Redland Road, Whitnash.'

Iron Railings

The Ministry of Works and Buildings caused some heart searching in the town by pressing the Council to schedule the removal of iron railings "for use in the manufacture of munitions". A [Special] Railings Committee took responsibility for this and at one of their meetings on 19th June 1940 they inspected the various railings on Corporation properties and then recommended that the following railings be removed:

[a] Jephson Villa and Hamilton House - From Arran Lodge the eastern corner of Hamilton House.

[b] Eagle Recreation Ground - Along the whole of the western boundary of the recreation ground and along the eastern boundary of the small piece of adjoining land. The gates across the footpath at the ends of Clarence Street and Shrubland Street to remain.

[c] Prince's Drive [east side] - Along the front of Messrs. Flavel's Works, from Old Warwick Road to the railway [subject to the necessary consents].

[d] Adelaide Road [east side] and York Road - From the gate in Adelaide Road to the College playground in York Road.

[e] Public Library - From the entrance to the Girls' College to the west side of the entrance door to the Art Gallery.

[f] Art Gallery - Along the whole of the eastern boundary, except the length closing the yard to the back entrance. [The dwarf railings removed from the west side of the gallery entrance to be refixed on the eastern boundary, from Avenue Road to the south-east corner of the building].

[g] Shrubberies - Avenue Road, L.M.S. Station Approach - The whole except the fence along the eastern boundary.

[h] Pump Room - Short length in front of the north annexe.

[i] Pump Room Grounds - All except those along the river side and the western boundary.

[j] Victoria Park - Along the shrubbery on the eastern boundary between Archery Road and Avenue Road [subject to any necessary consents].

That the following railings were not to be removed: - Regent Grove, Holly Walk [including the public lavatories], Jephson Gardens, Shrubland Recreation Ground, Victoria Park except those already referred to and Beech Lawn.

The committee also recommended that an old shell lying in the Town Hall and the 'old guns' [and surrounding railings] in Holly Walk and Victoria Park also be disposed of.

On 24th June 1940, the report was adopted subject to Jephson Villa and Hamilton House being moved to the list of railings not to be removed.

An 'old gun' in Holly Walk.

This postcard shows the cannon in situ in Holly Walk. Captured in Sebastopol during the Crimean War, it arrived in Leamington in 1857 and was originally placed in Jephson Gardens following a request by the Gardens Committee to the Secretary of War.

However, the Local Board of Health had made a similar request and claimed that it was really intended for them. After a 'war of words' between the two committees it was placed in Holly Walk, where it remained until 1940.

The Morning News dated 5th July 1940 reported: - **Hospital Railings to Remain**. The railings in front of Warneford Hospital are not to be removed as part of the town's move to provide scrap metal for the war effort. The reasons are that they act as a barrier to the public when ambulance cases are being unloaded in the drive and that in view of the close proximity of Clapham Terrace Schools the railings serve a useful purpose by keeping children off the premises.

The details of a Direction under Defence Regulations 54B from the Ministry of Supply dated 11th September 1941 was read to the Railings Committee on 14th November. It required the local authority to carry out a survey and make a schedule of iron railings, gates, posts, chains, bollards, and similar articles in the Borough. Exceptions were railings that had to be maintained for safety reasons, railings necessary to prevent cattle from straying, railings of special artistic merit or of historic interest, and railings which, if removed, would require to be replaced by a substitute. Appeals on the grounds of artistic merit or historic interest would be considered by local panels of architects set up by the Government.

The Morning News dated 5th March 1942 reported: - **Emergency Powers [Defence] Acts, 1939 and 1940 – Requisition of Unnecessary Railings** – I am directed by the Minister of Works and Buildings to give notice that all unnecessary iron or steel railings, posts, chains, bollards, gates, stiles, etc., in the Borough of Royal Leamington Spa will shortly be removed and collected for use in the national war effort in iron and steel works and foundries. The work of removal will commence on or after the 9th March, 1942, and will affect premises in almost all the streets and places in the Borough. - A. F. Greenwood Town Clerk, Town Hall, Leamington Spa, 27th February, 1942.

At the Railings Committee meeting on 23rd March 1942, the Town Clerk read a letter from Mr. Raikes, the local Emergency Works Officer of the Ministry of Works and Buildings. He queried the omission of railings from the schedule of unnecessary railings at the Jephson Gardens, Victoria Park and Priory Nursery and suggested that they should be included. A special meeting would be convened with Mr. Raikes.

On 26th March 1942, the committee met with Mr. Raikes. He agreed that the railings at Priory Nursery could be retained and that the railings on the south side of Victoria Park may be retained if they were being used for the protection of ground devoted to food production. The issue regarding the Jephson Gardens and surrounding bowling greens was referred to the Ministry for a final decision.

On 27th March 1942, the press recorded the resistance of the Railings Committee to the removal of railings from the Jephson Gardens. "The gardens are of great value as a refreshing place of resort for thousands of jaded war workers...the removal of the railings would make the gardens an unrestricted playground for children and dogs in the day-time, and a resort of disorderly persons at night". It was recalled that in 1848, "Before the gardens came into the possession of the present trustees they were found to be almost a nuisance in the neighbourhood, through being trespassed upon by dissolute persons."

The Morning News dated Wednesday 14th October 1942 reported: - **Jephson Gardens Railings - Ministry Order Their Removal**. The Ministry of Works and Planning have informed Leamington Town Council that the railings surrounding the Jephson Gardens must now be removed to provide scrap metal for the war effort.

In March 1943, the railings were removed by the Corporation rather than the official contractors as this was seen as "a guarantee against ruthless damage to the coping stones".

Bomber Crash at Whitnash on Thursday 26th April 1945

On 26th April 1945 an American pilot prevented a catastrophic air crash that would have devastated Whitnash. Lieutenant Jean Anderson, 23, was flying a Liberator Bomber from Chipping Campden to Germany when his plane came into difficulties.

Pilot Lt. Jean Anderson courtesy of the late Jean Field.

The Leamington Spa Courier dated 27th April 1945 reported: - **Bomber Crashes at Whitnash** – Last evening, shortly after 9 o'clock, pedestrians in the centre of Leamington were alarmed at seeing a bomber flying low and evidently in difficulties. The pilot was trying to avoid descending on the town, but a few moments later he crashed at Whitnash. The crew of nine managed to bail out, but one man is unaccounted for. The machine caught fire and was completely burnt out. A Courier representative viewed the wreckage in a field near Ashford Road this morning, and reports that smoke was still issuing from the ruins of the machine, some of the remains of which were scattered over a wide area. Some bits fell into the gardens of nearby houses. There can be no doubt that the presence of mind and bravery of the crew averted the danger of a plane crash in the middle of the town. That one of the crew lost his life appears to be an established fact. The N.F.S. engines turned out with remarkable promptitude and worked on the flames.

The crew of B-24 42-51251 406 Bomb Squadron, 492nd Bomb Group were pilot Lt. Jean Anderson, radio operator S/Sgt Robert G. Davis, gunner S/Sgt William L. Blackard, gunner Sgt Robert J. Sullivan, gunner Sgt Robert W. Roos, engineer S/Sgt Harold F. Wesley Jr, bombardier 2/Lt Melvin H. Davis, co-pilot 2/Lt Richard L. Halle and navigator 2/Lt Richard C. Klenoski.

[www.aviationarcheology.org.uk/marg/crashes1945.htm]. Photo taken at Casper, Wyoming on 12th January 1945 before flying out to England. Courtesy of Tom Ensmingers USA. Pilot Lt. Jean Anderson is on the front row second from the left.

Whitnash Bomber Crash – "I noticed with interest the letter of Mr. E. P. Hines, of Tachbrook Road, in the Morning News suggesting that something should be done in the way of starting a fund to assist the widow and relatives of the pilot who lamentably was killed in the Liberator aircraft which crashed in the vicinity of Whitnash on April 26. Much as I would like to make it my duty as Mayor of the borough to sponsor any worthy cause, I learn after being in touch with the U.S.A.A.F., that this particular scheme is unfortunately impracticable. I understand that no information is allowed to be given with regard to this pilot's nearest relatives and with regard to the crash. I am further informed that at no time was there any danger of this bomber falling on the town. Apparently the pilot could himself have bailed out except that certain circumstances prevented his being able to do so. No information as to the details of the accident, for obvious reasons can be made public, and I trust that all those friends who with public-spirited generosity kindly suggested and offered to support this scheme will understand my position in the matter, and the reasons for my inability to do anything in this way. C. W. Gardner [Mayor]."

Keith Douglas was stationed at the Harbury Lane aerodrome as a flight engineer when he saw the accident happen. He said, "I heard this noise which was obviously an aeroplane in trouble and then suddenly it appeared between Mallory Court and Whitnash and went into the field with a tremendous explosion. I was there in a few minutes. All that was left was some burning debris and four huge craters where the engines had gone in. We only found part of the pilot and there was no other sign of human remains." It was some years later that Mr. Douglas remembered the bravery he had witnessed and decided to tell the pilot's family what had happened. He said, "It was a long time before I thought about it and it crossed my mind that the pilot had been extremely brave having steered the aeroplane away from Whitnash. Living through the war one accepted that these sort of things happened as I had friends in the airforce that lost their lives. It was in the 1970s that it occurred to me that he had been a boy from America who had given his life and I wondered whether his family knew what happened. As I was a regular visitor to the States I decided to meet them." After contacting the American Embassy Mr. Douglas visited Lt. Anderson's family in Michigan to tell them his story.

Photo courtesy of Alan Griffin.

The Millennium News edition of the Leamington Spa Courier dated 24th December 1999 reported: - In 1984, Whitnash honoured a war hero when a new road was named Anderson Drive. Lt. Jean Anderson of the US Air Force died in 1945, sacrificing himself to stop his out of control plane hitting houses in the village. Resident Gerald Cox witnessed the fatal crash and campaigned for Lt. Anderson to be remembered.

The unveiling of the name board was carried out by Lt. Col. Frederick Bush, Assistant Air Attaché at the American Embassy in London. The photo on the previous page shows Gerald Cox and Lt. Anderson's brother Gail Anderson.

The Leamington Spa Courier dated 7th July 1995 reported: - '**Personal Thanks To War Hero** – A war hero whose bravery saved Whitnash from disaster has been honoured 50 years after he sacrificed his life. A plaque marking the event was handed over to his homeland on VE Day by an eye-witness from Whitnash. Lt. Jean Anderson, a 23-year-old USAAF pilot, ordered the crew of his badly-crippled Liberator bomber to bale out, while he remained at the controls to steer the aircraft away from houses. It crashed in open countryside on the outskirts of the town and Lt. Anderson was killed. A road on the South Farm estate, which was built on the spot, has been named after him. James Savage, 14, was with friends when he heard the plane fly over on April 26, 1945. "There was the roar of a plane in trouble flying much too low over the roof tops, then an explosion. My friends and I knew it had crashed nearby. As we rode our bikes towards the sound of the crash we saw parachutes coming down and assumed the crew had bailed out. The plane had crashed about two miles away in a field behind the last row of houses and was totally engulfed in flames when we got there. That scene is clearly etched in my memory."

James grew up, married and emigrated first to Canada and then to the United States. Now retired, he revisited Whitnash in 1994 and stood in Anderson Drive. He was concerned that Anderson's heroism was marked in Whitnash but not in his own birthplace, of Mason, Michigan. He contacted a newspaper in Detroit which tracked down Anderson's younger brother Gail who still lives in Mason. He told James the local Veterans of Foreign Wars Hall is named after his brother. On VE Day, James, a member of the British Commonwealth Club arranged for the club to hand over a plaque in memory of Lt. Anderson to the VFW Post. He said, "It is with a great deal of personal satisfaction that after 50 years I can say thank you to Lt. Anderson."'

Home Thoughts From Abroad – The following article was written by John Yarwood for the winter 2011 edition of the Leamington History Group newsletter, 'The Leamington Omnibus'. John was raised in Whitnash, and after leaving Warwick School trained as a journalist with the Leamington Spa Courier. He continued his career in journalism in Australia.

John recalls his boyhood memories of the bomber crash in Whitnash: - The sudden, deafening roar overhead threatened to shake our two-storey home in Heathcote Road, Whitnash, to its foundations. Seconds later...a massive explosion. My brother Paul, five, and I, eight, leaped from the bed we shared at No.31 [otherwise known as Marton House] to peer through the south-facing window in the direction of the blast. Blinking in the fading late evening light, we focussed on a bizarre scene, what looked like nine candles, with umbrella-shaped tails, floating to earth.

The parachutists had parted company from the United States bomber less than a minute before it slammed into a field half a mile away, gouging a massive crater at the eastern end of Ashford Road, miraculously just beyond the nearest house. Eight of them landed safely in the fields directly at the back of our long garden. The ninth became entangled in a tree from which he was later rescued unharmed. What none of the nine knew in the confusion of the moment was that the tenth member of the crew had not been as lucky on that evening of 26th April, 1945. Twenty-three-year-old pilot, Lieutenant Jean Anderson, perished while battling with the controls as he tried to steer the plane away from houses in the then thinly populated village.

The crew was part of the 406th Bombardment Squadron, based at Harrington, about 30 miles away in Northamptonshire. They had set out on a mission to drop propaganda leaflets in north-western Germany. Just before nightfall the bomber became uncontrollable because of icing and when the ailerons locked at 6,000ft. the crew was ordered to bail out. Pilot Anderson was ready to jump but in waiting – hoping to save the lives of villagers on the ground, he left it too late. A tidal wave of parishioners streamed across the fields to the crash site to be confronted by smouldering wreckage deeply embedded in the earth. The pilot's remains were later recovered and buried in the American Cemetery in Cambridge. The US Government awarded him the Purple Heart for Military Merit.

Extraordinarily, it was another 39 years before British authorities responded to villagers' pleas for Jean Anderson's supreme sacrifice to be recognised locally. On 16th April, 1984, a new road situated only 100 yards from the crash site, was named Anderson Drive. The formal unveiling of the name board was attended by the dead pilot's younger brother, Gail, and his wife, Donna, who flew from Michigan for the ceremony. It is thought that Jean Anderson's parents had died some years earlier.

One of the villagers who had witnessed the crash from his Lammas Terrace [Heathcote Road] home was a 16-year-old youth at the time, the late Gerald Cox. He became an enthusiastic local historian and recalled that he had entered into a lengthy correspondence with the bereaved parents. In one poignant letter, he said, they had referred to Jean Anderson as "our boy who now sleeps in England."

V. E. Day and after the War

On 27th April 1945, the General Purposes Committee discussed plans for celebrations once the announcement that war was over had been made. They recommended a service in All Saints Parish Church, a combined open-air service in the Pump Room Gardens, the illumination of Linden Avenue and open-air dancing in the Pump Room Gardens, music being provided by means of public address amplifying equipment.

At 02.41am on 7th May 1945, Germany surrendered bringing to an end six years of war in Europe. The unconditional surrender documents were signed in the French city of Reims by Chief-of-Staff of the German Armed Forces High Command, General Alfred Jodl.

World War Two officially came to an end on the 8th of May 1945. The day was declared a national holiday to mark Victory in Europe Day [VE Day]. The following day [9th May] was also a national holiday.

On 8th May King George VI made a broadcast to the nation from Buckingham Palace. He started by saying, "Today we give thanks to Almighty God for a great deliverance. Speaking from our Empire's oldest capital city, war-battered but never for one moment daunted or dismayed - speaking from London, I ask you to join with me in that act of thanksgiving." He asked the people to remember those who would not come back, to remember the men and women in all the services who had laid down their lives. He said, "Armed or unarmed, men and women, you have fought and striven and endured to your utmost. No-one knows that better than I do, and as your King, I thank with a full heart those who bore arms so valiantly on land and sea, or in the air, and all civilians who, shouldering their many burdens, have carried them unflinchingly without complaint."

At 3.00pm on the same day, the Prime Minister, Winston Churchill, made a broadcast to the nation from the Cabinet room at 10 Downing Street. In it he said, "The act of unconditional surrender is to be ratified in Berlin today - but in the interest of saving lives the ceasefire came into effect yesterday." He paid tribute to the men and women who had laid down their lives for victory as well as to all those who had "fought valiantly" on land, sea and in the air. He said, "We may allow ourselves a brief period of rejoicing; but let us not forget for a moment the toil and efforts that lie ahead. Japan with all her treachery and greed, remains unsubdued."

Churchill followed the broadcast with a statement in the House of Commons. He then led a procession of MPs to St. Margaret's Church for a service of thanksgiving. At Buckingham Palace, huge crowds had gathered outside and there was much excitement and cheering as King George VI, Queen Elizabeth, Princess Elizabeth and Princess Margaret came out onto the balcony.

In preparation for VE Day the local press carried an advertisement on 7th May 1945 from the Ministry of Food under the heading: - 'Food Supplies for VE-Day. The Ministry of

Food is confident that food traders, having served the public well throughout the war years, will provide a service during the V Holiday that will enable the public to obtain their essential minimum food supplies. The Ministry makes the following suggestions to food traders and housewives: -

Grocers - Should remain open on VE Day for at least one hour after the Victory announcement has been made and if possible two hours. If VE Day is a Friday grocers should open on Saturday and close on Monday but grocers selling bread and milk should act in accordance with the following paragraphs.

Dairymen - Are expected to deliver milk on both VE Days just as they normally do on Good Friday or a Bank Holiday.

Bakers - Should make arrangements in advance to ensure that after the announcement bread will be made and delivered to private houses and retail shops in sufficient quantities to provide at least for normal requirements. Wherever possible bakers should in addition make bread as usual for sale on VE+1 Day and on this day open their shops for one hour or possibly two hours for the sale of bread only. Although it is expected that the public will be able to obtain bread supplies during the V Holiday housewives are advised to carry in their homes slightly more bread than usual.

Shops dealing in perishable foods - Should remain open on VE Day long enough after the official announcement to ensure that perishable goods are not wasted.

Restaurants and cafés are expected to be open on both VE Days.

Every food trader is asked to display in his shop a notice telling his customers at what hours his shop will be open during the V Holiday, together with any further details useful to his customers. Retailers expecting deliveries from wholesalers on VE Day should arrange for the reception of these goods.'

VE Day was celebrated by street parties throughout the land. Everyone put on some sort of show. Tables were set up in the streets, flags and bunting decorated houses and shops, and everyone, young and old, danced in the streets. The hokey-cokey was one of the most popular dances of the day. Fancy dress competitions were popular too, with mums making clever use of everything from black-out fabric to prized parachute silk. The Eagle Street Recreation Ground was the venue for a particularly glamourous parade. Children in Villiers Street celebrated VE Day by tucking into a slap-up meal, watched by their happy mums as did the children and parents in Norfolk Street.

Norfolk Street.

The Leamington Spa Courier dated Friday 11th May 1945 reported: - 'News of the end of hostilities in Europe was officially announced by Mr. Churchill at 3 o'clock on Tuesday, a day proclaimed as VE-Day, to be marked by heartfelt thanksgivings and rejoicings. The announcement was somewhat in the nature of an anti-climax for we had been told overnight that it would come at the time mentioned. Indeed, the manner in which the war ended confounded the prophets and confused the planners.

However, the celebrations lost nothing of their spontaneity in consequence, and the people of Leamington and district shared with the rest of their countrymen a sense of profound relief that the dangers and hazards of war were no more to be endured in the European theatre.

The first impulse of a lot of people was to attend one or other of the many places of worship which had made special arrangements for the holding of thanksgiving services. As night came crowds gathered in the street to "celebrate".

A huge crowd in the Pump Room Gardens listened to the relay of the King's speech at 9.00pm. Dancing followed and the crowds then moved to the brightly-lighted thoroughfares where there was more dancing and singing to the music of accordions.

In the absence of any officially-organised festivity, the townspeople rose to the occasion marvellously, and in their own ways expressed their jubilation that the end of the war had come. The flood-lighting of the Parish Church attracted much admiration and it was noted that the inclusion of the north side added greatly to the beauty of the scene. The fountains in the Jephson Gardens were illuminated as also was the War Memorial.

Flags and bunting were to be seen everywhere. The Parade was modestly treated and was easily eclipsed by several minor streets which sported national emblems, the like of which have probably never been previously seen in Leamington. Where all the flags came from is something of a mystery but residents went to great pains to make attractive displays. Satchwell Street, Kenilworth Street and Shrubland Street were outstanding but they had many rivals in their efforts for gaiety. Church Street, too, was well beflagged, and it had another attractive feature in Bob Chimes' band, which officiated at a street party for children. Some 50 were taken to a cinema on Wednesday, and, out of the money subscribed, a substantial balance remains for a future visit. Gaveston Road celebrated by burning an effigy of Hitler, and well and truly they rejoiced in the process.

Admission to the Jephson Gardens on both days was free and they remained open until a late hour. Many people made their way to Stoneleigh Park where in the American camp they joined in the celebrations with our allies.

Wednesday was gloriously fine, and "everywhere was crowded", especially the dancing in the Pump Room Gardens. Licensed houses had an extension of half-an-hour on Tuesday evening, with the result that some were unable to "stay the course" on Wednesday. The beer had gone.

Preparations to illuminate Linden Avenue had been made but there was a disappointment on Tuesday night. Owing to a technical hitch the fairy lights could not be turned on but come Wednesday evening, they appeared in all their pristine glory.

Avondale Road

Street tea parties for children were very enjoyable and jolly affairs. A Victory Party held in Taylor Avenue was organised by Mrs. Farey and Mrs. Collins, assisted by all the neighbours. Miss Sheila Butler was crowned the Victory Queen by A.B. Seaman Eric Platt. She was attended by the Misses Geraldine Mullis, Carol Farey, Jean Harris and Master Maurice Norton was page boy. After the ceremony, the 'Victory Queen' declared the Victory Party open. Approximately 40 children sat down to tea. There was a two-tier Victory cake. The party went on until 9.00pm when each child was given a present, a bag of sweets and an orange and the winners of races were presented with their prizes. After the children had gone to bed the grown-ups indulged in dancing and games to music provided by Mr. Farey. Cheers were given for the boys in Burma.

Avondale Road

A very happy party was held in Clapham Street for all children and grown-ups living south of the canal bridge. The children sat down to tea at 3.30pm., the Vicar the Rev. F. A. Bunn and Mrs. Bunn took part. Tea and light refreshments were also served to the older folks and onlookers, and the working party later had theirs. There was an absolute profusion of good things. Music was provided by wireless and piano, and games were joined in by young and old. Sports and races were held and various prizes given.

Finally, there was an enormous bonfire with a very realistic effigy of Hitler which burnt merrily, while everybody sang all the old favourites. The party was organised by Mrs. Jenkinson and Mrs. D. Langley, assisted by Mrs. Rea, Mrs. Dingley, and Mrs. Henn, with the hearty co-operation of the neighbours.'

Barbara Buckley who during the war lived in Milverton Terrace recalls, "Leamington went mad on VE Day. It was such a relief that the war was over, it was such a fantastic feeling. The strangest thing I remember is that the street lights were all on at night for the first time, they hadn't been on at night time for such a long time. The Parade was absolutely packed, I couldn't even get to the Pump Room Gardens, there were just so many people on the streets. The dance band who played at the Town Hall were playing outside the Haunch of Venison on the Parade, and the bugler from the band was playing whilst hanging from the lamp post. The Haunch of Venison was so busy, but I knew Betty and Charles who ran the pub and so I was let in. By midnight the streets were empty as everyone had gone home."

Brunswick Street

Another local said, "On VE Day we had a street party in Gunnery Terrace. There was a table all down the middle of the road, with white tablecloths and we had paper hats. The children were in fancy dress, there was a lot of red, white and blue, one girl went as an Hawaiian in a grass skirt. At night, the grown-ups had a party in the Raffia factory, upstairs, with singing and dancing. Before the war, the factory made raffia baskets and cradles and during the war it was used as a store by a Coventry firm."

The Morning News dated Friday 11th May 1945 reported: - '**How the Spa Celebrated VE-Day** – Leamington was early astir on VE Day and in streets which were liberally bedecked with flags and bunting, large crowds fittingly celebrated the great news that hostilities in Europe had ceased. At the outset, the scenes in town constituted a curious mixture of business and pleasure. This was because the official announcement that the German Army had capitulated was not received until late in the day on Monday, with the result that most people had left work before the news came through. Consequently, many were puzzled as to what extent the statement that the following day would be a public holiday affected them.

Villiers Street.

Althorpe Street

Happily, the weather, which threatened to go back on the holidaymakers when a storm broke shortly before 11 a.m., improved considerably later on so that the celebrations were for the most part favoured with warm sunshine, which permitted the menfolk to discard their macs and the women to array themselves in their brightest of bright summer frocks.

One of the most popular items in the Spa's celebrations was the open-air dancing in the Pump Room Gardens. Here several hundred-people gathered on VE night and an atmosphere of gaiety was maintained until a late hour.

In several parts of the town informal dances were staged in the streets, a typical example being at Lillington, where neighbours ran out their loud speakers on long pieces of flex and dancing was indulged in to the strains of a B.B.C. orchestra. Traffic in the upper part of the Parade was stopped on VE night while an impromptu "band" played for dancing.

Althorpe Street

The working-class districts of the town did especially well with regard to decorations. These are the neighbourhoods which can always be relied upon to rise to the occasion and VE Day provided no exception to the rule. Kenilworth Street, Park Street, and Satchwell Street, in particular, caught the eye for the gaiety of their appearance, but they had close rivals in several other quarters.

The town's rejoicings were not wholly confined to the more exuberant forms of entertainment. As soon as the Victory announcement was made the various churches were opened for services of thanksgiving, which were continued throughout VE Day. These were attended by large congregations, which joined together to offer praise and thanks to Almighty God for the many blessings bestowed upon this nation during its time of trial and for its great deliverance from the forces of evil. There is to be a public act of worship on Sunday, when the Mayor and members of the Corporation will attend a combined service in the Pump Room Gardens at 3.15p.m. This will also be made the occasion of a Victory parade of military and civil defence units.'

The Leamington Spa Courier dated 18th May 1945 reported: -

Shrubland Street

'Mayor and Mayoress at Shrubland Street Victory Party

Shrubland Street held a Victory Party on Saturday, thanks to a number of generous donors. During the proceedings, Lance Corporal Bugden, a prisoner of war for five years, arrived home and was promptly "overwhelmed". A collection realised £3, and this was handed to him by the Mayor, [Alderman C. W. Gardner]. The Mayoress was also present, but the Rev. J. R. Simpson the Vicar of St. John's could not be accompanied by his wife owing to her indisposition. From start to finish the proceedings were of a happy character, concluding with dancing.

L-R George, Ethel and Emma Jones outside No.20 Shrubland Street.

Mr. Pritchard, Midland Electric, provided floodlights and Mr. Wilson the radiogram for dance music.

On Friday, a very happy and successful party was held in Brunswick Street. A children's street party was held at Campion Green on Monday, with 25 children sitting down to a sumptuous meal followed by games. During the evening there were performances of Punch and Judy and a magical show by Teddy Godfrey. Sweets and American popcorn were distributed and adults joined in the fun until 11.00pm. Fireworks ended the celebrations.

A fancy-dress parade, races and games, followed by tea, took place in Avondale Road for the local children. In the evening, the elder folk had a supper and dance.'

Offa Road

Ladder Bridge – Althorpe Street Estate. Photo courtesy of Ken Walter.

The photo on the previous page shows a street party close to the Ladder Bridge between the Althorpe Street estate and the Flavel's factory. It was actually a Coronation street party in 1953. However, it is interesting as to the left of the Union Jack is a Second World War air-raid shelter. The path leads to Warneford Terrace and to the right White Street. L-R: Mrs. Palmer [Piano player], Terry Walker, Edward Timms, and Trevor Young.

Thanksgiving Sunday for Victory in Europe was marked in Leamington, on Sunday 13th May 1945, by a unified service in the Pump Room Gardens, where an exceptionally large parade was witnessed by a very big crowd. The parade was led by the band of the Royal Warwickshire Regiment, and consisted of a platoon of the R.W.R., followed by two companies of the Home Guard, the A.T.S. Army Cadets, wounded soldiers, members of the British Red Cross, contingents of the R.A.F., the W.A.A.F., the A.T.C, Sea Cadets, W.R.N.S., W.L.A., Belgian Army, Police and W.A.P.C., N.F.S, St. John Ambulance Brigade, the band of the Salvation Army, Civil Defence and W.V.S., Fire Guards, nurses from the Warneford Hospital and the Royal Midland Counties Home, the British Legion, Boy Scouts, Girl Guides, Girls' Training Corps, Blue Triangle Service Corps, Church Lads' Brigade, Old Contemptibles, Kigass and Imperial Foundry.

LEAMINGTON'S THANKSGIVING FOR VICTORY

On the left the Rev. A. S. Beaty is seen addressing the united thanksgiving service in the Pump Room Gardens on Sunday. An impression as to the size of the crowd may be gained from the picture below. Report on page 7.

C. H. SOANS & SON, LTD.
MAIN FORD DISTRIBUTORS
DORMER PLACE ROYAL LEAMINGTON SPA
Phone 2205 (2 lines)

THIRTY YEARS in this town We must be capable. RAE Furriers, 10, Clarendon Avenue Top of Parade, turn left. Phone 1842.

BURTON
Leamington Spa, 140—142, Parade.

The service, which commenced with the National Anthem, was conducted by the Mayor's Chaplain the Rev. J. A. Carter who read the lesson. The Rev. Stanley Beaty gave the address, and prayer was offered by the Rev. W. W. Evans. After the service the Mayor said, "I share with you a great feeling of thankfulness to Almighty God that we have been spared to see this day. In many hearts there will be grief at the loss of dear ones, but to those we hope it will be some comfort to know that their sons and husbands did not die in vain. I feel it would be the wish of the Town Council to thank you all for the part you have played during the past six years. We are proud to salute the members of the Armed Forces, men and women, the Home Guard, the Civil Defence in all its branches, the youth organisations and the war workers, both those from factories and those who have worked on the land. To those who have not been in uniform, particularly the womenfolk, I would say you have all played your part splendidly." The Mayor afterwards took the salute outside the Town Hall.

At the Town Hall, on Wednesday 6th June 1945, a party of repatriated prisoners-of-war received an official welcome home from the Mayor and Mayoress Alderman and Mrs. Gardner. They were entertained to "an excellent meal, and enjoyed the delights of being in Leamington once again". The Mayor expressed the hope that the men would soon be back in 'Civvy Street'. Wing-Commander Peter Olver responded on behalf of the men, who included: - Cfn. G. F. King, L/Cpl. C. Holmes, Pte. David E. Rowlston, Dvr. A. Ayres, Sgt. W. Stocks, C.S.M. Galvin, Pte. J. Quelch, Dvr. W. J. Smith, Pte. F. G. Fruser, L/Cpl. F. A. J. Watson, Pte. Phipps, Sgt. S. G. Walsh, Pte, A. E. Cash, Pte. Foley, Pte. C. Reading, Pte. W. Hughes, Rfm. E. Reading, B. W. Whiteley, Capt. A. E. Barker, W.O. R. P. Heard, F/O Boniskowski, Cpl. T. Frost, Bdr. W. J. Batchelor, Lt. P. H. Judd, L/Bdr. Joe Bugden, Capt. L. E. H. Henning and Pte. Godfrey.

On Tuesday 29th June 1945, the Leamington branch of the newly formed Fireman's and Civil Defence Legion held its first meeting at the Pump Room where the aims and objectives of the organisation were outlined. It was formed to help all those who served in the National Fire Service, and the Civil Defence Services along with all those who were engaged on the Home Front including the W.V.S and Auxiliary Police. It was hoped to keep alive the spirit of brotherhood developed during the war period. It was said that it would be a social and welfare organisation with charitable aims and not aligned to politics, trade unions or other sectional interests.

The war with Japan continued until Tuesday 14th August 1945.

The then Prime Minister Clement Attlee [he became Prime Minister on 26th July 1945] announced the surrender on the BBC. He said, "Japan has today surrendered. The last of our enemies is laid low."

This effectively ended the Second World War. The 14th and 15th August 1945 were declared VJ [Victory over Japan] days.

On 2nd September 1945, a formal surrender ceremony was performed on board the battleship USS Missouri in Tokyo Bay, Japan.

The Daily Sketch

RADAR SECRETS —PAGE 5

JAPAN SURRENDERS

To-day And To-morrow To Be VJ-Holidays—Mr. Attlee

MR. ATTLEE BROADCASTING LAST NIGHT ANNOUNCED THE SURRENDER OF JAPAN.

The Prime Minister said: Japan has to-day surrendered. The last of our enemies is laid low. Here is the text of the Japanese reply to the Allied demands.

THE BRIDGE OF TEARS

YOU'LL GET THESE 'MADE IN JAPAN'

AMERICA STOPS FOR WHOOPEE

CABINET PLANS OUT TO-DAY

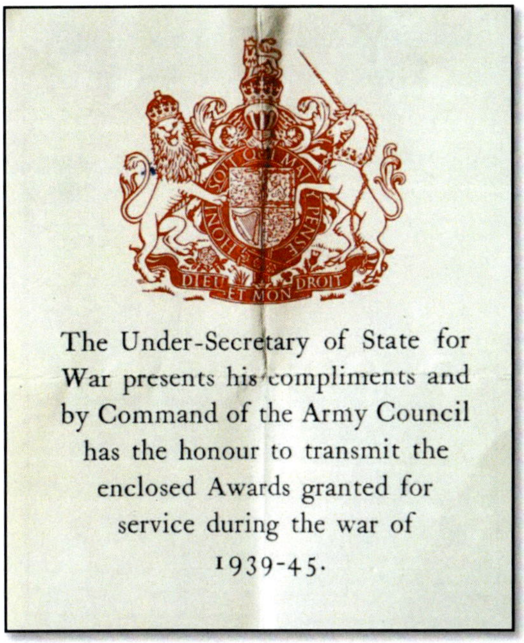
DIEU ET MON DROIT

The Under-Secretary of State for War presents his compliments and by Command of the Army Council has the honour to transmit the enclosed Awards granted for service during the war of 1939-45.

Following the end of the war, medals were issued, but not immediately.

The 1939-45 War Medal was a British decoration awarded to those who had served in the Armed Forces or Merchant Navy full-time for at least 28 days between 3rd September 1939 and 2nd September 1945.

The British issue medals were made of cupro-nickel and designed by Edward Carter Preston. The medal in the following photo, courtesy of Glynis Jennings, was issued to her father Victor Davies who served in the Middle East.

On the Home Front, the 1939-45 Second World War Defence Medal was awarded for non-operational service in the Armed Forces, the Home Guard, the Civil Defence Service and other approved civilian services during the period from 3rd September 1939 to 2nd September 1945.

The Voluntary Workers for the Forces Badge [right] was issued by the Directorate of Voluntary Services [1940-1945]. The badge was produced by J. R. Gaunt of London. To qualify for the badge and a certificate, volunteers had to provide three months' voluntary work [approximately 600 hours] in aid of the war effort.

On 8th June 1946, following the defeat of Germany and Japan, a victory celebration parade took place in London. The parade, which was over four miles in length and included over 500 vehicles, included representation from many of our allies.

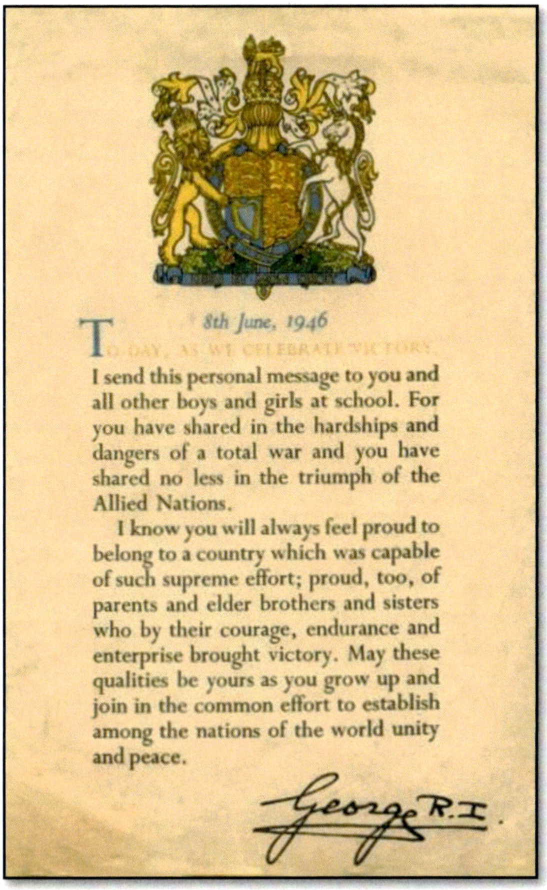

8th June, 1946

TO-DAY, AS WE CELEBRATE VICTORY, I send this personal message to you and all other boys and girls at school. For you have shared in the hardships and dangers of a total war and you have shared no less in the triumph of the Allied Nations.

I know you will always feel proud to belong to a country which was capable of such supreme effort; proud, too, of parents and elder brothers and sisters who by their courage, endurance and enterprise brought victory. May these qualities be yours as you grow up and join in the common effort to establish among the nations of the world unity and peace.

George R.I.

At the same time, all schoolchildren were given a certificate with a printed signature of King George VI.

"Today, as we celebrate victory, I send this personal message to you and all other boys and girls at school. For you have shared in the hardships and dangers of a total war and you have shared no less in the triumph of the Allied Nations."

"I know you will always feel proud to belong to a country which was capable of such supreme effort; proud, too, of parents and elder brothers and sisters who by their courage, endurance and enterprise brought victory. May these qualities be yours as you grow up and join in the common effort to establish among the nations of the world unity and peace."

Montgomery of Alamein

Field Marshall Bernard Law Montgomery, 1st Viscount Montgomery of Alamein.

The Morning News dated Thursday 20th August 1942 reported: -

New Eighth Army Commander – General B. L. Montgomery An Ex-Royal Warwick – Lieutenant-General B. L. Montgomery, who at the age of 54, has been appointed Commander of the Eighth Army in succession to General Ritchie, commanded the 1st Battalion of the Royal Warwickshire Regiment from 1931 to 1934. He is the son of Bishop Montgomery, and grandson of a Lieutenant-Governor of the Punjab. Since November, 1941, he had been G.O.C. [General Officer Commanding] South-Eastern Command in which he introduced Spartan methods of training. He ordered 15 minutes P.T. at 7 o'clock every morning for all men at his headquarters who were under 40. All ranks from private to brigadier had to run six miles each week over a course that was changed from time to time by the General, who often covered it himself. General Montgomery had a distinguished record of service in the last war, in which he won the D.S.O. and was mentioned six times in despatches.

The following letter was sent on 17th June 1947 to Mr. J. N. Stothert, the Town Clerk of Leamington Spa: -

Dear Town Clerk, Thank you for your letter of 12th June. I gladly accept the offer of the Hon. Freedom of your Borough; it will be a great honour for me. I would suggest Saturday 4 October as being a suitable date for me to attend to receive the honour; in the afternoon, after luncheon. Yrs sincerely Montgomery of Alamein, Field Marshall.

Field Marshall Montgomery entered the town from Radford Road and was then driven up Willes Road before coming down the Parade from Clarendon Avenue. Thousands of onlookers stood many deep on the pavement and onto the road along the whole length of the Parade.

This photo and the next one are courtesy of Ian Mitchell and show Montgomery being driven in Leamington on 4th October 1947 by Ian's father, local man, John Mitchell. Christ Church can be seen in the background in Upper Parade.

Bottom photo: Field Marshall Viscount Montgomery in his staff car accompanied by Leamington Mayor Councillor Oswald Davidson outside the Royal Pump Room. Photo courtesy of Leamington Art Gallery and Museum [Warwick District Council].

Field Marshall Montgomery receiving the honorary Freedom of Leamington Spa Borough from Mayor Councillor Davidson. Photos courtesy of Leamington Spa Art Gallery and Museum [Warwick District Council].

Top: The scroll bearing the Freedom of the Borough was presented to Montgomery inside a tank shaped casket. Bottom: Meeting the crowds at the Midland Oak. Photos courtesy of Leamington Spa Art Gallery and Museum [Warwick District Council].

Sir Winston Churchill

[30th November 1874 - 24th January 1965]

Winston Churchill was first elected to Parliament in 1900 and during his career held the most important of offices of state. From 1929 until 1939 he was out of office and politically was considered to be 'in the wilderness'.

In the years before the war started he constantly warned of the danger of Hitler's Germany and campaigned for rearmament. At the outbreak of war he was appointed First Lord of the Admiralty. Following the resignation of Neville Chamberlain on 10th May 1940, he became British Prime Minister. There is no doubt that his inspirational speeches and radio broadcasts as well as his leadership of the country were vital components in the eventual Allied victory.

On Monday 25th June 1945, wartime leader Sir Winston Churchill was seen in Leamington as he visited the town. He spoke to between five and six thousand people at the Pump Room Gardens in support of local M.P. Anthony Eden, the Earl of Avon, standing in the forthcoming general election. Dormer Place was packed with pedestrians and vehicles and some overflowed into Bedford Street. Mr. Churchill was due to arrive at 12.30pm, but the waiting crowds had to wait in the summer heat until 2.00pm before he arrived smoking his traditional cigar.

The election on 26th July 1945 resulted in a sweeping victory by the Labour Party and saw Clement Attlee become Prime Minister, this was despite Churchill having a personal approval rating of 83%. Following the election, Leamington's local Member of Parliament Anthony Eden became deputy leader of the Conservative Party.

Acknowledgements

I would like to thank the following without whose help and support this book could not have been produced. I would also like to extend special thanks to Nigel Briggs and Glynis Jennings for their considerable efforts in editing this book: -

- Anthony Allcock
- Jane Arnold
- Derek Billings - Leamington History Group
- Reg Boucher
- Barbara Buckley née Gee
- Janet and Steve Carvell
- Peter Chater - Leamington and Lillington History Groups
- Jeff Clarke - Leamington History Group
- Joe Claydon - Leamington History Group
- Peter and Janet Coulls - Leamington and Lillington History Groups
- Coventry Transport Museum
- Marion and Alan Crossan
- Hazel Davis née Parkes - Ex Women's Land Army
- Martin Ellis [Melbourne] - Leamington History Group
- Barry Franklin - Leamington History Group
- Terry Gardner - Leamington History Group
- David Goulding
- Pete Grenfell
- Alan Griffin - Leamington History Group
- Pete Griffin
- Judith Harridge - Leamington Spa Library
- Frank James - Leamington History Group
- Mick Jeffs - Leamington History Group
- Glynis Jennings - Sydenham History Group
- Helen Kerr - Estate Manager Abbey Park Kenilworth
- Richard King - Leamington History Group
- Patrick Kingston
- Leamington Spa Art Gallery and Museum [Warwick District Council] - Jeff Watkin Heritage and Arts Manager, Vicki Slade, Alice Swatton, Imogen Frost and Huw Jones
- Leamington Spa Courier - Chris Lillington, Phil Hibble and Peter Gawthorpe
- Leamington Spa Library staff and photo collection
- David G. P. Morse -Warwickshire Home Guard Living History Group
- Alan Orton
- Kenneth Owen - Leamington History Group
- Alec Riman
- Margaret Rushton - Leamington and Lillington History Groups
- Eva Sabin née Kilby
- Kit Smith - Leamington History Group

- Richard Soans
- Paul Springthorpe - Sydenham History Group
- Betty Still
- Neil Tew
- Ron and June Tew
- John Underhill
- Pauline, Lindsey and Tony Ward
- Mike Wardle
- Warwick County Records Office - Rob Eyre, Amanda Williams, Merima Hadzic, Karen Moulder, Samantha Ryan and all of the staff

I am very conscious of copyright issues and have endeavoured to establish ownership of, and gain permission to use all such material quoted and/or reproduced herein. If there are any omissions, please contact me, and I will correct the error at the earliest opportunity.

Camouflage Directorate Acknowledgements & Bibliography

- Fergus Durrant
- Virginia Ironside
- Barbara Buckley née Gee
- Pauline Ward née Hopkins
- Leamington History Group website - Mick Jeffs
- Leamington Spa Observer article 26th February 2015
- Leamington Spa Courier - Nostalgia article 13th September 2013
- The Bombing of Royal Leamington Spa by Allan Jennings
  Published in 2015 ISBN: 978-0-9932980-4-2
- The Springs, Wells & Baths of Royal Leamington Spa by Allan Jennings
  Published in 2015 - ISBN: 978-0-9932980-3-5
- People & Pubs of Royal Leamington Spa by Allan Jennings, Martin Ellis & Tom Lewin.
  Published in 2014 - ISBN: 978-1-85858-522-2
- Victorine Anne Foot information - courtesy of Wikipedia
- Camouflage and art design for deception in World War 2 - Henrietta Goodden - published in 2007 - ISBN: 978-0-906290-87-2
- http://www.leamingtoncourier.co.uk/news/local-news/light-shed-on-secret-wartime-camouflage-work-1-1057752
- http://www.ww2f.com/topic/14310-team-that-hid-wartime-factories/
- http://www.artbiogs.co.uk/2/organizations/camouflage-unit
- Story of the Artists International Association - Museum of Modern Art, Oxford 1983
- Concealment & Deception - The Art of the Camoufleurs of Leamington Spa 1939-45.
  Published by Warwick District Council 2016.

Photo Acknowledgements

- Derek Billings - Leamington History Group
- Nigel Briggs - Sydenham and Leamington History Groups
- Barbara Buckley
- Bernard Cadogan and Southam Cardell Collection
- Steve and Janet Carvell
- Peter Coulls - Leamington and Lillington History Groups
- Fergus Durrant
- John and Caroline Evetts
- Jean Field *[deceased]* collection - original from Michael Jacobs
- Carol Fitzsimon née Davies
- Ian Frost
- Bill Gibbons *[deceased]* photo collection
- Alan Griffin - Leamington History Group
- Barry Hickman and Sid Savage
- Maggie Hurlow and the late Jean Field collection
- Virginia Ironside
- Frank James - Leamington History Group
- Betty Jennings née Jones *[deceased]*
- Colin Jennings
- Richard King - Leamington History Group
- Patrick Kingston
- Leamington Spa Art Gallery and Museum
- Leamington Spa Library - Judith Harridge
- Leeds Museums and Galleries [Henry Moore Institute Archive]
- Len Lount - Leamington Spa Home Guard Club
- Wendy Lucey
- Claire Mayoh - Henry Moore Institute
- Jock McVarish
- David G. P. Morse - Warwickshire Home Guard Living History Group
- Vivienne Owen
- Kate and Robin Rourke
- Richard Soans
- Paul Springthorpe - Sydenham History Group
- St. John's Church and Joyce Heath
- Sebastian Tennant
- Ron and June Tew
- John Underhill
- Ken Walter
- Lindsey Ward
- Warwickshire County Record Office
- Les Woodfield - Leamington Spa Home Guard Club

- Portrait of 'Clip' Gammon painted by Bernard Hailstone - courtesy of Leamington Spa Art Gallery and Museum [Warwick District Council]
- Picture Post Cover - courtesy of Leamington Spa Art Gallery and Museum [Warwick District Council]
- Home Guard Camouflage Manual Cover - courtesy of Leamington Spa Art Gallery and Museum [Warwick District Council]
- Lockheed poster – courtesy of Leamington Spa Art Gallery and Museum [Warwick District Council] Ref: M.4736.2012.7
- Concealment and Deception Exhibition exhibits - courtesy of Leamington Spa Art Gallery and Museum [Warwick District Council]. A.R.P. First Aid Box and Tunic, W.V.S. Uniform Jacket and Skirt and Arthur Smith's Civil Defence items. Refs: LEAMG:M3676.1991, LEAMG:M4563.2001, LEAMG: M4375.1995.8 & 9, LEAMG: M4705.2011.24/25/2/12.1/13.16
- Leamington Spa Civil Defence Team – courtesy of Leamington Spa Art Gallery and Museum [Warwick District Council] Ref: LEAMG: M4197.1994
- Field Marshall Viscount Montgomery photos taken on 4th October 1947 - courtesy of Leamington Spa Art Gallery and Museum [Warwick District Council]. Ref: LEAMG: M3965.1993.25 by H. R. Clayton, LEAMG: M3965.1993.1 by H. R. Clayton and LEAMG: M3965.1993.66
- No.3 Platoon outside the Town Hall in 1945 - courtesy of Warwickshire County Record Office Ref: PH(N)600-720-12
- A.R.P. Control Centre on 22nd June 1945 - courtesy of Warwickshire County Record Office. Ref: PH(N)600/720/25 Img:4884
- A.R.P. Control Centre on 22nd June 1945 – courtesy of Warwickshire County Record Office. Ref: PH(N)600/720/26 Img:4885
- A.R.P. Control Centre on 22nd June 1945 – courtesy of Warwickshire County Record Office. Ref: PH(N)600/720/27
- A.R.P. Control Centre on 22nd June 1945 – courtesy of Warwickshire County Record Office. Ref: PH(N)600/720/29
- Butlins Shadow Factory on 15th September 1942 - courtesy of Warwickshire County Record Office Ref: CR3581a,1735 (5 photographs)
- Post Office in 1940 - courtesy of Warwickshire County Record Office Ref: PH(N)600/334/2
- Members of Home Guard No.6 Platoon circa 1943 - courtesy of Warwickshire County Record Office Ref: CR2134/6
- Civil Defence Parade - courtesy of Warwickshire County Record Office Ref: PH(N)600/720/30 & 31
- Home Guard Stand Down - courtesy of Warwickshire County Record Office Ref: PH(N)600/720/33-39 & 46
- N.F.S. Presentation to Chandos Street Messengers in 1944 - courtesy of Warwickshire County Record Office Ref: PH(N)600/720/22
- A.F.S. Adelaide Road - courtesy of Warwickshire County Record Office Ref: PH852/4-5
- Members of the A.F.S. based at Adelaide Road - courtesy of Warwickshire County Record Office Ref: PH852/3

- Fire Guard Service November 1944 - courtesy of Warwickshire County Record Office Ref: PH(N)600/720/15 & 17
- Ambulance Group at Central Depot on 29th May 1945 - courtesy of Warwickshire County Record Office Ref: PH(N)600/720/13
- Anthony Eden at Civil Defence Stand Down in 1945 - courtesy of Warwickshire County Record Office Ref: PH(N)600/720/42
- Flavel's Women in staff canteen in 1942 - courtesy of Warwickshire County Record Office Ref: PH,919/1
- Field Marshall Montgomery on 4th October 1947 - courtesy of Warwickshire County Record Office Ref: PH(N)600/833/1 & PH(N)600/832/9
- Telephone Exchange on 28th November 1949 - courtesy of Warwickshire County Record Office Ref: PH(N)600/335/3 & PH(N)600/335/1

Bibliography

- Leamington Spa Courier 1939-1945
- Leamington Spa Courier 19th May 1989
- Leamington Spa Courier Supplement June 1998
- Leamington Spa Courier - Warwickshire at War 1st September 1989
- Morning News 1939-1945
- Royal Leamington Spa Town Council Proceedings of Committees 1939-1945
- The Women's Land Army - V. Sackville-West 1944
- For U.S. Armed Forces in U.K. [Booklet] - courtesy of Peter Coulls
- Agriculture - the Journal of the Ministry of Agriculture December 1950
- Precision - Lockheed Hydraulic Brake Co. Staff magazine [October 1947]
- Precision - Lockheed Hydraulic Brake Co. Staff magazine [1960]
- Twentieth Century Defences in Warwickshire - Steve Carvell 2007 - ISBN: 9780752442686
- AP Jubilee book - 50 years of progress 1920-70
- This Noble Duty: A History of Fire-Fighting in Warwickshire - Alan Griffin 1987 ISBN: 0951447807
- We You Salute – Roy Rowberry 1990
- Leamington's Czech Patriots and the Heydrich Assassination - Alan Griffin 2004
- Leamington Lives Remembered - Alan Griffin 2012 - ISBN: 095144784X
- The Leamington we used to know - Leamington Literary Society 1977 ISBN: 0-900093-65-x
- More Looking Back - Leamington Literary Society 1980 - ISBN: 0950717517
- A Last Look Back - Leamington Literary Society 1983 - ISBN: 0950717525
- The Story of Jephson Gardens by W. G. Gibbons - 1996
- Rangemaster of Royal Leamington Spa 1777-2005 - Jean Field - ISBN: 185858289X
- A Celebration of Sydenham - Sydenham History Group 2014
- Bridging the Gap - Fran and Martin Collins. Published in 2014 by Brewin Books Studley ISBN: 978-1-85858-525-3
- Camouflage and Art – Design for Deception in World War 2 by Henrietta Goodden

- The Ash Grove - Jean Field 1996 - ISBN: 0952819104
- Pubs of Royal Leamington Spa - Two Centuries of History - Allan Jennings, Martin Ellis and Tom Lewin 2014 - ISBN: 978-1-85858-522-2
- http://www.bbc.co.uk/history/ww2peopleswar
- http://aufhimmelzuhause.com/id101.htm
- http://kigassaero.co.uk/
- www.royalvoluntaryservice.org.uk
- http://www.staffshomeguard.co.uk/
- http://www.stareton.co.uk/
- British Welcome Club - Leamington Spa Courier's dated 2nd June, 4th August, 13th October 29th December 1944 and 3rd May 1946
- Ashdown WWII Camp
- Banner Hill Camp Kenilworth
- Article 'From New York to Omaha Beach' by Alan Griffin. Originally in the Summer 2010 Leamington History Group newsletter - since inserted on their website
- Civil Defence Messenger Service - courtesy of Warwickshire County Record Office Ref: CR4159
- Messages to and from Air Raid Precautions - Warwick County Control - courtesy of Warwickshire County Record Office Ref: CR1499
- Shrubland Street School Admissions Register courtesy of Warwickshire County Record Office Ref: CR831/2/2

Lest We Forget.